ALGOL 68 IMPLEMENTATION

IFIP Working Conference on ALGOL 68 Implementation
Munich, Germany, July 20–24, 1970

organized by
IFIP Technical Committee 2, Programming Languages
International Federation for Information Processing

Organizing Committee
F.L. Bauer (Chairman), A. Caracciolo, M. Paul,
J.E.L. Peck, T.B. Steel, H. Zemanek

1971

NORTH-HOLLAND PUBLISHING COMPANY – AMSTERDAM · LONDON

ALGOL 68 Implementation

Proceedings of the
IFIP Working Conference on ALGOL 68 Implementation,
Munich, July 20–24, 1970

edited by
J. E. L. PECK
University of British Columbia, Vancouver, Canada

1971

NORTH-HOLLAND PUBLISHING COMPANY — AMSTERDAM · LONDON

© IFIP, 1971

All Rights Reserved. No part of this publication may be reproduced, stored in a retrieval system, or transmitted, in any form or by any means, electronic, mechanical, photocopying, recording, or otherwise, without the prior permission of the Copyright owner.

Library of Congress Catalog Card Number: 79–146198
ISBN: 0 7204 2045 8

Published by
NORTH-HOLLAND PUBLISHING COMPANY – AMSTERDAM
NORTH-HOLLAND PUBLISHING COMPANY, LTD. – LONDON

PRINTED IN THE NETHERLANDS

PREFACE

From 1963, Working Group 2.1 on ALGOL of the International Federation for Information Processing has discussed the development of a new language as a sucessor to ALGOL 60. Eventually A. van Wijngaarden was commissioned to prepare a document defining a new language. This document, designed in collaboration with B. J. Mailloux, J. E. L. Peck and C. H. A. Koster, was accepted as a defining document for the language ALGOL 68 by a meeting of the Working Group held in Munich in December of 1968. It was reviewed by Technical Committee 2 and finally recommended by the General Assembly of IFIP for widespread publication. It now appears as "Report on the Algorithmic Language ALGOL 68" (see the bibliography).

In order to stimulate the production of ALGOL 68 compilers and thus to put the new language to the test of use, Technical Committee 2 agreed to hold a Working Conference on ALGOL 68 Implementation in Munich in July of 1970. Some forty persons were present, by invitation, and twenty papers were presented. These papers discussed various aspects of implementation and ranged from the examination of detailed facets of compiler construction to the more general questions. There were also two panel discussions.

The conference was intended to reveal the current status of implementation efforts in many countries and to provide for the interplay of ideas. Of particular interest was the fact that a working compiler for ALGOL 68-R, a variant of ALGOL 68, was already in operation at the Royal Radar Establishment in Malvern, England.

That the conference was a success, can be seen from the lively discussions which followed the presentation of the papers. Naturally, numerous contacts were made and ideas exchanged outside of the meeting rooms. It was held at the Mathematical Institute of the Technical University of Munich. All sessions were carefully recorded. The participants were grateful for the excellence of the facilities and the hospitality provided by the local organizing committee.

The material in this volume has been edited in an attempt to make it more readable. To this end, all references to the participants, during the discussions, are by last name only, but, of course, many first names were used, while others preferred to use titles where appropriate. The editor must therefore apologize to those participants who find themselves addressing their long-time friends by the last name and to those young participants who may be surprised to read that they addressed their superiors with apparent disrespect. The discussion following each of the presentations keeps as closely as possible to that which is recorded, but, in some cases, much work was done to make it intelligible to one who was not present. Thus, some illustrative examples now appear, of which the conference participants did not, at the time, have the benefit. The editor is grateful for the help of those participants who made these revisions possible.

The members of the organizing committee, and especially Professor F. L. Bauer and Professor M. Paul, are to be thanked for the excellent arrangements for recording and transcribing the conference. It made the editorial work much lighter. The use of the facilities of the Technical University of Munich for later editorial work eased the burden even more. For the excellence of the dual set of recordings, the conference is indebted to Mr. Hellmuth Haag and Mr. Udo Schampel, and for assistance in the transcription, to Mr. Th. Ströhlein. Special thanks should go to Miss Margot Vogg and to a band of typists whom she supervised. Her good humour and dedicated efficiency were much appreciated.

Because of the desire to have this volume in the hands of the reader as soon as possible, an upper limit was set on its size and some papers presented at the conference could not be included. Moreover, limitations of time, prescribed by this goal, meant that many pieces of ALGOL 68 programs included here could not be put to the test of syntactic analysis or compilation.

A bibliography, current at the time of going to press, and prepared with the help of participants, is included.

J. E. L. Peck,
Vancouver,
November 1970.

CONTENTS

Preface ... v
Opening Session ... ix

Session 1 (*Chairman*: *M. Paul*)

A symbol table with scope recognition for the B-6500
    H. J. Bowlden ... 1
ALGOL 68-R
    I. F. Currie, Susan G. Bond, J. D. Morison ... 21

Session 2 (*Chairman*: *J. E. L. Peck*)

Analysis of the parenthesis structure of ALGOL 68
    P. Branquart, J. Lewi, J. P. Cardinael ... 37
An implementation of identifier tables in a multipass
ALGOL 68 compiler based on a hash-code technique
    J. Král, J. Moudrý ... 77
Syntax and mode check in an ALGOL 68 compiler
    H. Scheidig ... 83

Session 3 (*Chairman*: *B. J. Mailloux*)

Affix grammars
    C. H. A. Koster ... 95
On identification of operators in ALGOL 68
    H. Wössner ... 111
An attempted definition of an extensible system
    L. Trilling, J. P. Verjus ... 119

Session 4 (*Chairman*: *A. van Wijngaarden*)

A multilanguage programming system oriented to
language description and universal optimization algorithms
    A. P. Ershov ... 143
On description of syntax of ALGOL 68 and its national variants
    A. A. Bährs, A. P. Ershov, A. F. Rar ... 163
Some problems in compiling ALGOL 68
    G. Goos ... 179

Session 5 (*Chairman*: *C. H. A. Koster*)

A scheme of storage allocation and garbage collection
for ALGOL 68
    P. Branquart, J. Lewi ... 199
An ALGOL 68 garbage collector
    S. Marshall ... 239

Methods of garbage collection for ALGOL 68
P. L. Wodon   245

Session 6 (Chairman: G. Goos)

Panel discussion - ALGOL 68 sublanguages (Part 1)   265
Some ALGOL 68 sublanguages
C. H. Lindsey   283
Panel discussion - ALGOL 68 sublanguages (Part 2)   289

Session 7 (Chairman: A. P. Ershov)

A garbage collector to be implemented on a CDC 3100
P. Goyer   303

Session 8 (Chairman: F. L. Bauer)

Panel discussion - Implementation   321

Session 9 (Chairman: W. L. van der Poel)

Making the hardware suit the language
C. H. Lindsey   347

Conference participants   367
Bibliography   369

OPENING SESSION

Bauer (Conference chairman):
   Ladies and Gentlemen, welcome to Munich, welcome to this conference. I welcome all the participants. This is a restricted conference, and we have only invited participants here. I hope it will be for the benefit of the conference. We are a small group, your discussion can be very open, very lively, and we will do our best to record it so that everything you say may be used, for or against you! My particular greetings go to Professor Zemanek from Vienna, IFIP Vice-President. I should also give you the greetings of the Rector of the Technische Universität München. He asks me to convey his very best wishes for the success of this conference.
   Munich is not a new place for IFIP activities. We have had the IFIP congress here. With the start of the IFIP working group 2.1 activities, we have had a meeting (I think it was 1964) in Tutzing, near Munich and we have had the dramatic meeting of December 1968. We have a certain tradition. We are glad to have you here. In some sense you are all tied into the ALGOL activity, although not all of you belong to the working group. As those who have been here before may have noticed, we have moved into a new building, the building in which you are now. We are very happy that not only do we have better rooms but we can have a conference in nicer rooms than before. You may observe that opposite this building, another building is under construction and is about finished. It is the new Leibniz computing center building, and it will be open in a few weeks.
   Before I ask Professor Zemanek to open the conference, I would like first to mention one thing. I have had the help of Professor Paul in preparing this conference to such a large extent that I personally consider him to be more the chairman of the conference than myself, and I would like to express my thanks to him now, at this moment, quite clearly. Our thanks also go to our colleague members of the organizing committee, A. Caracciolo, M. Paul, J. E. L. Peck, T. B. Steel and H. Zemanek.

Zemanek:
   Mr. Chairman, Ladies and Gentlemen, Dear Friends,
The President of IFIP has charged me to represent him at this working conference and to give you the greetings of IFIP. As the responsible Vice President, it is my great personal pleasure to be here and to wish you a successful week. Most of you know that this is the fourth of this type of working conference organized by TC-2:

Vienna/Baden	1964	Formal Language Definition Language
Pisa	1966	Symbol Manipulation
Oslo	1967	Simulation
Munich	1970	ALGOL 68 Implementation.

In fact, these working conferences are much more than their titles convey. They play an important role in the general development of programming languages. It is generally true that our conferences take place only partly in the meeting rooms. Sometimes the even more important section happens in the corridors, parks and coffeeshops. Working conferences of our type are intended to create a family of scientists or to develop such a family further. This is why we usually invite an abstract community: one formed by mutual reading of publications and singular visits. At the working conference, the abstract community is turned into a real community.

With ALGOL, everything is more dense. A kind of community already existed before IFIP, and we only had the opportunity to host it under the IFIP umbrella. But then it grew, extended the field of ALGOL 60 and decided to start work on ALGOL X and Y. This is not the spot to tell the ALGOL 68 story. I have invited the former chairman of WG 2.1 to write this story and I hope that all his obligations will one day allow him time to do it.

Like any good scientific creation, ALGOL 68 initiates discussions and controversy. If I were more cynical, I would say that if controversy were a measure of its scientific value, ALGOL 68 has outstanding value. I think, however, that WG 2.1, by developing ALGOL 68, has become a focus-point of the programming language problematics and if the controversy has not been a measure of the importance of the ALGOL 68 of today, it is a measure of the creativity of the ALGOL community.

WG 2.1 and WG 2.3 will now have to elaborate the outcome of the discussions. WG 2.1 will deal with ALGOL 68 and WG 2.3 will have to show what else can be done.

In the opening letter of TC-2 for the ALGOL 68 report, we said that ALGOL 68 has to pass "the crucial tests of implementation and subsequent use by the computing community".

Since the publishing of the ALGOL 68 report, this conference is the first important step in the direction TC-2 and WG 2.1 are hoping our language is going to take. I am particularly grateful to Professor Bauer, chairman of the conference, and Dr. Paul, chairman of WG 2.1, and the other organizers of this working conference, who bore all the burdens of preparing our meeting, which is to be a working conference where the accent is on *working*.

A language, whether natural or constructed, is a social tool. A one-user language is no real language, and the importance of a language is directly proportionate to the number of its users. This number naturally increases with the successful applications of the language - and this again depends on the availability and the quality of the compilers for that language. ALGOL 68 implementation, therefore, is the most important subject for the growth of the ALGOL 68 community at this time.

There is a long list of places where implementation of ALGOL 68 is intended. The future of ALGOL 68 will depend very much on the success of these implementation groups. And the present working conference has the first purpose of supporting these groups and - consequently - the success of ALGOL 68.

It is therefore not only a polite remark or pleasure expressed ex officio to wish all of you a good working conference, in my own name, on behalf of the IFIP President and for IFIP as a whole. Because, as I always say, IFIP consists only of the work of its people, the remainder is overhead. You are the active part of IFIP this week. Make good use of it and enjoy it.

I. F. Currie, Susan G. Bond and J. D. Morison, Implementers of ALGOL 68-R

SESSION 1

(Chairman: M.Paul)

A SYMBOL TABLE WITH SCOPE RECOGNITION FOR THE B-6500

HENRY J. BOWLDEN
Westinghouse Res.Labs., Pittsburgh, Pennsylvania, USA

INTRODUCTION

The Burroughs B-6500 provides a specialized environment for computer programs, including compilers. The following three significant features of this environment are of concern here:
a) the stack hardware makes a recursive program organization feasible (with respect to efficiency), but at the same time restricts certain capabilities, such as "deep-stack" addressing;
b) the character manipulation hardware influences the design of source scanners;
c) the multiprogrammed operating system allocates space for a program entirely on demand, and therefore suggests a symbol table organization which is dynamic, and in which the "inner loops" of searches are confined to a small and isolated portion of the symbol table space.

The algorithms which we present here have been designed to operate efficiently in this specialized environment. Special consideration has also been given to the demands of a recognizer for a class of languages, including ALGOL 60 [1], Extended Algol for the B-6500 [2], and ALGOL 68 [3]. The recognizer is also suitable for LISP [4], and with a few modifications in the source scanner could be made to handle other languages, such as FORTRAN and PL/I.

The algorithms are presented in ALGOL 68, partly to test the suitability of this language for applications of this type, but primarily as a phase of a project to bootstrap an implementation of ALGOL 68 for the B-6500 written in ALGOL 68. A primary purpose of the formalization of this paper is to illustrate the manner in which the use of a general-purpose language can be combined with a knowledge of the computing environment to produce efficient programs.

The algorithms included in this paper are those for source scanning and symbol table handling. The method by which the scope concept is treated is designed to simplify the "identification" problem of ALGOL 68.

OVERVIEW AND SUMMARY

The presentation emphasizes a number of points which should be itemized.

In the first place, the design of a package such as this needs to take into account special hardware features of a given computer which may be applied to the problem. Any language which is to be suitable for efficiently implementing such a package must allow the programmer to establish control over such features. The scanner described here leans heavily on the character manipulation features of the B-6500; any clumsiness observed in the statements controlling these features may indicate a language deficiency in these areas. In many compilers, the "atoms" which are considered are the individual source characters, and the innermost level of the defining grammar governs the composition of characters into significant elements (identifiers, etc.). The B-6500 hardware, by its provision of efficient methods for isolating such elements, leads us away from that level and towards the level described here.

The ability to pack information (fields of structured data) into machine words for reasons of efficient handling or storage economy is important. This topic has not been considered in detail here, because extensions to the language would be required to handle it properly; the only change in the algorithm would, however, be in the declarations of the data modes.

In the organization of the tables, it is important that the search strategy should not be required to perform complicated tests too frequently. The tasks of high frequency should be made as simple as possible. Another example of the use of knowledge of the hardware to improve efficiency is contained in the organization of the various dictionaries into arrays containing elements of static size. This enables efficient referencing of an entry and packing of a reference as a subscript value. It also relieves the system of considerable overhead, letting the compiler (which knows the structural characteristics of its data base) handle the allocation.

The algorithms described here have been coded in Burroughs Extended Algol and the basic efficiency of the organization has been justified on a preliminary basis by the results of tests.

DESIGN OF THE SOURCE SCANNER

The scanner, which is presented in detail in Appendix B, must depend heavily on the character-handling capabilities of the B-6500. Its design also reflects some of the characteristics of the class of languages for which it is to be used. It treats the source as a continuous string of characters, broken arbitrarily into records or "lines" by the demands of the hardware. This source string is made up of the following "basic atoms".

<u>identifier</u>: letters and/or digits beginning with a letter. Blanks may or may not be embedded, depending on a global flag.
<u>integer</u>: digits; embedded blanks are allowed.
<u>string</u>: a sequence of characters beginning with $lqch$ and ending with $rqch$. These global quantities are assumed to contain the desired string delimiters.
<u>symbol</u>: a) a sequence of characters beginning with $lsymbch$ and ending with $rsymbch$. If $lsymbch$ contains a blank, no symbols of

this type exist. If *rsymbch* contains a blank, then the sequence is terminated by any character not a member of *symbcset*.
b) any single character other than a letter or digit, or *lqch*, *lsymbch*, or *eorch*.

The scanner is provided with two parameters, a pointer into a fixed string to which the scanned atom is to be moved, and the address of an integer variable in which the number of characters moved is to be stored. The scanner returns an integer result whose value indicates the class of atom:

0 = end-of-file, 1 = identifier, 2 = integer, 3 = string, 4 = symbol.

The details of the *fetch* routine are very much dependent on the external medium and hardware. The routine given in Appendix A assumes that source records contain 80 characters, of which the last eight are used as an identification field and are not part of the source program string. On the B-6500, this field is used as a control for merging separate streams of input records ("patch decks").

Two global variables, the pointer *iptr* and the integer *icnt*, are used to keep track of the scan position in the input record. The procedure *rescan* enables atoms to be restored to the input. It is not always possible simply to back up the pointer, because an atom may be split over more than one record. The *fetch* routine is therefore designed to move the records to the right-hand end of a fairly large fixed string in which the scanning is performed, allowing a reasonable amount of space for backing up the input pointer.

DESIGN OF THE DICTIONARY

The details of this dictionary and its lookup routines are given in Appendix C. Many techniques have been proposed for organizing a dictionary or "symbol table" [5]. The dynamic nature of the dictionary requirement for a compiler gives preference to hashing (scrambling) techniques for the table-lookup. This consists of the generation of a fairly small integer by some manipulation of the characters of the character string being considered, for use as an index into the table. Since this transformation cannot be unique, some mechanism is required to handle conflicts. The environment of the B-6500, in which data space is not allocated until requested, and in which "pages" are maintained in a "virtual memory" organization for recall to core on demand, suggests that the primary table in which searching is to be performed should be kept as small as possible. We accomplish this goal by two basic techniques. In the first place, entries in the basic table are designed so that they can be packed into a single word. In the second place, the scramble index is confined to a value less than the size of a single page. Conflicts are handled by chaining additional entries in an overflow area. Space for the latter is provided by the Operating System in page-size chunks, only as the program requires it. The entries in this basic table also contain the first few (one or more, depending on the word and byte size) characters of the representation. This assures rapid retrieval of short atoms, which tend to predominate in typical programs of the contemplated language class, and also decreases the frequency of required references to the main dictionary.

A "main dictionary" is provided in which the full representation of the entry is maintained. This dictionary also contains controls to allow the lookup routines, operating in conjunction with the scanner, to collect the components of "complex symbols", such as := in ALGOL, by a recursive look-ahead technique with rescan provided in the case of failure.

SCOPE ANALYSIS AND IDENTIFICATION

The languages of the contemplated class all have some concept of "scope", which allows a single source atom (specifically, an identifier, although ALGOL 68 extends the capability to symbols) to take on more than one meaning within a program. We refer to the portion of a program which controls scope as a "range". Its actual identity depends on the specific language (a block in ALGOL 60, a subprogram in FORTRAN, a range in ALGOL 68). We regard these ranges as forming a recursive nest; in some languages this degenerates into two levels only, global (e.g. FORTRAN COMMON) and local. We can now provide a separate entry, for any given atom, for each range in which it occurs. These entries are kept in a separate table, formulated as the "ragged array" *info* (a two-dimensional array with rows of varying lengths) with one row for each range.

Appendix D includes declarations of the two procedures, *rangebegin* and *rangend*, which maintain the scope analysis. They are called by the recognizer under appropriate conditions. These procedures develop a tree structure of ranges, with each range being linked to its father, first and last son, and nearest brother on each side. *Info* rows for completed ranges are copied into the file *stack* and removed from main memory.

In *rangend* each *info* entry for the range just completed which is not flagged as local (meaning that no defining occurrence has been processed) is copied back into the surrounding range if an entry does not already exist in that range. Also, all entries from this range are delinked from the *maindict* entry. This guarantees that each *maindict* entry will point directly to the most immediate *info* entry. The intermediate string created by the recognizer for use by subsequent passes contains pointers to *info* entries. In all cases, except for "reserved" (non-redeclarable) words, these will point to an entry belonging to the current range. The process of "identification" (3, sec. 4.1.2) then consists of linking back from this entry until one is found which is flagged as *local*.

After the first pass, the *maindict* entries are used only for regenerating the representation (in diagnostic messages, for example), and are recovered from the *mainlink* field of the *info* entries. It is therefore never necessary to reconstitute the *range* and *link* fields in the *maindict* during the following passes.

THE DICTIONARY ROUTINES

The routines appearing in Appendix B are driven by the procedure *next*, which returns, at each call, the class field of the proper *info* entry for the next atom in the source. It also ensures that a pointer to this *info* entry is stored in the global variable *thisinfo*.

The coding shows the three separate basic tables *iddict*, *symbdict* and *dendict* which contain entries for atoms recognized by the scanner as identifiers, symbols and denotations respectively. The particular table name is passed via parameters to the procedure *find*. The primary purpose of these multiple tables is to expedite the search for symbols, which are usually fewer in number but occur more frequently.

The process for handling complex symbols is incorporated, making use of the procedure *explore*. This procedure provides a recursive look-ahead under table control.

If an *info* entry is not found in the present range, a new entry is made automatically unless the global boolean *stopentry* is *true*. The use of this feature is not illustrated here; it would be used, for example, in scanning comments. The complete structure of the *info* entry is dependent on considerations outside the scope of this paper; other fields may be added to those shown as required for a specific application.

The algorithms provide for special context-dependent meanings applied to words; an example is the special use of words like SKIP and SPACE in *write* statements in B-6500 Extended Algol; these words have specialized interpretations which are not connected with any declared identification. The global variable *context*, if non-zero, causes an exhaustive search of the info entries for one whose *class* has the value *contx* and whose *mode* is equal to the value of *context*. Otherwise, the operation of the procedure *rangebegin* and *rangend* ensures that the first *info* entry belongs to the current range if any does.

ABSTRACT

The algorithms which are presented in this working paper are designed to provide an efficient source scanner and symbol table for a recognizer for a class of languages including those of the ALGOL family. The design criteria take into account the environmental characteristics of the B-6500, for which this recognizer is being developed. The mechanism for handling scopes is described, and the solution of the identification problem is outlined.

APPENDIX A. CHARACTER MANIPULATION ON THE B-6500

A.1. *Introduction*

The character manipulation facilities of the B-6500 are described in detail elsewhere [6]. A set of "library declarations" will be developed, giving to the ALGOL 68 programmer the ability to control these features. The purpose of this appendix is to provide sufficient tutorial background to enable the reader to understand the scanner presented in Appendix B. The formulas presented here do not represent an addition to ALGOL 68; they are implemented within the ALGOL 68 extension framework, and any clumsiness which is observed may be attributed to the fact that the hardware operators are basically non-procedural in nature (providing as many as three result values, apart from the side effects of transferring characters).

A.2. *Pointers and pointer arithmetic*

The basic data mode *pointer* is a reference to an element of a *string*. A pointer value can be created by a formula of the form *pointer (S, I)*, where S and I are of modes *ref string* (or *ref* [ ] *char*) and *int* respectively.

The pointer value generated by *pointer (x, 5)* is a reference to the fifth character of the *string x*. Given a pointer P, the formula $P+I$ gives a reference to the character which is *abs (I)* characters to the right of that referred to by P. Similarly, $P-I$ moves the reference point to the left by *abs (I)*. The formula $P1-P2$, where $P1$ and $P2$ are pointers, has an integer value (n) such that $P2+n$ and $P1$ refer to the same character position.

A.3. *Relations and character sets*

The standard ALGOL 68 syntax provides character comparisons according to an unspecified table of binary equivalents (R2.2.3.1f)*. We extend these comparisons to pointers; for example, $P1=P2$ has the same value as $C1=C2$, where $C1$ and $C2$ are the characters referenced by $P1$ and $P2$ respectively. The formula $P=C$ compares the indicated characters, and the formula $P=S$ compares the characters beginning at P with the characters of S. In the above, the equal sign may be replaced by any of the relational operators.

We provide "character-sets" (mode *charset*) such that any character is either *among* or *notin* a given set. Built-in sets are *letters*, *digits*, *alpha* (= *letters or digits*) and *blanks*. The programmer may also create additional sets.

The operator *abs* of ALGOL 68 is extended, and several more are provided, for obtaining numeric values from strings. The formula *abs p*, where p stands for a pointer primary, gives the same results as *abs* applied to the character pointed to by p. The procedure *extract*, given two parameters, a pointer and an integer, yields a reference to the slice of the string beginning at the pointer and containing the designated number of characters. The formula *abs s*, where s denotes a string (or slice), yields an integer value uniquely derived from the first N characters of the string, where N is implementation-dependent.

---

* References in this form are to sections in the ALGOL 68 Report [3].

The formula s *mod* n, where s is a string and n is an integral value, yields an integer k ($0 \leq k < n$) derived in some appropriate manner from the characters of the string. The formula *pchar (p)* yields a value of mode *ref char* designating the same character designated by the pointer p.

A.4. *Scanning a source string*

The operators *scan* and *seek* are used to scan a substring. The clause *scan blanks source (P, I) save (pp, n)* will scan the substring of I characters beginning at P until it finds a character not in the *charset* blanks. The operator *seek* is used in place of *scan* for a character which is in a set. In other words, *seek not blanks* is equivalent to *scan blanks*. In this connection, the phrase *not* "x" may be used, but this is not efficient in other contexts. The variables pp (mode *ref pointer*) and n (mode *ref int*) in the above example receive a pointer to the character at which the scan stops and the number of characters remaining in the source, respectively. The *save* clause may be replaced by *save* pp or *save* n or omitted entirely depending upon what information is to be retained. The right operand of *source* may be a string name (in which case the entire string is used) or a pointer (in which case the portion of the string beginning at the pointer is used). In these cases, no "remaining number of characters" is available so only the *save* pp form is meaningful.

If the above scans are terminated by the end of the substring (P, I) the global boolean variable *toggle* is set to *true* (otherwise, it is set *false*). This value may be tested programmatically. The corresponding action for a source string or pointer (only) is undefined.

A.5. *Character transfers*

Characters are transferred into a destination string by the operator *receives* (which may be abbreviated *rcv*).

For example, the formula

    p *receives* "abc"

causes the transfer of the characters "abc" to the character positions beginning with that referenced by p. The value of the formula, which may be used for further transfers, is a reference to the position in the destination string following those which have been altered. The formula

    dp *receives* (sp, n)

transfers n characters starting at sp.

The formula

    dp *receives* digits *source* (sp, n)

transfers *digits* (maximum = n) from sp to dp. The variations described above for the scan statements are acceptable here.

As an example, the following sequence finds the first identifier in the 80 characters beginning at *iptr* and transfers it to *acp*, followed by three blanks. The value left in *iptr* refers to the character following the identifier, the value left in *icnt* is the number of characters unscanned, and the value in *length* is the number of characters in the identifier. Embedded blanks are not considered in this simplified example.

>   *seek* letters *source* (iptr, 80) *save* (iptr,i);
>   acp *rcv* alpha *source* (iptr,i) *save* (iptr,icnt) *rcv* "...";
>   *if* toggle *then* icnt := 0 *fi*; length := i - icnt;

APPENDIX B. THE SOURCE SCANNING ROUTINES

The basic scanning facilities are incorporated in the procedures *scan* and *fetch* which are presented in this appendix, together with the global declarations which are assumed. The procedure *fetch* is a basic skeleton which assumes that the input string is presented in 80 character lines (records) of which only the first 72 contain source characters. The remaining 8 characters are used on the B-6500 as a control for merging separate files ("patch decks").

```
bool      eoftog            ¢ end-of-file flag ¢,
          blanks delimit    ¢ blanks delimit identifiers ¢,
          q2                ¢ """ is the 'quote-image' ¢;
int       min string        ¢ shortest string-this many characters are
                              taken without examination ¢,
          length            ¢ length of current atom ¢;
int       bsz = 1000        ¢ sufficiently large so that the "undefined"
                              path in rescan does not occur ¢;
[1:bsz]   char inbuff;
char      lqch              ¢ "left-quote" ¢,
          rqch              ¢ "right-quote" ¢,
          lsymbch           ¢ "shift-to-bold-face" ¢,
          rsymbch           ¢ "shift-to-light-face" ¢,
          eorch             ¢ end-of-record character ¢;
charset   symbcset=alpha    ¢ allowed characters in symbols ¢;
int icnt;
int maxicnt = bsz -8;
pointer iptr;
proc fetch = bool:
    if eoftog|true|:
        logical file ended (standin)|eoftog := true
    else read (inbuff [bsz-79:bsz]);
        iptr := pointer (inbuff,bsz-79);
        icnt := 72;
        false
    fi;
proc rescan = (pointer p, int n) :
    if(icnt plus n+1) > maxicnt then
        undefined
    else
        (iptr := iptr - (n+1)) rcv (p,n) rcv "."
    fi;
[1:100]char accum;
        ¢ limits identifiers and denotations.  could be increased ¢
pointer acptr := pointer (accum,0);
```

SYMBOL TABLE FOR THE B-6500

```
proc scan = (pointer sp, ref int n) int :
begin
    ¢scans "element" starting at sp and returns report as follows:
    failure     : 0 (end-of-file)
    identifier  : 1 (deblanks if not blanks delimit)
    integer     : 2 (always deblanks)
    string      : 3 (delimited by lqch and rqch, minimum length given
                  by minstring. If q2 then treats rqch lqch combination as
                  "quote-image").
    symbol      : 4 (single character or group delimited by lsymbch and
                  rsymbch. If lsymbch = null character then there are no
                  group symbols. If rsymbch = null character then the
                  charset symbcset specifies allowed characters in symbols.
                  Group symbols must exist in a single record.)
    eorch is the end-of-record character and is treated as a blank.
    ¢
    int result := 0,i;
    char ch; pointer p := sp;
    n := 0;
    (icnt <1|:fetch|xt);
debl: scan blanks source (iptr,icnt) save (iptr,i);
    if toggle then (fetch|xx|debl)fi;
    if (ch := pchar(iptr)) among digits then
        result := 2;              ¢ integer found ¢
int: p := p rcv digits source (iptr,i) save (iptr,icnt);
    if toggle then
        n plus i;
        (fetch|xt);
        i := icnt;
        go to int
    fi;
    n plus  i - icnt;
dbn: if (ch := pchar(iptr)) = "." then
        scan blank source (iptr,icnt) save (iptr,i);
        if toggle then (fetch|xx|i := icnt;dbn)fi;
        if (ch := pchar(iptr))among digits then int fi;
        icnt := i
    fi;
    if ch = eorch then (fetch|xt|i := icnt;int)fi;
    go to xt
    fi;
    if ch among alpha then
        result := 1;              ¢ identifier found ¢
id: p := p rcv alpha source (iptr,i) save (iptr,icnt);
    if toggle then
        n plus i;
        (fetch|xt);
        i := icnt;
        go to id
    fi;
    n plus i - icnt;
    (blanks delimit|xt);
dbi: if (ch := pchar(iptr)) = "." then
        scan blanks source (iptr,icnt) save (iptr,i);
        if toggle then (fetch|xx|i := icnt;dbi) fi;
        if (ch := pchar(iptr)) among alpha then go to id fi;
        icnt := i
```

```
            fi;
            if tp = eorch then (fetch|xt|i := icnt;id) fi;
                go to xt
         fi;
         if ch = lqch then
               result := 3;                    ¢ quoted string ¢
               p := p rcv (iptr,1) save iptr;
               if min string > 0 then
                     if (icnt := i - min string) < 1 then
                           if i > 1 then
                              p := p rcv (iptr,i-1) save iptr;
                              i := min string +1-i
                           else i := min string
                           fi;
                           (fetch|xt)
                     else i := min string
                     fi;
                     p := p rcv (iptr,i) save iptr;
                     n := min string +2
               else n := 2
               fi;
qs:            (icnt < 2|(fetch|xt); i := icnt|i := icnt -1);
               p := p rcv not rqch source (iptr,i) save (iptr,icnt);
               (toggle|n plus i; qs);
               n plus i-icnt;
               p := p rcv (iptr,1) save iptr;
               if (icnt minus 1) > 0 and q2|:iptr = lqch then
                     p := p rcv (iptr,1) save iptr;
                     n plus 1;
                     qs
               fi;
               go to xt
         fi;
         result := 4;                          ¢ symbol found ¢
         if ch = lsymbch and i > 1 |: iptr + 1 among symbcset then
               if rsymbch = null character then
                  p := p rcv symbcset source (iptr+1,i-1)save(iptr,icnt)
               else p := p rcv not rsymbch source (iptr+1,i-1)
                     save(iptr,icnt)
               fi;
               (toggle|icnt := 0);
               n := i-1-icnt;
               go to xt
         fi;
         (ch = eorch|result := 0; (fetch|xx|debl));
         ¢ simple special character ¢
            spec: p rcv (iptr, n := 1)save iptr;
               icnt := i-1;
            xx: icnt := 0;
            xt: result
end ¢ scan procedure ¢;
```

APPENDIX C. THE DICTIONARY STRUCTURES AND ALGORITHMS

The procedure *next* given here, with its auxiliary routines, yields as "atoms" the identifiers, integral-denotations, string-denotations and symbols of the source. The method of handling comments and pragmats is shown, indicating that they are triggered by symbols with *class* = *symbolv* and *mode* = *lcomv* or *lpragv* respectively. The scanners, *commenter* and *pragmatter*, are not given in full. They make use of the context feature.

In the actual processor, integral- and real-denotations are handled by a special version of *find* which performs the necessary look-aheads, making use of globally defined variables for recognizing the decimal-point, the powers-of-ten-symbol, and the plusminus. The format-denotations of ALGOL 68 could be handled either by making the *scan* procedure recognize them as it does with strings, or by having *next* recognize the formatter-symbol and calling a special routine. The latter is probably more satisfactory, since the syntax of formats is more complex than that of strings.

Some of the fields and values are used for parsing purposes. The *range* and *level* values are manipulated by procedures called for the purpose. The algorithms presented here show only the portion of this mechanism which is pertinent to the dictionary. An efficient first-pass table-driven parser will be described separately.

```
        ¢ the following declarations set up the dictionaries and their scanning
        algorithms. It is assumed that certain entries are set into the dic-
        tionaries initially; the most flexible method involves the reading of
        a "language" file from tape or disk ¢

        struct firstent = (int     firstchars  ¢ contains first characters ¢,
                                   mainlink    ¢ index into maindict ¢,
                                   link        ¢ list-link for hash conflicts ¢),

               mainent   = (bool   reserved    ¢ not redeclarable ¢,
                                   cxf         ¢ context definition exists ¢,
                                   csymbf      ¢ look-ahead activator ¢,
                            int    backup      ¢ return look-ahead ¢,
                                   length      ¢ length of repr ¢,
                                   range       ¢ current entry¢,
                                   link        ¢ addr. of current entry¢,
                            ref[ ] char repr   ¢ representation ¢),

               info      = (int    class       ¢ primary class ¢,
                                   mode        ¢ mode pointer or subclass ¢,
                                   rnglink     ¢ range of prev. entry ¢,
                                   range       ¢ range of this entry ¢,
                                   level       ¢ lexical level of entry ¢,
                                   link        ¢ addr. for prev. entry ¢,
                            bool   local       ¢ declared in current range ¢);

        int maxsd, maxdd, maxid, maxmain, maxrange, maxinf
        ¢ these values are set by the implementation to control table sizes.
          If the operating system can handle it, they may be left small with
          provision for automatic lengthening as needed ¢;
```

```
[0:maxsd]   firstent symbdict;        int nextsd := scram;
[0:maxdd]   firstent dendict;         int nextdd := scram;
[0:maxid]   firstent iddict;          int nextid := scram;
[1:maxmain] mainent maindict;         int nextmain := 1;
[0:maxrange] ref [1:0 flex] info info; int nextrange := 1;


¢ range "0" contains the preludes and postludes ¢

int scram = 125 ¢ the hash modulus ¢,
int range := 0 ¢ current range value ¢,
    lexlevel := 0 ¢ current lexical (range) level ¢,
    nextinfo := 1 ¢ for current range ¢,
    context := 0 ¢ controls "context" searches ¢;
ref info thisinfo ¢ most recently scanned atom ¢,
bool contextog ¢ signals success of "context" search ¢,
    stopentry ¢ prevents new table entries ¢;
info eofinf ¢ specially initialized end-of-file symbol ¢;
    ¢ the following values of class are somewhat arbitrarily chosen ¢
int denotv  = 36¢ denotations "local" ¢,
    declv   = 16¢ mode-indications ¢,
    transym = 12¢ transition symbols for parser ¢,
    opsym   = 10¢ operator-indication ¢,
    contx   =  9¢ context-dependent definition ¢,
    symbolv =  8¢ other symbols ¢,
    localv  =  4¢ may be "or-ed" with others ¢,
    forwardv=  2¢ "forward" declaration ¢,
    identv  =  0;

proc addinfo = (ref mainent mde, int c, m) ref info:
begin
    int ir = range of mde, iadd = link of mde;
    int cl = (c ≠ symbolv or ir + iadd = 0|c|
        class of info [ir][iadd]);
    int i := ninf [range];
    range of mde := range;
    link of mde := nextinfo;
    info [range] [nextinfo] := (ch,m,ir,range,lexlevel,iadd,false);
    nextinfo +:= 1
end ¢ addinfo proc ¢;
proc explore = (pointer p, int nn) int:
begin
    int j, result,n := nn;
    (scan (p+n,j) = 0|bu1);
    ref [ ] char s = extract (p,(n := n+1));
    int fc = abs s[1:2];
    int i := s mod scram, mp;
    ref mainent mde;
    ref firstent fde := symbdict [i];
    (fde :=: nil|rescan(p+n-j,j); result := 0; xt);
    mp := mainlink of fde;
lfc: if firstchars of fde = fc then
    mde := maindict[mp];
        if length of mde = n then
            (n < 3|fm);
            (repr of mde = s|fm)
        fi
```

SYMBOL TABLE FOR THE B-6500

```
        fi;
        ((i := link of fde) > 0|fde := fd[i]; lfc);
bul:  rescan (p+n-j,j);
        0 exit
fm:   (not csymbf of mde|lcs);
        ((i := explore (p,n)) = 0|lcs);
        (i > 0|i|rescan(p+n-j,j);i+1) exit
lcs:  ((i := backup of mde) = 0|mp|rescan(p+n-j,j);1-i) exit
xt:   result
      end ¢ explore proc ¢;

proc find = (pointer p, int n, m, c, ref int nd, ref [ ] firstent fd) int:

begin
      ref[]char s = extract (p,n);
      int fc = (n > 1|abs s[1:2] abs s[1]);
      int i := s mod scram, mp, r;
      ref firstent fde := fd[i];
      ref mainent mde;
      ref info t;
      contextog := false;
      (fde :=: nil |:stopentry|xn|nmd);
      mp := mainlink of fde;
lfc:  if firstchars of fde = fc then
          mde := maindict[mp];
          if length of mde = n then
              (n < 3|fm);
              (repr of mde = s|fm)
          fi
      fi;
      ((i := link of fde) > 0|fde := fd[i]; lfc);
      (stopentry|xn);
      link of fde := nd;
      fde := fd[nd];
      nd := nd+1;
nmd:  (ref firstent fde) := (fc,nextmain,0);
      mde := maindict [nextmain];
      (ref mainent:mde) := (false,false,false,0,n,0,0,s);
      nextmain := nextmain+1;
      thisinfo := addinfo (mde,c,m);
      go to xt;
fm:   if csymbf of mde then
          ((j := explore (p,n)) > 0|mde := maindict[(mp := j)])
      fi;
      if context > 0 thef cxf of mde then
          r := range of mde; i := link of mde;
          while r+i > 0 do
              begin
                  (class of (thisinfo := info [r][i]) = contx|:
                      contextog :=  mode of t = context|xt);
                  r := rnglink of thisinfo;
                  i := link of thisinfo
              end
      fi;
      thisinfo := info [range of mde][link of mde];
      (reserved of mde|xt);
      (range of thisinfo ≠ range|:not stopentry|thisinfo := addinfo (mde,c,m));
```

```
xt: class of thisinfo exit
xn: -1
end ¢ find proc ¢;
proc next = int:
begin
    int cl, m;
    ¢ here we can handle the end-comment and extended parameter separators
       of ALGOL 60 by looking at previous item scanned ¢
    cc: case scan (acptr,length)+1 in
           cl := class of (thisinfo := eofinf),
           cl := find (acptr,length,unknownv,identv,nextid,iddict),
           cl := find (acptr,length,intv,denotv,nextdd,dendict),
           cl := find (acptr,length,stringv,denotv,nextdd,dendict),
           cl := find (acptr,length,unknownv,symbolv,nextsd,symbdict)
        esac;
        if cl = symbolv then
           ((m := mode of thisinfo) = lcomv|commenter; cc);
           (m = lpragv|pragmatter; cc)
        fi;
        cl
end ¢ next proc ¢;
int ¢ arbitrary values for certain modes ¢
    unknown = 0,
    intv    = 1,
    realv   = 2,
    stringv = 3;
```

APPENDIX D. RANGES AND SCOPES

The procedures *rangebegin* and *rangend* represent the mechanism for the handling of ranges in the first pass. The *struct* called *range* maintains all the useful information about a range. These are kept in the row-of-*range ranges*. The fields have the following interpretations.

nextinfo	The value of the global *nextinfo* for this range (valid in first pass only when it is not the current range).
proclevel	The procedure nesting level.
rnglevel	The range nesting level.
father *firstson* *lastson* *oldbrother* *youngbrother*	These fields contain range numbers, and link the ranges into a tree.
stackpos	Beginning of the entry in the scratch file *stack* for this range (set in *rangend*).
present	Indicates presence of the row of *info* in core.
actual	If true, the range has at least one local identifier. (Valid in first pass only when the range is not current.)

The coding in *rangebegin* saves the values of *nextinfo* and *actualrange* and

SYMBOL TABLE FOR THE B-6500   15

creates and properly links an entry for the new range. Ranges are serially numbered, using *nextrange* as the counter.

The coding in *rangend* completes the *range* fields. It also locates all *info* entries for the range which are not marked *local* (i.e. no defining occurrence was found in the range) and copies them, with necessary adjustments, into the containing range if necessary. The *maindict* entry for every *info* entry in the range is then altered to point to the previous *info* entry. The *info* row is written into the scratch file *stack* and the core space is returned. Values of *nextinfo*, *actualrange* and *proclevel* are "popped", restoring the context of the containing range.

Recursion is not used for range manipulation because of the occasional need to reference the surrounding range. This requires a "deep-stack" addressing capability, in which it would be necessary for one level of a routine to address stack cells belonging to a lower level of the same routine. Neither the language nor the hardware provides such a capability.

Rows of *info* are written into the file *stack* for two reasons. In the first place, this makes it possible to return the memory space to the system. In the second place, the contents of this file may be preserved, along with the other tables and the intermediate program string, for use by other routines (for example, cross-reference programs, documentation programs, and the compiler itself).

```
  struct range = (int nextinfo, proclevel, rnglevel, father, firstson,
                  lastson, oldbrother, youngbrother, stackpos, bool present,
                  actual);
[0:maxrange] range ranges;
proc rangebegin = (bool act):
begin
    int rn = range;
    ref range rr = ranges[rn];
    int bro = lastson of rr;

    nextinfo of rr := nextinfo;
    actual of rr := actualrange;
    range := nextrange;
    nextrange +:= 1;
    ((lexlevel +:= 1) > lvlcnt|lvlcnt := lexlevel);
    (bro > 0 |youngbrother of ranges[bro] := range
             |firstson of rr := range);
    lastson of rr := range;
    ranges[range] := (1,proclevel,lexlevel,rn,0,0,bro,0,0,true,
                      (actualrange := act));
    info[range] := [1:maxinf] info;
    nextinfo := 1
end rangebegin;

proc rangend =:
begin
    int r,il,md;
    ref[]info info1 = info[range];
    ref range rr = ranges[range];
    ref info ip;
    int n = nextinfo -1, rn = range;
```

```
        actual of rr := actualrange;
        nextinfo of rr := nextinfo;
        range := father of rr;
        ref range rf = ranges[range];
        proclevel := proclevel of rf;
        lexlevel := rnglevel of rf;
        nextinfo := nextinfo of rf;
        actualrange := actual of rf;
        ref[]info info2 = info[range];
        for i to n do
        begin
            md := mainlink of (ip := info1[i]);
            (local of ip|il := infolink of ip;r := rnglink of ip
            |:rnglink of ip = (r := range)|il := infolink of ip
            |info2 [(il := nextinfo)] := ip;
                range of info2[il] := range;
                level of info2[il] := lexlevel;
                nextinfo +:= 1);
            link of maindict[md] := il;
            range of maindict[md] := r
        end;
        stackpos of rr := stackpos;
        present of rr := false;
        putbin (stack, info1[1:n]);
        stackpos +:= n;
        info[rn] := ¢ empty row ¢
    end rangend;
```

REFERENCES

[1] Naur, P. (Editor), Revised report on the algorithmic language ALGOL 60, Comm. ACM 6 (1963) 1.
[2] B 6500/B 7500 Extended ALGOL reference manual, Rep. No. 1039559, Detroit (Burroughs Corp.), January 1970.
[3] Van Wijngaarden, A. (Editor), Report on the algorithmic language ALGOL 68, Numer. Math. 14 (1969) 80-218.
[4] LISP 1.5 Programmer's Manual, Cambridge (MIT Press) 1966.
[5] Morris, R., Scatter storage techniques, Comm. ACM 11 (1968) 38.
[6] B 6500 Reference Manual, Rep. No. 1043676, Detroit (Burroughs Corp.) rev. January 1970.

DISCUSSION

Paul:
  You have pointed out that modularity is one of the strong pros for high level languages. Is there any place for thinking of having a compiler modular, not only in order to get a better oversight over it, not only to get a

good documentation, but also to get clues for finding those modules that later on, if you define a new language, can serve as basic bricks in building a new compiler for another language that relates somehow to this language that you had compiled before. In other words, I would think of some future in which you are not satisfied with having one high level language that does every job but where you would have many more or less specialized languages, very special and restricted in some cases, in other cases maybe more flexible and less restricted. To do this of course, you would have to find the problem solver for getting all these compilers without using always six or ten man-years to produce such a thing. You would try, consequently, to relate a new language in some way to parts of languages for which you have constructed compilers before. And there I think you find another aspect of compiler modularity that may become very important.

Bowlden:
   Well, we have done something like this. We have developed a preprocessor with essentially a macro facility added to ALGOL to translate into ALGOL, a preprocessor which is ALGOL-like (the declaration structure of the thing is ALGOL-like), and it is a string manipulation language basically. You can scan part of texts; you can mix them up, you can change them around, you can keep them and collect them and spit them out later. You can do anything you want pretty well. You can set compile time variables and test them. It is a very flexible affair. We have used it for implementing a simulation language. It runs out of tables which are stored on disk, and one mode of operation is to say, "All right, I have gotten up to this point. Dump me some new tables". It then produces a set of tables on disk, and you can use those as a starting point for future compilation. Indeed this process is working. The same thing I am sure can be done in ALGOL 68. Now when you come to this kind of generality, enabling people to twist strings around to this extent, I think it defies the idea of producing a syntactic description of the resulting beast. It might be an interesting task.

Lindsey:
   If you consider *info*[5], for example, which you can extend one unit at a time as you discover new identifiers, this is a thing which in your hardware you can do very easily. How do you describe that in ALGOL 68? Have you got some operator in your library prelude? I presume you declare these things to be flexible? Have you defined some operator for saying, "Add a new element into this multiple value"?

Bowlden:
   This is one place where we intend to cheat. We intend to let the operating system do the job. It has the facilities for an interrupt on invalid index, and we intend to teach it that if the thing is one more than the current upper bound, it is intended to increase the array. Now it does not increase it by 1 of course; it would increase it by, say, 256 or something like that.

Lindsey:
   When you declared that *info*[5] for example, did you declare it with some remark to the operating system that it was to be interpreted in this way

Bowlden:
This we have not decided yet, how we intend to communicate. I think probably simply saying *flex* on the upper bound will tell the system what is necessary. That is our intent. It may not be enough, I do not know yet.

Lindsey:
So all you do in fact is to assign something to an element which does not exist yet, and lo and behold, it appears!

Bowlden:
That is right.

Prentice:
You say you are prepared to sacrifice machine independence, and you have described some ways of doing this. What would be your feelings about allowing procedure bodies in code, or in line code say, as a unitary-clause in ALGOL 68?

Bowlden:
I guess that depends on what you mean by code, you see. My background prohibits me from even thinking of this because there is not any. For example, our biggest goal that we are asking for at the moment on the 6500 is the ability to include ALGOL procedures, to link ALGOL procedures with all programs. That is our code.

Lindsey:
You have invented some operators which will cause code to be generated. How do you create these operators in your library-prelude?

Bowlden:
It is clear that the compiler must generate code. That is correct. What we have done, for example, on the 5500, which is where we have been doing this until we got our 6500, is that there are provided intrinsic procedures, in other words, library-prelude procedures. The 5500 does not have the same character manipulation hardware at all. It is entirely different, and so there are provided a set of procedures and the code that is generated for these statements calls on these procedures. It is of course much less efficient. Now, you ask what the body of these procedures is written in. It is written in ALGOL. Again, the ALGOL was extended on the 5500 to give control over the character manipulations on the 5500. It is a different kind of extension. I agree, somewhere down the line there is a point beyond which you cannot go. There is a point at which you have to be able to say, "Here we produce code". We produce code, we do not write code. For example, on the 6500 there are a number of facilities which are provided in the executive system, for example, to control interrupts, which the typical programmer is not about to use. And so there is a special compiler for the executive system. That is, it is the same ALGOL compiler with a few extra procedure identifiers stored in its tables initially. These are parameterless or sometimes one or more parameter procedures. The point is, you see, that bad code cannot be produced by an unwary programmer. You cannot hang the system. And indeed we just do not have system hangs,

caused by programmer's producing bad code, because they cannot produce code except through the compilers. Now, of course when you are testing a compiler, that is another game because there you are testing the code that it produces.

Lindsey:
   So, your compiler would, in fact, eventually produce something in the core?

Bowlden:
   Eventually it produces machine code, and essentially what is done here is to provide a set of constant declarations which give mnemonic names to the various op codes, which are passed as parameters to an emit procedure.

Paul:
   You said that after the first pass you do not need the identifiers. You are using only the pointers, and that is fine. But I take it that information about the identifiers will go into lists for post mortem dump routines in case of a breakdown at runtime.

Bowlden:
   This part is not entirely planned. I can tell you how it is currently being done in the extended ALGOL compiler. We planned to do something similar, although it is not as easy. The addresses in the generated code are printed in the compilation listing beside the source. If a person wishes, he can produce a table of the display register relative assignments for his variables. And thus the dump can be read. The error terminate message gives the segment number and relative address in his programs, so normally he does not have to read the dump at all.

Paul:
   But still, I should say it is very interesting if you can produce, so to speak, a dump on the spot in case of a runtime failure. Your breakdown happens somewhere in the dynamic structure of your program, and what you want is not a complete core image. What you really wish to see is only a listing of those variables that are living at this point and you want their names and their values in some way. So providing something of this sort, I think, should still be a goal for a compiler, and that is what I could call a comfortable post-mortem dump.

Bowlden:
   I think indeed this is desirable. We have given some thought to it and have not got very far. What this would mean is carrying some of these tables over into the run. Of course, there are systems that do this sort of thing, and I see no reason why it could not be done. But the point is that it is not needed for the rest of the compilation.

ALGOL 68-R

I. F. CURRIE, SUSAN G. BOND and J. D. MORISON
Royal Radar Establishment, Great Malvern, Worcs., England

ALGOL 68-R is a language based on ALGOL 68. It has been implemented for the general service computer at the Royal Radar Establishment, an ICL 1907F. It is intended that 68-R shall be the main language for the computing service, and all local software support will be directed towards its use. At RRE, programmers are mainly scientific, but there is also a requirement for business data processing such as payrolls and stock control.

ALGOL 68-R was chosen because we felt it could be implemented so as to produce reasonably efficient object code for number-crunching, while possessing some advanced features for more sophisticated users.

THE LANGUAGE

The context-free shape of a 68-R program is given by the included syntax. The main differences between ALGOL 68 and 68-R are:

1. Identifiers, modes and operators must be specified before use. (To declare mutually recursive modes X and Y we have to say "MODE X;" before the declaration of Y.)
2. No automatic proceduring. This leads to the use of a 68 cast as a 68-R routine-denotation while the 68-R cast is Mode VAL Clause.
3. The mode VOID is explicit.
4. Formal-declarers are the same as virtual-declarers.
5. No parallel processing.
6. GOTO may not be omitted.
7. Uniting is only applicable in strong positions.

Other minor differences exist; whether these can be considered as bugs in the compiler is largely a matter of taste.

THE COMPILER (MARK 1)

The Mark 1 compiler is written in a local dialect of ALGOL 60 with only integer types and some peculiar features to aid address manipulation and list-processing. It is a one-pass compiler, translating a source text segment directly into a form of relocatable binary suitable for subsequent loading into core with linkage to other independently compiled segments.

The compiler makes use of a package of routines which allow stack manipulation (independent of the normal ALGOL 60 stack) and a heap of chunks of core which are kept alive by special list pointers or by pointers in the stack or in other chunks.

The compiler operates as follows. A pre-processor reads in text characters and transforms them into terminal symbols which are fed to the syntax analyser. The syntax analyser operates on a one-track syntax (Knuth's LR(1)), with embedded functions to perform the necessary compiling actions of producing code, setting up declarations lists and so on. The terminal symbols produced by the pre-processor can be affected by the actions performed in the syntax; for example, an operator in an applied occurrence produces its priority as a terminal symbol.

The syntax actually used has the same effect as the syntax included with this paper. With the present choice of terminal symbols, this syntax cannot be transformed into LR(1) and yet still preserve a reasonable structure for embedding the functions. The syntax therefore incorporates a look-ahead, which does nothing but queue terminal symbols and their associated values until a decision-point has been reached, whereupon it reverts to the normal analysis. This look-ahead is expressed using the same analyser and is invoked by function-calls embedded at critical points in the syntax. The LR(1) syntax is produced from a more legible syntax by the program SID which transforms an input syntax (with embedded functions) and produces an LR(1) analyser for that syntax.

A mode is held in the compiler as a unique entry in an array which contains the description of the mode. The particular representation we chose is not a very good one. All the mode information is in the array itself, making it necessary to use a different representation for incomplete modes (with attendant difficulties in identification etc.). As a further complication, we also made it a rule that mode M must be inserted before REF M, PROC M or [ ]M. This ordering makes it easier to do balancing etc. with the limited 68-R coercions, but whether it is worthwhile depends on which part of the compiler one is writing.

The compiler runs in 32K of 24-bit words. About 20K of this is program, which we feel is too large. Next time we could reduce it considerably and also produce a more elegant compiler. A Mark 2 version is still little more than a twinkle in its implementers' eyes, but we hope that its conception will be complete by July and that its delivery will be early next year.

THE OBJECT CODE

The Object Code produced by the Mark 1 compiler produces a new environment on the stack for each block (routine-denotation or serial-clause) entered. Each environment consists of a space whose length can be determined at compile time (e.g. for locals) and above that, space which can be grabbed dynamically. As well as the normal pointers to other environments for non-local accessing (etc.), the environment contains a word which points to a map which determines which of the entries in the compile-time known space of this environment are volatile (e.g. references which could point to the heap). The map is a fixed area of core which consists of control information (e.g. skip the next few entries) and words which give a key and a displacement from the base of the environment for each current volatile entry. The key consists of information giving the level of refs in the entry and what is to be found at the end of the ref chain (e.g. array, structure or union). Each structure-mode which can contain volatile fields has a portion of map to itself, and in the first word of each structure of that mode there is a pointer to that portion of the map. Each array descriptor contains the key for the elements of that array and each united value has the key for its current value.

Chunks of core are grabbed from the heap (by generators etc.) in stack fashion from the other end of the store. At each grab the address of the end of the chunk is noted in a limit-area, which is a special chunk in the heap. The limit-area thus consists of a monotonic sequence of addresses delimiting the chunks grabbed from the heap since the last garbage collection.

When the stack meets the end of the heap, the heap is scavenged by (1) tracing through the volatile entries in the stack and their consequences, marking the words in the limit-area corresponding to chunks encountered in the trace, (2) computing the amount that each chunk can be moved, (3) retracing to update the volatile elements before (4) compacting the live chunks in the heap (and of course the marked words in the limit area).

As a large number of programs will not require the heap, considerable care is taken by the compiler to make sure that code concerned with heap manipulation, map pointer updating and scavenging is not included in any program which does not need it. This implies that the relocatable binary code produced by the compiler is capable of dealing with the optional omission (and insertion) of code on loading. The same feature is used to provide load-time diagnostic options. Also in the relocatable binary is diagnostic information used by the loader to construct a storage map of the loaded program. This map is used by fault routines to provide meaningful diagnostic information on errors at run-time.

Any comparison of efficiency of object program is difficult, but the compiler compares favourably with ALGOL 60 compilers for programs which use only ALGOL 60 features - procedure calls being considerably faster and simpler. Only array indexing (in positions where the array could be a slice) compares unfavourably as fixed point multiplication is slow on the 1907F.

LIBRARY AND ALBUMS

As mentioned above, the unit of compilation is a segment. Identifiers, modes and operators declared globally can be "kept" by mentioning them in a "KEEP-list" at the end of the segment text. This segment can then be loaded and run, or included in an album. An album is a hierarchy of files of segments where both the relocatable binary code of segments and the specifications of their kept names are held. The kept names of any segment in an album are then available without further declaration to any further segments which have included the name of the segment in their "WITH-lists". A segment, with any included segments, is loaded and run in the natural order, remembering that the rule of no usage before declaration is adhered to rigorously.

The hierarchy of files in an album means that we can have an album inside another album, provided that segments within the inner album do not refer to segments in the outer album. Albums can therefore be shared between users. The only criterion for inserting a segment into an album is that the segment must have been compiled using either that album or one of its included albums. The base-level of every album is the system library, segments from which need not be prespecified.

The operating system environment is GEORGE 3, albums being GEORGE files. At present the compiling system is driven by GEORGE macros, but it is hoped that subsystems will be written to provide more efficient machine usage for various operating needs, such as batch-processing.

68-R SYNTAX

```
Things inside {} are optional.
Words starting with a capital are expanded.
Words in lower-case are explained elsewhere.

---        means repeatable from last unmatched { ( or [
-,---       last entity may be repeated (with comma separation)
--,---      last two entities may be repeated etc
---,---     last three etc

"Entity" is word, symbol, thing inside {}, or repeated entity.
Upper-case words and other symbols stand for themselves.
```

```
Segment      seg{WITH seg-,--- FROM album}(Sec){KEEP name-,---}

Sec          {Dec;{Unc;---}---}Unclist

Unclist      {{label:}Unc;---}{label:}Unc{EXIT label: Unclist}

Unc          Expn := Unc
             Expn ::= Unc
             Expn :: Unc
             Expn IS Unc
             Expn ISNT Unc
             {FOR id}{FROM Unc}{BY Unc}{TO Unc}{WHILE Sec}DO Unc
             Routineden
             Mode VAL Unc
             Expn

Expn         formula
             Primary

Primary      id
             den
             Primary(Unc-,---)
```

ALGOL 68-R

```
                  Primary[indexers]
                  selector OF Primary*
                  {LOCAL}Boundmode
                  IF Sec THEN Sec {ELSE Sec} FI**
                  CASE Sec IN Sec-,--- {OUT Sec} ESAC
                  (Sec)
                  (Sec,Sec-,---)
                  GOTO label

Dec               Boundmode id {:= Unc}--,---
                  PROC id := Routineden
                  Mode id = Unc---,---
                  PROC id = Routineden
                  MODE modename = Boundmode---,---
                  PRIORITY op = digit---,---
                  OP op = Routineden
                  OP(Mode){Mode}op = Unc
                  OP(Mode,Mode){Mode}op = Unc

Routineden        Mode:(Sec)
                  (Mode id-,--- --,---){Mode}:(Sec)

Boundmode         [Unc:Unc{FLEX}----,---]Boundsingle
                  Boundsingle

Boundsingle       STRUCT(Boundmode selector-,--- --,---)
                  Simplemode

Mode              [{,}---]Single
                  Single

Single            STRUCT(Mode selector-,--- --,---)
                  Simplemode

Simplemode        primitivemode
                  modename
                  VOID
                  REF Mode
                  PROC Mode
                  PROC(Mode-,---){Mode}
                  UNION(Mode-,---)
```

Abbreviations:

```
              den             denotation
              Expn            Expression
              id              identifier
              op              operator
              Routineden      Routine denotation
              Sec             Serial clause
              Unc             Unitary clause
              Unclist         List of Unitary clauses

              ( ... )         may be written   BEGIN ... END
```

*   Brackets bind more tightly than OF.

** "THEN IF ... FI FI" may be written "THEF ... FI"
    "ELSE IF ... FI FI" may be written "ELSF ... FI"

EXAMPLES OF ALGOL 68-R IN ACTION

program 11p10

```
BEGIN

OP / = ([] REAL a, b) REAL :
     {the value of  a/b  is that of the continued fraction
          a1 / (b1 + a2 / (b2 + . . . + an / bn...)) }
   ((UPB a = 0 | 0 | a[1] / (b[1] + a[2: ] / b[2: ])));

FOR n BY 2 TO 25 DO
   BEGIN
     [1:n] REAL a;
     FOR i TO n DO a[i] := 1;
     print((a / a, newline))
   END;

print((newline,
       "should approach (sqrt(5) - 1) / 2 = ", (sqrt(5)-1)/2,
       newline))

END
FINISH

****


10.31.33_ compile program11p10
10.31.55   4.07    CORE GIVEN 32768
  4.11  :HALTED :     COMPILED PROGRAM11P10
10.32.23_ online *lp0 (identify)
10.32.33_ execute
10.32.51   4.13    CORE GIVEN 5888
DISPLAY : LD
*LP0   +1.0000000000& +0
*LP0   +6.6666666667& -1
*LP0   +6.2500000000& -1
*LP0   +6.1904761905& -1
*LP0   +6.1818181818& -1
*LP0   +6.1805555556& -1
*LP0   +6.1803713528& -1
*LP0   +6.1803444782& -1
*LP0   +6.1803405573& -1
*LP0   +6.1803399852& -1
*LP0   +6.1803399017& -1
*LP0   +6.1803398896& -1
*LP0   +6.1803398878& -1
*LP0
*LP0   SHOULD APPROACH (SQRT(5) - 1) / 2 =  +6.1803398875& -1
*LP0
```

```
program 11p4

BEGIN

   PROC innerprod3 = (REF INT i, INT n, PROC REAL xi, yi) REAL :
      BEGIN
         REAL s := 0;
         FOR k TO n DO (i := k;   s PLUS xi * yi);
         s
      END;

   [1:8] REAL x1 := (1, 2, 3, 4, 5, 6, 7, 8);
   [2:9] REAL y1 := x1[AT 2];
   INT j, n;

   print((newline,
          innerprod3(j, 8, REAL : (x1[j]), REAL : (y1[j+1])),
          newline, newline));

   PROC ncos = REAL : (cos(twopi * j / n));
   PROC nsin = REAL : (sin(twopi * j / n));

   FOR i TO 20 DO
      print((i, "     ", innerprod3(j, n:=i, nsin, ncos), newline))

END
FINISH

****

10.15.25_ compile program11p4
10.15.49    2.21    CORE GIVEN 32768
  2.26  :HALTED :      COMPILED PROGRAM11P4
10.16.32_ online *lp0 (identify)
10.16.46_ execute
10.17.06    2.27    CORE GIVEN 6912
DISPLAY : LD
```

*LP0		
*LP0	+2.0400000000& +2	
*LP0		
*LP0	+1	+0.0000000000& +0
*LP0	+2	+0.0000000000& +0
*LP0	+3	+1.8189894036&-11
*LP0	+4	+0.0000000000& +0
*LP0	+5	-1.8189894036&-11
*LP0	+6	+1.4551915228&-11
*LP0	+7	+9.5070358763&-11
*LP0	+8	+4.3655745686&-11
*LP0	+9	-3.6379788071&-11
*LP0	+10	-4.0017766878&-11
*LP0	+11	+2.9103830457&-11
*LP0	+12	+6.9121597336&-11
*LP0	+13	+1.4551915228&-11
*LP0	+14	+1.4236408325&-10
*LP0	+15	+1.7098500393&-10
*LP0	+16	+5.4569682107&-11
*LP0	+17	+1.2369127944&-10
*LP0	+18	-4.7293724492&-11
*LP0	+19	+1.1641532183&-10
*LP0	+20	+0.0000000000& +0
*LP0		

INTRODUCTIONS

Woodward:

I would like to introduce to you Mr. Ian Currie, who with Miss Bond and Mr. Morison has written our compiler at the Royal Radar Establishment - a government laboratory which has a centralized computing service serving about 200 regular programmers. Mr. Currie has told me he would prefer to stimulate a discussion on his implementation of ALGOL 68 rather than give a formal lecture, but I will leave that to him. I suppose that our implementation should strictly be described as a "variant" because there are several ways in which the language differs from the formal definition. Mr. Currie will be telling you about this. The reason we are so glad to be here in Munich is our enthusiasm for ALGOL 68; we have called our version ALGOL 68-R, and it is now in everyday use at RRE. We already have some experience, not only of the compiler writing problems, but of users' reactions. It may interest you that I have myself found little difficulty in teaching the language to users: what may interest you far more is the way the users have become keener and keener on ALGOL 68 once they have started using it on real applications. Their initial difficulties were much eased by the fact that they had all been brought up on ALGOL 60. Our recent history is this: we started working in ALGOL with a compiler for ALGOL 60 which we wrote ourselves at RRE, and began using in 1963. For seven years, ALGOL 60 has been the sole language for our scientific and engineering users. This era will end in October of this year, when our old computer goes out of service. Our new machine opened operations in April of this year (1970). Two years previously, we had to decide what language in future to support. It was quite clear that we needed something more powerful than ALGOL 60, and there seemed little choice but to go for ALGOL 68. It was not an easy decision to make at the time, but we decided to go ahead. In the event, we were able to open operations in April this year with a servicable ALGCL 68-R compiler. I would like to stress the fact that we at RRE are not language theorists. We are concerned with practical utility, and with questions of maximizing throughput. This has meant that whenever we could see ways of reducing compilation time or improving object code efficiency in some obvious way, we felt bound to do something about it, if we could do so without departing from the spirit of the language. We aimed, in fact, that ALGOL 68-R should be a sublanguage of ALGOL 68, but I am sure that minor transgressions can be discovered. The compiler was started in January 1969, and during the overlap period between ALGOL 60 on the old computer and ALGOL 68-R on the new one, we are getting the cream of our clientele - users with rather big problems who need the bigger language and the bigger machine. In October this year, we shall be presenting our entire Establishment with little option but to program in ALGOL 68-R, as this will be the only language we shall actively support.

Currie:

I do not think I can add much more to what Mr. Woodward has said as far as the history is concerned, except for the facts, by way of explanation, as to why we started off doing the ALGOL 68 compiler in the way that we did. The ALGOL 60 compiler that we had on our old machine, was a one-pass compiler written all in machine code. Since then, we have written several compilers for a variety of different machines. They have all had the property that they were essentially one-pass, i.e., going from one source text to some kind of relocatable binary to load into the machine. So virtually all of our experience has been in writing one-pass compilers. I would not know how to set about writing a multi-pass compiler. I would regard it as a major intellectual exercise, not the least of which is having to work out n more intermediate codes. The writing of a one-pass compiler, influenced us quite a lot in the subset of ALGOL 68 that we wanted to implement.

(The paper was presented, by Currie, at this point.)

DISCUSSION

Griffiths:
You have just said that there is no parallel processing. I deduce that means you have no semaphores.

Currie:
No semaphores, right.

Griffiths:
Do you make use of the fact that the user might put commas instead of semicolons?

Currie:
No.

Van der Poel:
How do you do your explicit proceduring? What sort of operator do you use to procedure?

Currie:
Remember that in MR93 we had a thing called *val*. We have extended that slightly so that you write, for instance, *(real* : 2 × *random)* for a routine-denotation. To make a cast, you replace the cast-of-symbol by *val*. It comes back to ALGOL 68 proper if you translate that *val* as a colon.

Van der Poel:
Why do you find independent compilation of procedures so difficult?

Currie:
I did not say that. I want independent compilation of rather more than procedures. I do not think independent compilation of procedures is enough. I think you have got to be able to compile structures and all the rest of it

independently, as well as procedures. If you have only got procedures, then you find that writing packages to insert into the library is very difficult. It means that the users have always got to do something other than just declaring something.

Mailloux:
You said that declaration before use is not much of a restriction. I wonder if you handle mutually recursive procedures?

Currie:
Well, it is not really much of a restriction, is it? Of course, we handle mutually recursive procedures. We just put an extra reference in, e.g.:

```
proc p1,q1;
proc p = void: (...;q1;...);
proc q = void: (...;p1;...),
p1 := p; q1 := q;...
```

It is not nearly the same restriction as it was in ALGOL 60. In ALGOL 60 you always had to declare one procedure within the other procedure in our implementations, which always got a bit messy with scopes. But in ALGOL 68 it makes so little difference. You assign the procedure later instead of declaring it.

Mailloux:
What do you do with mutually recursive modes?

Currie:
We have extended the language slightly. You see, to declare mutually recursive modes x and y, we have to say *mode* x somewhere, e.g.:

```
mode x;
mode y = struct (int a, ref x x);
mode x = struct (real r, ref y y)
```

It is not strictly necessary.

Paul:
It is just a warning for the compiler then?

Currie:
Yes, that is right. It just helps in some of the bookkeeping inside the compiler.

Mailloux:
I notice, in some of your sample programs, that you are not underlining or stropping anything. Is this significant?

Currie:
We use two different representations. For the usual bold-face you can use upper case, with normal identifiers in lower case, or else make it case independent and put bold-face between primes, e.g., 'begin'.

Mailloux:
   I would be interested to know how you do coercions, in particular balancing, all in one pass.

Currie:
   Balancing in our subset is far easier than in full ALGOL 68. In most positions you are only doing either dereferencing or deproceduring in order to find the mode that you are trying to get to. You do not have to try uniting and proceduring as well, all at the same time. There is always a goal mode to look for and you can just apply your total coercions to the whole lot.

Mailloux:
   You deviate from the official definition though?

Currie:
   I am not so sure what you mean by deviation. I have said I have deviated already. I do not allow automatic proceduring at all.

Mailloux:
   Well, for instance, do you allow a jump as one half of a conditional-clause? For example:

   $x + \underline{if}\ y \geq 0\ \underline{then}\ sqrt(y)\ \underline{else}\ \underline{goto}\ alarm\ \underline{fi}$

Currie:
   That is O.K. That still comes by the same method. When you are in any position at which there is some element of balancing to go on, with this set of coercions, then all you need ever do is to take off *refs* and *procs* until you reach something that satisfies you.

Mailloux:
   Well, what about widening?

Currie:
   That is the one that is done at the base level, as it were. You cannot go any further down after widening. Perhaps if you would write down something.

Mailloux:
   Well consider: $random + \underline{if}\ x > 0\ \underline{then}\ i\ \underline{else}\ z\ \underline{fi}$
Clearly, given the standard prelude, this + is the one operating on a *real* as left operand and a *compl* as right operand. Thus, the left operand must be deprocedured, but the right operand is more difficult - i must be dereferenced to *int* widened to *real* and widened again to *compl*, whereas z need only be dereferenced to *compl*: that is to say, a different number of machine instructions will almost certainly be required to perform each of these coercions. Now space must be left in the object-code stream for each of these coercions, but, in a single scan, we cannot determine which coercions, and hence, how much space, until the scan has advanced to the *fi*.

Currie:
   Let us write down the input text and the corresponding code produced as it is read in.

input	code
random	
+	
if	
x	
>	
0	Load x
then	Branch <=0 to *l*1
i	
	Load reference i
else	Branch to *l*2
z	*l*1:
fi	(At this point we can balance the if-clause to complex since 68-R allows only dereferencing and deproceduring of operands)
	Load complex z
	*Branch to *l*3
	*l*2: Dereference and widen ref int to complex in register
	*l*3: (We can now identify the + as operating between real and complex)
	*Store complex in w1
	Deprocedure random
	Add real result and complex in w1

In this "translation" there are two extra "instructions" marked with a * which can be regarded as the one-pass penalty. Both of these instructions could be avoided by re-ordering the evaluation in a way which cannot be done in one pass. Of course, the presence or absence of the extra store instruction probably depends more on the availability of sufficient hardware registers.

Paul:

I should say the hard core of Mailloux's question of course is not that anyone doubts that everything can be done in one pass if you just make it complex enough, but the question is, how complex does it have to be in order to insist on doing it in one pass. I think the main flavour of your answer is that your restrictions allow you to cut down the complexity in a considerable way, but it is still somewhat unclear to me that the complexity is so much cut down.

Currie:

Consider what would happen if I allowed uniting in this position. Then we could not have reduced the operands to single values <u>before</u> identifying the operator. If there had been conditional-clauses on both sides of the operator, then none of the branches in the conditionals (like the one to *l*2 in the example) could be resolved until all the formula had been absorbed and the operator identified. Besides being against one-pass philosophy, this would produce a terrible complexity of branches in fairly simple situations.

These restrictions in the coercions do not help much in evaluating collateral-clauses since, except in trivial situations, a branch is required from each element to do the necessary coercions etc., and then a branch back to evaluate the rest of the collateral.

Van der Meulen:

Could you please explain why automatic proceduring is so difficult in one pass compiling. You have already partly answered it, but I should just like to know the difficulty in automatic proceduring as such.

Currie:

There are two main reasons for this difficulty. First, it is difficult to avoid obeying the code of expressions that are to be procedured. This implies that branches must be inserted before expressions which require proceduring and a lot of messiness occurs in getting rid of branches which are not required. Secondly, because of a shortage of index registers, I produce markedly different code for accessing locals and non-locals. Locals are accessed simply as a displacement on an index register, while non-locals require several instructions to get to the correct level. Since automatic proceduring would alter the local level, you can see the difficulties that would arise in attempting to produce efficient code compatible to the two situations.

Mailloux:

Let me give an example to see whether I understand correctly.

```
begin real a,b,c;
      proc real p;
      ...
      p:=a+b×c;
      ...
      begin compl x,y,z;
            ...
            x:=p;
            ...
      end;
      ...
end
```

Here, the routine created by proceduring $a+b\times c$ is "smuggled" into the inner range by the variable p, and elaborated there. The variables a, b and c in the routine would be accessed as specific displacements on the "most-local" index register, this register being updated at entry to, and exit from, each range. The call of the routine in the inner range then malfunctions, since this register then contains the address appropriate for accessing most-local variables like x, y and z, whereas the coding of the routine depends upon the register containing the address appropriate to the outer range. Is this the problem?

Currie:

Yes.

Mailloux:

Thus, in a machine sufficiently richly endowed with index registers that it is possible to allocate a different one to each depth of range nesting, the whole problem vanishes, even for one-pass compilation.

Currie:

Yes, except for getting rid of the branches inserted to avoid obeying the code, in the cases where you do want to obey the code at this point.

Branquart:

I should like to point out that the difficulty of proceduring in a one-pass compiler is less in a strong position. In other positions you can have balancing and if you are allowed to mix proceduring and deproceduring you have to wait until having in hand all modes of the balanced clauses before taking a decision. I think it one of the main reasons why it is difficult.

Currie:

There is a point that nobody has raised, and that is why proceduring anyway?

Paul:

I would like to hear the answer to this provocative question, but I should say that all those who have used more than one pass have not been so wrong after all because they have gained some better handling of complex things. You cannot postpone decisions very easily in a one-pass compiler because you have to put information into some lists and then to struggle your way through those lists back up again. You save that if you do the compiling by two or three or more passes.

Currie:

You struggle your way through three or four different representations instead.

SESSION 2

(Chairman: J.E.L.Peck)

ANALYSIS OF THE PARENTHESIS STRUCTURE OF ALGOL 68

P. BRANQUART, J. LEWI and J. P. CARDINAEL
MBLE, Res. Lab., Brussels, Belgium

1. INTRODUCTION

For the time being, no mechanical solution, directly using the definition of ALGOL 68 [1] has been found for solving the problem of syntactic analysis of this language. However, from this definition, it is rather easy to deduce a context-free syntax [7] describing a superset of the language; such a syntax defines a very useful structure for the compiler builder.

It remains to find out a deterministic algorithm of analysis based on this syntax, but this seems difficult to be done in a completely automatic way. The difficulty comes from the high degree of recursivity in which all program constructions are defined and from a lack of redundancy at the level of the representation language.

One solution consists in researching more ad hoc processes of analysis, which, among other things, try to split the problem into more simple ones. As far as we are concerned, we tried to use an algorithm generating bounded-context decision tables, already used for an ALGOL 60 compiler [3-6]. The results yielded have obviously not solved the whole problem of analysis for ALGOL 68 but they have given interesting information which has guided the choice of more ad hoc solutions. These solutions are based on the considerations given below.

Roughly speaking, the context-free structure of ALGOL 68 can be split up into three parts:
(i) The *edition structure* which separates entities of information such as identifiers, indications, some denotations and tokens.
(ii) The *parenthesis structure* which closely corresponds with the parentheses * used in the language.
(iii) The *operator structure* which corresponds with program constructions generally associated with language defined operators (:=, :=:, ...) or with program defined operators (formulas).

The edition structure is rather easy to detect by means of a finite state automaton.

---

* Throughout this note, the stress has been laid on parentheses proper; the other tokens playing a similar part have been treated as well; such are: "<u>begin</u>", "<u>end</u>", "<u>if</u>", "<u>fi</u>", "<u>case</u>", "<u>esac</u>", "[",")", "<u>then</u>", "<u>else</u>", "<u>thef</u>", "<u>elsf</u>", "<u>in</u>", "<u>out</u>", "|" and "|:".

The parenthesis structure is partly explicit, because it corresponds with the parentheses of the language, and partly hidden, because the same parenthesis tokens are used for surrounding many kinds of syntactic constructions; the goal of this note is precisely to develop a method for allowing the recognition of these constructions and to add this information to the corresponding parentheses. These may then be regarded as phrase markers.

The further detection of the operator structure is straightforward and is easily obtained in a deterministic way.

Though apparently trivial, the problem of recognition of parentheses is rather intricate if it is solved in its whole generality and in the absence of entirely mechanical solutions. For this reason, the solution described in this note cannot be qualified as fool-proof and we would be only too glad to acknowledge any kind of corrections and ameliorations.

However that may be, our purpose is twofold: on the one hand, to propose a particular solution issued from the experience gained [2] in closely following the evolution of ALGOL X, and on the other hand to produce a document displaying the complications inherent to the problem.

Finally we should like to recall that some aspects of this problem have already been treated [8]; the approach which is given here has been developed independently.

2. CRITERIA

The method of recognition which is developed in this note applies to the most general ALGOL 68 programs, only supposing they have been edited beforehand; thus, it admits all kinds of representations allowed in [1], even inconsistently mixed, and it does not suppose that the mode and operator indications can be distinguished. This last assumption is at the origin of some intrinsic indeterminations about the nature of parentheses; these indeterminations are solved in a trivial way during the next phases of the compilation.

The method uses three criteria which are based on specific syntactic features of the language. In practice, these criteria are not independently used, and in particular, the order in which they are applied is relevant.

(i) The first criterium is based on the bounded-contexts surrounding left and right parentheses; it has been checked starting from a context-free syntax [7] by means of an algorithm generating bounded-context decision tables [3, 5, 6].

Examples: - in "struct (int i, real r)", the context "struct" of the left parenthesis determines its nature (FIELDS declarator pack);

- in "(int i, real r) a: ... " the contexts "real r" and "a:" of the right parenthesis determine the nature of the construction: formal PARAMETERS pack.

(ii) The second criterium is based on particular characters of the program texts comprised between left and corresponding right parentheses, to the exclusion of the texts surrounded by inner parentheses; such characters are the comma, the colon and the semicolon.

ANALYSIS OF THE PARENTHESIS STRUCTURE   39

   Example: - in "<u>begin</u> *a*, *b* <u>end</u>" the appearance of a comma determines
   the nature of the construction, collateral CLAUSE, as opposed to "<u>be-
   gin</u> *a*; *b* <u>end</u>" which is a 'closed CLAUSE'.
(iii) The third criterium is intended to take the extensions into account, by
   which the characters "<u>struct</u>", "<u>union</u>" and "<u>op</u>" need not always be repeated inside some program constructions (collateral declarations, formal PARAMETERS, FIELDS declarators). This problem is solved by
   setting up some states when the characters "<u>struct</u>", "<u>union</u>" and "<u>op</u>"
   appear in the programs under certain circumstances. These states are
   reconsidered each time a comma or a semicolon is met.
   Example: - in "<u>struct</u> *s* = (<u>real</u> *a*, *b*), *t* = (<u>int</u> *i*, <u>real</u> *r*), ... " the nature of the last left parenthesis (FIELDS declarator pack) depends on
   the state dictated by the presence of "<u>struct</u>".
  The above criteria are not sufficient to eliminate all indeterminations on
parentheses; two kinds of indetermination do subsist:
(i) The first kind corresponds with making the difference on the one hand
   between 'ROWS rower' or 'formal PARAMETERS pack' and 'CLOSED
   clause', on the other hand between 'ROWS rower' and 'routine denotation', in some difficult contexts:

$$\begin{bmatrix} (\underline{int}:2)\ \underline{a}\ i \\ \text{cast} \\ \text{formula} \end{bmatrix} \quad \text{and} \quad \begin{bmatrix} (\underline{int}:2)\ \underline{a}\ i \\ \text{declarer} \\ \text{identity declaration} \end{bmatrix}$$

$$\begin{bmatrix} ((\underline{a}\ a):3)\ \underline{b}\ b \\ \text{routine denotation} \\ \text{formula} \end{bmatrix} \quad \text{and} \quad \begin{bmatrix} ((\underline{a}\ a):3)\ \underline{b}\ b \\ \text{declarer} \\ \text{identity declaration} \end{bmatrix}$$

and also between 'void cast pack' and 'ROWS rower':

$$\begin{matrix} (:3)\ \underline{a}\ a=\ldots \\ \text{void cast pack} \\ \text{formula} \end{matrix} \quad \text{and} \quad \begin{matrix} (:3)\ \underline{a}\ a=\ldots \\ \text{declarer} \\ \text{identity declaration} \end{matrix}$$

   These indeterminations can always be solved when the nature of one
   single indication appearing in the bounded contexts of a right parenthesis is known; a fortiori, it can be solved as soon as a table of indication
   declarations is available; such a table can be built up at the same time
   as the present algorithm is performed; this one already deals with a
   number of extensions of mode declarations, thus facilitating the construction of the table. Among these indeterminations, some are completely unsolvable without knowing the nature of the indications:
   "$((\underline{a}a):3)\ \underline{b}\ b$" or "$(\underline{int}:2)\ \underline{a}\ i$"; other ones could be solvable at the price
   of introducing intricate complications in the criteria: "$(3:x+y*z)\ \underline{b}\ b$".
(ii) The second kind of indetermination corresponds with making the differ-

ence between 'slices' and 'calls': it will be solved during the processing of modes and coercions. In some cases it is impossible to solve these indeterminations before this last process has been performed: "$a(3)$" or "b (int : 3)"; in other cases they could be solved at the price of changing the criteria: "$a(3:4)$".

Remark finally that the criteria which are generally very specific could be misleading when errors appear in programs. Obviously some redundancies can be introduced by combining several criteria or by enlarging the contexts, or even by finding out other criteria. Nevertheless the difficulties of the problem of error handling seem to be inherent to the language. This problem has not been tackled here.

3. GENERAL FORM OF THE ALGORITHM

The algorithm of recognition proceeds in a single left to right pass through the programs, without backtracking.

Given the nested structure of parentheses, the passing on of the information issued from the three criteria can be performed by means of a pushdown stack. The elements of this stack may be regarded as structured values having as many fields as there are informations of different nature. For example, the informations resulting from the contexts of the left parentheses, from the states, the commas, the colons and the semicolons, have to be transmitted to the right until the corresponding right parenthesis is met; to each of these informations corresponds a field in the stack elements. Conversely the informations available at the right parenthesis should be transmitted to the corresponding left parenthesis; this can be obtained either by storing the address of the left parenthesis in a new field of the stack elements or by performing a further right to left pass. For reasons of simplicity the transmission of informations to the left parenthesis has not been implemented in the sequel of this note.

The general form of the algorithm is the following:
(i) At each left parenthesis its context is analyzed; this generally allows one to restrict the class to which this parenthesis belongs; a new stack element is then set up, where in particular, information about the class of the left parenthesis is stored.
(ii) To the field 'state' of the upper stack element, an appropriate state is assigned in the following cases:
   a) the state '<u>op</u>', when the character "<u>op</u>" is met
   b) the state '<u>structm</u>' or '<u>unionm</u>' when the character "<u>struct</u>" or "<u>union</u>" followed by a mode indication is met
   c) the state '<u>structd</u>' or '<u>uniond</u>', when the right parenthesis of a declarer '<u>struct</u>(...)' or '<u>union</u>(...)' followed by an identifier is met.
This field is analyzed when a comma is met at the same level of the nested structure. The context of the comma sometimes indicates if an extension corresponding with the state is present. In some difficult cases such as

ANALYSIS OF THE PARENTHESIS STRUCTURE   41

and
$$\underline{\text{struct}} \ (\underline{\text{int}}\ i, \ \underline{\text{real}}\ r)\ s, \ (\underline{\text{int}}\ i, \ \underline{\text{bool}}\ b)\ t, \ldots$$

$$\underline{\text{struct}} \ (\underline{\text{int}}\ i, \ \underline{\text{real}}\ r)\ s, \ (\underline{\text{int}}:2)\ \underline{a}\ a, \ldots$$

the decision has to be postponed (to the last right parenthesis in the examples).
(iii) The appearance of a comma, colon and semicolon brings about the overwriting of the corresponding field in the upper stack element.
(iv) At each right parenthesis, the information accumulated in the upper stack element, and possibly some context are examined in order to determine with more precision the class to which the parenthesis belongs. As said above, there may remain some indeterminations.

The explicit algorithm of recognition is given in section 5 by means of an ALGOL 68 program. This program uses the table of section 6 where all situations are displayed. It must be emphasized that this table has to be consulted in a sequential order. On the other hand, in a practical implementation, a less interpretive and consequently more efficient algorithm can easily be deduced from the table.

We remark at last that the introduction of some restrictions simplifies the problem a great deal (see appendix); for example the following restrictions can be envisaged:
(i) The use of square brackets as 'sub' and 'bus symbols' can be required
(ii) More consistency in the use of the representations may be required (as already done in the language in the use of the pairs"[,]", "(/,/)" and "(,)" for the 'sub' and 'bus symbols').
(iii) The possibility of recognizing mode indications from operator indications may be required, for example by means of a preliminary pass.

4. THE USE OF THE ALGORITHM IN A COMPILER

In the compiler under implementation in our laboratory, the syntactic analysis of ALGOL 68 programs has been split up into three parts as explained above: the edition structure, the parenthesis structure and the operator structure.

This compiler proceeds in six phases, where no backtracking is allowed:
(i) The first phase takes place during the loading of the program, it comprises the detection of the *edition structure*, and of the *parenthesis structure*, using the algorithm described in this note. Moreover, a table of indication declarations is established. This table is intended to be used for performing the identification process of indications during the next phase; hence, these declarations have to be connected with a range. The trouble is that the ranges cannot be detected before parentheses have been recognized; a solution consists in regarding all parentheses as defining a kind of range which, though not corresponding with the ranges of the language, can however be used for identifying the indications. These ranges differ from those of the language in two respects: some constructions such as 'collateral clauses' and 'formal

PARAMETERS' are regarded as ranges but the 'routine denotations', the parentheses of which have been dropped, are not. This does not bring about any problem, because no one of these constructions may have constituent indication declarations.

(ii) The second phase has the table of indication declarations at its disposal, and is able from the outset to identify the indications and to eliminate the first kind of remaining indeterminations on parentheses. Moreover, the previous recognition of the parentheses of the 'formal PARAMETERS packs' easily allows one to restore the parentheses of the routine denotations which have been dropped; some distinctions among routine denotations, made in the preceding phase, allow one to detect the dropping of the 'plans' in the procedure and operator declarations (see section 7 - 15). This phase is systematized by means of a deterministic top-down syntactic analyzer, which can be easily obtained once parentheses have been recognized. Such an analyzer detects the *operator structure* and inserts in the program texts the corresponding phrase markers in *postfix form*. The detection of 'empty' as rowed coercend is also performed and this 'empty' is replaced by a special symbol, greatly facilitating the performance of the next phases. At last, during the second phase a table of declarers and of identity declarations is established, and the ranges which have no constituent declarations are marked in a special way.

(iii) The main goal of the third phase is to insert the markers corresponding with the *operator structure* in *prefix form*; this phase proceeds from right to left and is also systematized by means of a top-down analyzer. In this way, the coercions and thereafter the translation proper can be performed each during a single left to right pass. The identification of identifiers is also performed during this phase.

(iv) The fourth phase deals with modes, coercions and performs the identification of operators [9]. It also eliminates the second kind of indetermination on parentheses (difference between 'slices' and 'calls') and collects information for scope checking.

(v) The fifth phase translates the program into an intermediate code closely depending on the storage allocation scheme which has been adopted [11-16].

(vi) At last the sixth phase translates the intermediate code into machine code while some optimizations are performed.

5. THE ALGORITHM OF RECOGNITION

begin
comment
1. This algorithm accepts ALGOL 68 'source programs', and transforms them into equivalent 'object programs' where supplementary information has been attached to parentheses, thus connecting each of them with a particular class. These classes correspond with the following program constructions, the parentheses of which will be given a charcteristic representation:

ANALYSIS OF THE PARENTHESIS STRUCTURE

FIELDS declarator pack	(s	)s
procedure symbol, virtual PARAMETERS pack	(p	)p
operation symbol, virtual PARAMETERS pack	(o	)o
LMOODS MOOD and box pack open LMOODS MOOD and box pack	(u	)u
sub symbol, VICTAL ROWS rower, bus symbol	(b	)b
formal PARAMETERS pack	(f	)f
routine denotation	(r	)r or (rl)rl
sub symbol, ROWS leaving ROWSETY indexer, bus symbol	(sl	)sl
actual PARAMETERS pack	(call	)call
void cast pack	(v	)v
closed CLAUSE	(cl	)cl
collateral CLAUSE	(col	)col
conditional CLAUSE	if then else fi thef elsf	
case CLAUSE	case in out esac (*)*	

After the process, some indeterminations on right parentheses remain between:

)b and)col   )b and)rl   )sl and)call
)b and)cl   )f and)cl   )b and)v

2. The following conventions will be used throughout this program:

    ν : indicant
    μ : mode indication
    ρ : ADIC indication
    δ : identifier
    α : any character a declarer may begin with in the source program, with the exception of "(", "[" and "ν". These characters are:

long	char	union	bytes
int	format	struct	string
real	proc	compl	sema
bool	ref	bits	file

they determine without any context consideration the presence of a declarer in the source program; only long may also begin a denotation or an operator, but this can be detected in a trivial way.

ω: any character a declarer may end with in the object program with the exception of "ν". These characters are

int	format	)s	string
real	proc	compl	sema
bool	)p	bits	file
char	)u	bytes	

they determine without context consideration the presence of a declarer in the object program

π : any character a primary may end with in the object program, with the exception of the characters representing right parentheses on which some indetermination subsists; π represents the following set, the elements of which, that must not end the primary of a slice or of a call, have been crossed out; actually, these elements need not to be considered:

)cl   esac   ~~nil~~   ~~)v~~
)~~col~~ ~~)*~~   δ   )r
fi   )sl   ~~skip~~   )rl
PLAIN denotation
BITS denotation
row of character denotation
format denotation

3. The characters K, S, and F represent each a single parenthesis on which some indetermination subsists; the indetermination associated with each such character is described hereafter by enumerating the possible specific parentheses it may represent:

K: (col, (cl, if, case, (b, (f
S:)sl,)call
F:)f,)cl

comment
char rchar co   rchar possesses a name which refers to the last edited character which has been read in *co*;
proc EDIT = (*rchar* := *co* the next edited character of the source program *co*)

comment
            EDIT works as a finite state automaton; it reads ALGOL 68 source programs sequentially from left to right and it groups their characters into atoms of information from a semantical point of view. Comments, spaces, carriage returns and other irrelevant characters are disregarded.

ANALYSIS OF THE PARENTHESIS STRUCTURE

Those regarded as atoms are:
- the identifiers
- the indications
- the denotations except the routine denotations and the dynamic replications of format denotations
- the action tokens
- the declaration tokens
- the syntactic tokens
- the sequencing tokens
- the hip tokens
- the extra tokens

Actually, "identifiers", "indications", and "denotations" are transformed into structures with two fields: a 'class field' (identifier, indication or denotation) and a 'specification field' where a pointer to a table is stored. In this table more specific information can be found: alphanumerical representations for identifiers and indications, and machine representations of the values possessed by denotations.

The present algorithm is only concerned with the first field which is regarded as the character delivered by EDIT.

comment
proc STORE = (char c) : co stores c into the object program co;
mode stackelem = struct (char parenthesis,
                            state,
                            consistency,
                        bool comma,
                            colon,
                            semicolon)

comment
'stackelement' represents the mode of the elements which are stored on the stack used in this program.
- in the field 'parenthesis' is stored a character representative of the information available at each left parenthesis; such characters are

(s	(p	if	out	(sl
(u	(col	then	while	
(o	(:	else	thenin standing for then or in	
(b	(*	in	ifcase standing for if or case	
(slcall standing for			(sl or (call	
(bsl	"	"	(b or (sl	
(bsc	"	"	(b, (sl or (call	
(rb	"	"	(r, (b or (rl	
(colcl	"	"	(col or (cl	
(sb	"	"	(s or (b	
(ub	"	"	(u or (b	

(ob	standing for		(o or (b
(r	"	"	(r or (rl
(cr	"	"	(col, (cl, <u>if</u>, <u>case</u>, (b, (f, (r or (rl
(c	"	"	(col, (cl, <u>if</u>, <u>case</u>, (b or (f
(ck	"	"	(col, (cl, <u>if</u>, <u>case</u>, (b, (r or (rl
(c2	"	"	(col, (cl, <u>if</u>, <u>case</u> or (b

- in the field 'state' is stored a character representative of the information allowing one to take some of the extentions 9.2 of [1] into account; such characters are:

<u>structm</u>   <u>structd</u>
<u>unionm</u>   <u>uniond</u>
<u>op</u>   <u>empty</u>

- in the field 'consistency' is stored the source program token of each left parenthesis; it is intended to give the possibility of checking an abusive mixing of representations of parentheses, for example "begin a)".
- the fields 'comma', 'semicolon' and 'colon' indicate whether, respectively, at least one comma, one semicolon or one colon has been met after the last encountered left parenthesis, disregarding the text comprised between inner parentheses.

comment ;

　　mode stack = [1:*flex*] *stackelem ;*

　　stack S := ;

　　struct context = *(string left, char char, string right);*

　　struct conditions =　　*(char　　rchar,*

　　　　　　　　　　　　　　　　　parenthesis,

　　　　　　　　　　　　　　　　　state,

　　　　　　　　　　　　context　context,

　　　　　　　　　　　　bool　　comma,

　　　　　　　　　　　　　　　　semicolon,

　　　　　　　　　　　　　　　　colon   );

　　struct actions =　　*(string　part action,*

　　　　　　　　　　　　char　　parenthesis,

　　　　　　　　　　　　　　　　state,

　　　　　　　　　　　　　　　　classes   );

ANALYSIS OF THE PARENTHESIS STRUCTURE

struct <u>tableelem</u> = *(conditions* conditions,

actions   actions   );

<u>int</u> n;

<u>mode</u> <u>table</u> = [1:n] <u>tableelem</u>;

<u>table</u> TABLE
   <u>co</u> TABLE (see section 6) will be interpreted by the present algorithm, it is composed of a number of elements (lines) which are scanned sequentially. Each element consists of a number of execution of a number of actions. The entry points in TABLE correspond with the last edited characters; such characters are:

struct	union	op	
(	)	|	|:
[	]		
begin	end		
while	do		
if	then	else	fi
thef	elsf		
case	in	out	esac
:	;	,	

The following declarations define procedures which will be used in TABLE

<u>co</u> ;

<u>proc</u> INS = (:(<u>co</u> add one element at the top of S <u>co</u>

   [1: ⌈S+1⌉] <u>stackelem</u> IT;

   IT [1: ⌈S⌉] := S;

   IT [⌈S+1⌉] := ("empty", "empty", "empty",

      <u>false</u>, <u>false</u>, <u>false</u>)

   <u>co</u> empty is regarded as one character <u>co</u>;

   S := IT));

<u>proc</u> OUTS =   S := S[1: ⌈S-1⌉] <u>co</u> delete one element from S <u>co</u> ;
<u>proc</u> OPEN = (:(INS;

$$consistency\ \underline{of}\ S[\ulcorner S] := rchar));$$

$\underline{proc}\ CLOSE = (:(\ OUTS\ ;$

$\quad\quad \underline{if}\ \ulcorner S=0\ \underline{then}\ stop\ \underline{fi};$

$\quad\quad \underline{if}\ parenthesis.\underline{of}\ S[\ulcorner S] = "(cr"$

$\quad\quad \underline{then}\ parenthesis\ \underline{of}\ S[\ulcorner S] := "(c"\ \underline{fi}));$

$\underline{proc}\ CLOPEN = (:(\ CLOSE;\ OPEN));$

$\underline{proc}\ SUPScm = (\underline{bool}\ b)\ :\ comma\ \underline{of}\ S[\ulcorner S] := b;$

$\underline{proc}\ SUPScn = (\underline{bool}\ b)\ :\ colon\ \underline{of}\ S[\ulcorner S] := b;$

$\underline{proc}\ SUPSsc = (\underline{bool}\ b)\ :\ semicolon\ \underline{of}\ S[\ulcorner S] := b;$

$\underline{proc}\ ROUT = (\underline{char}\ c)\ :\ (OUTS;$

$\quad\quad \underline{if}\ \ulcorner S=0\ \underline{then}\ stop\ \underline{fi};$

$\quad\quad \underline{if}\ parenthesis\ \underline{of}\ S[\ulcorner S] = "(cr"$

$\quad\quad \lor\ parenthesis\ \underline{of}\ S[\ulcorner S] = "(ck"$

$\quad\quad \underline{then}\ parenthesis\ \underline{of}\ S[\ulcorner S] := "(c"\ \underline{fi});$

$\underline{proc}\ EXTD = (:(\ STORE\ (",");$

$\quad\quad SUPScm\ (\underline{true});$

$\quad\quad EDIT;$

$\quad\quad OPEN));$

$\underline{proc}\ EXTM = (\underline{char}\ c)\ :\ (\ STORE\ (",");$

$\quad\quad SUPScm\ (\underline{true});$

$\quad\quad rchar := c);$

$\underline{co}$ the algorithm proper is the following: $\underline{co}$

$newchar\ :\ EDIT;$

$\quad\quad \underline{for}\ I\ \underline{to}\ n\ \underline{do}$

$\quad\quad (\underline{tableelem}\ T = TABLE\ [I];$

$\quad\quad \underline{conditions}\ conditions = conditions\ \underline{of}\ T;$

$\quad\quad \underline{actions}\ actions = actions\ \underline{of}\ T;$

ANALYSIS OF THE PARENTHESIS STRUCTURE

  if (*rchar of conditions* = "skip" *co* see section 6, step 6 *co*
    ∨ *rchar of conditions* = *rchar*)
   &(*parenthesis of conditions* = "skip"
    ∨ *parenthesis of conditions* = *parenthesis of* $S[\lceil S]$)
   &(*state of conditions* = "skip"
    ∨ *state of conditions* = *state of* $S[\lceil S]$)
   &(*left of context of conditions* = "skip"
    ∨ *left of context of conditions* = *co the string corresponding*
      with the last characters stored in the object
      program, in number equal to the number of
      characters in "left of context of conditions"
      co)
   &(*right of context of conditions* = "skip"
    ∨ *right of context of conditions* = *co the string corresponding*
      with the next characters to be read in the
      source program, in number equal to the num-
      ber of characters in "right of context of
      conditions" co)
   &(*comma of conditions* = "skip"
    ∨ *comma of conditions* = *comma of* $S[\lceil S]$)
   &(*colon of conditions* = "skip"
    ∨ *colon of conditions* = *colon of* $S[\lceil S]$)
   &(*semicolon of conditions* = "skip"
    ∨ *semicolon of conditions* = *semicolon of* $S[\lceil S]$)
then proc EXECUTE = (*string s*) : *co consider s as an Algol 68 program*
     and elaborate it co;
 co here can be performed a check of consistency between rchar and
  consistency of $S[\lceil S]$ *co*
   EXECUTE (*part action of actions*);

>   *if* parenthesis *of* actions ≠ "skip"
>
>   *then* parenthesis *of* S[⌈S] := parenthesis *of* actions
>
>   *fi*;
>
>   *if* state *of* actions ≠ "skip"
>
>   *then* state *of* S[⌈S] := state *of* actions
>
>   *fi*;
>
>   *if* classes *of* actions = "skip"
>
>   *then* STORE (rchar) ;
>
>   newchar
>
>   *else* STORE (classes *of* actions);
>
>   newchar
>
>   *fi*
>
>   *fi*);
>
>   STORE (rchar);
>
>   newchar .
>
>   stop : *co* end of the process *co*

comment

> The problem of error detection and recovery has not been treated, no alarm is provided

comment

> *end*

6. THE DECISION TABLE

The table below is a condensed form of the decision table to be used by the algorithm described in section 5. This condensed form has the advantage of making some combinations apparent and of being more synthetic. On the other hand the algorithm is much simpler if a complete form of the table is used. It is rather easy to deduce the complete table from its condensed form, though the following rules to be applied for performing the transformation might seem intricate.

Step 1: delete the last column N^o (this column is only constituted by num-

ANALYSIS OF THE PARENTHESIS STRUCTURE

bers referring to the examples of section 7); go to step 2.

Step 2: if several characters (lines) appear in one same rectangle of the column classes, replace these characters by a single one representative of the set of original ones (the characters of the set have been enumerated in order to make the indeterminations more clear) and go to step 2; otherwise go to step 3.

Step 3: if a symbol α, ω or π which stands for n ($n>1$) characters, appears in some line of some rectangle of the table, replace in this rectangle, this line by n lines. These lines are copies of the original line where the symbol α, ω or π has been replaced in the n respective lines by the respective n characters for which this symbol stands, go to step 3; otherwise go to step 4.

Step 4: if n lines of text ($n>1$) appear in the same rectangle, combine each of these lines with all rectangles at the right of the original one, go to step 4; otherwise go to step 5.

example:

a	b	d	f
	c	e	g

becomes

a	b	d	f
		e	g
	c	d	f
		e	g

Step 5: if a rectangle, now necessarily containing at most one line of text, corresponds with n ($n>1$) rectangles at its right, divide the original one into n rectangles at the height of the right ones, repeat the line of text in each of the new rectangles, and go to step 5; otherwise go to step 6.

example:

a	b	d
		e
	c	d
		e

becomes

a	b	d
a	b	e
a	c	d
a	c	e

step 6: if a rectangle is empty, write "<u>skip</u>" in it, and go to step 6, otherwise the process is finished.

NB. Vertical dotted lines appearing in the table will be explained in the appendix.

TABLE I

	conditions									actions			
rchar	parenthesis	state	left	context char	right	comma	semi-colon	colon	part action	parenthesis	state	classes	N°
struct				struct	μ						structm		1
union				union	μ						unionm		2
op				op							op		3
(			struct	(					OPEN	(s		(s	4
			structμ=	(					OPEN	(s		(s	4'
			union	(					OPEN	(u		(u	5
			unionμ=	(					OPEN	(u		(u	5'
			op	(					OPEN	(o		(o	6
			proc	(	⌒...				OPEN	(b		(b	7
				(					OPEN	(p		(p	8
			par	(					OPEN	(col		(col	9
			= s	(					OPEN	(sl(call		(sl (call	10
			F	(					OPEN	(bsc		(b (sl (call	11
				(	:				OPEN	(:		(v (b	12

ANALYSIS OF THE PARENTHESIS STRUCTURE 53

TABLE II

N°	conditions									actions			
	rchar	parenthesis	state	left	context char	right	comma	semi-colon	colon	part action	parenthesis	state	classes
13	‿				‿	*				OPEN	(*		(*
14					‿	/*				OPEN	(*		(*
15					‿					OPEN	(cr		(col (cl (if (case (b (r (rl
16										OPEN	(c		(col (cl (if (case (b (f
17		(c ::(c2					true	false		CLOPEN	in		in
18		ifcase								CLOPEN	thenin		then in
19		if								CLOPEN	then		then
20		thenin					true	false		CLOPEN	out		out
21		then thenin								CLOPEN	else		else
21'		in								CLOPEN	out		out

TABLE III

rchar	parenthesis	state	conditions context left	context char	context right	comma	semi-colon	colon	part action	parenthesis	state	classes	N°
|:	(c (c2 ifcase if								CLOPEN	if		thef	22
	then thenin								CLOPEN	if		elsf	23
)			*/ */	)					CLOSE			)*	24
	(bsc		/	)	α ν:				ROUT("(r")			)b	25
			/	)					ROUT("(c2")			)sl	26
									ROUT("(c2")			)sl)call	26'
	(b								CLOSE			)b	27
	(s			)	δ				CLOSE		structd	)s	28
					δ				CLOSE			)s	28'
	(u			)					CLOSE		uniond	)u	29
									CLOSE			)u	29'
	(p								CLOSE			)p	30
	(o								CLOSE			)o	31
	then else								CLOSE			fi	32

TABLE IV

ANALYSIS OF THE PARENTHESIS STRUCTURE

rchar	conditions										actions			
	parenthesis	state	context			comma	semi-colon	colon	part action	parenthesis	state	classes	N°
			left	char	right								
	in/out								CLOSE			esac	33
	thenin					true	false		CLOSE			esac	34
									CLOSE			fi	35
	(col								CLOSE			)col	36
	(slcall								CLOSE			)sl	37
									CLOSE			)sl/call	38
	(colcl					true	false		CLOSE			)col	39
									CLOSE			)cl	40
	(:			)	α				CLOSE			)b	41
					⊃				CLOSE			)b/)⊃	41'
			/	)					CLOSE			)⊃	42
	(c		K	)	α/⊃:				CLOSE			)b	43
			,						CLOSE			)b	44
				)	α/⊃:			true	CLOSE			)b	45

TABLE V

rchar	parenthesis	state	conditions context left	context char	context right	comma	semi-colon	colon	actions part action	parenthesis	state	classes	N°
)	(c		κ	)	α ν:				ROUT(''(r'')			)f	46
				)	ν				CLOSE			)b	47
			,	)	ν				CLOSE			)b)col	48
				)	ν	true	false	false	CLOSE			)col	49
							false	false	CLOSE			)cl	50
						true	false	true	CLOSE			)b)col	51
								true	CLOSE			)b)cl	52
			,δ	)	.. ⌣				ROUT(''(r'')			)f	53
			ωδ	)	.. ⌣				ROUT(''(r'')			)f	54
			νδ	)	..				ROUT(''(rb'')			)f)cl	55
					⌣				ROUT(''(ck'')			)f)cl	56

ANALYSIS OF THE PARENTHESIS STRUCTURE

TABLE VI

rchar	conditions									actions				N°
	parenthesis	state	context			comma	semi-colon	colon	part action	parenthesis	state	classes	
			left	char	right								
)	(c					true	false		CLOSE			)col	57
									CLOSE			)cl	58
									CLOSE			)b	59
	(c2			)	α	true	false	false	CLOSE			)col	60
				)	∨		false	false	CLOSE			)cl	61
						true	false	true	CLOSE			)b)col	62
								true	CLOSE			)b)cl	63
						true	false		CLOSE			)col	64
									CLOSE			)cl	65
	(sb			)	δ				CLOSE		empty	)s	66
									CLOSE			)b	67
	(ub			)	δ				CLOSE		empty	)u	68
									CLOSE			)b	69

TABLE VII

	conditions										actions				
rchar	parenthesis	state	context		comma	semi-colon	colon	part action	parenthesis	state	classes	N°
			left	char	right									
⟩	(ob		(;	⟩				CLOSE		empty	⟩b	70
							true	CLOSE		empty	⟩b	71
								CLOSE			)o	72
	(r			⟩	; ;			CLOSE			)r	73
								CLOSE			)rl	74
	(rb			⟩	α			CLOSE			)b	75
					∨			CLOSE			)rl)b	76
					; ;			CLOSE			)r	77
								CLOSE			)rl	78
			proc	[				OPEN	(b		(b	79
			π S	[	*			OPEN	(*		(*	80
				[				OPEN	(sl		(sl	81
			F	[				OPEN	(bsl		(b (sl	82
[								OPEN	(b		(b	83

ANALYSIS OF THE PARENTHESIS STRUCTURE

TABLE VIII

	conditions									actions				
rchar	parenthesis	state	left	char	right	comma	semi-colon	colon	part action	parenthesis	state	classes	N°
⌐				⌐					CLOSE			)*	84
	(sl								CLOSE			)sl	85
	(bsl			⌐	α ν:				ROUT("(r")			)b	86
									ROUT("(c2"))			)sl	87
	(b								CLOSE			)b	88
begin			par	begin					OPEN	(col		(col	89
									OPEN	(colcl		(col (cl	90
end	(col								CLOSE			)col	91
	(c ::(c2					true	false		CLOSE			)col	92
	(colcl								CLOSE			)cl	93
while									OPEN	while		while	94
do									CLOSE			do	95
if case									OPEN	ifcase		if case	96

TABLE IX

	conditions									actions				
rchar	parenthesis	state	context			comma	semicolon	colon	part action	parenthesis	state	classes	N°
			left	char	right								
then in	if								CLOPEN	then		then	97
	ifcase (c ;(c2					true	false		CLOPEN	in		in	98
									CLOPEN	thenin		then in	99
else out	in								CLOPEN	out		out	100
	then								CLOPEN	else		else	01
	thenin					true	false		CLOPEN	out		out	02
									CLOPEN	else		else	03
fi esac	in								CLOSE			esac	04
	then								CLOSE			fi	05
	out								CLOSE			esac	06
	else								CLOSE			fi	07
	thenin					true	false		CLOSE			esac	08
									CLOSE			fi	09
thef									CLOPEN	if		thef	10
elsf									CLOPEN	if		elsf	11

ANALYSIS OF THE PARENTHESIS STRUCTURE

TABLE X

	conditions									actions				N°
rchar	parenthesis	state	context			comma	semi-colon	colon		part action	parenthesis	state	classes	
			left	char	right									
:										SUPS$_{cm}$(true)				112
;										SUPS$_{sc}$(true)		empty		113
,		structm		,	μ=					FXTM("struct")				114
		unionm		,	μ=					FXTM("union")				115
		structd		,	(					EXTD	(sb		(s,b)	116
				,	δ					SUPS$_{cm}$(true)				116'
		uniond		,	(					EXTD	(ub		(u,b)	117
				,	δ					SUPS$_{cm}$(true)				117'
		op		,	p=					FXTM("op")				118
				,	(					EXTD	(ob		(o,b)	119
										SUPS$_{cm}$(true)		empty		120

7. EXAMPLES

In this section are given a few examples relevant to a number of situations which may occur when trying to recognize the parentheses of a program. These examples are linked to the table of section 6 by means of their numbers which correspond with the column N^o. They are intended to facilitate the understanding of the table but by no means do they represent an exhaustive study.

Information about parentheses has been added under the examples and the underlined arrows point to the characters which are supposed to have been read last.

1) (struct s = (int i, real r), ...
          ↑
          ĭ

2) (union u = (int, real), ...
         ↑
         ĭ

3) (op o = ((real x) real : - x), ...
       ↑
       ĭ

   (op (real) real o = ((real x) real : - x), ...
    ↑
    ĭ

4) (struct (int i, real r) s, ...
           ↑
           s

5) (union (int, real) u, ...
          ↑
          u

6) op (real) real o = ((real x) real : -x);
      ↑
      o

7) proc (:,) int p;
        ↑
        b

8) proc (real) int p;
        ↑
        p

9) par (a, b, c);
       ↑
       col

10) a (3);   a (3)   (4);   [1:3] int a; a (3);
      ↑   ↑ ↑   ↑   ↑
      sl   sl sl   sl   sl
      call   call call call   proc (int) a; a (3);
                                                                     ↑
                                                                     call

11) ((a a) (...
    ↑   ↑ ↑   ↑
    r   f f   b
    cl   cl cl sl
    col   call
    b
    if
    case

ANALYSIS OF THE PARENTHESIS STRUCTURE

$$\begin{bmatrix} \text{mode } \underline{a} = \ldots, \ \underline{c} = \ldots, \\ (\ (\ \underline{a}\ a\ )\ (\ :\ )\ \underline{c}:5\ )\ ; \\ \uparrow\ \uparrow\quad\ \ \uparrow\ \uparrow\quad\quad \uparrow \\ \text{r f}\quad\ \ \text{f b}\ \ \text{b}\quad\quad\ \text{r} \end{bmatrix}$$

$$\begin{bmatrix} \text{op } \underline{a} = \ldots, \ \underline{c} = \ldots;\ \text{mode } \underline{f} = \ldots; \\ (\ (\ \underline{a}\ a\ )\quad (\ 1:3\ )\ \underline{c}\ 7:5\ )\ \underline{f}\ a; \\ \uparrow\ \uparrow\quad\quad\ \uparrow\ \ \uparrow\quad\quad\ \uparrow\quad\quad\quad \uparrow \\ \text{b cl}\quad\quad \text{cl sl}\quad\quad \text{sl}\quad\quad\quad \text{b} \\ \quad\quad\quad\quad\ \text{call}\quad\quad \text{call} \end{bmatrix}$$

$$\begin{bmatrix} \text{op } \underline{a} = \ldots, \ \underline{c} = \ldots,\ \underline{f} = \ldots;\ \text{mode } \underline{d} = \ldots; \\ (\ (\ \underline{a}\ a\ )\quad (\ 1:3\ )\ \underline{c}\ 7;\underline{d}:5\ )\ \underline{f}\ a; \\ \uparrow\ \uparrow\quad\quad\ \uparrow\ \ \uparrow\quad\quad\ \uparrow\quad\quad\quad\ \uparrow \\ \text{cl cl}\quad\quad \text{cl sl}\quad\quad \text{sl}\quad\quad\quad\ \text{cl} \\ \quad\quad\quad\quad\ \text{call}\quad\quad \text{call} \end{bmatrix}$$

The indetermination between, on the one hand "bound" and on the other hand "slice/call" could be solved without identifying the indications, but not always by using the criteria defined in section 2 (see also 26 and 27 in this section). However, the indetermination is more intrinsic in "a (3)" and "a ($\underline{b}$:3)" which may be either "slices" or "calls".

12) $(\ :\ 3\ \ldots$
    $\uparrow$
    v
    b

$$\begin{bmatrix} (:3\ ); \\ \uparrow\ \ \uparrow \\ \text{v} \\ (:3\ )\ \text{int } a = \ldots \\ \uparrow\ \ \uparrow \\ \text{b}\ \ \text{b} \end{bmatrix}$$

13) $(*\ x,\ y\ ::\ w\ *);$
    $\uparrow\quad\quad\quad\quad\ \uparrow$
    $(*\quad\quad\quad\quad *)$ not allowed?

14) $(/\ *\ x,\ y\ ::\ w\ *\ /);$
    $\uparrow\quad\quad\quad\quad\quad\ \uparrow$
    $(*\quad\quad\quad\quad\quad *)$ not allowed?

15) ((
    $\uparrow$
    col
    cl
    if
    case
    b
    f
    r
    rl

$$\begin{bmatrix} (\ (\ 1,\ 2\ )\ ,(\ 3,\ 4\ )\ )\ ; \\ \uparrow\ \uparrow\quad\quad\quad\ \uparrow\ \uparrow\quad\quad\quad\ \uparrow\ \uparrow \\ \text{col col}\quad\ \text{col col}\quad\ \text{col col} \\ (\ (\ 1,\ 2\ )\ )\ ; \\ \uparrow\ \uparrow\quad\quad\quad\ \uparrow\ \uparrow \\ \text{cl col}\quad\ \text{col cl} \\ (\ (\ b = \text{true}\ )\ |\ 3\ |\ 4\ )\ ; \\ \uparrow\ \uparrow\quad\quad\quad\quad\quad\ \uparrow\quad\quad\quad\ \uparrow \\ \text{if cl}\quad\quad\quad\quad\ \text{cl}\quad\quad\quad \text{fi} \\ (\quad (\ i+1\ )\ |\ 3,\ 4\ |\ 5\ )\ \ ; \\ \uparrow\quad\quad\quad\ \uparrow\quad\quad\ \uparrow\quad\quad\quad\ \uparrow \\ \text{case cl}\quad\ \text{cl}\quad\quad\quad\quad \text{esac} \\ (\ (\ i+1\ )\ :4\ )\ \text{int}; \\ \uparrow\ \uparrow\quad\quad\quad\ \uparrow\quad\ \uparrow \\ \text{b cl}\quad\quad\ \text{cl}\quad\ \text{b} \end{bmatrix}$$

```
       ( ( ( , ) int x) real : ... ) ;
         ↑ ↑ ↑ ↑      ↑            ↑
         r f b b      f            r
       ( ( ( , ) int x) real : ...) ( 3 ) ;
         ↑ ↑ ↑ ↑      ↑             ↑  ↑   ↑
         r1 f b b     f             r1 call call
```

NB. The differentiation between '(r' and '(r1' will be useful to detect extension 9.2.e in the next phase:

proc p = ((real x) : ...); corresponding to
          ↑   ↑
          r   r proc (real) p = ...

proc p = ((real x) : ...) (3.14); no extension.
          ↑   ↑
          r1   r1

16) See 15 except '(r' and '(r1' because these parentheses are necessarily followed by another one: '(f'

17) (x, y :: z | ...   parenthesis of S[ΓS] = (c
                ↑
                in

    if x, y :: z | ...   parenthesis of S[ΓS] = ifcase
                  ↑
                  in

    ((a a) (b : 3)   c 7, y :: Z | ... parenthesis of S[ΓS] = (c2
      ↑ ↑   ↑ ↑   ↑   ↑
      if cl   cl sl   sl   in
              call   call

18) (b | ...   parenthesis of S[ΓS] = (c
        ↑
        then
        in

19) (b | : d | ...
        ↑   ↑
        thef then

20) (x | 3 , 4 | ...
        ↑   ↑
        then   out
        in

21) (x | 3 | ...
        ↑   ↑
        then else
        in

21') (x, y :: z | 3 , 4 | ...
                  ↑   ↑
                  in   out

22) (x | : ...
        ↑
        thef
```
```

23) $(\ x\ |\ 3\ |\ :\ ...$
    $\quad\ \ \uparrow\quad\ \ \downarrow$
    $\quad$ then elsf
    $\quad$ in

24) see 13 and 14

25) $(\ (\ \underline{a}\,a\ )\ (\ \underline{b}:3\ )\ \underline{c}\ :\ ...$
    $\qquad\qquad\quad\uparrow\qquad\ \ \downarrow$
    $\qquad\qquad\quad$b$\qquad\ \ $b
    $\qquad\qquad\quad$sl
    $\qquad\qquad\quad$call

    see also 11

26) $(\ (\ \underline{a}\,a\ )\ (\ \underline{b}:3\ )\ \underline{c}\ a\ ...$
    $\qquad\qquad\quad\uparrow\qquad\ \ \downarrow$
    $\qquad\qquad\quad$b$\qquad\ \ $sl
    $\qquad\qquad\quad$sl$\qquad\ \ $call
    $\qquad\qquad\quad$call

27) see 7
28) see 4
29) see 5
30) see 8
31) see 6

32) $(b\ |\ :d\ |\ e\ )\ ;$ $\qquad\qquad$ (see 19)
    $\qquad\quad\ \ \downarrow\quad\ \uparrow$
    $\qquad\quad\ $then fi

33) $(\ x,\ y\ ::\ z\ |\ 3,\ 4\ )\ ;$ $\qquad$ (see 17)
    $\qquad\qquad\ \uparrow\qquad\ \downarrow$
    $\qquad\qquad\ in\qquad$esac

34) $(\ x\ |\ 3,\ 4\ )\ ;$ $\qquad\qquad$ (see 18)
    $\quad\ \ \uparrow\quad\ \ \downarrow$
    $\quad$ then$\quad$esac
    $\quad$ in

35) $(\ x\ |\ 3\ )\ ;$ $\qquad\qquad\quad$ (see 18)
    $\quad\ \ \uparrow\quad\downarrow$
    $\quad$ then fi
    $\quad$ in

36) see 9

37) $a\ (/\ 3/)\ ;$
    $\quad\ \ \uparrow\quad\ \downarrow$
    $\quad$ slice slice
    $\quad$ call

38) see 10

39) begin x, y) ;
    ↑   ↑
    col col
    cl

40) begin x) ;
    ↑   ↑
    col cl
    cl

41) (: 3) int a = ...
    ↑ ↑
    b b

41') (: 3) $\underline{a}$ a = ...
     ↑ ↑
     b b
     v v

42) see 12

43) ; (... /) ...   see 15 and 16
         ↑
         b

44) ( ) int a = ...
    ↑ ↑
    k b

45) (3 : 4) int a ;
         ↑
         b

46) ((int x) int : 3) ;
    ↑   ↑
    r   f

    (int x) $\underline{a}$: ...
             ↑
             f

47) ( ) $\underline{a}$ a = ...
    ↑
    b

48) ($\underline{b}$: a ,) $\underline{a}$ b ;
              ↑
              b
              col

49) (3 , 4) $\underline{a}$ a ;
          ↑
          col

50) (3) $\underline{a}$ a ;
      ↑
      cl

51) ($\underline{b}$: 4, $\underline{c}$: 5) $\underline{a}$ a ;
                ↑
                b
                col

ANALYSIS OF THE PARENTHESIS STRUCTURE

52) (<u>b</u> : 4) <u>a</u> a ;
      ↧
      b
      cl

53) (<u>a</u> a , <u>b</u> b) : ... ; ... (<u>a</u> a , <u>b</u> b) (...
                ↧   ↧
                f   f

no collateral clause neither as strict lower bound nor in weak position,
nor as primary of a call.

54) (<u>a</u> a ; int b) : ... ; ... (<u>a</u> a ; int b) ( ) int : ...
                ↧   ↧
                f   f

no declaration at the end of a closed clause

55) ((<u>a</u> a) : ...   ⎡ mode <u>a</u> = ... ; ((<u>a</u> a) : ...
    ↑   ↑   ↑   ↧
    b   cl   r   f
                                            op <u>a</u> = ... ; ((<u>a</u> a) : ...
                                                                   ↑   ↧
                                                                   b   cl

56) ((<u>a</u> a) (...   ⎡ mode <u>a</u> = ... ; ((<u>a</u> a) ( ) int : ...
   ↑   ↑   ↑   ↧
  col f   r   f
  cl cl
  if   op <u>a</u> = ...;((<u>a</u> a) (3)
  case   ↑   ↧ ↑
  b   b   cl sl
  r   call

57) (a , b) ;
        ↧
      col

58) (a) ;
    ↧
    cl

59) ((<u>a</u> a) (1 : 3) <u>c</u> 7 : 5) int ...
   ↑   ↑   ↑   ↑ ↑   ↑   ↧
  cl cl   cl sl   sl   b
  col   call   call
  b

60) ((<u>a</u> a) (1 : 3) <u>c</u> 7,5) <u>d</u> 3 ...
   ↑ ↑ ↑ ↑ ↑   ↑   ↧
  cl cl cl sl   sl   col
  col   call   call
  b

61) ((*a* *a*) (1 : 3) *c* 7) *d* 3 ...
   ↑ ↑   ↑ ↑   ↑   ↑
   cl cl   cl sl   sl   cl
   col   call   call
   b

62) ((*a* *a*) (1 : 3) *c* 7 : 5, 1 : 2) *d* ...
   ↑ ↑   ↑ ↑   ↑   ↑
   cl cl   cl sl   sl   b
   col   call   call   col
   b

   ((*a* *a*) (*b* : 3) *c* 7, *d* : 2) *e* 3 ...   │ the distinction between '(b' and
                                      ↑   │ '(col' is not possible using the
                                     col   │ criteria of section 2.
                                      b

63) similar to 62

64) ((*a* *a*) (*b* : 3) *c* 7, 2) *d* 3 ...
                                ↑
                               col

65) ((*a* *a*) (*b* : 3) *c* 7) *d* 3 ...
                                ↑
                               cl

66) struct (...) *a*, (...) *b*, ...
              ↑   ↑
              s   s
              b

67) struct (...) *a*, (...) int *b*, ...
              ↑   ↑
              s   b
              b

68) similar to 66

69) similar to 67

70) op ... , (, ,) int *a* ...
             ↑   ↑
             o   b
             b

71) op ... , (3 : 4) int *a* ...
             ↑   ↑
             o   b
             b

72) op ... , (int) int *o* = ...
              ↑   ↑
              o   o
              b

73) ((int *a*) : ...) ;
                ↑
                r

ANALYSIS OF THE PARENTHESIS STRUCTURE   69

74) ((int a) : ...) (3) ;
            ↑
            r1

   see remark under 15

75) (($\underline{a}$ a) : ...) int ...
    ↑ ↑   ↑   ↑
    r f   f   b
    b cl   cl

76) (($\underline{a}$ a) : ...) $\underline{b}$ b ...
    ↑ ↑   ↑   ↑
    r f   f   r1
    b cl   cl   b

77) (($\underline{a}$ a) : ...);...
    ↑ ↑   ↑   ↑
    r f   f   r
    b cl   cl

78) (($\underline{a}$ a) : ...) (...
    ↑ ↑   ↑   ↑
    r f   f   r1
    b cl   cl

79) proc [,,,] ...
         ↑
         b

80) [* x, y :: z *] ;
    ↑
    (*

81) a [3] ; a (3) [4] ;
        ↑   ↑
        sl   sl

82) ($\underline{a}$ a) [...
          ↑ ↑
          f b
          cl sl

83) ([ ] ...
    ↑
    b

84) see 80

85) see 81

86) ($\underline{a}$ a) [,,,] int : ... ; ... ($\underline{a}$ a) [,,,] $\underline{b}$: ...
          ↑ ↑   ↑ ↑
          f b b   f b b

87) ($\underline{a}$ a) [...] ;
             ↑
             sl

88) see 79

89) to 113) obvious

114) <u>struct</u> <u>a</u> = (<u>int</u> i, <u>real</u> r) , <u>b</u> = (...
                          ↑

115) similar to 114

116) <u>struct</u> (<u>int</u> i, <u>real</u> r) a, (...
                                ↑
                                s
                                b

117) similar to 116

118) <u>op</u> <u>o</u> = ... , <u>p</u> = ...
          ↑

119) <u>op</u> <u>o</u> = ... , (...
                        ↑
                        o
                        b

8. CONCLUSION

The results of this study have shown that it is possible to detect the almost complete parenthesis structure of the most general ALGOL 68 programs in a deterministic way during the first pass of the compilation. The remaining context-free structure, i.e. the operator structure, can then be obtained in a rather trivial way.

In the whole this study has not been easy at all and the absence of mechanical solutions does not allow one to guarantee its correctness in an absolute way. Moreover, the problem of error detection and recovery, which has not been treated here, seems to be still more difficult. These problems are simplified a great deal by the introducing simple syntactic restrictions.

ACKNOWLEDGMENTS

The authors wish to acknowledge the invaluable contributions of their colleagues J. P. Delescaille and M. Vanbegin in the programming and debugging of the algorithm.

ABSTRACT

First the part played by parentheses in the syntactic structure of ALGOL 68 and the problem of their recognition are settled, then the criteria used for solving this last problem are explained (section 2). Thereafter, the main lines of the algorithm of recognition are sketched (section 3) and this is placed in the general frame of a compiler (section 4).

The algorithm is then expressed under the form of an ALGOL 68 program (section 5). This algorithm uses a decision table which is displayed (section 6) while a few examples illustrating the most difficult cases are given (section 7). At last, the simplifications subsequent to some restrictions are enumerated (appendix).

REFERENCES

[1] Van Wijngaarden, A., (Editor), Mailloux, B.J., Peck, J.E.L. and Koster, C.H.A., *Report on the algorithmic language ALGOL 68*, Mathematisch Centrum, Amsterdam, 1969.
[2] Sintzoff, M., (Editor), Branquart, P., Lewi, J. and Wodon, P.L., *Remarks on the Draft Reports on ALGOL 68*, Report R96, MBLE Res. Lab., Brussels, January 1969.
[3] Branquart, P., *A program generating a decision table for a bounded-context syntactic analyzer, (The algorithm of Eickel)*, Technical Note N31, MBLE Res. Lab., Brussels, May 1967.
[4] Branquart, P., *The ALGOL 60 - P3 compiler*, Report R73, MBLE res. Lab., Brussels, January 1968.
[5] Loeckx, J., *An algorithm for the construction of bounded-context parsers*, Report R99, MBLE Res. Lab., Brussels, March 1969.
[6] Branquart, P., Delescaille, J.P. and Lewi, J., *An implementation of an algorithm for the construction of bounded-context decision tables*, Technical Note N52, MBLE Res. Lab., Brussels, April 1969.
[7] Branquart and Lewi, J., *A context-free syntax of ALGOL 68*, Internal Note, MBLE Res. Lab., Brussels, September 1968.
[8] Koch, F., *The recognition of ranges in ALGOL 68*, Thesis, University of Calgary, September 1969.
[9] Branquart, P. and Lewi, J., *On the implementation of coercions in ALGOL 68*, Report R123, MBLE Res. Lab., Brussels, January 1970. (Presented at the "International Computing Symposium", Bonn, May 1970.)
[10] Sintzoff, M., *Calculating properties of programs by evaluations on specific models*, MBLE Res. Lab., Brussels, April 1970.
[11] Branquart, P. and Lewi, J., *On object language and storage allocation*, Proceedings of an Informal Conference on ALGOL 68 Implementation, University of British Columbia, August 1969.
[12] Branquart, P. and Lewi, J., *A scheme of storage allocation and garbage collection for ALGOL 68*, MBLE Res. Lab., Brussels, April 1970.
[13] Wodon, P.L., *Methods of garbage collection for ALGOL 68*, MBLE Res. Lab., Brussels, April 1970.
[14] Branquart, P. and Lewi, J., *On the implementation of local names in ALGOL 68*, Report R121, MBLE Res. Lab., Brussels, November 1969. (Presented at the International Computing Symposium, Bonn, May 1970.)
[15] Branquart, P. and Lewi, J., *Structure d'un compilateur ALGOL 68*, MBLE Res. Lab., Brussels, April 1970 (presented at the AFCET Congress, Paris 1970).
[16] Branquart, P. and Lewi, J., *Local generators and the ALGOL 68 working stack*, Technical Note N62, MBLE Res. Lab., Brussels, April 1970.

APPENDIX: SIMPLIFIED TABLE

The simplifications to the table of section 6, given below, are obtained by supposing that the mode and operator indications are distinguished.

1. Modifications to the conventions:
    α stands for the union of the old set α and μ
    ω stands for the union of the old set ω and μ
2) Modifications to the table
    {- the numbers between parentheses are references to the column N^o of the table;
    - the arrows stand for "has to be replaced by";
    - the lines which have to disappear are marked in the table with vertical dotted lines}
    (11), (25), (26), (26'), (41'), (47) to (52), (55), (56), (59) to (65), (75) to (78), (82), (86), (87) →
    in (17), (18), (22), (92), (93), (98), (99) : (c2 →
    in (44), (45), (46) : r: →

DISCUSSION

Mailloux:
    I am going to try and hang myself I think by asking whether, on the basis of your study, you can come to any conclusion about how many different kinds of brackets would have been necessary or highly desirable as distinct kinds, supposing we had round ones, square ones, braces, and so on.

Branquart:
    I think if you drop the possibility of using normal parentheses instead of square brackets, it would greatly simplify the problem.

Mailloux:
    I think you still have the difficulty of discovering whether you have a routine denotation or not, which has always bothered me.

Branquart:
    Yes, but it would be less difficult if specific square brackets were used.

van der Meulen:
    As a matter of fact, the square bracket is in the language, and replacing it by a round bracket is an extension, isn't it?

Branquart:
    But for descriptive reasons, I think.

van der Meulen:
    Yes, but the trouble arises from using an extension that nobody will use, I hope.

Branquart:

I am not sure that nobody will use it.

Mailloux:

I do not have square brackets on my keypunch (Amusing rejoinders about manufacturers.)

Peck:

Your methods of analysis of the parenthesis structure involves using a stack, and I think this stack contains six elements in it. Do you think that this could possibly be simplified, that some of these stack elements might be left out and that the remaining analysis could be left to the parsing stage?

Branquart:

Some of the stack elements are only useful in very particular cases, which perhaps can be treated in the following passes, I agree.

van Wijngaarden:

May I make one remark in defense of the ALGOL 68 Report? It has been said that the sub-symbol, or the bus-symbol may be represented by an ordinary opening and a closing parenthesis by virtue of the extensions and not the representations. As far as I remember, it is only in the extensions for purely aesthetical reasons, namely to prevent a programmer from using a square opening parenthesis combined with a round closing parenthesis. But as far as I can see, there is no problem whatsoever for the computer. It is just an aesthetical problem rather than any problem of substance.

Branquart:

Moreover the problem of brackets is not the only problem arising from the extensions; if you drop all extensions, the whole compiler will be simplified a great deal. (Laughter.)

Lindsey:

On this same subject, there is another remark one could make. Generally speaking, if you meet an opening parenthesis and you are not sure what is going to follow, then it does not particularly matter if you do not know, provided that things that may follow are roughly similar in nature. Generally speaking, what is going to follow, for example after an *if* or an *elsf* in a conditional, is some sort of serial-clause, and what is going to follow after an open bracket in a closed-clause is some sort of serial-clause and it does not really matter terribly. You are not sure which is at this stage. But where it does matter is where the beast which is about to follow may turn out to be something very unlike a serial-clause, such as where it turns out that what you are embarking on is in fact a row-of-mode-declarer. So there are some cases, and I think this is one of them, which are going to be rather embarrassing, as Branquart has said. I think there are other cases where it does not matter particularly that you do not know. But certainly this opening round parenthesis, which turns out to be a row-of-mode-declarer is an unpleasant thing to have to deal with. It is a pity, but it is there. Are there any observations to make upon the case where you get an opening round bracket followed by a slash, which means that you are either starting on a thing where the slash is a monadic-operator, or it may be that you are starting simply on another representation of the sub-symbol.

Branquart:
I think that the use of a round bracket followed by a slash facilitates the solution of the problem, compared to the use of only square brackets without the slash.

Lindsey:
Yes, but if you have a round bracket followed by a slash, it may be a round bracket followed by a monadic-operator slash, and you do not know until you get to the matching bracket.

Branquart:
Yes O.K., but in many cases of recognition of parenthesis, you have to wait until the right parenthesis is met, and parenthesis-slash is only a particular case, which enters into our system without difficulty. The principal advantage of having recognized parentheses is that you have more information in prefix form, and the further use of a deterministic top-down syntactic analyzer is very much simplified thereafter.

Lindsey:
Can you give us a summary of the passes you are going to have and into which pass this particular recognition process fits?

Branquart:
Well, we have a six pass compiler, the first of which takes place during the reading of the program. During this first pass we recognize a part of the parenthesis structure in the most difficult cases; the reason is that during the next pass we want to recognize the ranges of the program and to make a table of the declarers. For that purpose we have to recognize the routine-denotations, the formal-parameters-packs and the bounds-packs beforehand. During the second pass, the remaining parentheses are recognized, but this becomes rather trivial. Moreover, in thia pass we are able to recornize the operator structure of the program and to put the corresponding phrasemarkers in postfix form. Then we have a right to left pass in which these phrasemarkers are put in prefix form, and this permits us to deal with the coercions in one single left to right pass, I cannot say without backtracking but with a rather restricted backtracking only dealing with modes. The last two phases are related to the translation into machine code.

Prentice:
If a person who is rather perverse chooses to write a program, perhaps unintentionally, which has one of these constructions, and the whole of his program is one procedure, you could end up with a very large amount of material on your stack. Will this not present problems?

Branquart:
The length of the stack only depends on the depth of the nesting of parentheses; practically such a depth cannot be so large as to cause storage problems. So we store the stack in the core store but the program in the

backing store. The storage problem is now how to add complementary information to the left parentheses already stored in the backing store; you can imagine two solutions. The first is to make a right to left pass after the first pass. Of course, this is time-consuming. The second one consists in storing in the program, not refined parentheses, but pointers to a part of the core store where the refined information is stored.

program: (...)

refined information: parenthesis of bounds

We have the same features when dealing with coercions, which after all, are also discovered after a whole coercend has been treated. And it is important to have this information in prefix form in case of proceduring.

Prentice:
The thing that slightly worries me is that if I had done something like this, someone would find a construction which my decision table did not take account of, and that using the same sort of entries in the decision table, I could not resolve it. Is it that you have tried enough cases to convince yourself that this is all right or have you got some sort of a more formal way of demonstrating this?

Branquart:
No. We have learned the language for a long period, but we are not sure of our table of decision. The proof is that we found two errors recently. However, I can say we are more and more sure.

Griffiths:
The trouble surely goes a lot deeper than this because like most implementers, or at least most of the ones I know, you are using a grammar which is not the grammar written in the Report. We have thus no formal proof that the grammar we start with contains the grammar that is in the Report. However, it is reasonably simple to prove from your grammar that what you are doing is correct, that is to say that the character on which you perform discrimination is actually sufficient. The only formal problem would then be to prove that ALGOL 68 is properly contained in the language defined by your context-free grammar.

Branquart:
I can say we are more convinced of the correctness of our starting grammar than of the correctness of our decision-table. Because after all you have already a context-free frame in the Report. However, I am not at all convinced that it is so easy to prove the correctness of our decision table.

Peck:

Could I ask whether, as a result of this study, there is one single thing you would like to have changed in the language in order to make this analysis easier?

Branquart:

My answer would be rather trivial: to impose the use of a specific symbol for some kind of parenthesis, in the case of 'sub' and 'bus symbols' for example.

Goos:

May I answer your question? We should recognize that language parsing is from left to right and that the right context in parsing has not the same weight as the left context. Some of these parentheses use some kind of "postfix" to distinguish between the different meanings. They do not use a "prefix" form and that is what is really wanted for the parsing.

Branquart:

In my opinion, it would be very difficult to make it possible to discriminate parentheses by means of left context, without imposing the use of specific brackets in most of the cases.

AN IMPLEMENTATION OF IDENTIFIER TABLES IN A MULTIPASS ALGOL 68 COMPILER BASED ON A HASH-CODE TECHNIQUE

J. KRÁL and J. MOUDRÝ

Prague Tech. Univ. and Czech.Acad.Sci., Prague

1. TERMINOLOGY

We shall use the terminology of the ALGOL 68 Report. By the 'meaning' of an identifier Id in its applied occurrence O we shall understand the mode associated with it at its defining occurrence O_1 identified by O. We shall say that the identifier Id is declared on the level of the range R, if R is the least range containing O_1. We shall assume that each pass scans its input (or source) text from left to right. We shall say that the compiler enters (leaves) a range R if it reads the first (last) symbol of R.

In this paper the question of whether the boundary symbols belong to the range R is not important.

2. MAIN FEATURES OF THE COMPILER

The compiler under discussion will be of three-pass type (it is not excluded, however, that the third pass will be split into more passes). The compiler will translate a source program into an assembly language. A rough description of the compiler is given below. Only the details important for the technique discussed are given.

Pass 1

1a. Range enumeration. An integer j, the range number of R, is associated with each range R. In the following, R_j is a range with range number j. (In [2], j is called a 'cumulative block number'). A range is uniquely determined by its range number. Ranges are numbered from left to right according to the occurences of their left most symbols.
1b. Transformation of tokens into an internal representation.
1c. Elaboration of mode- and operation-declarations.
1d. Substitution of implicit identifiers for denotations.
1e. Syntactic analysis I (context conditions for modes, bracketing, form of denotations).
1f. Transformation of identifiers into 'standard form'.

Pass 2

2a. Elaboration of identity declarations (i.e., construction of identifier tables, including the meaning of identifiers).

2b. Syntactical analysis II (context conditions for identifiers).
   Pass 3
   Translation into assembly language (including the search for the meaning of all identifiers at their applied occurrences).

3. TRANSFORMATION OF IDENTIFIERS IN PASS 1

The basic idea of a 'standard form' of an identifier is to make as easy (and as quick) as possible any search in identifier tables (which will be constructed later). This is achieved by renaming the identifiers used. New identifiers form a sequence $Q1, Q2 \ldots Q'k'$, where $Q'k'$ means an identifier, obtained as a result of the concatenation of letter Q and the current numerical value of k. A hash table may be used to perform the transformation efficiently.

The meaning of any ALGOL 68 program P does not change if identifiers in P are systematically changed, provided a one-to-one correspondence between the original and the changed identifiers exists. Let $T = \{T_0, T_1 \ldots T_N\}$ be a hash table containing all the identifiers occurring in the program P. Let the structure $T_i = \{Id_i, N_i\}$ be a pair consisting of an identifier and a positive integer, which will be used in the transformation

$$Id_i \rightarrow Q'N_i'.$$

The number N_i is associated with the identifier Id_i at its first occurrence; its value is equal to (number of distinct identifiers met so far) -1.

A simple program

   begin real i, j, k ; .... *(int* i, j) .... *end*

will be transformed into

   begin real Q1, Q2, Q3 ; .... *(int* Q1, Q2) .... *end*

The transformation algorithm may be described in ALGOL 68 as follows:

   begin int NID := 0 ; ¢ *NID will contain the number of identifiers in*

   the program ¢

   struct item = *(bytes* id, *int* n) ;

   [1:1023] *item* T ;

   for i *from* 0 *to* 1023 *do* T [i] := (empty bytes, 0) ;

   bytes empty bytes = *c* *any pattern which cannot correspond to an*

   identifier c ;

   proc hash : *(bytes* a) *int* : *c* *a procedure generating a nonnegative*

   integer less than 1024 c ;

```
proc transformation = (string orig) string :
    begin bytes a = ctb orig ; int i := hash (a) ;
    e: if id of T [i] = a then i := n of T [i]
        elsf id of T [i] = empty bytes then ¢ new
                            identifier ¢
        NID := NID + 1 ;
            T [i] := (a, NID); i:= NID
        else i := h(i) ¢ h is a function determining what item of
        T will be examined in the next step ¢ ;
            go to e fi ;
"Q" + int string (i, 4, 10)
end ;
 . . . . . .
```

Here, of course, only the procedures implementing the basic features of the idea are given. The generalisation is not complicated. For example, it is quite easy to allow identifiers and the table T to be of variable length and so on. To each identifier in the source program the procedure *transformation* is applied.

4. CONSTRUCTION OF DECLARATION LISTS (PASS TWO)

In pass two, for each range Rj, a declaration list Lj is constructed. Each list Lj is a sequence of pairs $(Q'k', M)$, where $Q'k'$ is an identifier in the standard form declared on the level Rj and M its meaning (a pointer to the corresponding 'mode descriptor'). For the sample program given above the declaration lists may be written in and ad hoc notation as follows:

L_1 = { (Q1, *real*), (Q2, *real*), (Q3, *real*) }
L_2 = { (Q_1, *int*), (Q2, *int*) }

When leaving a range Rj the corresponding list Lj may be transferred into an auxiliary memory. The symbols Q are clearly redundant in Lj lists and can be omitted. The construction of Lj is straightforward and causes no problem.

5. THE USE OF DECLARATION LISTS (PASS THREE)

In pass three a table Tl of the size NID is created (NID has the value obtained in pass one, the value of NID is therefore equal to the number of different identifiers in the program). Elements of Tl are the 'meanings' of identifiers and the 'addresses' associated with them. At the start of pass three all the members of Tl have a value indicating that the meaning of the corresponding identifier is yet undefined. When a range Rj is entered, its declaration list Lj is transferred into the main memory. For each item $I(Q'i',M)$ in Lj the value of M in I and the value of $Tl\,[i]$ are exchanged (note that the value of i is given in $Q'i'$). When leaving the range Rj the reverse change is made so that after the completion of the elaboration of Rj, Tl has its initial contents. It can easily be verified that during the elaboration of Rj the meaning of any identifier $Q'k'$ in all its applied occurrences may be found in $Tl\,[k]$ (note again that k is given in $Q'k'$).

Another very similar technique stores a pointer to a list structure in $Tl\,[k]$. This structure contains the meanings of $Q'k'$ from all the ranges entered but not left up to now. The last (i.e., valid) meaning of $Q'k'$ is in front of $\mathcal{L}k$. Handling of such structures may be described as follows. At the start of pass three each member of Tl contains <u>nil</u>. When a range Rj is entered the following transformation is performed. For each item $l = (Q'k',M)$ in Lj a copy of M is placed in front of $\mathcal{L}_k$. When leaving Rj the reverse transformation is performed, i.e., the lists $\mathcal{L}_k$ are made to have the content before entering Rj. The reverse transformation can easily be made by a systematic examination of the first members in all $\mathcal{L}_k$ or using the list Lj again.

It can be shown that the technique discussed can be applied to the handling of mode tables and that there are modifications of it using ideas described in [2].

SUMMARY

A simple straightforward technique for the construction of the identifier tables is given. The technique is particularly efficient in multipass compilers. It will be used in a three-pass ALGOL 68 compiler for the TESLA 200 computer. The search time is independent of the number of identifiers in a program and needs no complicated machinery.

REFERENCES

[1] Van Wijngaarden, A., Mailloux, B.J., Peck. J.E.L., and Koster, C.M.A., Report on the algorithmic language ALGOL 68, MR101, Mathematisch Centrum, Amsterdam, 1969.
[2] Kanner, H., Kosinski, P., and Robinson, C.L., The structure of yet another ALGOL compiler, in: Programming systems and languages, S. Rosen (Ed.), McGraw-Hill, New York, 1967.
[3] Morris, R., Scatter storage techniques, Comm. of ACM, Vol. 11 No. 1 (1968) pp. 38-44.

[4] Král. J.. Some very effective methods of searching in tables. Aplikace matematiky. Vol. 14. No. 1 (1969).
[5] Mailloux. B.J.. The implementation of ALGOL 68, Thesis. Mathematisch Centrum, Amsterdam. 1967.

SYNTAX AND MODE CHECK IN AN ALGOL 68 COMPILER

H. SCHEIDIG
Technical University, Munich

INTRODUCTION

The major tasks which must be dealt with by an ALGOL 68 compiler are syntax check and mode check - apart from the activities which serve to prepare the run-time organisation.

In short, we give here a summary of how these problems are treated in the Munich implementation of ALGOL 68.

1. SYNTAX CHECK

If we consider the methods of syntax checking which are developed - for example for ALGOL 60 - and ask for the most efficient methods amongst these, we will no doubt get to the methods working with some kind of transition matrices. In general, the condition which a language has to fulfil to make this technique acceptable is that the language is (1,1)-context bounded. This condition is not fulfilled in the case of ALGOL 68 - in ALGOL 68 the context which is needed to identify a syntactic construction can be of any length; in certain critical cases, namely, if we have to handle a so called alternative component a we cannot come to any decision without the knowledge of whether the indication *ind* constituting this alternative component a, is a mode-indication or an operator-indication (a can be a declaration, a generator, a parameter or a formula, see [1]). Therefore, the task to make a syntax check for ALGOL 68 is divided into two tasks:
1. the handling of alternative components, the syntactic correctness of which we can not check without further 'semantic' information and
2. the check of all other constructions of the language for syntactic correctness.

1.1. *The handling of alternative components.*
To handle the alternative components, Mailloux makes the obvious proposal to have a preliminary run before the syntax check which collects all mode-declarations. By this collection the syntax checker in the next pass immediately comes to the appropriate decisions.

The advantage of this method is that the syntax check can then handle the alternative components in a very simple manner; the obvious disadvantage is that the compiler will be lengthened by one pass.

In the Munich implementation we have taken another way:

a) Each alternative component a which is found during the run of the syntax check is treated as a declaration (this means, that the indication(s) constituting a is (are) considered as a mode indicant(s)).

Moreover, certain additional information is collected which allow us to regenerate the original language construction (i.e. the formula) in the next pass, that is, after the syntax check is finished, and especially after all (mode) declarations are elaborated, if a is not a declaration (generator, formal-parameter; generators and formal-parameters are treated like declarations in this part of the compiler).

b) For the further pass of the syntax check we have to guarantee that, although we cannot identify the alternative components, all syntactic errors will be detected. Also at this point the error recognition is to be recovered in pass 2 for some well defined kinds of errors (for example, if a is the last element of a closed serial-clause then a may not be a declaration).

The disadvantage of this method is that the syntax check is complicated and much lengthened by this treatment of alternative components and that the following pass has to recover certain activities; on the other hand, we save a complete pass.

Practical experience and comparison of these methods will have to point out which of them is the better.

1.2. *Syntax check for the other language constructions.*

As remarked in the introduction, the method of using a transition matrix for the syntax check cannot, or at least not immediately and in a simple manner, be transferred to ALGOL 68 (experiments in this direction seem to be useful first after we have more experience of the language and of compilers for the language respectively).

In the Munich implementation of ALGOL 68 the basis for the syntax check is the so called Floyd-Evans Production Language (see [2], [3]). The syntax check is a program in this language and this means an ordered sequence of productions $P_1, \ldots, P_n$.

At execution of this program the productions $P_1, \ldots, P_n$ are examined for 'applicability':

let P_i $(1 \leq i \leq n)$ be the first applicable production (such a production always exists) then this production fulfils the following condition:

the first n symbols in the stack are the same as the n 'state'-symbols given in P_i (these symbols can be ALGOL 68 symbols or local symbols).

If such a production P_i is found then the following is done:
1. The first n symbols in the stack are replaced by m symbols given in P_i $(m \geq 0)$.
2. So called 'semantic routines' given in P_i are executed.
3. If specified in P_i the next symbol of the program string is read into the stack.
4. Either, the execution of the program is finished after execution of P_i or in P_i is given a j $(1 \leq j \leq n)$, so that the examination of applicability begins at production P_j.

By means of this method we can hold in the stack a context of any length to come to decisions, and the semantic routines perform the further activities (such as making entries in lists and so on).

Apart from this, a program in the Floyd-Evans Production Language yields a good and well readable documentation of the syntax check.

2. MODE CHECK

In ALGOL 68 the task of making the mode chack is equivalent to the task of making the syntax check with regard to the extent as well as the difficulty of these problems. But, the problem of mode checking appears in ALGOL 68 for the first time, whereas the methods for making a syntax check are (at least partly) well established.

Therefore, one of the most important goals of the Munich implementation of ALGOL 68 is to find an efficient method for mode checking; we describe shortly the method which we have developed.

2.1. *Coercing instructions*.

The following elements we denote as coercing instructions:
a) operators.
b) the elements of
   P_1 = {for-symbol, from-symbol, by-symbol, to-symbol, case-symbol}
   and
   P_2 = {if-symbol, while-symbol, thef-symbol, elsf-symbol}
c) slices and calls.

Always, when in an ALGOL 68-program the 'own modes' $m_1, \ldots, m_k$ are connected by coercing instructions coercing operations are produced.

We denote as operators:
(i) standard operators and operators defined in the program by operation-declarations.
(ii) internal operators out of
   $I = \{:=, :=:, :\neq:, ::, ::=, \underline{of}, : \text{(cast-symbol)}, = \text{(in declarations)}\}$.

2.2. *Coercing functions*.

Each coercion A is a mapping - depending of the coercing instruction x which produces A - which transforms the own modes $m_1, \ldots, m_k$ into the 'target modes' $m'_1, \ldots, m'_k$:

$$A(x, m_1, \ldots, m_k, m'_1, \ldots, m'_k) : m_1, \ldots, m_k \to m'_1, \ldots, m'_k$$

(if $k > 2$ this transformation proceeds simultaneously and not independently for all modes $m_1, \ldots, m_k$).

The target modes m'_i ($i = 1, \ldots, k$) either are given directly (in the cases $x \in P_1 : \underline{int}$ or $x \in P_2 : \underline{bool}$) or they are to be determined from the corresponding operator-declaration (procedure declaration, row-of ... declaration; we do not say anything here about operator identification).

We call $A(x, m_1, \ldots, m_k, m'_1, \ldots, m'_k)$ a coercing function; the result of such a function are k 'coercing sequences' $CS_1, \ldots, CS_k$ each of which consists of a sequence of 'coercing words'.

ercing words serve to denote the single elementary coercions such as
rencing, deproceduring, proceduring and so on.

2.3. *The coercing function* $A(:=, m_1, \ldots, m_k, m_1', \ldots, m_k')$.

First of all, let us consider the simplest case $k = 2$ with m_1 as 'left own mode' (that is, m_1 appears on the left-hand side of $:=$) and m_2 as 'right own mode' (that is, m_2 appears on the right-hand side of $:=$).

2.3.1. The following elements are denoted as mode-indicators:

void, int, real, compl, bool, bits, bytes, char, string, formal, file, union$(u_1, \ldots, u_n)$ with $n > 1$, *struct*$(f_1, \ldots, f_n)$ with $n > 0$, *proc*$(p_1, \ldots, p_n)$ with $n \geq 0$, $[\ldots]$, $\text{ref}(n) = \underbrace{\text{ref} \ldots \text{ref}}_{n}$ with $n > 0$ and $\text{long}(n) = \underbrace{\text{long} \ldots \text{long}}_{n}$

with $n > 0$.

Each element out of the set of admissible ALGOL 68 modes consists of a sequence of mode-indicators.

2.3.2. *The coercing matrix* $\mathfrak{A}$.

The row and column entries of $\mathfrak{A}$ are the mode-indicators introduced above apart from *ref* and *long*.

Each matrix element $\mathfrak{A}_{i,j}$ is a pair $(\mathfrak{A}^1_{i,j}, \mathfrak{A}^2_{i,j})$ with:

$$\mathfrak{A}^k_{i,j} = CS^k_{i,j} \, S^k_{i,j} \quad \text{or} \quad \mathfrak{A}^k_{i,j} = S^k_{i,j} \, CS^k_{i,j}, \quad k = 1, 2;$$

thereby $CS^k_{i,j}$ is a coercing sequence (possibly empty) and $S^k_{i,j}$ is empty or a statement.

2.3.3. *Definition of the coercing function* $A(:=, m_1, m_2, m_1', m_2')$.

If we remove the prefix from m_1 and m_2, that is, some long's or ref's in front of them, then the first following mode-indicator of m_1 and m_2 specifies exactly one matrix element $\mathfrak{A}_{i,j}$ of $\mathfrak{A}$; the function A selects this element: if $\mathfrak{A}_{i,j}$ contains a statement $S^k_{i,j}$, then this statement is elaborated; in the normal case the effect of $S^k_{i,j}$ is a new call of the function A and this means a new access to the matrix $\mathfrak{A}$. In this way the coercing sequences CS_1 and CS_2 for m_1 and m_2 are determined by successive rowing of the coercing sequences $CS^k_{i,j}$ given in $\mathfrak{A}_{i,j}$ in the corresponding order.

Example: Let the assignation $x := y$ be given, let m_1 be the own mode of x and m_2 the own mode of y and let:

$m_1 = \text{ref}(n) \, \text{proc} \, \overline{m}_1$
$m_2 = \text{ref}(m) \, w_1 \ldots w_r$ with $w_1 \notin \{\text{proc}, [\ldots]\}$,

then all matrix elements $\mathfrak{A}_{i,j}$ have the form:

SYNTAX AND MODE CHECK 87

$$\mathfrak{A}_{i,j} = \begin{cases} (\phi,\ \text{proceduring } A^2(:=,\overline{m}_1,m_2,\overline{m}'_1,m'_2)),\ \text{if } n=1 \\ (A^1(:=,\overline{m}_1,m_2,\overline{m}'_1,m'_2)\ \text{deproceduring},\ A^2(:=,\overline{m}_1,m_2,\overline{m}'_1,m'_2)) \\ \qquad\qquad\qquad\qquad\qquad\qquad\qquad\qquad\qquad\qquad\qquad \text{if } n=0 \\ \text{undefined in all other cases.} \end{cases}$$

Thereby, A^i ($i = 1, 2$) denotes the ith element of the pair which is the result of A. This means the following:
If the prefix of m_1 is <u>ref</u> then we have to apply the operation 'proceduring' after we have found some further coercing words, if any, which must be determined recursively. If the prefix of m_2 contains no reference symbol then the operation 'deproceduring' is to apply to m_1 and then some further operations which are still to be found. In each of the other cases the assignment is not allowed.
In this way the definition of the matrix elements $\mathfrak{A}_{i,j}$ succeeds for all combinations of modes, with the exception of union modes alone; for union modes a special treatment must take place.

2.3.4. The coercing function $A(:=, m_1, \ldots, m_k, m'_1, \ldots, m'_k)$ for $k > 2$.
Let $m_1, \ldots, m_l$ be the left modes and $m_{l+1}, \ldots, m_k$ the right modes, then the following holds:
a) Let $m^* \in \{m_1, \ldots, m_l\}$ be a special mode, the so called 'soft mode', which meets the following conditions:
   (i) There exists an $m_r \in \{m_1, \ldots, m_l\}$ with:
       $f_r(m_r) = m^*$, whereby f_r is a soft coercion.
   (ii) $f_i(m_i) = m^*$, for $i = 1, \ldots, l$ ($i \neq r$), whereby f_i are strong coercions.
   (iii) $m^* = \text{ref}(n)\ \overline{m}$ (with $n > 0$).
b) The function $A(:=, m_1, \ldots, m_k, m'_1, \ldots, m'_k)$ is then defined in the following way:
$$A(:=, m_1, \ldots, m_k, m'_1, \ldots, m'_k) = \begin{cases} A(:=, \text{ref } m^*, m_i, \text{ref } m^*, m'_i),\ i = 1, \ldots, l \\ A(:=, m^*, m_i, m^*, m'_i),\ i = l+1, \ldots, k. \end{cases}$$

It is easy to see that we can find an algorithm which determines a soft mode out of a set of modes $\{m_1, \ldots, m_l\}$. Thus, the function $A(:=, m_1, \ldots, m_k, m'_1, \ldots, m'_k)$ is reduced to the functions $A(:=, m, m_i, m', m'_i),\ i = 1, \ldots, k$.

2.3.5. Definition of the functions $A(x, m_1, \ldots, m_k, m'_1, \ldots, m'_k)$ for the coercing instructions $x \neq :=$.
In each case, that is, for each other coercing instruction x, the function $A(x, m_1, \ldots, m_k, m'_1, \ldots, m'_k)$ succeeds in reducing them to the functions $A(:=, m^*, m_i, m^*, m'_i),\ i = 1, \ldots, k$, whereby m^* is a special mode which is to be determined in a similar way as the soft mode. For example, this is simple to see for $x \in P_i$ ($i = 1, 2$). Here we define:
$$A(x, m_1, \ldots, m_k, m'_1, \ldots, m'_k) = A(:=, m, m_1, \ldots, m_k, m, m'_1, \ldots, m'_k)$$
with the 'left mode' $m = \underline{\text{ref int}}$ or $m = \underline{\text{ref bool}}$ for $x \in P_1$ and $x \in P_2$, respectively.

By this we first get a lucid description of all coercions and second a very efficient method to implement them.

REMARK

The functions $A(x, m_1, \ldots, m_k, m'_1, \ldots, m'_k)$ also depend on the syntactic structure $t_1, \ldots, t_k$ of the objects the own modes of which are $m_1, \ldots, m_k$. This means, more precisely, that they depend on whether or not the t_i are collateral. The decisions between collateral 'carriers' t_i and non-collateral carriers t_i is easy to take into consideration by the definition of $A(x, m_1, \ldots, m_k, m'_1, \ldots, m'_k)$; we do not however give details of that in this informal description.

REFERENCES

[1] Mailloux, B.J., On the implementation of ALGOL 68, Mathematisch Centrum, Amsterdam, 1968.
[2] Floyd, R.W., A descriptive language for symbol manipulation, J.ACM. 8 (1961) 579.
[3] Evans, A., An ALGOL 60 compiler, Annual Review in Automatic Programming, Vol. 4, ed. by R. Goodman (Pergamon Press, Oxford, 1964).

DISCUSSION

Currie:

I am a bit confused about the size of the coercion array. Does it contain all possible modes?

Scheidig:

No, I would say it is a twenty by twenty matrix. You can make it smaller, perhaps twelve by twelve, by coalescing such matrix-elements as belong to modes, the handling of which is similar. We have for instance, that the elements *nil*, *skip* and the jumps may be treated as special modes. We can, therefore, collapse the matrix by superimposing these elements.

Currie:

I was not clear, from what you are saying, whether or not you had litterally one row or column per mode. Is it one row and column per primitive mode and so on?

Scheidig:

Of course you have entries in this matrix for the primitive modes: *void*, *int*, *real*, ..., *file*, and *union*(...), *struct*(...), *proc*(...), [...] .... Then we can have references in front, or longs in front. To determine the matrix entry for the two modes, we remove the prefix and then we always have a mode of this sort. Of course this function must be recursive, because we can have a row of *proc*s, *ref*s, and so on.

Van Gils:

Do you determine the process of coercion of the left side and the right side of an assignment at the same moment? It seems to me it would be easier to deduce the mode of an assignation by deducing the mode of the left hand side first and using this to give the mode of the right hand side. Why have you combined these two processes?

Scheidig:

Well, in the first place, we have only soft operations on the left hand side of an assignation. Thus, only deproceduring is possible. We can do it beforehand or we can do it at the same time, it does not matter which. In the second place, it is simple to reduce all coercing functions to this particular function. Therefore we have a matrix for exactly the soft coercions on the left hand side and the strong coercions on the right hand side. But it is not difficult to separate them.

Van Gils:

How do you determine your soft mode?

Scheidig:

It is quite obvious what you must do if we have only one mode on the left hand side, but also in the general case we can easily determine the soft mode to which we can apply the function $A(:=,\ldots)$.

Van Gils:

How do you reduce the weak coercion to this scheme?

Scheidig:

It seems to me that it would be better if I explain the scheme for determining our soft mode. The determination of the "weak" mode proceeds in quite a similar manner. Let $M = \{m_1, \ldots, m_m\}$ be the left hand side modes, the soft mode of which is to be determined. Now we see whether we have to apply the operation deproceduring on the modes $m_i \in M$. If we have to, then we do it; in consequence, no mode $m_i \in M$ begins with *proc* (*proc* without parameters). Then we see whether a union mode $m_i = p_i$ *union* $(\ldots)$ exists (p_i is the prefix consisting of *ref*s and *proc*s, but not beginning with *proc*). If we find only one union mode m_i, then we take this mode m_i. If we have more than one union mode, then we take the one with the maximum number of components. If we have more than one with the same (maximum) number of components, then we consider the length of the prefixes and take the union mode with the longest prefix. Now if we have more than one union mode with these properties, then we take that with the minimum number of references in front of it.

We have a similar method if we find row modes instead of union modes; in this case we consider the dimension of the multiple values instead of the number of components. Of course, we have to combine these two processes if we have modes in M of the kind $p_i[\ldots]\ldots$ *union*$(\ldots)$. If we find in M neither union modes nor row modes, then we first introduce an "order" for the other modes in the following way:

modes	counting number
p _void_	0
p _int_	1
p _real_	2
...	...
p _file_	...
p _struct_	...
p _proc_(...)	...

Now, we take the mode with the highest corresponding counting number (the prefix p does not influence the ordering process) and after this we consider the length of p in the same way as above.

For a mode $m*$ which we have determined in this way the following holds:
(1) the function $A(:=, m_1, \ldots, m_n, \overline{m}_1, \ldots, \overline{m}_r, m'_1, \ldots, m'_n, \overline{m}'_1, \ldots, \overline{m}'_r)$ can be reduced to the functions
$A1 = A(:=, \underline{ref}\ m*, m_i, \underline{ref}\ m*, m'_i)$ for the left hand side modes m_i ($i = 1, \ldots, n$) and
$A2 = A(:=, m*, \overline{m}_i, m*, \overline{m}'_i)$ for the right hand side modes $\overline{m}_i$ ($i = 1, \ldots, n$).
(2) if the assignation is not correct (in the sense of the Report), then one of the following cases can occur:
   (a) $m*$ does not have any reference before it: then $A1$ is possibly defined but not $A2$.
   (b) M contains two non-compatible modes, for instance $\underline{ref\ int}$ and $\underline{ref\ real}$: then the determination of $m*$ always works, but $A1$ is not defined.

Thus, if we determine $m*$ in this way, we get all coercions if the assignation is correct. Otherwise we get an error message. Moreover, to $m*$ only soft coercions can be applied since to each other mode $m_i \in M$ strong coercions can be applied.

Peck:

May I ask you about your syntax checker which is written in the Floyd-Evans language. Did you obtain this by mechanical means from a context-free syntax, or did you develop the reduction rules by hand?

Scheidig:

We have an assembler which accepts a program in Floyd-Evans production language. By means of these productions you can express the syntax of ALGOL 68.

Peck:

But from what did you get the reduction rules?

Scheidig:

From our heads in the same way as the decision tables of Branquart.

Branquart:

I have one more question about the Floyd-Evans production language. You said that you are allowed to take contexts of any length into account.

That is to say that you are provided with a look ahead. If you take the right context of any length into account, I think you have the equivalent of a look-ahead. Have you an idea about the relative efficiency of such a look-ahead and of a compiler which would do the same job in two passes? We had to make the same choice. That is why I am asking this question.

Scheidig:

Well, that is an interesting question, especially in connection with what we call "alternative components", and in connection with the use of brackets. I can say only that I would be glad to hear about other methods, for instance the method which was proposed by Mailloux, and to compare these methods. For myself, I can say nothing about efficiency.

Branquart:

Do you analyze your program completely during the first pass?

Scheidig:

Yes, in the first pass.

Branquart:

When you meet an alternative component, it is treated as a declaration. What do you mean by treated as a declaration? To what extent does this assumption influence the object program of your first pass?

Scheidig:

Of course, it does. Therefore we have to collect some other information to regenerate the original language construction if we detect that this construction was not really a declaration. Moreover, if we treat this construction as a declaration it means that we make entries in some lists which contain the mode of this entity and the name and so on.

Branquart:

Is it a trick which allows your parser to come to the end of the program? When you have an expression such as $\underline{a}\ a$ you can imagine that a context-free parser would be ambiguous. You could choose, let's say, one alternative of this ambiguity, for example, a declaration. My question is, what is the further influence of such a decision?

Scheidig:

It is not only a trick. Perhaps I should explain it. First, if we handle an alternative component like a declaration then we are right in 50% of the cases. Moreover, the organization of our first two passes makes it necessary to generate an entry in our declaration list of a declaration which occurs. So, we cannot take the other possibility, namely, to do nothing if we cannot decide during the syntax check whether an alternative component is a declaration or not. At least, this handling of an alternative component is very easy. The only thing we have to do is to collect some information which allows us to regenerate the original construction if it is a formula. This information is small and we do not have any trouble at all in connection with this method. Apart from this, we have trouble in connection with alternative components, but this fact does not depend on which method we use to handle them. If we have a construction such as $(\underline{ind1}\ x_1, \underline{ind2}\ x_2, \ldots, \underline{indn}\ x_n)$ then it can be a formal-parameters-pack for instance, or it can be a collateral-clause. What is not allowed is that it is a closed-declaration. We cannot detect that in the first pass. We can detect it instantly after we have collected all mode declarations. That is, after the syntax check in our pass 2.

Peck:
Have you a context-free syntax for ALGOL 68?

Scheidig:
We have tried to get a context-free syntax and we have done this by means of the language called Euler. Goos has written a compiler for it and one of the first large jobs was to read in context-free productions. But this approach did not work because we have a relatively small machine and, moreover, at this time we have no possibility in Euler to save information in backing store.

SESSION 3

(Chairman: B.J.Mailloux)

AFFIX-GRAMMARS

C. H. A. KOSTER
Mathematisch Centrum, Amsterdam

INTRODUCTION

The purpose of this paper is to present a type of two-level grammar, akin to that used in the definition of ALGOL 68, but better suited for syntax-directed parsing techniques.

1. DEFINITION AG

An affix grammar AG is a 9-tuple

$\langle V_n, V_t, A_n, A_t, Q, E, R, S, P \rangle$, where

V_n = a finite nonempty set of *nonterminal* symbols,
V_t = a finite nonempty set of *terminal* symbols,
A_n = a finite set of symbols, the *nonterminal affixes*,
A_t = a finite set of symbols, the *terminal affixes*,
Q = a finite set of symbols, the *primitive predicate symbols*.

(V_n, V_t, A_n, A_t and Q are mutually disjoint, and do not include the symbol ω, the *forbidden symbol*.)

E = the *initial symbol* $\in V_n$,
R = *affix rules*, a finite subset of $A_n \times (A_n \cup A_t)^*$.

(Observe that for every $a \in A_n$, the 4-tuple $G_a = (A_n, A_t, a, R)$ forms a CF grammar. Define for $a \in A_n$, $L_a = \mathcal{L}(G_a)$.
Let $L = \bigcup_{a \in A_n} L_a$.)

S = *control*, a collection of 5-tuples $S_x = \langle x, N_x, \alpha_x, \alpha_x, F_x \rangle$, one for every $x \in Q \cup V_n$, where:
  x = *head* $\in Q \cup V_n$,
  N_x = *number of affixpositions* $\in N$,
  τ_x = *types of the affixpositions* $\in \Pi^{N_x}\{\delta, \iota\}$, where δ and ι are special symbols
  α_x = *domain of the affixpositions* $\in \Pi^{N_x} A_n$,
  F_x = *associated function*, a total recursive function

$$F_x : L_{\alpha_{x,1}} \times L_{\alpha_{x,2}} \times \ldots \times L_{\alpha_{x,N_x}} \to \{\epsilon, \omega\},$$

(When $x \in V_n$, then this function is irrelevant.)

$P = rules$, a finite collection of pairs $(\mathcal{U}\mathcal{V})$, where every $\mathcal{U}$ is of the form $(v, a_1, a_2, \ldots, a_{N_v})$ where $v \in V_n$ and $a_i = \alpha_{v,i}$ of S_v, and where every $\mathcal{V}$ is of the form $(m_1, m_2, \ldots, m_k)$ where $k \geq 0$ and $m_i \in M$, where $M = (Q \cup V_n) \times \Pi^*(A_n \cup L)$, the set of *affix expressions*.

2. NOTATION

When $(x, y) \in R$ where $y = y_1 y_2 \ldots y_n$, then we write

$x : y_1 y_2 \ldots y_n$. .

When $(x, y) \in P$ where $y = (y_1, y_2, \ldots, y_n)$, then we write

$x : y_1, y_2, \ldots, y_n$. .

When $x \in M$ where $x = (x_0, y_1, y_2, \ldots, y_n)$, then we write

$x_0 + y_1 + y_2 + \ldots + y_n$ for x.

When both $x : y_1$. and $x : y_2$. we write $x : y_1 ; y_2$. .

3. TERMINOLOGY

For strings x, y and z, let subst (x, y, z) denote the result of substituting x for every occurrence of y in z.

When $\mathcal{R} = \mathcal{X} : \mathcal{Y}$., then we term $\mathcal{X}$ the *left hand side* and $\mathcal{Y}$ the *right hand side* of the rule or affix-rule $\mathcal{R}$

The right hand side of a rule or affix-rule whose left hand side is $\mathcal{X}$ is termed an *alternative* for $\mathcal{X}$

When an affix expression $\mathcal{X} = x + y_1 + y_2 + \ldots + y_n$ then x is termed the *head* of $\mathcal{X}$ and y_i its *ith affix-position*.

When all affix positions of an affix expression $\mathcal{X}$ are members of L, then $\mathcal{X}$ is termed a *concrete affix expression*.

In particular, the initial symbol E is a concrete affix expression.

A *predicate* is either a concrete affix expression, and is then termed *productive*, or is a terminal symbol, or is the forbidden symbol ω, or is empty.

The *direct production* of a concrete affix expression $\mathcal{X}$ whose head is a primitive predicate symbol $\mathcal{P}$ is the value of the function associated with $\mathcal{P}$ evaluated with as its *i*th parameter the *i*th affix position of $\mathcal{X}$. A direct production of a concrete affix expression $\mathcal{X}$ whose head is a nonterminal symbol, is a list of predicates $\mathcal{Y}$ such that there is a rule $\mathcal{R} = \mathcal{U} : \mathcal{V}$, and there are terminal production $\overline{m}_1, \overline{m}_2, \ldots, \overline{m}_n$ of the nonterminal affixes $a_1, a_2, \ldots, a_n$ occurring in $\mathcal{R}$ such that

subst$(\overline{m}_1, a_1,$ subst$(\overline{m}_2, a_2, \ldots$ subst$(\overline{m}_n, a_n, \mathcal{U})\ldots)) = \mathcal{X}$, and

subst$(\overline{m}_1, a_1,$ subst$(\overline{m}_2, a_2, \ldots$ subst$(\overline{m}_n, a_n, \mathcal{V})\ldots)) = \mathcal{Y}$.

If a predicate other than a terminal symbol or empty has no direct production, then it is termed a *blind alley*.

A *production* of a concrete affix expression $\mathcal{X}$ is either a direct production of $\mathcal{X}$ or a list of predicates obtained by replacing in a production of $\mathcal{X}$ some productive predicate $\mathcal{Y}$ by a direct production of $\mathcal{Y}$.

A *terminal production* of a concrete affix expression $\mathcal{X}$ is a production of $\mathcal{X}$ all of whose predicates are either a terminal symbol or empty.

A *sentence* of an AG $\mathcal{G}$ is any terminal production of the initial symbol of $\mathcal{G}$. The language of $\mathcal{G}$ is the set of sentences of $\mathcal{G}$.

4. PROPERTIES

Let us call a Finite State grammar all of whose rules are of the form $A \to a$, where A is nonterminal and a is terminal, a Finite Choice grammar FC.

We thus have a hierarchy of grammars

$$FC \subset FS \subset CF \subset CS.$$

If in some AG grammar $\mathcal{G}$, for every $a \in A_n$, G_a is a grammar of type $\mathcal{T}$, we will indicate $\mathcal{G}$ as a $(\mathcal{T}_{CF})$ grammar.

Proposition 4.1. For every $(\mathcal{T}_{CF}^{FC})$ grammar $\mathcal{G}$ there exists a (weakly) equivalent CF grammar.

The nonterminal axis x can be removed from $\mathcal{G}$ by expanding every rule in which it occurs into as many rules as x has terminal productions (which is a finite number).

Proposition 4.2. For every Turing Machine $\mathcal{T} = \langle Q, S, q_0, R \rangle$ there exists a $(\mathcal{T}_{CF}^{CF})$ grammar $\mathcal{G}$ which generates the language recognized by $\mathcal{T}$.

This can be demonstrated by simulating $\mathcal{T}$ as follows:

Its tape

| blank | s_{-n} | ... | s_{-1} | s_0 | s_1 | ... | s_m | blank |

can be contained in two strings

and

$$L = \boxed{s_{-n} | \ldots | s_{-1} | s_0}$$

$$R = \boxed{s_1 | s_2 | \ldots | s_m}.$$

The control of $\mathcal{G}$ contains:

$\langle \text{attach}, 3, (\iota, \iota, \delta), (C, s, C), F_{\text{attach}} \rangle$,

$\langle \text{detach}, 3, (\iota, \delta, \delta), (C, s, C), F_{\text{detach}} \rangle$ and

$\langle \text{equal}, 2, (\iota, \iota), \quad (s, s), \quad F_{\text{equal}} \rangle$ where

s and C are nonterminal affixes with as terminal productions the symbols S and the strings over S respectively, and where

$$F_{\text{attach}} = \lambda_{x \in L_C} \lambda_{y \in L_S} \lambda_{z \in L_C} \; [xy = z \to \epsilon, \; xy \neq z \to \omega]$$

$$F_{\text{detach}} = \lambda_{x \in L_C} \lambda_{y \in L_S} \lambda_{z \in L_C} \; [x = zy \to \epsilon, \; x \neq zy \to \omega]$$

$$F_{\text{equal}} = \lambda x, y \in L_S \; [x = y \to \epsilon, \; x \neq y \to \omega].$$

The rules of $\mathcal{G}$ are transliterations of the rules of $\mathcal{T}$ along the following pattern:

$\mathcal{T}$-rule $\qquad\qquad\qquad$ $\mathcal{G}$-rule

$\langle q_i, S_i \rangle \to \langle S_f, q_f, 0 \rangle \quad q_i + L + R:$
$\qquad\qquad\qquad\qquad$ detach $+ L + s + L'$, equal $+ s + S_i$,
$\qquad\qquad\qquad\qquad$ attach $+ L' + S_f + L''$, $q_f + L'' + R$.

effect: $\quad$ [$\;\;$ | S_i | $\;\;$] $\Rightarrow$ [$\;\;$ | S_f | $\;\;$]

$\langle q_i, S_i \rangle \to \langle S_f, q_f, -1 \rangle \quad q_i + L + R:$
$\qquad\qquad\qquad\qquad$ detach $+ L + s + L'$, equal $+ s + S_i$,
$\qquad\qquad\qquad\qquad$ attach $+ R + S_f + R'$, $q_f + L' + R'$.

effect: $\quad$ [$\;\;$ | x | S_i | $\;\;$] $\Rightarrow$ [$\;\;$ | x | S_f]

$\langle q_i, S_i \rangle \to \langle S_f, q_f, +1 \rangle \quad q_i + L + R:$
$\qquad\qquad\qquad\qquad$ detach $+ L + s + L'$, equal $+ s + S_i$,
$\qquad\qquad\qquad\qquad$ attach $+ L' + S_f + L''$, detach $+ R + x + R'$,
$\qquad\qquad\qquad\qquad$ attach $+ L'' + x + L'''$, $q_f + L''' + R'$.

effect: $\quad$ [$\;\;$ | S_i | x | $\;\;$] $\Rightarrow$ [$\;\;$ | S_f | x | $\;\;$]

In this way $\mathcal{G}$ can be constructed.

It is clear that the power of an AG depends to a great extent on the functions occurring in its control. Therefore it is interesting that the simple functions detaching one symbol from a string, attaching a symbol to a string and comparing two symbols suffice for realizing a Turing Machine.

5. ADDITIONAL TERMINOLOGY

Any nonterminal affix which occurs in the left hand side of some rule is termed a *bound affix* of $\mathcal{R}$.

Any nonterminal affix which occurs in the right hand side of some rule and which is not a bound affix of $\mathcal{R}$ is termed a *free affix* of $\mathcal{R}$.

An affix expression $\mathcal{X}$ occurring in the right hand side of some rule is termed an *application* of the rule $\mathcal{R}$ if the head of $\mathcal{X}$ is the same as the head of the left hand side of $\mathcal{R}$.

The ith bound affix of a rule $\mathcal{R} = \mathcal{U} : \mathcal{V}$. is termed *inherited* (*derived*) if the type of the ith affix position of the control of the head of $\mathcal{U}$ is equal to $\iota(\delta)$.

An occurrence of a nonterminal affix in an affix expression $\mathcal{X}$ in the right hand side of some rule is termed inherited (derived) if the corresponding bound affix of any rule of which $\mathcal{X}$ is an application is also inherited (derived).

6. UNDERLYING CF GRAMMAR

The *underlying* CF *grammar* of an AG $\mathcal{G}$ is the grammar $G_u = (S', T', E', P')$, obtained as follows:

$S' = V_n$,
$T' = V_t$,
$E' = E$,
P' = the set of all different rules, obtainable by taking a rule $\mathcal{R}$ of P, replacing every affix expression in $\mathcal{R}$ whose head is a nonterminal symbol by that symbol, and deleting all other affix expressions from $\mathcal{R}$

Clearly, $\mathcal{L}(G_u) \supset \mathcal{L}(\mathcal{G})$.

By making slight changes in a given AG, it is possible to get an equivalent AG with a different G'_u and $\mathcal{L}(G'_u)$. Thus, the present notion of underlying CF grammar is of no great formal interest, but a convenient way of getting an impression of the language of some AG. In particular, it is of interest that the G_u of an AG be unambiguous, even though that hardly gives an indication of possible ambiguities in AG.

7. WELL-FORMEDNESS

An affix grammar AG will be termed *well-formed* if the following conditions c_1-c_5 hold:

c_1) $\forall \langle N, \tau, \alpha, F \rangle \in S \quad \forall_{i,j \in [1,N]} [i \neq j \rightarrow \alpha_i \neq \alpha_j]$.

This condition ensures that no nonterminal affix occurs twice in the left hand side of any rule.

c_2) $\forall \mathcal{X} = x_0 + x_1 + x_2 + \ldots + x_n \in \text{LHS} \quad \forall \mathcal{Y} = y_0 + y_1 + y_2 + \ldots + y_k \in \text{RHS}$
$[x_0 = y_0 \rightarrow (n = k \wedge \langle x_0, k, \tau, \alpha, F \rangle \in S \wedge$
$\quad i \in [1, k] \rightarrow (\tau_i = \delta \rightarrow y_i \in A_n \wedge Lx_i \subseteq Ly_i,$
$\quad \quad \tau_i = \iota \rightarrow y_i \in A_n \wedge Lx_i \supseteq Ly_i$
$\quad \quad \vee y_i \in Lx_i))]$.

This condition cuts off 'invisible' blind alleys.

c_3) $\forall \langle q, N, \tau, \alpha, F \rangle \in S \ [q \in Q \rightarrow$

> Define $C(k) = \sum_{j=1}^{k} (\tau_j = \delta \rightarrow 1, \tau_j = \iota \rightarrow 0)$.
> Let $n = C(N)$.
> Let $l = N - n$.
> Separate α in two lists $D = (d_1, d_2, \ldots, d_n)$ and $I = (i_1, i_2, \ldots, i_l)$ such that $\alpha_k = (\tau_k = \delta \rightarrow d_{C(k)}, \tau_k = \iota \rightarrow i_{k-C(k)})$, $k = 1(1)N$.
> Then there is given a total recursive function
> $$\widetilde{F} : L_{i_1} \times L_{i_2} \times \ldots \times L_{i_l} \rightarrow L_{d_1} \times L_{d_2} \times \ldots \times L_{d_n} \cup \{\omega\}$$
> such that $\forall j \in [1, N] \ \forall x_j \in L_{i_j} \ \forall y_j \in L_{d_j}$:
> $$\begin{cases} \text{Let } z_k = (\tau_k = \delta \rightarrow x_{C(k)}, \ \tau_k = \iota \rightarrow y_{k-C(k)}); \\ F(x_1, x_2, \ldots, x_l) = (y_1, y_2, \ldots, y_n) \hookleftarrow F(z_1, z_2, \ldots, z_N) = \epsilon]. \end{cases}$$

This condition makes the separation between derived and inherited affixes meaningful. The $\widetilde{F}$'s are functions from the inherited to the derived affixes of the head.

c_4) i) If the bound affix $\mathcal{X}$ of $\mathcal{R}$ is inherited, then all occurrences of $\mathcal{X}$ in the right hand side of $\mathcal{R}$ are inherited.
  ii) If the bound affix $\mathcal{X}$ of $\mathcal{R}$ is derived, then the first occurrence of $\mathcal{X}$ in the right hand side of $\mathcal{R}$ is derived, and all others are inherited.
  iii) The first occurrence of a free affix in a rule is derived, all others are inherited.

This condition makes that the inherited affixes can be seen as 'input parameters' and the derived affixes as 'output parameters' to the rules.

c_5) The underlying CF grammar of the AG is not left-recursive and its language does not contain ϵ.

This condition prevents endless cycling in parsing.

For well-formed AG's the following terminology is useful:
A *primitive predicate* is an affix expression whose head is a primitive predicate symbol.
A *nonterminal precidate* is an affix expression whose head is a nonterminal symbol.
A *terminal predicate* is a terminal symobl.
The symbol ω we will term the *false predicate*.
We will term ϵ the *true predicate*.
With these extra definitions, one might define a *predicate* as either a primitive predicate, or a nonterminal predicate, or a terminal predicate, or the false predicate, or the true predicate.

Proposition 7.1. It is undecideable whether or not a given AG is well-formed.

Proposition 7.1 follows from the undecideability of condition c_2. In practice, 7.1 is no restriction, since in constructing an AG one will stick to grammars for which c_2 can easily be decided.

In a given AG, the condition c_4 may often be brought about by suitable rewriting of the rules.

The grammar in 4.2 is not well-formed since c_5 is not satisfied.

8. PARSING PROBLEM FOR AG

A *parsing step* $\mathcal{S} = (\mathcal{X}, \mathcal{Y})$ consists of two lists of predicates $\mathcal{X}$ and $\mathcal{Y}$ such that $\mathcal{Y}$ is the result of substituting for the leftmost productive predicate $\mathcal{I}$ of $\mathcal{X}$ a direct production of $\mathcal{I}$.

A *parse* $\mathcal{P}$ according to an AG $\mathcal{G}$ for a sequence $\mathcal{T}$ of terminal symbols is a sequence of lists of predicates $\mathcal{P} = p_1, p_2, \ldots, p_n$ such that $p_1 = E$, for $i = 1(1)n - 1$ the couple (p_i, p_{i+1}) is a parsing step, and $p_n = \mathcal{T}$, disregarding comma's and empty's.

Recognition problem
Given a sequence $\mathcal{X}$ of terminal symbols and an AG $\mathcal{G}$, is $\mathcal{X}$ a sentence of $\mathcal{G}$?

Parsing problem
Given a sentence $\mathcal{X}$ of an AG $\mathcal{G}$, determine a parse according to $\mathcal{G}$ for $\mathcal{X}$.

Proposition 8.1. Every well-formed AG $\mathcal{G}$ can be brought into a (Greibach-like) Normal Form such that the right hand side of every rule starts with a terminal symbol.

Assume an ordering of the rules. Take the first rule $\mathcal{R}$ of $\mathcal{G}$ which is not in the required form. If there is no such rule, the grammar has been brought into the required form. Look at the leftmost member $\mathcal{M}$ of its right hand side which is a terminal or is an affix expression whose head is a nonterminal symbol.

To the left of $\mathcal{M}$ only affix expressions occur whose head is a primitive predicate symbol.

Case 1 $\mathcal{M}$ is a terminal symbol. Now $\mathcal{M}$ can be shifted to the left in $\mathcal{R}$ without affecting $\mathcal{L}(\mathcal{G})$, until the right hand side of $\mathcal{R}$ starts with the terminal symbol $\mathcal{M}$.

Case 2 The head of $\mathcal{M}$ is a nonterminal symbol. Replace $\mathcal{R}$ by a number of rules, substituting for $\mathcal{M}$ its alternatives only by one. Start all over.

Case 3 There is no such $\mathcal{M}$ in $\mathcal{R}$. Replace every occurrence in the rules of the left hand side of $\mathcal{R}$ by the right hand side of $\mathcal{R}$, delete $\mathcal{R}$ and start all over.

Proceeding in this way, the rules can be brought into the normal form one by one. Case 2 cannot lead to cycling of the algorithm since otherwise the underlying CF grammar of $\mathcal{G}$ would be left recursive, contrary to c_5.

Proposition 8.2. Every parse according to a well-formed AG *in Normal Form* $\mathcal{G}$ *of a sequence* $\mathcal{T}$ *contains at most* $1 + (N-1) \times M$ *parsing steps where N is the maximum number of members of any right hand side of a rule* $\mathcal{G}$ *and where M is the number of symbols in* $\mathcal{T}$.

Proposition 8.3. For a well-formed AG, *the recognition and parsing problem are both solvable.*

Because of c_1-c_4 the rules of the AG describe a top-down parsing algorithm in terms of (mutually) recursive functions corresponding to the predicates. Proposition 8.2 ensures that this algorithm always terminates.

9. PARSING

In [2] it was shown how, from an affix grammar $\mathcal{G}$, a parser in, e.g., ALGOL 60 or ALGOL 68 could be obtained by a mechanical transcription process. This parser then consists of a parser-body obtained by transcribing the rules of $\mathcal{G}$, embedded in an environment containing in effect its control. The parser will terminate provided $\mathcal{G}$ is well-formed.

10. PARSER-BODY

The parser-body consists of one procedure-declaration for every rule of $\mathcal{G}$. As a transcription of a rule

    identity declaration: declarer + mode, identifier + tag,
                  define identifier + tag + mode; contracted id decl.

the parser-body might contain

    proc *bool* identity declaration = *bool* :

    begin *int* mode, tag;

        if declarer (mode)

        then *if* identifier (tag)
            then define identifier (tag, mode) *else* *false* *fi*
        else contracted id decl *fi*
    end

The head of the rule is transcribed as the procedure-identifier, bound affixes passed as parameters, free affixes declared locally and also passed as parameters.

This transcription is merely the extension of a well known top-to-bottom parsing method for CF grammars by the addition of parameters and locals. The usual techniques for removing circularity, backtracking and local ambiguity can be applied also to AG's [3].

11. ENVIRONMENT

An environment could contain the following:

a) declaration for some stacks with pointers to their beginning and top, e.g.

$[\,1:10000\,]\,\underline{int}\ stack1;\ \underline{int}\ start1\ =1;\ \underline{int}\ top1\ :=1;$

b) declaration for a reading procedure *read (x)* which assigns to x the key of the next symbol on the input tape.

c) two complementary procedures to access elements of a list, declared as

$\underline{proc}\ get\ =\ ([\ ]\ \underline{int}\ L,\ \underline{int}\ p,\ \underline{ref}\ \underline{int}\ x):x:=L[\,p\,];$

$\underline{proc}\ put\ =\ (\underline{ref}\,[\ ]\ \underline{int}\ L,\ \underline{int}\ p,\ \underline{int}\ x):L[\,p\,]:=x;$

d) procedures for simple arithmetic with pointers

$\underline{proc}\ incr\ =\ (\underline{ref}\ \underline{int}\ p)\ :p+:=1;$

$\underline{proc}\ decr\ =\ (\underline{ref}\ \underline{int}\ p)\ :p+:=1;$

e) a procedure for assignment of pointers

$\underline{proc}\ make\ =\ (\underline{ref}\ \underline{int}\ x,\ \underline{int}\ y):x:=y;$

f) procedures for comparing pointers

$\underline{proc}\ equal\ =\ (\underline{int}\ x,y)\ \underline{bool}:x=y;$

$\underline{proc}\ less\ \ =\ (\underline{int}\ x,y)\ \underline{bool}:x<y;$

g) a procedure *out (x)* for outputting the symbol corresponding to the key x.

12. APPLICATION TO ALGOL 68

Making use of only those primitives, a compiler-compiler has been written, defined by an affix grammar, that constructs from an AG its parser. This compiler-compiler is being used to construct an ALGOL 68 translator. For most of the syntax of ALGOL 68, rewriting it as an AG is straightforward, but as with every syntax-directed technique the real problems are caused by local ambiguities and unnecessary backtracking.

13. DEFINITION OF PROGRAMMING LANGUAGES

From the point of view of definition of programming languages, affix grammars present a special interest in that they may describe both syntax and semantics. In fact, the semantics is represented by the functions occurring in the control of the grammar. More involved tools are defined syntactically in terms of those primitive functions. Affix grammars are well-suited for describing the context-conditions of ALGOL 68, e.g., the identification condition, in a syntactic way. One is left with the bare bones of semantics.

REFERENCES

[1] MR 101
[2] Koster, C. H. A.: Syntax-directed parsing of ALGOL 68 programs, Proceedings of Informal Conference on ALGOL 68. Implementation, U.B.C., Vancouver B.C., August 1969.
[3] Foster, J. M.: A syntax improving program, Computer Journal, Vol. 11, 1968, p. 31.

APPENDIX: IDENTIFICATION OF IDENTIFIERS

As an application of affix grammars, consider the problem of determining the mode of an identifier in an ALGOL 68-like language.

Every occurrence of an identifier in a formal-parameter is termed *defining*, all other occurrences are termed *applied*. The mode of an applied occurrence of an identifier is the mode of the defining occurrence identified by it according to the process described in [1] 4.1.2.b.

We will treat this identification process in a syntactic way. Let the environment (see section 11) also contain the arrays B, T and W and the pointers pb, db, pt and pw.

During the first scan all information about the nesting of blocks has to be put into the array B, where the ith element of B contains the number of the block directly surrounding the ith block. Blocks will be numbered through, like, e.g.:

  0 *begin* 1

      1 *begin* 2

      2 *end* 1

      1 *begin* 3

          3 *begin* 4

          4 *end* 3

      3 *end* 1

  1 *end* 0

In the process, use is made of the pointers pb (present blocknumber) and db (dynamic blocknumber, the last blocknumber handed out).

This information is collected by:

E 1) blockbegin: incr + db, put + B + db + pb, make + pb + db.

E 2) blockend: get + B + pb + pb.

T will contain one entry for each identifier. In the stack W with pointer pw, for every defining occurrence of an identifier an element is added to a chain, containing present blocknumber and associated mode. For example, if a is defined in block 1 as *integer* and in block 3 as *real*, we want the structure:

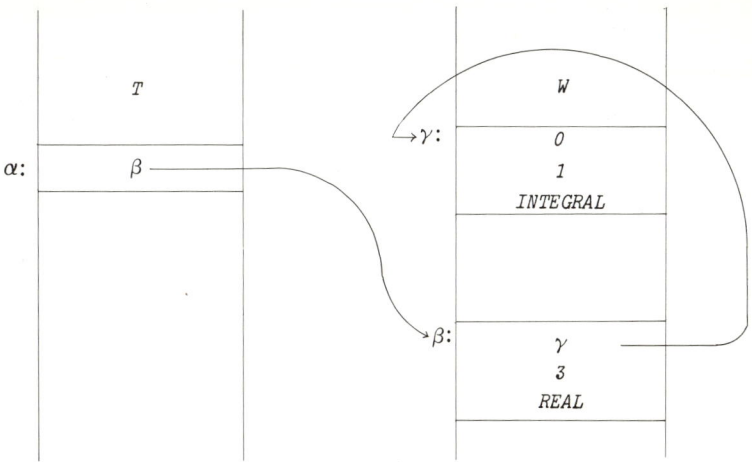

Fig. 1.

In syntax:

E 3) declaration:
    declarer + mode, identifier + tag, define + tag + mode.

E 4) define + tag + mode:
    get + T + tag + ch, put + T + tag + pw, stack + ch, stack + pb,
    stack + mode.

E 5) stack + x:
    put + W + pw + x, incr + pw.

Note that in E 3, tag and mode are free affixes, in E 4 tag and mode are bound affixes but ch is free.

Now we come to the identification process proper, which mirrors R 4.1.2.b:

E 6) identify + tag + mode:
    make + home + pb, get + T + tag + ch,
    find + ch + home + mode.

E 7) find + ch + home + mode:
    equal + ch + zero, make + mode + ERRONEOUS;
    make + p + ch, incr + p, get + W + p + bldef,
    rest find + ch + home + bldef + mode.

E 8) rest find + ch + home + bldef + mode:
    equal + bldef + home, incr + ch, incr + ch,
            get + W + ch + mode;
    less + bldef + home, get + B + home + home,
            rest find + ch + home + bldef + mode;
    get + W + ch + ch, find + ch + home + mode.

In E 7, if an identifier turns out to have no defining occurrence it gets as mode ERRONEOUS. In E 8 the three alternatives are:
1) The home contains the definition and a mode is obtained.
2) Block of definition outside the home; the home is enlarged.
3) Home outside block of definition; another definition is taken from the chain.

This example demonstrates that a complicated matter like identification can wholly be 'programmed' at the level of syntax.

DISCUSSION

Lindsey:
 The example you have would presumably work only for a language where definitions preceded applications?

Koster:
 No, actually the treatment of declarations is in a second scan. Really I have shown three scans; one is the treatment of parenthesis structure, or at least part of the treatment of parenthesis structure. The second is the entering of the information contained in declarations, and the third is the acting upon that information.

Lindsey:
 If you just took the grammar as you have written it, then it would work with that restriction, or a grammar of that nature would?

Koster:
 Then, with that restriction, it would work, yes.

Lindsey:
 Now the next thing that is bothering me is this business of the inherited and derived occurrences. It seems to me that it is perfectly possible to have a derived occurrence on your bound side and then the first thing on the right might be inherited and the next one derived. It seems to me that so long as there is one instance of a derived thing somewhere on the right side, you can make a sensible deduction.

Koster:
 I agree that you might relax the condition, C4, a lot. For one thing you might allow more than one derived occurrence for some non-terminal affix. That means that for one part of the rule you use one meaning and for the rest of the rule you use the other. Things like that. But from a descriptional point of view that is not very neat. From a practical point of view, of course you would do it and I have done it in the syntax given in the appendix.

Lindsey:
 The sort of thing I had in mind was: suppose that the affix concerned was MODE and you had a whole string of things on the right hand side separated

by commas's, then at the first one it met as it went down the production rule concerned, it might conclude that the object that was in the source string was of some subset of mode, like NONPROC. So it would come back and say "Yes, we recognize this affix expression. We do not know what the value of the affix is (we have not derived it entirely) but we know that it is at least NONPROC." It now goes along to the thing after the next comma and looks at the source object and it may conclude that is is NONSTOWED or something. So we now know that the thing is the intersection of these two and eventually we shall either find that it is something which is an intersection of those, in which case we have parsed it, or we will find that it is not, in which case we have a failure. It seems to me that you need not even insist, in the bound affix, that you know whether it is derived or inherited.

Kosler:
Yes, I agree with you that you can certainly relax this condition, especially by having mixed cases where you cannot say that your bound affix is either inherited or derived. The fact is that you must be sure that an affix never gets no value and it helps perhaps that in an article of Knuth on semantics of CF languages he has derived conditions under which those mixed cases are non-paradoxical.

Griffiths:
Is it not true that you can do all those things that you were trying to suggest without relaxing the condition c4, just by defining new class names and going down a level in the grammar?

Kosler:
It is, I think.

Lindsey:
Yes, you can always make bigger and bigger grammars to do the same thing.

Kosler:
There is to this a theoretical and a practical aspect. From a theoretical point of view, you'd better stick to that rule. It is cleaner; then you have a description that you can trust. On the other hand, from a practical point of view, why spend storage for nothing? Lindsey is trying to save storage.

Lindsey:
I have in fact got a parsing routine, but I have not gotten any technique for proving that any given grammar will terminate in this parsing routine.

Yershov:
I have several questions. The first question is about the underlying context-free grammar. Is the procedure for obtaining this underlying grammar really automatic? My question is especially about the reducing of superfluous rules after elimination of unnecessary information.

Kosler:
The definition of the underlying context-free grammar, as I gave it, is

very rough. If somebody would start thinking about this problem, then he could derive much more. For instance, an interesting question is the relationship between the ambiguity of the original grammar and that of the underlying context-free grammar. Well, I must simply say that the definition I have given is very bad, but it tells you something already.

Yershov:
Could you say something about the difficult points in reducing the ALGOL 68 grammar to an affix grammar?

Koster:
Of course, there are the practical difficulties of backtracking, which I will not now mention. But the difficult point is where, in the ALGOL 68 grammar, the full power of the van Wijngaarden two-level system is used. An example of that is in the beginning of Chapter 8 of [1] where you, let us say, reparse hyper-notions a number of times. The automaton which treats the united declarations is really a context-sensitive automaton, a full-blown context-sensitive automaton. And you'd better not write it that way for the affix grammar. You even cannot

Yershov:
What about the formalization of other context conditions? For example, the prohibition to have two declarations for one identifier?

Koster:
This is easy, because you can check it easily. As in the appendix you are filling in that list W, you have now simply to move chain elements in there, but of course you can check whether a specific block number had already occurred.

Yershov:
Could you program your affix grammar to control the number of scans and agree to nesting the loops during the work of the parser? In other words, could you predict how long your parser will work during parsing?

Koster:
Well, the affix grammars more or less dictate a top to bottom algorithm for parsing, and many techniques developed for that can be used.

Yershov:
The question is really a programming question. Would you control how your parser will actually work during parsing and reflect your control in selecting specific grammar rules?

Koster:
I can tell for instance this. You can write every single rule in such a way that it starts with a non-terminal symbol. And if you do that, then you know that if you have n symbols in your text, you can have at most n rewritings, but you have a very long syntax here.

Griffiths:
Surely you can apply any of the techniques which are known for context-free grammars to your affix grammars?

Koster:

I think this is an extension of context-free grammars which is useful in the sense that, well, context-free grammars are manageable. Everybody knows how to interpret them and how to work with them, and most of their properties go along with this extension.

Scheidig:

How many rules do you get for ALGOL 68?

Koster:

When I first tried, I had 250, and I could fit the thing into my machine.

Scheidig:

Do you have some mechanical way to translate such a grammar into some sort of code?

Koster:

Yes.

Branquart:

As far as I can see, there are similarities between your way of writing a compiler with the help of affix grammars and the formalism introduced by Irons in this article on ALGOL 60 compilation. Are you aware of it? In that case, what are the essential differences between affix grammars and his formalism?

Koster:

There is of course the matter of notation in that you write something which still looks like a grammar and where your primitive functions do not fit in in a strange place but are really there. Then there is the fact that you have both bound and free affixes, that is, you have both parameters and local variables. I think that the last one is more than Irons used. The third thing would be that in this way you have a tendency for using as few semantic primitives as possible. In this article I give a list of some which suffice well for constructing Turing machines etc., for instance, constructing ALGOL 68 parsers. There may also be a point for all this in defining programming languages.

Mailloux:

It was not quite clear to me whether the arrays T, W and B are inherent in your system or whether these are defined in it.

Koster:

I have to elaborate slightly on that because I cheated: all the rules that I wrote down have to be provided with some extra affixes for the environment. In our compiler-compiler this is more practical. There is a macro facility which allows you to define your functions in ALGOL 60 and furthermore a specification possibility by which you can ask for some number of stacks with various identifiers. So it is a self-contained compiler-compiler.

ON IDENTIFICATION OF OPERATORS IN ALGOL 68

H. WÖSSNER
Technical University, Munich

INTRODUCTION

In presenting some results from [1] we will, in contrast with [2], restrict ourselves to the more complicated cases of those operands which are not directly coercends and even require firm balancing of modes.

As a consequence of the overloading concept in ALGOL 68 [3], the identification is, in general, an iterative process. Efficient algorithms for it can therefore only be achieved by unburdening its successive stages from all activities which can be done beforehand and once and for all. One such separable activity turns out to be, in nearly all cases, the balancing.

We begin with the classification of the "composite" clauses to be considered as operands or, more generally, in firm position:
(1) We denote as "noncollateral clauses" those conditional- and closed-clauses C with the following property:
There are at least two units which possibly, by elaboration of C, yield the value of C; and no such unit, called a (direct) component of C, is a collateral-clause[‡].
(2) Collateral-clauses (which we sometimes call "directly collateral").
(3) Conditional- and closed-clauses "containing" at least one component which is a collateral-clause are finally called "indirectly collateral clauses".

1. NONCOLLATERAL CLAUSES

Before starting to consider case (1) we introduce some abbreviations. Let M be a set of modes, $M_1 \subseteq M$, $m \in M$, and let $\overline{m}$ denote an arbitrary mode. Then we define:

D1) $\text{fc}(m) := \{\overline{m} \mid \overline{m} \text{ firmly coerced from } m \}$,

$\text{fc}(M_1) := \bigcup_{m \in M_1} \text{fc}(m)$.

[‡] Note that the term "component" here is defined for external objects.

D2) $\text{sc}(m) := \{\overline{m} | \overline{m} \text{ strongly coerced from } m\}$,

$\text{sc}(M_1) := \bigcap_{m \in M_1} \text{sc}(m)$.

D3) $\text{fb}_M(M_1) := \text{fc}(M_1) \cap \text{sc}(M)$,

$\text{fb}(M) := \text{fb}_M(M)$,

$\text{fb}_M(m) := \text{fb}_M(\{m\})$. *

D4) $\text{fm}(M) := \{m | \text{fb}(M) = \text{fb}_M(m)\}$,

the set of the "f-modes" of M.

Now, let C be a noncollateral clause and M the set of different a priori modes of its components. Then we can give our first statement in the following form:

S1) $\text{fm}(M) \neq \phi$, that is,

$\exists m \in M : \text{fb}(M) = \text{fb}_M(m)$.

In other words, there is at least one component (with mode m) of C to which, in all cases and without any restrictions on the coercing possibilities, the firm position of C can be passed, since all parameter modes agreeing with the operand C are elements of

$$\text{fb}(M) = \bigcup_{\overline{m} \in M} \text{fb}_M(\overline{m})$$

and, from S1, even of $\text{fb}_M(m)$. Obviously, $\text{fb}_M(m)$ is the set of all modes which can be reached from C, if a component of mode m is chosen as firm, while the other components are to be strong. We remark that S1 does not imply $\text{fb}(M) \neq \phi$.

In view of an algorithm delivering such an f-mode of C,

$$\text{fm}^o(M) \in \text{fm}(M),$$

the following is important:

S2) $M = M_1 \cup M_2$, $m_1 \in \text{fm}(M_1) \Rightarrow \text{fm}(m_1 \cup M_2) \subseteq \text{fm}(M)$,
or, constructively,
$\text{fm}^o(M) := \text{fm}^o(\text{fm}^o(M_1) \cup M_2)$.

To prove S2, let $m \in \text{fm}(m_1 \cup M_2)$. Then we have, by an easy computation,

$$\text{fb}(M) = \text{fb}_M(m), \quad \text{i.e., } m \in \text{fm}(M),$$

as stated. S2 reduces S1 to the following statement for two given modes m_1 and m_2:

S1r) $m_y \in \text{fm}(m_1 \cup m_2)$, or $\text{fc}(m_x) \cap \text{sc}(m_y) \subseteq \text{fc}(m_y)$, $x \neq y \in \{1, 2\}$.

* Further we will identify a set $\{m\}$ with its element m.

Instead of giving now the detailed proof (which consists of a suitable distinction of cases) we will consider some examples. First, we define

D5) $u(a) := \{\underline{\text{union}}\,(m_0, \ldots, m_n)\,|\,m_\nu \in \text{fc}(a) \text{ for one } \nu,\ 0 \leq \nu \leq n\}$,

$u(a, \bar{a}) := u(a) \cap u(\bar{a})$.

In connection with D5 we remark that always before uniting only firm coercions are possible.

E1) $\text{fm}(\underline{\text{int}} \cup \underline{\text{compl}}) = \underline{\text{compl}}$.

It is clear that

$\text{fc}(\underline{\text{int}}) \cap \text{sc}(\underline{\text{compl}}) = \text{fc}(u(\underline{\text{int}}, \underline{\text{compl}}))$
$\subseteq \text{fc}(\underline{\text{compl}})$,

but an exchange of <u>int</u> and <u>compl</u> is, of course, not allowed.

E2) $\text{fm}(\underline{\text{ref}}\ \underline{\text{row}}\ \underline{\text{real}} \cup \underline{\text{row}}\ \underline{\text{row}}\ \underline{\text{real}}) = \underline{\text{row}}\ \underline{\text{row}}\ \underline{\text{real}}$.

Here we have to see that no <u>row</u> can disappear by (strong) coercion.

E3) $\text{fm}(\underline{\text{real}} \cup \underline{\text{ref}}\ \underline{\text{real}}) = \underline{\text{real}} \cup \underline{\text{ref}}\ \underline{\text{real}}$.

In this last example, we have

$\text{fc}(\underline{\text{real}}) \subset \text{fc}(\underline{\text{ref}}\ \underline{\text{real}})$

(but not vice-versa). Therefore, the choice of <u>real</u> as $\text{fm}^0(\underline{\text{real}} \cup \underline{\text{ref}}\ \underline{\text{real}})$ minimizes, in general, the tentative coercions needed for identifying an operator, if we presume that the firm coercion is tried first.

2. COLLATERAL-CLAUSES

In the case (2) of collateral-clauses C we have to take notice of
i) the proper recursion introduced by those units of C which are directly or indirectly collateral clauses and
ii) the restrictions on the coercions available for coercends on any level which also contains a collateral component.

Here we have denoted, in an obvious manner, as a (direct) component on level 1 of C, any unit of C which is a coercend or a collateral-clause and any component of another composite unit of C. The (indirect) components on level 2 are then the direct components of any direct component of C, and so on.

Further, we term an "f-level" any level of (components of) C which under all circumstances contains a firm component. For instance, if the units of C are all collateral, we have at least the f-levels 1 and 2. Now we can easily see:

S3) The minimum level l which contains (as a component) a coercend is also the maximum f-level.

his is trivial if l is at the same time the maximum level L of C. Otherwise, suppose $l < L$: if we now choose a collateral component K on level l as firm, the value of K must be an array of a mode †

1) <u>row</u> m, with lower bound lwb = 1 and upper bound upb ≥ 2.

Then, however, any coercend $\overline{K}$ on level l can only be firmly coerced. For, a properly strong coercion of $\overline{K}$ would, in this case, end with rowing and so lead to an array of a mode

2) <u>row</u> $\overline{m}$ with lwb = 1 and upb ≤ 1,

where upb = 0 occurs only for a vacuum $\overline{K}$ (which we consider as a coercend, too). Obviously, for such values of K and $\overline{K}$, the further elaboration of C is undefined (see [3] 6.2.2.c, Step 6).

It turns out that the set of possible modes for C is, in the case $l = L$, of the form

$\qquad$ row(l) fb(M_l)

where row(l) is a sequence of l <u>row</u>'s and M_l the set of a priori modes of the coercends which are components on level l. In the other case, $l < L$, this set of reachable modes consists of one and only one element (for correct C). This mode can, of course, be determined by only considering C and does not depend at all on any parameter mode specified for the operator which is applied to C.

As examples for C we give (representing the coercends by their a priori modes):

E4) (<u>int</u>, <u>real</u>, (<u>real</u>, <u>real</u>))

$\qquad$ with the unique mode <u>row compl</u>.

E5) (<u>ref proc row</u> m, (m, <u>ref</u> m))

$\qquad$ with the mode <u>row row</u> m.

3. INDIRECTLY COLLATERAL CLAUSES

In our third case of indirectly collateral clauses C we have to distinguish between clauses C, all direct components (on level 0) of which are collateral, and others. For the first of these two classes it can generally be shown that:

S4) there is a unique maximum f-level l in C with a coercend as firm component both of which depend only on C.

For example, let

E6) $C \equiv $ <u>if</u> b <u>then</u> C_1 <u>else</u> C_2 <u>fi</u>,
$\qquad$ where C_1 is one of the following collateral clauses:
$\qquad$ a) (<u>int</u>, <u>real</u>)
$\qquad$ b) (<u>real</u>, <u>compl</u>)
$\qquad$ c) (<u>real</u>, <u>row real</u>)
$\qquad$ and C_2 is always
$\qquad\qquad$ $C_2 \equiv ((\underline{int}), \underline{real}), (\underline{int}, \underline{int}))$.

† The symbol <u>row</u> stands for the protonotion "row of".

Then we get as reachable modes for C and corresponding maximum f-level l, respectively (using the Kleene operation "*"):

a) **row** (2) {**proc**}* **real**, $l = 2$

   (on level 1 rowing is needed) ;

b) **row compl**, $l = 1$;

c) **row** (2) **real**, $l = 1$.

In the example a), $l = 1$ would not deliver a mode for C. In the other examples, $l = 2$ would not allow other modes than $l = 1$. It is generally true that l is the minimum level of C which, although it contains a coercend as firm component, yields a mode for C.

In the second class of indirectly collateral clauses the maximum f-level l is, by our definition of f-levels, $l = 0$. But here, for the first time, this level does not necessarily contain a coercend on a firm position. The reason for this exception is that the restrictions mentioned above (see 2) do not hold for the coercends on level 0 and only for these coercends. Especially, rowing may be performed on these coercends on level 0.

As example we consider the following particular program E7:

0) **begin**
1) **struct** $\underline{s}$ = *(**int** i, **bool** b)* ; $\underline{s}$ s = *(0, **true**)* ;
2) **union** $\underline{u}$ = *(**int**, **bool**, $\underline{s}$)* ;
3) **op** ? = *($\underline{s}$ x) **int** : **skip** ;*
3a)   ? *if b of s then s else (1, false) fi ;*
3b) **begin**
4) **op** ? = *([1 : **flex**] $\underline{u}$ x) **int** : **skip** ;*
5)   ? *if b of s then s else (1, false) fi*
3c) **end**
6) **end**

Here, the applied occurrence of the monadic operator "?" in line 3a identifies the defining occurrence in line 3 where s, the then-clause, is firm. The equally applied "?" in line 5 identifies, on the other hand, the defining occurrence in line 4, where s is necessarily strong. The remainder results from the earlier cases.

4. AN AMBIGUITY

Obviously, the modes $\underline{s}$ and **row** $\underline{u}$ in E7 are not loosely related. By eliminating the lines 3a, b, c we should, therefore, get a proper program. But, as we have seen, the identification of "?" is ambiguous.

This ambiguity could be avoided by the following definition of the relation "loosely related".

Let us define (for mode m)

D6) $fc_n(m) := row(n) \; fc(m), \; n \geq 0$,

then we say

D7) $m_i, \; i = 1, 2$, are loosely related whenever there exists a mode m and an integer $n \geq 0$ so that one of the following conditions holds:

(i) $m_i \in fc_n(m) \quad , \quad i = 1, 2 \;$;

(ii) $m_1 \in fc(m) \land m_2 \in fc_n(u(m)), \quad n \geq 1.$ ‡

5. CONCLUSION

In conclusion we remark that the first printing of [3] contained only the condition (i) of D7. For the reason that collateral-clauses are not coercends, this condition is, of course, sufficient (for a unique identification of operators) in all cases except the last one considered. This follows from the uniqueness of the a priori mode (m) and the level (n) of the firm coercend which we have shown for these cases. Only in the last "critical" class deviating from this, the balancing process cannot be completely separated from the identification of operators.

POSTSCRIPT

In the discussion it was presented that N. Yoneda has found another ambiguity in the critical class. This ambiguity is caused by recursive modes and is not solved by D7. Now, instead of further extension of D7, we propose to reduce it to its earlier form (with only condition (i)) and to require, for instance, that collateral components of critical clauses must be strong (so that the firm balance would be restricted to the coercends on level 0).

REFERENCES

[1] Wössner, H.: Operatoridentifizierung in ALGOL 68, Thesis, Technische Hochschule München, July 1970.
[2] Goos, G., Scheidig, H. and Wössner, H.: Mode representation and operator identification in ALGOL 68, Proceedings of an Informal Conference on ALGOL 68 Implementation, University of British Columbia, August 1969.
[3] Van Wijngaarden, A., Mailloux, B.J., Peck, J.E.L. and Koster, C.H.A.: Report on the algorithmic language ALGOL 68, Mathematisch Centrum, Amsterdam, MR 101, 2nd print, October 1969.

---

‡ $n = 0$ is contained in (i), for $u(m)$ see D5.

DISCUSSION

Ershov:
What is the actual representation of modes?

Wössner:
We have a list of all modes occurring in a program, called the declarator-list, in which entries are made for all declarers. For manipulation of these modes we use, in part, a binary representation, which is very simply manipulated, at least in those cases which do not require uniting. We have defined simple modes to be those which, if you delete the prefixes, are not unions. For the representation of these modes we have given details in a paper presented in Vancouver. For example, the property of a mode to be firmly coerced from another is proved by simple binary operations on their representations. This method allows not only a proof of this property but also the determination of the coercing sequences to perform on the coercends.

Ershov:
You use a set theoretical terminology to explain the algorithmic approach. What is the actual technique for processing the sets of modes and lists of modes which appear during the algorithm? Do you use linear search or some special methods for addressing? And now a special question. What is the approach for generating modes? For example, if you have to check whether or not two modes are related? You have usually several samples to compare.

Wössner:
Yes, from the general list of modes, we take out just these modes to deal with and manipulate them in a special stack which is provided only for this purpose.

Sintzoff:
I would like to ask Kakehi to explain whether the ambiguity discovered in Japan is solved by Wössner's restriction.

Kakehi:
I suppose that the ambiguity which was found by Yoneda, is not excluded by such a restriction. I will write it down.

> mode a = [1 : 1] s ;
>
> mode c = [1 : 2, 1 : 1] s ;
>
> mode s = struct (ref a f, g) ;
>
> a a ; s s ;
>
> ... + if bool then s else (a, a) fi
>
> firm   strong → s
>
> strong firm   → c

Wössner:

You have no defined elaboration in the second case because the bounds are not right. See Report 0.2.0.2 and 6.2.2.c, if I remember right.

Kakehi:

Yes, the elaboration is undefined because of incorrect bounds.

Goos:

I do not see that this question of bounds changes the problem, because anyway, at compile-time you have to make a decision and you do not know the bounds.

Wössner:

Yes, you are right, but you can generally, at compile-time, anticipate consequences from the elaboration conditions given in the Report. You can for example see that in some cases rowing is not possible. You are certain, that, on the one hand, by rowing of a coercend, you can only obtain an array of mode <u>row</u> m with the bounds zero or one. On the other hand, if you make the "generalized rowing" of a collateral-clause, you must obtain a mode <u>row</u> m with an upperbound ≥ 2. Then, by the semantic conditions for the elaboration of collateral-clauses, you cannot build an array which contains as components two multiple values with different bounds.

Goos:

This means that you are able to solve the situation by using information which comes along at that time.

Wössner:

I am not sure for the given example.

Sintzoff:

But, you may use flexible arrays and a syntactic ambiguity still remains.

Bowlden:

The point is that this is an ambiguity and the question of bounds has nothing to do with it.

Sintzoff:

Exactly.

AN ATTEMPTED DEFINITION
OF AN EXTENSIBLE SYSTEM

L. TRILLING[*] and J. P. VERJUS[*]
Département d'informatique. Université de Montréal

1. INTRODUCTION

Our goal is to propose a "basic system" that admits to be extended as our needs grow.

Two kinds of computer users can be distinguished: those who care about the system and those who program applications. The first have to know the system deeply especially if they want to modify it accordingly to the wishes of the other group. The others have to know a programming language and at least some elements of the system.

Our goal is to ease the task of all these people by empowering them to use only one language: that is , to reduce as far as possible "systems orders".

ALGOL 68 has been selected mainly because:
- it includes all the facilities of modern programming languages,
- it is rigorously defined and it provides good means of communication between programmers,
- through mode declaration and operator declaration, it can be considered as extensible.

This will enable one to:
- construct oriented-systems for different needs,
- implement oriented-languages towards special applications.

An interesting feature will be that any user will have at his disposal an ALGOL 68 description (as complete as possible) of the environment in which his programs are executed.

A processor, called "Machine U", which can be addressed from a terminal (teletype or alphanumerical display) is presented under the form of an ALGOL 68 procedure.

Following this, user's library facilities are considered. A privileged user, called the "master", can access any book and controls users' requests (entries, exclusions ...).

Finally, some examples of context building, text edition and book manipulation are given.

---

[*] Present address: Département Mathématiques et Informatique, Université de Rennes, France.

2. THE KERNEL

2.1. *Notion of context*

2.1.1. Compiling in a context. Progressive compilation

Let us consider an ALGOL 68 compiler which accepts a source string s_2 and an initialisation as parameters. This given initialisation results from the compilation of a source string s_1 and is called "compilation state" resulting from the compilation of the source string s_1.

To compile s_2 in a context s_1 means to compile s_2 with an initialisation given by the compilation state of s_1 and to obtain another compilation state.

Example:

- let s_1 be the string (**int** x ;

From its compilation, we obtain a compilation state.

- let s_2 be the string x := x + 1

To compile s_2 in s_1 means to compile the string

(**int** x ; x := x + 1

and to obtain the resulting compilation state.

Only "satisfying" contexts will be considered here. A given context s_1 is said to be satisfying if the string s_1) is an ALGOL 68 program.

Example: (**int** x := 0   is a satisfying context but
       (**int** x := 1 + (**int** y   is not.

2.1.2. Execution in a satisfying context. Progressive execution

Execution in a satisfying context s_1 results in an "execution state" corresponding to the "objects" and their "relations" [1] prior to the elaboration of the statement

    e : <u>skip</u>

in the program:

    s_1 ; e : <u>skip</u>)

To execute a string s_2 in a context s_1 assumes that s_1 has been executed and means that the execution of

    s_1 ; s_2 ; e : <u>skip</u>)   (1)

will follow on from s_2 with the execution state corresponding to s_1. This resulting execution state is the one corresponding to the objects and their relations prior to the elaboration of

    e : <u>skip</u>

The string ;s_2 is compiled in the context s_1 and, of course, (1) has to be an ALGOL 68 program.

Example:

    Let s_1 be the string
    (**int** x := 0

ATTEMPTED DEFINITION OF AN EXTENSIBLE SYSTEM

Assume that this satisfying context has been executed. To execute the following string s_2

    print (x := x + 2)

in the context s_1 produces as an output the value 2. To execute the following string s_3

    print (x := x + 1)

in the same context after the preceding execution produces as an output the value 3.

2.1.3.

In the following, every context will have the same beginning, called the "basic context". It is formed in the following way

    (s (skip

where s is a declaration prelude sequence.

From now on:

    $(s(\underline{skip};s_1$ will be said to be a context and, by extension s_1 will be too if

    $(s(\underline{skip};s_1))$

is an ALGOL 68 program and

    s_1 will be said to be a program if

    $(s(\underline{skip};s_1)$

is an ALGOL 68 program *.

2.2. *The basic context and the Machine U*

The problem can be specified in the following terms:

- On a computer, we have at our disposal a compiler translating programs written in a given source language (ALGOL 68) into a given object language. Compiling is done in a context (cf. 2.1.1).
- A given string can be executed in a particular context (cf. 2.1.2).
- Communication with the computer is provided by terminals. Thus, each user can write on a book corresponding to his terminal.

We want a simple processor to which the user could address himself to order the following tasks:

- to compile a string in a choosen context,
- to execute a string in a choosen context,
- to "edit", that is to modify what has been written on the terminal,
- to interrupt an execution,
- to initialize and to close the communication.

---

* The execution of the string s_2 in a context s_1 will be now understood with the help of the ALGOL 68 program:
    $(s(\underline{skip};s_1;s_2;e:\underline{skip}$ q
where q is ")" or "))" according as s_1 ; s_2 is a program or a context.

Our solution is to provide the user with a processor (Machine U). It is described by an ALGOL 68 procedure working in a particular context called the "basic context". Some variables used by this processor are declared in this context.

The basic context is the "minimal" context in which the user can compile or execute a string. Thus, the variable declared in this context are accessible to the users (nevertheless some of these variables are "hidden").

An ALGOL 68 description (with many comments) of the basic context and of the Machine U is given below.

2.2.1. The basic context

The basic context can be described as follows*:

(*struct état comp*) = (*bool réussite, programme,*

     string source,

     int % adresse,

     état compilation) ;

  co "source" *is a source string which when concatenated to the basic context*

   string corresponds to the "compilation" state. "réussite" is true *when*

   the source string is a context or a program (cf. II.1.3) and "programme"

   is true *if "source" is a program.*

  co

struct % état =

  c a value of this mode gives the compilation state of a source language st

   The corresponding object string is included as one of its fields.

  c ;

état comp base comp =

  c result of the basic context compilation

  c ;

état comp % courant comp,

   courant 1 comp := base comp ;

proc p courant comp = état comp : courant comp ;

  co "courant comp" is the compilation state of the current context.

   "courant 1 comp" is used to change the current context. The user canno

---

* Symbol % before an identifier means that the last one is not accessible to the current user.

modify "courant comp", this to keep the correspondence between the compilation state of the current context ("courant comp") and its execution state ("courant ex"). However, the user has access to its value with the help of the procedure "p courant comp".

  co

priority compiler = 1 ;

op compiler = (string source, état comp initialisation) état comp :

  c *The operator's parameters are respectively a source language string and a given initial state of compilation. It compiles the string "source" in the context "initialization". It results in a new compilation state. The field selected by "adresse" in the result gives the starting point of the object program corresponding to the "source" string. In case of errors, a message is delivered and compilation is left.*

  c;

int % départ = adresse of (" " compiler base comp) ;

struct % état ex =

  c *a value of this mode gives the execution state of a context.*

  c;

état ex basex =

  c *result of the execution of the basic context.*

  c;

priority exécuter = 1 ;

op % exécuter = (état comp objet, état ex original) état ex :

  c *these operator's parameters are respectively a compilation state and an initial state of execution. It executes the object program starting at "adresse of objet" in the execution state "original" and gives the resulting execution state.*

  c;

int pc = *c* *c*,

  lc = *c* *c*,

  cc = *c* *these are the fixed dimensions of a book containing a compilation*

    state

    c ;

proc lirec = (*file* i) état comp :

    c takes the value of the compilation state read on the book specified

    by "i".

    c ;

proc ecrirec = (*file* i, état comp x) état comp :

    c writes the compilation state "x" on the book specified by "i"

    and returns this state.

    c ;

file terminal ;

string tampon, tampon 1 := " " ;

string % utilisateur courant ;

    co "utilisateur courant" is initialized by "Machine U" ; its value

      being a string representing the user. See III for application.

    co

(*skip*

    co this parenthesis is noteworth (cf. 1.3).

    co

2.2.2. The Machine U

This processor is activated as soon as the user asks for an access to the system from his terminal.

  Machine U proceeds as follows:

  It creates a book corresponding to the terminal (100 pages, 40 lines and 72 characters). Then, it asks for an identification (i.e. user's name) and checks his rights to work (i.e. user's password). This verification implies a search in the "répertoire" (i.e. repertory) (cf. 3). Once the user has been admitted to work, Machine U prints out the character → and conversing may begin.

ATTEMPTED DEFINITION OF AN EXTENSIBLE SYSTEM   125

Each character sent by the user is taken care of by Machine U. In fact, only six special characters are recognized and interpreted: those characters are:

$, ! , # , ↓ , ╪ and →

Any other character is stored in the string "tampon".
The effects of these special characters are:

$ - ends the processing,
! - causes compilation and execution in the current context of the string obtained by enclosing the string contained in "tampon" within parenthesis. The compilation state of the current context is not modified unlike its execution state. In other words, the source string contained in tampon is executed without inserting it in the current context.
- is identical to ! except that the source string is not enclosed between parentheses and is added to the current context whose compilation state is modified consequently.
↓ - is used to change the current context. The compilation state of the new current context is given by "courant 1 comp" this one being executed.
╪ - copies the string contained in "tampon" into "tampon1".
→ - interrupts the execution (this order is not described here).

The processor is now described:

proc Machine U = :

(*char* a ;

   establish (terminal, "terminal", 100, 40, 72, 2);

     co call for user's identification *co*

   tampon := " " ;

e_1: put (terminal, "qui êtes-vous?");

   while (get (terminal, a); a) ╪ "!" *do* tampon +:= a ;

   while (*ref des utilisateurs* : descripteur courant) :╪: *nil do*

     if nom utilisateur *of* descripteur courant ╪ tampon

       then descripteur courant := utilisateur suivant *of* descripteur
                                                            courant

     else e_2

   fi ;

e_1 ;

e_2 : utilisateur courant := tampon ;

   co checking the password *co*

e_3 : put (terminal, "donnez votre mot de passe");

   tampon := " " ;

```
while (get(terminal, a) ; a) ≠ "!" do tampon +:= a ;
if tampon ≠ mot de contrôle of descripteur courant
    then put (terminal, "→")
    else e₃
fi ;
tampon := " " ;
    co conversational part co
e₄: get (terminal, a) ;
    if a ≠ "$" then
    if a = "!" then
        état comp x = ";(" + tampon + ")" compiler courant comp ;
        if réussite of x then
            tampon := " " ;
            if programme of x then put (terminal, "execution impossible")
                else courantex := x exécuter courantex
            fi
        fi
    else
    if a = "#" then
        état comp x = ";" + tampon compiler courant comp ;
        tampon := " " ;
        if réussite of x then
          bool p = programme of x ;
          courant comp := if p then base comp else x fi ;
          courantex := (étatex r = x exécuter courantex ;
                        if p then r else basex fi )
        fi
    else
```

ATTEMPTED DEFINITION OF AN EXTENSIBLE SYSTEM

 if a = "↓" *then*

  courant comp := *courant 1 comp* ;

  adresse of courant comp := *départ* ;

  courantex := *courant comp exécuter basex else*

 if a = "⊥" *then*

  tampon 1 := *tampon* ;

  tampon := " " *else*

tampon +:= a ; e_4

fi fi fi fi ;

put (terminal, "→") ; e_4

fi ;

scratch (terminal)

  Thus, given a string sent from the terminal, it can be executed in a particular context (this context, in our view, would be written by the system programmer). This string can also be included in the current context, thus extending it.

  One can note that a string sent from a terminal is always considered as preceded by ";". Also, that if the current context is the concatenation of the basic context to a program (cf. 2.1.3), the current context becomes the basic context: this property is used in the example below.

  A context is changed by assigning to *courant* 1 *comp* the compilation state of the new context and activating the order "↓".

  Finally, one is able to modify a string on a terminal by copying it in *tampon* with the order "⊥". Then, one is free to use operators declared in his context to effect the desired modifications and to put back the modified string into *tampon*.

2.3. *Example*

  ¢ *the current context is the basic context* ¢

→ *int* x := 0

  ¢ *this declaration is added to the basic context* ¢

→ put (terminal, x +:= 1) !

 1

  ¢ *this statement has been compiled in the current context and*

   executed. The value 1 is printed ¢

→ put (terminal, x +:= 2) !

   3

     ¢ *this time, 3 is printed because the execution state of the current context was such that the value of x was 1* ¢

     ¢ *now, we will build, use and store a context and we will show how to call it back* ¢

→ <u>proc</u> replace = (<u>string</u> a, b, c) <u>string</u> :

     (<u>string</u> t ; <u>int</u> bsa =⌈a, bsb = ⌈b ;

     <u>for</u> i <u>to</u> bsa <u>do</u>

     <u>if</u> a [i : i + bsb - 1] b <u>then</u>

       t := a[1 : i - 1] + c + a[i + bsb : bsa] <u>fi</u> ;

     t)#

     ¢ *we introduce this procedure in the current context* ¢

→ <u>proc</u> fac = (<u>int</u> n) <u>int</u> : (m = 0 | 1 | m * fac(m - 1)) †

     ¢ *there is an error* ¢

→ tampon := replace (tampon1, "m", "n") !

     ¢*the correct text is assigned to "tampon"* ¢

→ ; put(terminal, fac(3)) !

   6

     ¢ *we have the good answer* ¢

→ <u>file</u> f1 ; establish(f1, "edition", pc, lc, cc, 2) ;

   ecrirec(f1, p courant comp) ; close(f1) !

     ¢ *the compilation state of the current context is stored in the book* ¢

→ <u>skip</u>)#

     ¢ *the current context is now the basic context* ¢

→ <u>string</u> s #

→ tampon := s := "<u>proc</u> fac = (<u>int</u> n) <u>int</u> : (z = 0|1| z * fac(z-1)) ; put (terminal, fac(3)) " !

→ !

ERREUR COMPILATION

　　¢ *an error has been detected at compile time* ¢

→ <u>file</u> f1 ; open(f1, "édition", 2) ;

　　courant 1 comp := lirec(f1) ;

　　tampon1 := s !

→ ↓

　　¢ *current context is the one which had been stored previously in the book "édition"* ¢

→ tampon := replace(tampon1, "z", "n"))#

　　¢*correction is made and the current context becomes the basic context* ¢

→ !

6

3. THE "MASTER" AND THE LIBRARY

The processor described previously enables one to create and use books. However, nothing has been provided to use these books for another elaboration. Also, it has not been anticipated that one could use other users' books or that one could restrict the utilisation of his own books.

A brief description of the repertory ("repertoire") is given below, that is books organization and means of access to them. Only one user, called the "master", can access this repertory without any restriction. He can thus manage users' admission, modify their password ... etc., with the help of ALGOL 68 programs written by him. Other users are limited by the basic context (where given variables are hidden) and by eventual restrictions on other users' books.

A presentation of the different authorizations one is able to get is given. Finally, means of access to a book during an elaboration are introduced, and that, accordingly to ALGOL 68.

3.1. *The repertory*

The repertory is a list of users, each user possessing his own list of books.

Three characteristics are attributed to each user: a control word, a "global authorization" (cf. 3.2) and a list of "partenaires" (partners).

To each user's book one finds characteristics of the ALGOL 68 bfile, a boolean indicating if the book is used and an "autorisation particulière" (particular authorization) for this book.

The following declarations are then to be added to the basic context:

struct des utilisateur = (*string* nom utilisateur,

(*string* mot de contrôle,

[1 : nmb channels] *ref des livre* catalogue des livres,

autorisation globale, [1 : 0 *flex*] *ref string* partenai

ref des utilisateur utilisateur suivant) ;

struct des livre = (*bool* attaché, *autorisation* particulière,

bfile livre,

ref des livre prochain livre);

struct autorisation = ([1 : 3] *bool* propriétaire, partenaire, anonyme) ;

struct bfile = ([1 : 3] *bool* autorisation d accès,

[1 : 0 *flex*, 1 : 0 *flex*, 1 : 0 *flex*] *int* book,

int lpage, llivre, lchar, page, livre, char, max page, max livre

max char,

string idf,

ref bfile next) ;

ref des utilisateurs % répertoire := *c* a particular initialisation given by

the master *c* ;

ref des utilisateurs % descripteur courant ;

The ALGOL 68 structure bfile is slightly modified: a row of boolean has been added, indicating if reading, writing or scratching are possible, depending on the will of the book's owner.

It has been shown in 2.2 how "descripteur courant" is initialized. Its value gives access to informations related to the user.

ATTEMPTED DEFINITION OF AN EXTENSIBLE SYSTEM 131

Example of a program (normally written by the master) to introduce "dupont" in the repertory:

répertoire := <u>des utilisateur</u> := ("dupont", "dup129zbxa",

<u>skip</u>,

((<u>true</u>, <u>true</u>, <u>true</u>),

(<u>false</u>, <u>false</u>, <u>false</u>),

(<u>false</u>, <u>false</u>, <u>false</u>)),

<u>skip</u>,

répertoire) !

This way a new user named dupont possessing a given password and a global authorization (the one given here could be considered as standard, cf. 3.2) is included in the repertory. At this point, dupont does not possess any book nor partner.

An example displaying the repertory:

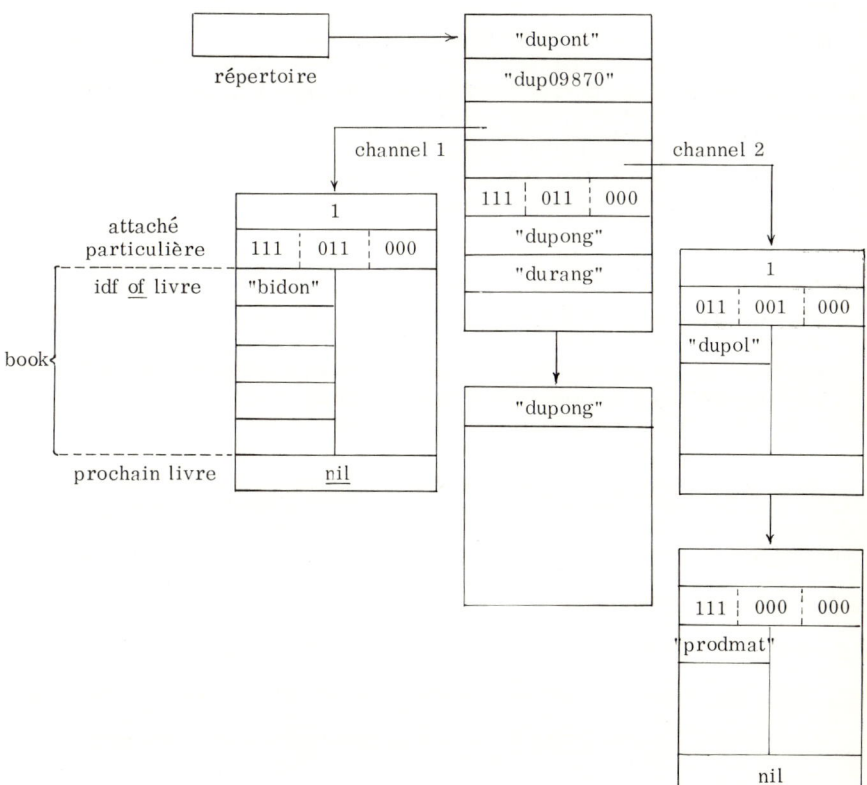

The user dupont possesses a book titled "bidon" on channel 1 and two others, "dup01" and "prodmat", on channel 2. The meaning of authorizations will be seen in the next paragraph. The book "prodmat" is being used in an elaboration.

3.2. *The authorizations*

When a book is requested, two pieces of information are considered:
- the relation between the applicant and the owner of the book. There are three kinds of applicant:
  . the requested book's owner
  . the owner's partners
  . others are anonymous applicants.
- the nature of the restrictions imposed to the applicant by the owner. Restrictions fall under one of the three followings:
  . reading allowed or not
  . writing allowed or not
  . scratching and modifying the *idf* allowed or not.

An authorization is represented by a triple of boolean rows, each having three elements. The first element of the triple is related to the owner, the second one to the partners and the third one to the anonymous.

The third element of a boolean row indicates the possibility to read a book (value *true*), the second one the possibility to write on it and the first one the possibility to scratch it and to modify the *idf*. For example, the value (*false*, *false*, *false*) prohibits any access to applicants and the value (*false*, *true*, *true*) permits reading and writing in the book.

There is one authorization per user and one per book. The first mentioned concerns all the owner's books and the other one is related only to a considered book.

Thus, in the last example of 3.1:
- dupont has complete access to the book "bidon" but it is not possible for him to scratch his book "dupol".
- durang, who is a partner of dupont, is at most allowed to read or write in his partner's books. This is exactly the case with the book "bidon" but "dupol" is accessible only through reading.

In order to protect his books, a user must be allowed to modify:
- his partners' list,
- his global or particular authorizations.

Thus, the basic context must include the following declarations:

<u>ref</u> <u>autorisation</u> *autorisation globale* = *globale* <u>of</u> *descripteur courant* ;

<u>ref</u> [1:0<u>flex</u>] <u>ref string</u> *mes partenaires* = *partenaires* <u>of</u> *descripteur courant* ;

<u>proc</u> *autorisation livre* = (<u>string</u> *nom livre*, <u>int</u> *canal*) <u>ref</u> <u>autorisation</u> :

 (<u>ref</u> <u>des livre</u> *i* := (*catalogue des livres* <u>of</u> *descripteur courant*) [*canal*] ;

 <u>co</u> *searching the book, the value* <u>nil</u> *is returned if not found* <u>co</u>

while (ref des livre : i) :≠: nil do

   if idf of livre of i ≠ nom livre then

      i := prochain livre of i else e fi;

nil .

e : particulière of i

) ;

The variables *autorisation globale* and *mes partenaires* can be used by the user. That is not the case of descripteur courant (cf. 2.2).
Example:

   autorisation globale := ((true, true, true), (false, false, true),
                                                         (false, false, false)) !

/allows at least:

   - to the user, reading, writing and scratching his own books,
   - to his partners, reading only.

No access is provided to the anonymous.
   Using the procedure *autorisation livre*, one can know the value of a particular authorization and modify it at his will.
   Example: (Mr. Dupont is at work)

   ref autorisation x = autorisation livre("dupol", 2) ;
   if x :≠: nil then x := ((true, true, true), (false, true, true),
                                                         (false, false, false)) !

Mr. Dupont has thus allowed himself complete access to his book "dupol" and permits his partners to read and write in it.

3.3. *Accessing the books*

In ALGOL 68, to open a book during an elaboration of a program it must be accessible through "chainbfile". The initialization of this row is left in the ALGOL 68 report to the implementer.
   A procedure is provided to enter a book in chainbfile. This procedure, called *mettre en chainbfile* (put chainbfile) is declared in the basic context. It possesses three parameters characterizing the book which are respectively the owner's name, the book's name and the channel on which it resides. It takes out the book from the repertory if possible; two cases may arise where the applicant is not allowed to put this book in his chainbfile, they are:
   - the book is already used (into current elaboration),
   - the owner has not allowed him to use it; that is, the opening authorization is not sufficient.

This opening authorization is computed the following way: the relation between the owner and the applicant is considered, let us call it the status of the applicant. Then, we intersect the parts of the global authorization of the owner and of the particular authorization of the requested book corresponding to this status. The entry into *chainbfile* is refused if the resulting value is (*false*, *false*, *false*).

Entering a book into an user's *chainbfile* implies that the boolean field *attaché* belonging to its *bfile* is adjusted to *true*.

In the standard prelude, the elements of *chainbfile* will be initialized to *nil*.

The procedure *lock* will disconnect a book from its channel and will enter it in the repertory. The procedure *scratch* will disconnect a book from its channel and will take it out from the repertory.

This is the procedure *mettre en chainbfile*:

<u>proc</u>   mettre en chainbfile =

   (<u>string</u> utilisateur, nlivre, <u>int</u> canal) <u>int</u> :

   <u>co</u> this procedure takes a negative or null value whenever the

   book "nlivre" of the user "utilisateur" is not accessible.

   The values it can take and their meanings are listed below :

      -3   :   owner does not exist,

      -2   :   the requested book does not exist,

      -1   :   the book is being used,

       0   :   no access is provided for this applicant,

    1 to 7:   access is allowed and number corresponds to the

   authorization from reading only ((0, 0, 1) :

   value 1) to complete access ((1, 1, 1) : value 7).

<u>co</u>

(<u>ref</u> <u>des utilisateur</u> i := répertoire ;

<u>ref</u> <u>des livre</u> j ;

<u>int</u> genre := 0 ;

   <u>co</u> searching the book owner <u>co</u>

ATTEMPTED DEFINITION OF AN EXTENSIBLE SYSTEM

```
if utilisateur = utilisateur courant then
    i := descripteur courant ;
    genre := 1 ;
    e
fi ;
while (ref des utilisateur : i) :≠: nil do
    if utilisateur ≠ nom utilisateur of i then
        i := utilisateur suivant of i else e
    fi ;
    - 3 .
e :   co searching the requested book co
    j := (catalogue des livre of i) [canal] ;
    while (ref des livre : j) :≠: nil do
        if idf of livre of i ≠ nlivre then
            j := prochain livre of j else f
        fi ;
        - 2 .
f :   co  availability of the book  co
    (ref bool x = attaché of j ;
        if x then x := false ; g fi) ;
        - 1 .
g :           co searching applicant's status co
    if genre ≠ 1 then
        for k to ⌈partenaires of i do
            if (partenaires of i) [k] = utilisateur courant then
                genre := 2 ; h fi ;
            genre := 3
        fi ;
```

h :   co computing the authorizations co

    (op η = ([1:3] bool x, y)[ ] bool :

        ([1:3] bool z ; for k to 3 do z[k] := x[k]∧ y[k] ; z) ;

   priority η = 9 ;

   ref autorisation gi = globale of i, pj = particulière of j ;

   [1:3] bool x = case genre in

        proprietaire of gi η prorietaire of pj,

        partenaire   of gi η partenaire of pj,

        anonyme   of gi η anonyme   of pj esac ;

   int 1 := 0 ;

   for k to 3 do 1 := 2*1 + (x[k] | 1 | 0) ;

   if 1 ≠ 0 then

      autorisation d accès of j := x ;

      next of j := chainbfile [canal] ;

      chainbfile [canal] := livre of j

   fi ; 1

)

)

3.4. *Example* (see figure on next page).

    Mrs. Dupont and Dupong are working:
    Mr. Dupont has written:
  mettre en chainbfile ("dupont", "prodmat", 2) !
then the book prodmat has been taken from the repertory to *chainbfile*.
    Mr. Dupont has written:
  mettre en chainbfile ("dupont", "bidon", 1) ;
  mettre en chainbfile ("dupong", "dupo2", 1) ;
  mettre en chainbfile ("dupont", "dupo1", 2) !
these books have been entered in this *chainbfile*. Being the owner, he can only read "dupo2" and as a partner of Dupont, he can only read "dupo1" and is allowed to read and write into "bidon".

ATTEMPTED DEFINITION OF AN EXTENSIBLE SYSTEM

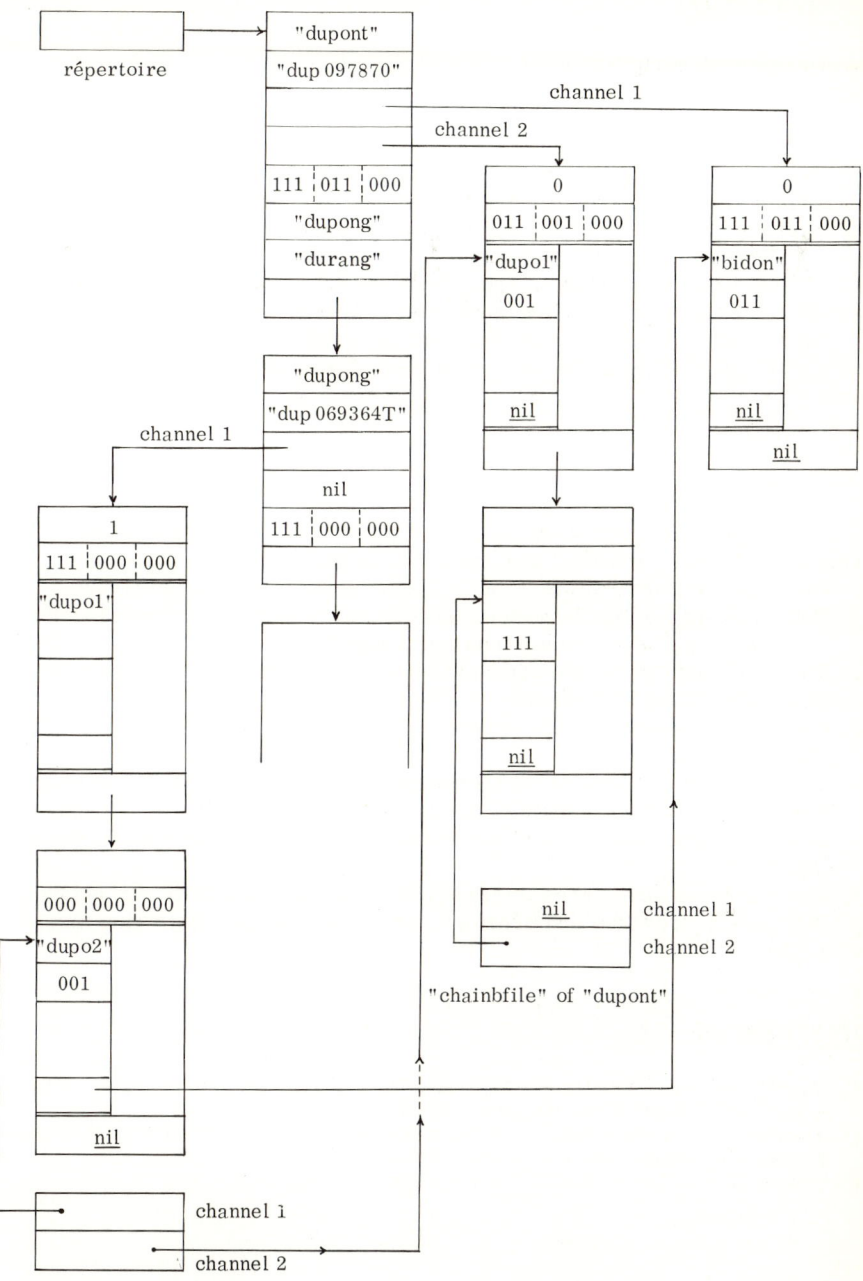

4. CONCLUSION

The given description of the system is not complete and a practical realization will help us to give a more detailed one. Thus, the order "→" which stops execution and returns control to the Machine U would require a description using semaphores.

Our choice to compile may be argued. To keep source string and object program is costly. However, ALGOL 68 is not readily interpretable but in our point of view a conversational system is an outstanding tool to build ALGOL 68 programs. LISP is readily interpretable but it is not as flexible as ALGOL 68 concerning data structures and we can expect ALGOL 68 programs to be more efficient and more readable than LISP programs.

We are now working towards the realization of the system described, with a subset of ALGOL 68, excluding procedures, multiple values and unions.

ABSTRACT

This paper deals with a system which gives to a user (whatever his speciality may be) powerful and adaptable means to work on a computer.
The main characteristics of the proposed system are the following:
1. The knowledge of one language, ALGOL 68, is sufficient to work at the "system" level and to write ordinary programs.
2. The processor which the user addresses to is described in an easy way by an ALGOL 68 procedure.
3. Concepts of modes and operators introduced in ALGOL 68 make this language extensible.
   With the help of "contexts" in which programs are executed, one can use this very important facility to define oriented-languages (simulation, numerical analysis ...) and particular systems (evolved towards editing, debugging ...).
4. Several users have access to the system and possess their own books. Adequate procedures are provided for exchanging and protecting these books.

REFERENCES

[1] Van Wijngaarden, A. (Editor), Mailloux, B.J., Peck, J.E.L. and Koster, C.H.A., Report on the algorithmic language ALGOL 68.
[2] Assabgui, M. and Trilling, L., Entrées-sorties ALGOL 68, Département d'informatique de l'Université de Montréal, Publication No. 13.
[3] Wilkes, M.V., Time-sharing computer systems, Mac Donald and Co. Ltd.

DISCUSSION

Ershov:
I have not understood whether the contexts have a linear or a nested structure. If it is linear, then there is no possibility of organizing the real block structure of an ALGOL 68 program.

Trilling:
Well, the contexts must have a linear structure but the programs that you execute under them may have a block structure.

Van Wijngaarden:
How do you repair an error which depends upon the context? For example, in your definition of *fac* you may have had an error in the third occurrence of the colon. Perhaps it was an equals-symbol instead.

Trilling:
You have to write another procedure in your context. In fact, what we want is that people should have several different contexts and several editing procedures.

Van Wijngaarden:
Perhaps I do not understand it quite. The use of your replace must be very rare because all your examples were such that the letter that you changed into another one occurred only once, but usually it will occur at many places. Could you use your int = which occurs only once. Could you use that in *replace* (*tampon* 1, "int =", "int :").

Trilling:
In this case you could use a new procedure *replace* taking into account the left or the right contexts of the string to be replaced.

SESSION 4

(Chairman: A.van Wijngaarden)

A MULTILANGUAGE PROGRAMMING SYSTEM ORIENTED TO LANGUAGES DESCRIPTION AND UNIVERSAL OPTIMIZATION ALGORITHMS

A. P. ERSHOV
Computing Centre, Siberian Division, AS USSR, Novosibirsk 90, USSR

INTRODUCTION

This paper relates to such an initial stage of the development when the investigator follows mainly his intuition and experience with less care about motivation, comparisons and references. The paper just reflects a current vision of that multilanguage programming system within the framework of which we are planning to implement ALGOL 68.

We want to build the multilanguage programming system for a specific computer but we hope that the computer will influence the system not so deeply and this influence will be concentrated in isolated parts of the translator.

The translator will be multilanguage in a sense that it will translate source programs written in one of several algorithmic languages. ALGOL 68 is definitely one of them. PL/1 and Simula 67 are highly probable candidates. Orientation of the translator to one or another language is performed by incorporation of some tables into appropriate places of the translator, those tables being written for each language by general rules. In a successful case there will be not so many such tables and their contents will be filled without great effort directly from the language specifications. An extreme failure is to have these tables in the form of a family of independent translators, one for each considered language.

Having in mind the reservations made at the beginning of the paper we shall not discuss here what the differences or similarities are between our approach and syntax-directed translators, compiler compilers, etc.

The key point in the organization of the translator is a specially designed algorithmic language which will be called "Internal Language" (IL). It could also be called "intermediate language", because it is an intermediate stage between a source language and an object computer language or "semantic language" because the semantics of the source languages will be described in a form of the IL constructs which elaborate notions of the source languages. It seems to us, however, that it is most important to stress the internal character of the language in a sense that the programming processor rather than the human being deals with texts in this language.

IL is also the medium in which an optimization of a translated program is carried out.

The general scheme of the translation is shown in fig. 1.

In what follows the main phases of the translation process will be discussed.

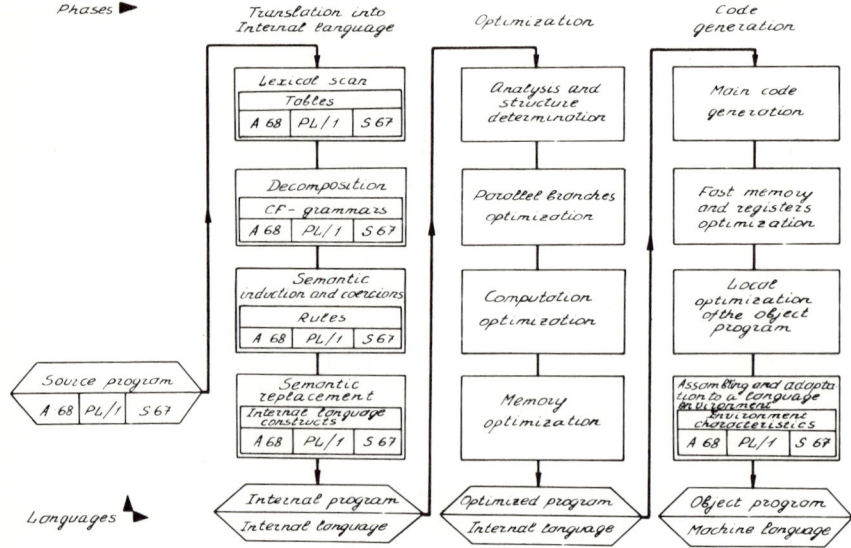

Fig. 1. Scheme of the joint implementation of the ALGOL 68, PL/I and Stimula 67 languages.

1. TRANSLATION INTO THE INTERNAL LANGUAGE

The translation into IL includes lexical analysis, context-free parsing and decomposition of some recursive notions of the source languages, identification of applied occurrences of denotations, semantic analysis of intermediate denotations, implementation of coercions and, finally, direct replacement of source languages notions by appropriate IL constructs.

1.1. *Lexical analysis*

It is appropriate at this point to note some specific IL features. Its grammar, like any phrase-structure algorithmic language grammar, is constructed over a set of its notions. These notions denote not only intermediate steps occurring during program parsing but also some important and selfcontained language units. It is necessary to stress that the set of IL notions is not built independently of the considered source languages. Turing machine language could well be an internal language if we cared only of the principal possibility to specify the process of elaboration of source languages notions. But it is not enough for us. We want to find and specify, by means of the internal language, those common things which really *exist* in all these source languages. We are looking for the commonness not only in their algorithmic equipower but also, and mainly, in details of their structure, in kinds of statements and expressions and in data types. In particular, this commonness will be materialized in many notions which will be common for IL as well as for the source languages (constants of various kinds, identifiers, subscripts, assignments, control transfers, formats, procedures, etc.).

It is supposed that IL will have a common representation of "lexemes" for all source languages, where lexemes are objects which are usually subjected to the lexical analysis (identifiers, numbers and strings). Replacement of the lexemes by their standard representation and filling of appropriate lexical tables is the contents of the lexical scan.

1.2. *Decomposition*

Decomposition is a context-free parsing of the program. This parsing which is carried out by means of a universal parser will be based on context-free grammars of the source languages, possibly reinforced by precedence matrices.

The standard output of the parsing will be a representation of recursive and nested structures in the form of a list structure, the elements of which will be linearly ordered following the logical order of their execution. Thus, for example:

$$y := f(a + b[i + j, 2 \times t])$$

will be transformed into a construction shown in fig. 2.

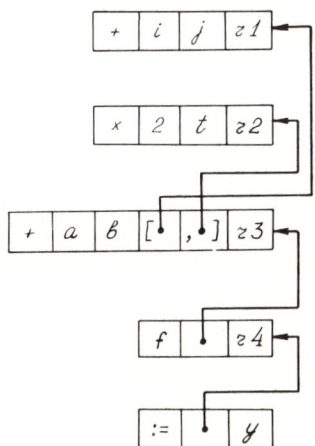

Fig. 2. List structure of a decomposed program.

Instead of the lexemes $+$, i, j, 2 etc., their standard IL representations will, naturally, appear in the decomposed program. These lexemes together with 'intermediate' lexemes $r1$, $r2$, $r3$ and $r4$, do not yet contain any semantic information in their representation but the identification rules and introduced references permit us to find and fill this information at the next passes. These references will be useful not only for the semantic analysis. For example, at a proper moment during loop optimization they will make it possible to discover that the address of the component of the array b contains in a subscript a linear dependence on variables i, j and l which could happen to be control variables of _for_ statements.

There is an unsolved problem in the decomposition of recursive notions. A literal application of the decomposition just described will transform, for example, a for statement

$$\underline{for}\ i := 1\ \underline{step}\ 1\ \underline{till}\ n\ \underline{do}\ \{a := a + b[i] \times c[i]\}\ *$$

into

$$\times b[i]\,c[i]\,r\underline{1};\ +a,a;\ \underline{for}\ i := 1\ \underline{step}\ 1\ \underline{till}\ n\ \underline{do}\ \{\ ,\ \}$$

Such a careless decomposition, besides some technical difficulties, can lead to the loss of the vitally important information that only the first and second statements are in the scope of the _for_ statement.

It means that the decomposition of recursive notions sometimes must not destroy the nesting caused by this recursiveness. It involves the consideration of two or even three kinds of recursiveness where recursive construction of linear sequences is regarded as the third kind. An additional complication consists in a fact that the kind of recursiveness cannot be made a univalued function of a language and notion. It depends sometimes on the character of optimization algorithms or even on specific properties of a notion. For example, two subscripted variables

$$a[sign\ (sin\ (l\uparrow 2))]$$

and

$$a[i+j]$$

where i and j are regular control variables of _for_ statements require quite different approaches to the implementation and decomposition.

A possible solution could be reached if the formal decomposition will be accompanied by a system of additional delimiters and special references which will make it possible to save all the information about nesting in order to collect things again into one nest if necessary.

The declaration parsing consists in inductive construction of the information, contained in the declaration and in passing it into the lexical tables. The format of the tables is defined by IL. It is highly desirable to have a united format which would be common for all source languages. This means that any position in the tables, for example plain modes position, must have a proper flexibility of formats providing the necessary variety of plain mode characteristics. If the source languages will happen to be too incompatible then it can enforce us to have quite separate lexical tables with separate processing procedures.

---

*{and} are abbreviations for _begin_ and _end_ respectively.

1.3. Context conditions and coercions

The implementation of context conditions and coercions is an inductive process of dissemination of prescribed information which is contained in the lexical tables over all occurrences of the lexemes in the program. This process begins with the defining occurrences of source language lexemes and then, by identification rules, is spread over all their applied occurrences. Inductive steps appear when intermediate lexemes are involved. The direction of the "semantical" induction is given by the references introduced by the decomposition.

In a general case supplying an intermediate lexeme with semantic information is not performed in a single way. From this point of view coercion is a comparison of several variants of the semantic induction for a lexeme-operand with a single possibility permitted by a given position. An ambiguity arises when the position permits several possibilities; an inconsistency takes place if no variant coincides with any possibility (fig. 3).

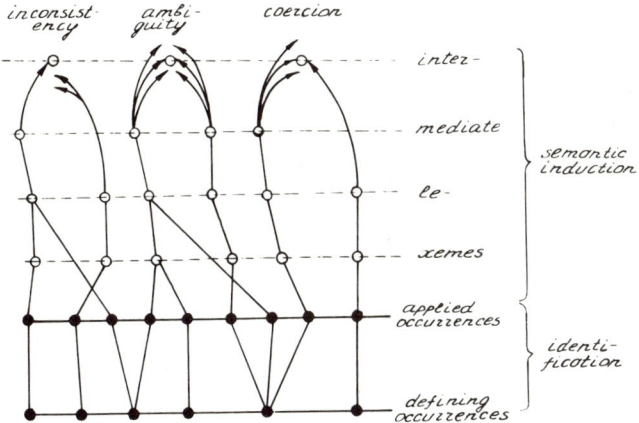

Fig. 3. Identification, semantic induction, and coercions.

We hope to develop some general theory of identification and coercion in which such notions as identifier, indicant, scope, region, intermediate lexeme, operand and position will be treated in a common-for-all-languages manner. This general treatment will allow us to define united formal and general rules of the processing of 'semantical tables' which will contain specific-for-each language rules of identification, semantic induction and coercion. These rules will be expressed in terms of some concrete actions for filling up or amendment of the lexeme-mode tables, the actions being directed by predicates of such type as "Has a lexeme (L) mode (M)?", "Are modes (M_1) and (M_2) related?" and so on.

All this technique will, seemingly, be close to the corresponding mechanism of ALGOL 68, where it is developed in an explicit and diverse way.

1.4. *Semantic replacement*

The transformation of a decomposed source program into an IL program is naturally called 'semantic replacement', because the transformation relates, to each executive notion N of a source language, an IL program that precisely describes the elaboration of the notion N. There are, in a general case, several versions of the program, each version being chosen depending on specific modes of operands of N. If these modes are already defined by previous passes then the corresponding predicates can be evaluated during translation and the notion is replaced by a most appropriate program. In some cases the reduction of a general program for an elaboration of N to a particular program can be done 'automatically' by means of universal optimization algorithms (see below).

2. INTERNAL LANGUAGE

Here we shall summarize some IL design specifications.

2.1. *Descriptive means*

Using an arithmetic analogy, IL has to be a collection of greatest common divisors of main notions of the source languages. We could make the analogy much deeper if we were able to answer what are the 'greatest', 'divisor' and 'main' in this case. Nevertheless this sentence has already shown an approach to the IL design: we refuse to construct any a priori system of basic notions of algorithmic languages but try to find it out after studying the candidate languages. We believe that there is a piece of the real world of programs, operating systems and machine architectures in the background of these languages. We believe that important aspects of these source languages such as parallelism and synchronization, channel control and formats, multiple precision computations, loop control, memory allocation technique - all this could be expressed adequately on some abstract level higher than machine instructions and bits-and-bytes language.

When we say 'abstract' we mean that IL should have some free parameters (details of the real-numbers arithmetics, quantitative restrictions, numbers value diapason, execution time, sequenching of parallel processes and so on) as they are in source languages.

IL might be considered as the instruction code of an abstract computer that elaborates source programs. Having introduced axiomatically some interpretation of the IL instruction we shall get a precise description of the source language semantics that itself could be of some interest. It should be noted that the semantics of the source languages must be taken into account at the first phase of the translation because some pieces of a program elaboration may be executed during the translation as it has already been mentioned. Most IL constructions are formally introduced into a program by replacement rules regardless of their meaning.

Regarding IL descriptive means it is necessary to mention the variety of 'control' actions which organize a proper allocation of data and computation in space and time. It does not mean that a computer model will be completely fixed (for example a specific method of indirect addressing) but conceptually all these actions (descriptor generation, copying of instances, memory reservation, referencing, substitution by actual parameters, parallel branches initiation) must be present in a program in the form of explicit instructions.

2.2. *Relation to the object computer*

We would like IL to be a machine-independent language. This independence could be defined quite precisely if one says, for example, that a change of an object computer changes nothing in the first two phases of the translator. But even if it were achieved it would not mean that there is no connection between IL and the computer. On the contrary, IL must be subjected to some quite definite hypotheses on a possible object computer. Continuing the arithmetic analogy used above, we can say that with respect to the object computer IL must be a collection of least common multiples of those machine patterns which are used during implementation of the chosen source languages.

It would be quite easy to satisfy this condition if we could be sure that all IL patterns were larger than machine instructions (case a) in fig. 4).

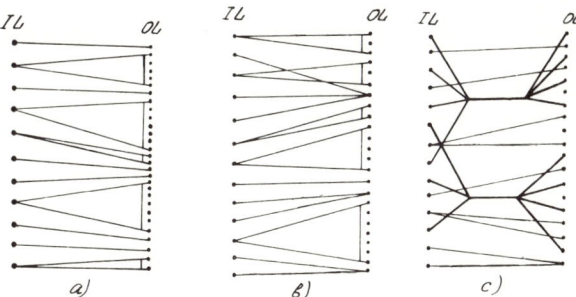

Fig. 4. Comparison of the detailness of the Intermediate and Object languages.

A computer usually contains such a 'nucleus' in its instruction repertoire that satisfies this condition, but to use only the nucleus means to lose efficiency which is potentially provided by combined machine instructions (for example, loop control, increment parts in arithmetic instructions and so on). This means that IL must provide specific possibilities to recognize such dispersed patterns in IL texts, for they could be composed in one combined machine instruction (case b) in fig. 4). But if we are faced with a necessity to apply irregular constructions of type c) in fig. 4, it will mean our failure in IL design.

2.3. *Language and program structure*

The main working usage of IL is to be a convenient medium for optimizing transformations of a program. The optimization is based primarily on an analysis of the information and logical connections between statements and on studying program structure. It imposes some specific requirements to the language. Statements must be simple, each easily identifiable with one another, and must not contain nested operands. Information and logical connections between statements have to be easily recognizable. This means that successors and predecessors must be shown by references but not found out by scanning. The same concerns the search for statements which supply arguments of a given statement. These requirements are rather burdensome but, on the other hand, they essentially reduce the time required. Another requirement is that the dependence of statements on the context should be as weak as possible, which greatly simplifies their transposition.

Requirements to those IL means, which make it possible to expose and study the program structure, are less trivial.

We understand the structure of a program as a partition of program variables and statements into subsets which are of special importance during the optimization, namely:
- potential subprograms and linear components
- repetition parts
- scopes
- parallel branches.

Potential subprogram - or 'hammock' - is a connected set H of program statements which contains two statements - entrance EN and exit EX such that any statement in H is reachable from the outside only through EN and any outside statement is reachable from H only through EX. An important special case of H is a linear component. That is the case when all statements from H, possibly except for EX, have only one successor.

We cannot yet give a precise definition of a repetition part but only can state that it is a connected set of program statements about which it is possible to say that they may be executed as a whole not less or not more frequently than some other set of statements. It is possible to make the following partial but important observations:
- a *for* statement body is executed not less frequently than the direct successor or predecessor of the *for* statement;
- any inside statement of a procedure body is executed not less frequently than the entrance or exit of the procedure;
- any call of a procedure is executed not more frequently than the body of the procedure;
- the translator when translating a program is executed not more frequently than the translated program.

Repetition parts play a fundamental role in the optimization algorithms as it will be shown below.

The precise definition of a scope S of variable V in a program also requires too lengthy abstract constructions to be formulated here. It is sufficient for our purposes to say that two sets of statements *Out* and *In* are connected with any variable V. *Out* is a set of the statements that supply with values as their results and *In* is a set of the statements that use a value of V as their argument. Then the scope S of the variable V is a set of the statements which are passed by during a 'transportation' of the values of V from statements from Out to statements from In. It is obvious that if, for a pair of variables V_1 and V_2, the set Out for one of them is not intersected with the set S for the other, then V_1 and V_2 may be allocated in a common part of the memory.

We say at last that a program has parallel branches $P_1, \ldots, P_n$ if a partition of program statements into subsets $P_1, \ldots, P_n$ is given such that for every pair P_i and P_j it is known whether statements from P_i and statements from P_j can be executed collaterally or not.

Probably, for every one of the structures just described universal recognizing algorithms could be developed. It is true at least for potential subprograms and scopes. But it would be quite unreasonable to rely only on universal algorithms and to consider an IL program before the optimization just as a 'uniform' graph of statements over a field of variables. The source language programs inevitably contain very useful information on their structure and this information has to be completely preserved after the modern algorithmic languages.

Let us list those structures which are introduced into programs by most of the modern algorithmic languages.

- Hammocks: every block or procedure body without jumps to non-local labels.
- Linear components: arithmetic expression without calls of declared procedures.
- Repetition parts: *for* statement and procedure bodies, blocks.
- Scopes: procedure bodies, blocks, *for* statement bodies for their control variables, arithmetic expression programs for their temporary locations, any hammocks for their internal values.
- Parallel branches: component serial phrases in collateral phrases, actual parameter programs in calls, arguments in any binary operations in ALGOL 68, branches in PL/I, blocks in Simula.

It is obvious that IL must preserve the variety of delimiters which make it possible to indicate explicitly the bounds of corresponding structures. There has to be a unified system of delimiters for every program regardless of its origin. For example a set of statements forming a procedure body in IL has to be singled out in a standard IL manner regardless of the denotations of procedure bodies in PL/I, Simula 67 or ALGOL 68.

Additional means for an indication of the program structure is a classification of variables or statements by their specific properties which make it easier to indicate the structures connected with them. Here are some of those means:
- specific notations for blocks or loops without exits to non-local labels;
- different notations for static and dynamic arrays;
- specific notations for temporary locations of arithmetic expressions;
- specific notations for variables which have more than one assignment in the program.

A unification of all such means at the IL level can become a considerable contribution in the recognition of those universal internal program structures which are important for an efficient program optimization.

3. OPTIMIZATION

The previous discussion shows obviously that the preservation of the structural properties of programs which have been introduced to them by means of the source language is a basis for the optimization algorithms. Until now optimization algorithms have been so tightly connected with specific properties of source languages that they even were described usually only in the context of a specific implementation of a given language.

An exposition of optimizing structures of programs at the IL level in a form which is invariant with respect to individual properties of the source languages allows us to put forward a problem of finding universal optimization algorithms providing the compilation of an efficient object program regardless of its source language. These universal algorithms include:
  computation optimization:
  - unloading of repetition parts
  - elimination of redundant computations
  - elimination of trivial computations
  - elimination of non-used computations
  memory optimization
  parallel branches optimization.

An optimization region corresponds to any specific application of an optimization algorithm that is the part of a program to which the algorithm is applied. It is reasonable to distinguish a) local, b) quasilocal and c) global algorithms which have as their optimization regions a) one or several neighbour statements, b) part of the program of a regular structure, c) the program as a whole, respectively.

3.1. *Unloading of repetition parts*

Unloading of repetition parts is in its universal application a highly effective algorithm. There exist universal algorithms which, for any statement and for any point of a program, can determine whether the statement may be transferred into this point without losing indispensable information connections. Then, it is possible, in principle, to develop algorithms which, for every statement S from repetition part R, can determine whether the computation of S is dynamic or static with respect to R, i.e., whether S produces one and the same or different values under different repetitions of part R. Then the unloading of a repetition part R is a systematic transfer of all its static statements into program parts whose execution frequency is not higher than that of R. It is generally a global algorithm though it can be quasilocal for some of its partial applications (cleaning up of loops) or even local (computation over constant operands during the translation).

If the operation of the translator is described in the same language as the language of the translated program, then, applying systematically the unloading of repetition parts to such parts as the translator itself and the translated program, it is possible to develop a philosophy of programming processors with a continuous spectrum of operation modes - from a pure interpretation to a pure compilation.

3.2. *Elimination of redundant computations*

Elimination of redundant computations consists of two parts: the recognition of equivalent expressions (textually identical or algebraically convertible to identical, for example, using the commutative law) and the determination of what occurrences of equivalent expressions are redundant for their subsequent elimination. This is a typical example of a combinatorial optimization long ago attacked by many softwaremen. There is a well developed technique of expression elimination along linear components and simple branches; there is one recent paper dealing with a global algorithm of elimination [1]. The implementation of the algorithm is close to the memory economy as regards the scope construction.

3.3. *Elimination of trivial and non-used computations*

Elimination of trivial and non-used computations is not of a main importance, at least for human-written programs. Their role is the collection of 'garbage' that appears as a secondary result of other optimization algorithms.

3.4. *Memory economy*

Memory economy is a highly importation kind of optimization because of the permanent lack of high-speed memory. It has two aspects: static, that is connected with an economic allocation of memory locations, and dynamic, that is connected with the concept and implementation of the virtual memory.

The static aspect requires a priori knowledge of scopes of variables. There exist universal algorithms of scope construction and some reasonable combinatorics of memory allocation. Algorithms of the static or - pushdown principle - dynamic memory allocation which are based on regular nested scopes of variables (blocks, hammocks, linear components - for temporary locations) seem, however, more realistic.

The dynamic aspect which deals mainly with various kinds of buffering depends highly on machine features and is not considered here.

3.5. *Parallel branches optimization*

We adopt the multiprogramming technique as a working version of the implementation of parallel computation. The main premise is that the computer system has a comparatively small number of processors (ones but not tens) and the allocation of a processor for a job is a comparatively rare event. Parallel branches in a program are not recognized automatically but are given explicitly by appropriate means of the source languages. Each parallel branch is a separate job which is a 'unit of work' for the operating system. Thus the program as a whole appears as a collection of job $J_1, \ldots, J_n$ (see fig. 5).

Any parallel branch begins in some branch point and ends in some meet point. If, for example, we have a branch point B which initiates two branches J' and J'', then at the point B a call to the operating system is inserted which signalizes the finalization of the job that proceeds B and the readiness for the execution of two new jobs J' and J''. Some characteristics

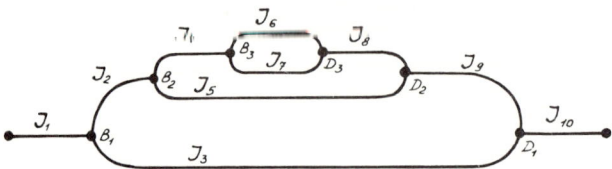

Fig. 5. Partition of a program into parallel branches and jobs.

of these jobs (start address, time required and so on) are also transferred to the operating system.

The finalization of all jobs having a common meet point leads to an execution in this point of a call to the operating system which initiates a new job next to the meet point.

Such an approach does not oblige the operating system to use any strategy of processor appointment but only supplies it through dynamic calls with consistent information about possible candidates for execution.

It is important, however, that in this case the number of parallel branches should not exceed considerably the number of processors and the branches themselves should be as long as possible. It will reduce the number of transactions with the operating system.

At the same time, for example, ALGOL 68 rules cause such a situation that a literal understanding of the semantics will produce a great many of too short parallel branches. It is known that there are the following sources of collateral elaborations in ALGOL 68: proper collateral phrases, procedure operand lists and array components. It is appropriate here to remember a critical remark by Dr. V. Turski at one of the W.G. 2.1. meetings that in ALGOL 68 there is no conceptual distinction between inner parallelism introduced 'automatically' in the program (array components, procedure operands) and parallelism introduced deliberately in the program (collateral phrases).

However, one can convert this possible deficiency of ALGOL 68 into its obvious merit by developing universal algorithms for reducing the number as well as the increasing length of parallel branches of the program with respect to that initial structure which will appear during parsing of the source program.

Then such 'too' parallel programs which are similar to those shown in fig. 6 will be converted by the considered optimization process into constructions which are more appropriate, for example, for a two-processor configuration (fig. 7).

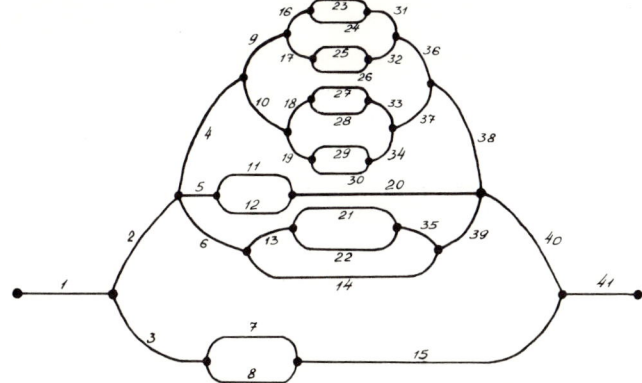

Fig. 6. Initial structure of a parallel program.

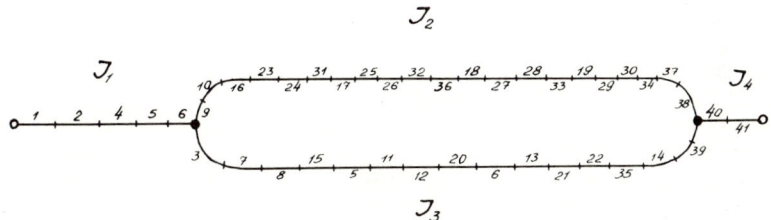

Fig. 7. Optimized structure of a parallel program.

3.6. *Implementation of the mixed programming strategy*

When using universal optimization algorithms an additional problem arises that is connected with the mixed programming strategy principle. This term has been introduced during the development of the ALPHA system [2]. It denotes that for the implementation of a complicated language notion (procedures or for statements, for example) a universal and, as a rule, uneconomical programming algorithm is supplemented by a series of simpler algorithms destined for various particular cases of the usage of these notions.

For example, in paper [3] which deals with the implementation of procedures in the ALPHA system five methods of actual parameter substitution are used when calling a procedure. These methods are shown in fig. 8 where the following notations are used. An example of a programming procedure F is taken. F has one formal parameter which occurs twice in its body and two calls for it. Each method occupies two lines in the figure: the upper line contains the two calls for F, the lower one represents its body. The inner brackets single out the procedure body proper and the outer ones embrace all the subprogram implementing the procedure. The box schemetizes a subprogram (thunk) which evaluates an actual parameter storing the

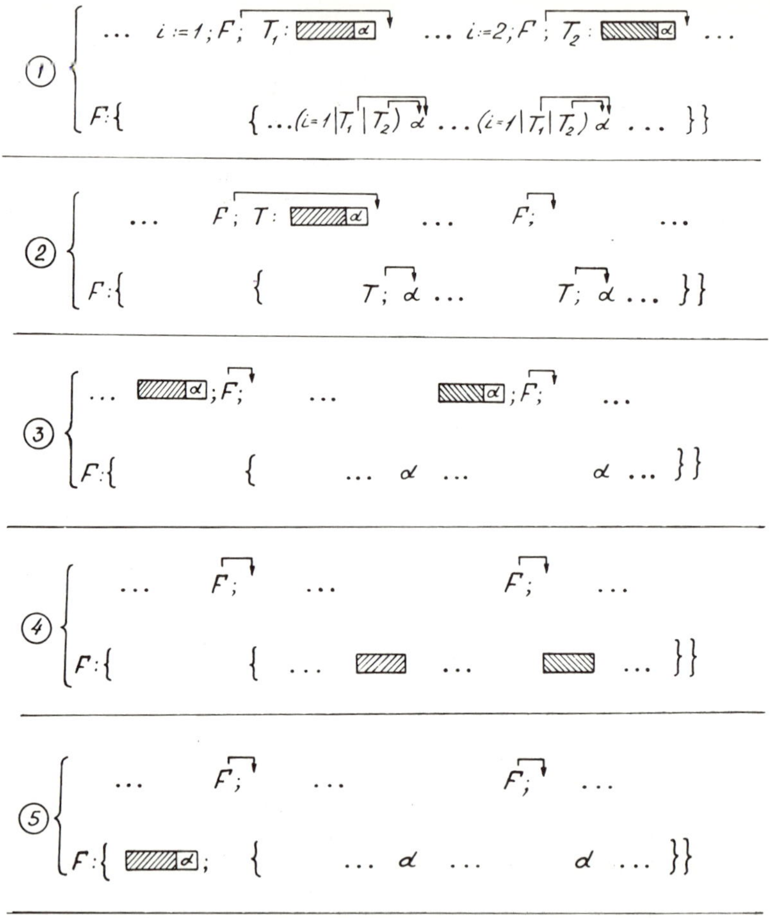

Fig. 8. Five methods of the implementation of procedures.

result in a location α. If T: is a subprogram label then T denotes a return control transfer to the subprogram (the arrow directs a return point).

The 1st method is a universal one. The 2nd method is applied when both calls have (graphically) one and the same actual parameter. The 3rd method is applied when it is known that for any call all formal parameter occurrences take one and the same actual parameter value which may be computed just before the call. The 4th method consists of an open substitution of the same actual parameter for all formal parameter occurrences. The 5th method is a particular case of the 4th method when it is known that the actual parameter value is not changed during the execution of the procedure body.

We can see that the choice of a most appropriate programming method requires an informal analysis of the translated program. This analysis exploits, on the one hand, such universal notions as graphical identity, existence or absence of assignments and on the other hand such specific characteristics of the source language as procedure, call, actual and formal parameter. It means that, in general, the translation which uses a mixed programming strategy (for example, for procedures) increases considerably that part of the translator which essentially depends on the source language.

Two solutions are possible here.

The first, not yet obvious solution, to unify, for all three languages, all the mentioned notions (procedure, call and so on) in order to make possible an implementation in a general form of the principle of mixed programming strategy for procedures.

The second solution, that will be demonstrated in the sequel on the example 5 of the above mentioned programming methods, consists in an argumentation that global universal optimization algorithms make the mixed programming strategy obsolete.

Let us return to the 1st method in fig. 8.

Suppose that the global elimination of redundant expressions has discovered that $\boxed{\alpha} = \boxed{\alpha}$. The second occurrence will then be removed as redundant and the switches in the procedure body will be converted into $(i = 1 | T | T)$. The elimination of trivial computations will transform this switch just into T, after that the assignments to i will become unused. As a result we will have the 2nd method.

If thunk T is very simple the translator, for the sake of economy of control actions, will perform an open substitution of T into every place where there is a call for it which will lead to method 4.

Application of the algorithm of elimination of redundant computations can reveal that in method 4 actual parameters introduced into the body compute the same value. Then only one thunk will be left in the procedure body. Unloading of the procedure body as some repetition part may remove it outside the internal block of the procedure body which yields method 5.

Return once more to method 1. If it turns out that the value α, computed by each actual parameter, does not change in the procedure body then, using the algorithm of elimination of redundant expressions and the unloading of the procedure body, we obtain in the procedure body the following construction:

$$F : \{(i = 1 | T_1 | T_2);^{\downarrow} \ldots \{ \ldots \alpha \ldots \alpha \ldots \}\}.$$

Logically analysing the program of the procedure, we find that the computation of T_1 is logically subjected to the first procedure call and that of T_2 to the second procedure call. This information will allow us to perform the selective unloading of the procedure body. As a result, the call of the procedure and its execution will take the form

$\ldots i := 1;\ \overline{T_1\ ;\ ^\downarrow F\ ;\ T_1\ :\ \text{\fbox{α}}}^\downarrow \ldots i := 2;\ \overline{T_2\ ;\ ^\downarrow F\ ;\ T_2\ :\ \text{\fbox{α}}}^\downarrow \ldots$

$\ldots F : \{ (i = 1 \mid \mid) \ldots \{ \ldots \alpha \ldots \alpha \ldots \} \}.$

A subsequent series of obvious simplifications will make this program take the form of method 3.

4. A PHASE OF CONSTRUCTION OF MACHINE INSTRUCTIONS

In its main part this phase does not put forward any essentially new problems and therefore it will not be discussed here. It will be reasonable to note only one peculiarity associated with putting an object program in the concrete environment of a source language. Among the elements of the environment are standard programs called at run-time, specific administrative systems, subprograms of execution of formats in input-output operations, special debugging facilities, editors of the bilisting, etc.

Any translated program has points of contact with this environment. At the first stage of constructing machine instructions these points of contact have a conditional, non-concrete form denoting but not being actual instructions of call and parameter transfer. The tables of the language environment have in this sense a form of dictionaries which, by a conventional code of the point of contact, yield actual instructions to be included in the program as well as some additional information to be used for a correct assimilation of these instructions.

5. CONCLUSION

The paper describes an attempt of a system approach to the development of a multilanguage programming system when the general outline of the system and its philosophy are fixed before the solutions of particular problems are accumulated. The multilanguage character of the system is ensured by orientation to the language description which controls the work of the initial stage of the translator.

The language description consists of the following parts:
1. Tables of lexical analysis
2. Context-free grammars for parsing
3. Tables of semantic induction and rules of coercions
4. Tables of semantical replacement by Internal Language constructions
5. Tables of the language environment.

The latter is used only at the final stage of translation.

The translator must ensure high quality of the translations due to the application of universal optimization algorithms. Efficiency of the algorithms essentially depends on how well we shall use the information on the program structure contained in the constructions of the source languages. The candidates for implementation are ALGOL 68, PL/1 and Simula 67.

In a successful case this approach may contribute to the solution of the following problems:

- economy of efforts and costs as compared with the development of three independent translators.
- elaboration of universal optimization techniques,
- finding of basic concepts of algorithmic languages,
- objective comparison of ALGOL 68, PL/1 and Simula 67.

REFERENCES

[1] Cocke, J., Global elimination of common subexpressions in programs. Proceedings of the 2nd All-Union Conference in Programming. Novosibirsk, February 3-6, 1970. Foreign participants reports (Russian).
[2] Ershov, A.P., Organization of the Alpha-translator. In the collection: "ALPHA - an automatic programming system". Novosibirsk, 1967 (Russian).
[3] Zagatskii, B.A., Procedures implementation in the Alpha-translator. Novosibirsk, 1967 (Russian).

DISCUSSION

Branquart:
I know you have a deep knowledge of the language ALGOL 68. Do you have the same knowledge of PL/I and SIMULA 67?

Ershov:
Well, not all of the group. We have two experts in PL/I; one of them translated the language specification, and so it is possible to believe that she knows the language rather well. Also we have two people who studied very carefully all the material of the Vienna group about the formal description of PL/I. We do not have considerable experience in the use of the languages for writing programs. Also we conducted a comparative study of the languages to try to find common patterns in these languages in order to understand better whether or not it is possible to have a united approach to implementation. We found that there are many similarities in the language structures. But there are also some difficult points for a unified approach, for example, multiple precision arithmetic is treated in a very different way and in this respect PL/I and ALGOL 68 are not so compatible. So, it is difficult to say that we have real experience with these languages, but we did everything that was possible.

Branquart:
At this time do you have the impression that an ALGOL 68 compiler, which is properly conceived, will automatically contain the necessary primitives?

Ershov:
No, definitely not. I am sure that the descriptive means which are necessary to describe the ALGCL 68 patterns are not enough to describe all the patterns for PL/I.

Branquart:

In your optimization scheme you eliminate all the things which are redundant and not useful; such things which seem to be bad programming. According to your experience, is it really worthwhile to eliminate these things?

Ershov:

Well, there are two aspects. First of all, it is a good thing to have an optimizing compiler because there are a lot of careless programmers. Especially when we use ALGOL, or even the ALPHA language, which is some considerable extension of ALGOL (it contains some multi-dimensional arrays, some kind of slices, complex arithmetic, and so on). So there are a lot of people, especially in open shop installations, who are careless. For example, they write a *for* clause in the form *for* $i := 1, 3, 5, 7$ and so on up to *37 do*.... Optimization algorithms can reduce the losses caused by such bad programming. That is one point. Another point is that, if you have some syntactically directed construction of a program then you necessarily have much redundance. That is, the replacement of the source language patterns by machine constructs is based on local rules and there are many boundary effects which cannot be recognized if you have no optimizing algorithm. So, if you have a syntactically directed compiler, there is more scope for subsequent optimization than if you have some programming scheme as for example in classical FORTRAN compilers, which are very carefully tailored for this particular language, for this particular machine, and so on. Thus, the importance of a universal optimization scheme is obvious to me if you have syntactically directed compilers.

Prentice:

Have you any estimate of the increase of cost at compile time of your optimization? I am thinking of the open shop which you described. In an open shop, my experience is that a lot of compiling is done and not so much running, and so time spent optimizing is likely to be wasted in these circumstances. I have another question. If I have understood you correctly, it appears that at the running of the compiler, a decision is being made which language it is compiling; whereas if you have three essentially separate compilers, then when the compiler is loaded, this decision is made once and for all. I may have misunderstood what you are envisaging, but if that is the case, how much would that cost as against the ease of writing the compiler through being able to use common parts well?

Ershov:

Of course, there is some optimum point in the balance between compile-time and execution time. If you have a well-organized open shop or any other installation, it is best to have two compilers for a language, one, I should say, a light compiler for one-run jobs and for debugging, and another, a massive compiler for more heavy works, for large programs repeated many times. I definitely understand that any multi-pass optimizing compiler will in some cases take in total more time passing through the operating system. It depends on the situation, but our experience shows us that we often lose more on the poor efficiency of compilers than on the compilation time. We have two compilers for ALGOL. If you have a computer which executes one million operations per second and if you have a job which runs on the optimizing compiler for one hour and through another non-optimizing compiler for five hours, it is a real piece of money, you see. So, it is an economic question. If you have good software, you should have at least two versions of your compiler. Actually, with this work which we have, it is supposed that there will be at least two versions of compilers for all languages. One of them, a high-speed compiler as I have just mentioned, and another, an optimizing one.

Now about the other question. I see no serious problem in it because if you have batch processing, you cannot avoid the reading of compilers from tape and introducing them into the memory. Actually, of course, we have three copies of the compiler with tables corresponding to each language and all three versions are available for the operating system. Any particular job knows what the language is in which it is written. So there is no dynamic change or mixture of languages in one particular job. The job is written in one language, and information about the language is written in the job control card.

Prentice:
Do you not envisage mixing languages in one problem?

Ershov:
No. That is not our approach.

Lindsey:
The example you wrote up said *for* $i := 1, 2, 3$, and all the way up to 37. Now if I had a compiler which was clever enough to optimize that, I would rather that I did not optimize it. I would rather that the compiler would recognize this state and print out a very rude message to the user and refuse to run the program! This is the only way that you would educate your users to write good programs in a high-level language.

Trilling:
You have to increment the variable and you have to compare with the bound and that is not so foolish.

Griffiths:
Can I protest against the idea, which is very paternalistic, of refusing to run somebody's program because you do not like it. You have defined a language in which this program is legal. Legal programs should be able to run, however bad they are. If you want to print out rude messages, then print out all the rude messages you like. I do not usually listen when people talk to me anyway.

Lindsey:
Yes, well, for "refuse to run it" at least substitute "refuse to optimize it".

van Wijngaarden:

If you write *for* $i := 1, 2$ *do*, would you reject it because 1 and 2 also form a part of an arithmetic sequence?

Bowlden:

Really, the question is: what is the responsibility of a computer center toward its users? Is its job to teach them how to write good programs, or is its job to teach them how to solve their problems?

Ershov:

I also would like to comment that this is a part of a more general and also technical problem to what extent the programmer or compiler is responsible for the strict and direct relation between the structure of written programs and the structure of executed programs. There are, of course, many smart programmers who would like to have a compiler in their hands as a tool and understanding its, in most cases, literal translation of the program structure, they prefer to use for their personal choice a selected language construction to better express their smart thoughts. But this is only a part of the real users of computers. Many of them ignore absolutely how to run and how to program. They simply express their thoughts, their problem, and they are careless about any consequences. It is a real part of users and if we want to consider money, we have to recognize their existence and overcome their deficiencies.

van Wijngaarden:

It is perhaps also true that a programmer is more or less punished for his inefficiency by the amount of time that is used by the computer and for which he has to pay in some form or another, either in the form of money, or in the form of losing time which is allotted to him.

ON DESCRIPTION OF SYNTAX OF ALGOL 68 AND ITS NATIONAL VARIANTS

A. A. BÄHRS, A. P. ERSHOV and A. F. RAR
Computing Centre, Siberian Division of the AS USSR, Novosibirsk 90

INTRODUCTION

In 1969 the authors of this report together with L. L. Zmievskaya fulfilled the translation into Russian of the Report on the Algorithmic language ALGOL 68 [1]*. The Translation and the Original were published in the form of a bilisting in the journal "Kibernetika" [2].

On the basis of this work we can formulate some problems regarding the international character of ALGOL 68 and make some suggestions on modification of the language itself as well as of the Report. The authors are aware that the suggested modification can be materialized only when editing the Revised Report and they hope that the principles of "internationality" of the international programming language can be discussed in the process of preparing it.

While studying the Original and working on the translation some efforts were made in the Computing Center of the Siberian Division of the USSR Academy of Sciences to find a more visual and suitable form for representation of ALGOL 68 syntax. As a result two variants of syntactic charts for ALGOL 68 were developed, viz. tree-like disjointed syntactic charts [3] and single-connected syntactic charts with collectors [4]. The two forms of the Charts were made in Russian and English variants. The first section of this report briefly describes the methods of constructing the charts and their characteristics**.

SYNTACTIC CHARTS

Tree-like charts. The rules given in sections under 'Syntax' in the Report on ALGOL 68 will be termed rules for hypernotions. Each hypernotion G will be brought to correspond to a set of notions $M(G)$ obtained as a result of replacing the metanotions contained in G by their terminal productions, in accordance with ALGOL 68 metasyntax.

---

* In what follows the Report will be referred to as the Original.
** The methods described are somewhat simplified as compared with a general case bur clearly enough demonstrate the idea.

The construction of a tree-like chart is made by induction starting with the rule for the hypernotion "program", and the chart itself is a graph whose nodes are brought to correspond to hypernotions. Each node of the chart is in a layer. In the uppermost layer there is one node, that is "program".

Let there take place a moment of construction of a chart. Consider in the lowermost layer the leftmost node with some hypernotion.

Let G be a hypernotion brought to correspond to a node V under consideration. If it is a terminal symbol, it is replaced in V by some of its representations, after which there takes place transition to the next node under consideration.

Otherwise, if G is also brought to correspond, in the chart, to some other node V', with outgoing arcs, then we put at the node V, for reference, coordinate of the node V' (the number of the layer and that in the layer) after which there takes place transition to the next node under consideration.

Otherwise, if for S there exists a production rule of the form

$G : A, B, C; K; L, M, N,$

then to the node V is added the following construction:

the ith layer,

the $(i+1)$th layer,

after which a given moment of constructing the chart is completed and there takes place transition to the next moment.

Otherwise, if for G there exists a hypernotion F, such that $M(G) \subset M(F)$, and for F there exists a production rule or F is already contained in the chart, then to the node V is added the following construction:

the ith layer,

the $(i+1)$th layer,

after which a given moment of constructing the chart is completed and there takes place transition to the next moment.

Replacement of G by F is termed operation of g e n e r a l i z a t i o n.

Otherwise, if for G there exists some hypernotions, e.g. F_1, F_2, F_3, such that $M(G) \supset M(F_i)$ for each F_i, production rules existing for all F_i, then to V is added the following construction:

the ith layer,

the $(i+1)$th layer,

after which a given moment of constructing the chart is completed and there takes place transition to the next moment.

Replacement of G by F_1, F_2, F_3 is termed operation of c o n c r e t i z a t i o n.

Transition to the next node under consideration consists in transition to

SYNTAX OF ALGOL 68 AND ITS NATIONAL VARIANTS

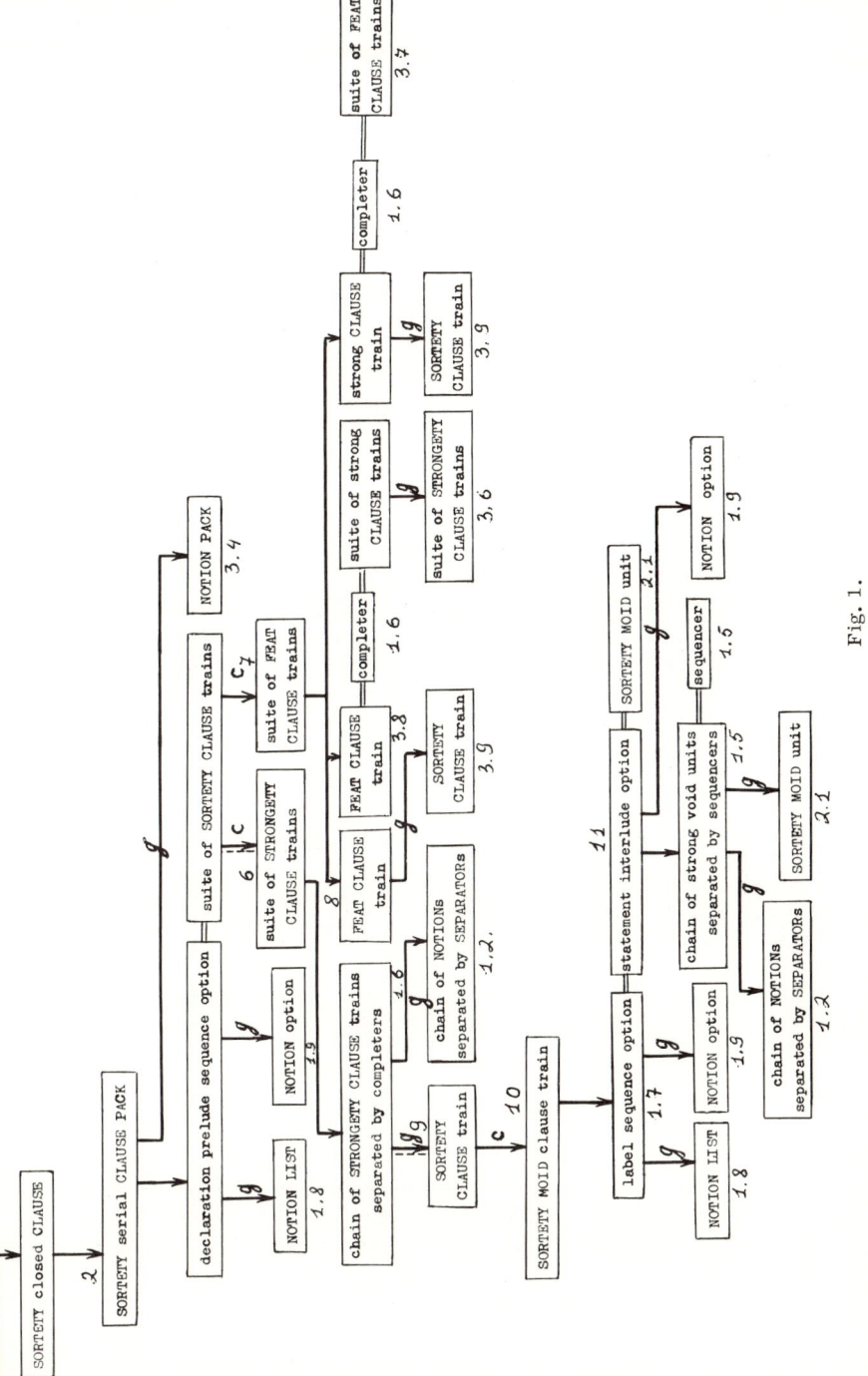

Fig. 1.

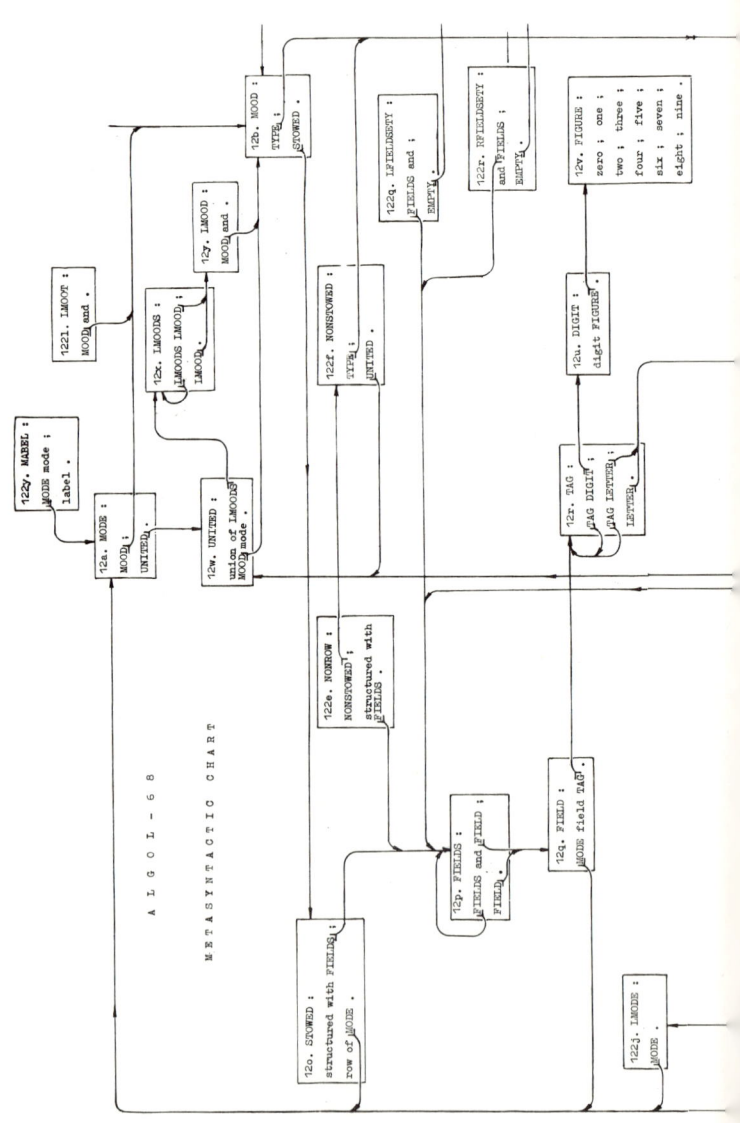

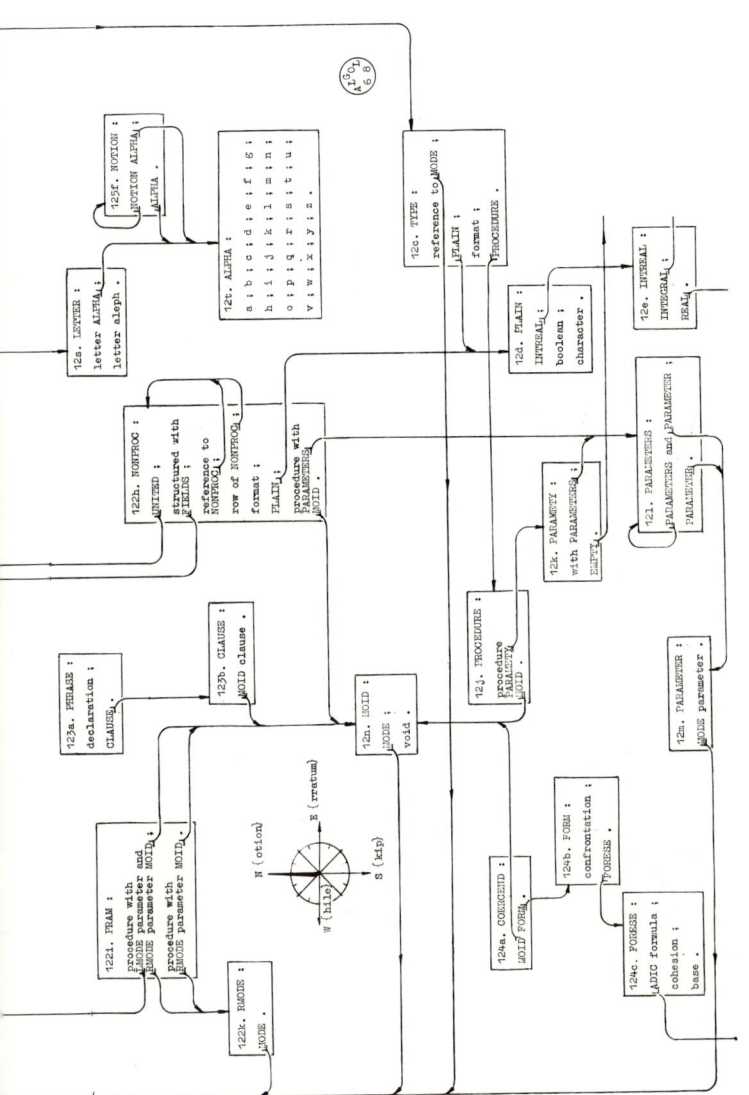

Fig. 2.

the nearest right-hand node in a given layer or, if the layer is terminated,
to the leftmost not yet considered node of the previous layer if any.

Fig. 1 shows a fragment of a tree-like syntactic chart.

Collector Chart. Two hypernotions G_1 and G_2 are assumed to be strongly
connected if $M(G_1) \cap M(G_2) \neq \Lambda$. G_1 and G_k are connected if there exists
sequence of hypernotions where G_1 is the beginning and G_k the end of the sequence and any neighbouring hypernotions in it are strongly connected. According to this definition, it is obvious that the set of all hypernotions used
in ALGOL 68 syntax decompose into a number of the components of connectivity.

The basis of a collector chart is a family of lines termed collectors.
Each of the above components of connectivity is brought to correspond to a
collector. In this way, each hypernotion G of ALGOL 68 has its own collector brought to correspond to the component of connectivity to which
belongs.

Rules of ALGOL 68 syntax are placed between collectors. Each hypernotion G, used in some rule R, is linked by an arrow with its collector. If
G is on the left-hand side in R the arrow goes from the collector towards
R, and if G is in the right-hand side of R the arrow goes from G towards
the collector.

In addition, for the sake of visualization, it is required that no collector
entry should be placed between any exits of the collector - it is one-sided
motion all along the collector. Besides, in arranging the rules of syntax,
an effort was made to reduce a number of intersections of arrows with outside collectors and intersections of collectors with one another. A fragment
of a collector chart is shown in fig. 2.

Each collector may be brought to correspond to a hypernotion T such that
all hypernotions forming the component of connectivity, corresponding to a
given collector, are obtained from T by concretization. A set of such hypernotions T can naturally be termed basic hypernotion of ALGOL 68. Selection
of a set of basic hypernotions is very essential in constructing national variants of ALGOL 68 syntax.

It is known from experience that syntactic charts are a convenient and
visual method for studying syntax and they are especially so as a source
material for constructing algorithms of syntactic analysis and tables for
them (e.g. obtaining of basic context-free grammar, construction of analyzing automaton and the like).

NATIONAL VARIANTS OF ALGOL 68

In the authors' opinion the international algorithmic language must satisfy the following conditions:

a) to provide possibility of developing national variants of the language
and translation of its canonical description into national languages, preserving the structure and mnemonics both of the language itself and its description;

b) to allow such translation both by the structure of the language itself
and by that of the Report;

c) to provide uniformity of executing any particular program written in the canonical language for any national variant of the language;

d) to stipulate, in the canonical description, rules regulating the translation so that the above requirements can be fulfilled.

Consider the structure of the language and the Original emphasising the points which are essential for the translation.

As mentioned in the Original (1.1.1.a,b), ALGOL 68 is defined in three stages: the "strict language", the "extended language" and the "representation language" - by means of the English language and a formal language defined in the Original. In this connection the text of the Original consists of the fragments of the three types: some fragments (FL type) are texts in this formal language - section 1.2 "Metasyntax" and all sections beginning with "Syntax", later on to be referred to as "quasisyntax"*, other fragments (AL type) are texts in ALGOL 68 itself (e.g. transput procedures in Chapter 10 and examples of programs in Chapter 11) and the rest of the fragments are written in English. The latter, in their turn, are divided into two parts: first - the phrases (of EF type) saying about the formal language and its objects, which are given here in " " or ' ' - for example, texts from 1.1.5.b.c.; the fragments (EA type), in which objects of the formal language are represented by means of paranotions, form the second part. Besides, some fragments of AL, EF, and EA types are enclosed in braces and, as mentioned in 1.3, are not part of the language description and play an auxiliary role.

The authors think that the definition of the language in three stages accepted in ALGOL 68 is the foundation which makes it possible to preserve in translating the stability of the language core, that is the strict language defined by the Original. However, this aspect of the language needs to be refined. The fact is that a variant of the strict language becomes fully fixed only after addition (allowed by the Original in 1.1.4, Step 2, 1.1.5.b.c.) of a number of production rules for the metanotion "ALPHA" (1.2.1.t.), whose every direct production is another small syntactic token, and addition of production rules for the notions 'indicant', 'dyadic indicant' and 'monadic indicant' (4.2.1.b.e.f.) and the notions 'other comment item' (3.0.9.c.) and 'other string item' (5.1.4.1.b.) whose every direct production is some symbol (with restrictions described in the Original). The question of who can add the above production rules, when and under what conditions they can be added, remains indefinite and causes contradictory interpretation (as, for example, was the case with the authors of this report). According to Professor A. van Wijngaarden (a personal communication), any user, introducing for example some new indicant when declaring a new mode offered by him, is likely to create, in this way, a new copy of the Original which contains the corresponding production rule. It seems to us that this interpretation contradicts the principle of stability of the international language.

On the other hand, all the advantages of ALGOL 68 in describing new modes and overloading operations reduce to zero if a user is forbidden to make use of the indicants which are not specified by an implementation. It

---

* The notion originated due to N. I. Zaritski.

is clear also that in practice the structure of indicants depends on a set of symbols contained in the transput devices and, consequently, is in fact defined by implementation.

Consider a possible regulation of the method of specialization and concrete definition of the language described by the Original.

We think that the Report on the Algorithmic Language ALGOL 68 must clearly state that it describes a canonical "variant" of the strict language, canonical "modification" of the extended language and canonical "version" of the representation language and indicates explicit methods for developing other variants, modifications and versions of the language.

First, let us consider the definition of the strict language and the development of its variants.

Introduce into the metasyntax the following production rules:

SPALPHA : ALPHA.
INDICANT : SPALPHA tag ; SPALPHA INDICANT.
CHARACTER : LETTER ; DIGIT ; point ; times ten to the power ;
    flip ; flop ; plus i times ; open ; close ; comma ; space.
COMMENT : CHARACTER.

Add to the quasisyntax the following rules:

indicant : INDICANT symbol.
dyadic indicant : INDICANT symbol.
monadic indicant : INDICANT symbol.;

besides, drop rules 3.0.9.c.d and replace rules 3.0.9.b and 5.1.4.1.b by

   comment : comment symbol, COMMENT symbol sequence option,
       comment symbol.

and

   string item : CHARACTER symbol ; quote image.

The context conditions should include the requirement that no proper program should have an indicant and a monadic indicant whose terminal productions contain one and the same terminal production of metanotion INDICANT.

If, for example, the representation of the symbol 'peace tag symbol' is peace and so on, the canonical variant of the language automatically allows the introduction of various indicants, dyadic and monadic indicants, which are sequences of bold-face letters. Collisions due to the use of the indicants of the type 'mode' can be avoided without difficulty with the help of context conditions and/or by introducing symbols of type 'mode' by means of the mechanism of indicant production.

Thus, development of new variants of the strict language suggests addition of new production rules for the metanotions 'ALPHA', 'SPALPHA', 'CHARACTER' and 'COMMENT', and, the contents of any of the four basic alphabets, can be enlarged, generally speaking, independently. In this way, the programmer does not develop a new variant by introducing his own indicant but acts within the framework of some existing variant of the strict language using a set of string and comment items and generally speaking an infinite set of indicants, which are available in this variant.

Let us consider now the representation language and versions. Besides the explicit enumeration of some symbols, the canonical version must also have a mechanism for creating representations of the symbols 'INDICANT symbol'. Transition to a new version consists, first of all, in indication of representations for new symbols (if this version refers to the language of representation of a new variant of the strict language and or a new modification of the extended language) and, secondly, maybe, in addition or removal of some representations for symbols from the canonical version. There is nothing new in it.

Now it remains to discuss the extensions of the strict language. We suggest that new modifications of the extended language could be developed by adding new rules of extension to Ch. 9 (this logically follows from the principles of the language definition). This will make it possible to develop, on the basis of the same strict language without changing it, different specialized languages in which some constructions, frequently occurring in a given class of applications could have convenient contracted forms. Besides, introduction of modification of the strict language will make the conception of the three-stage language structure logically completed.

Let us consider now ALGOL 68 adaptations to national languages. First of all it will be noted that the above methods of changing the language, i.e. development of variants, modifications and versions, which are necessary for this purpose, are nevertheless insufficient.

In fact the standard part of ALGOL 68 programs is part of the language description given in the Original. It follows that a choice of one or another variant, modification and version does not formally affect the identifiers, indications and field selectors, declared in the standard part and applied in the particular program, whose representations are meaningful English words.

Therefore ALGOL 68 is essentially oriented to the English language and it is more convenient to read and understand ALGOL 68 programs for those who know English. A similar assertion holds for the language description method since formal language objects are denoted in the Original by meaningful English words and phrases whose meaning, independently of their syntactic role, fills syntactic constructions with very important mnemonics.

The authors are convinced that in any country where the English language is not predominant among programmers the international algorithmic language ALGOL 68 will be adequately acknowledged only if it can be "loaded" by mnemonics of the native language.

In particular, in translating into Russian, "russification" of ALGOL 68 was performed in the following way:

first, small syntactic marks of the Original were supplemented by missing Russian letters (creation of the Russian variant of the strict language);

second, new rules of extension were added which makes it possible to use, in particular programs, Russian synonyms of field-selectors of the standard structured mode file (creation of the Russian modification of the extended language);

third, the collection of basic symbol representations of the canonical version was supplemented by suitable Russian words or abbreviations (creation of the Russian version of the representation language);

fourth, a transitive identity declaration was introduced for each standard "mode identifier", giving a Russian synonym of this identifier, and identifiers localized in the standard part declarations were replaced by suitable Russian identifiers (change of standard part of ALGOL 68 program);

fifth, Russian synonym ВЫХОД was introduced for the standard identifier *exit* and placed before the label *exit* : in the "exit" (2.1.e) (change of quasisyntax).

Thus, one of the important requirements to the international language is the ability to specify synonyms for objects represented by meaningful words of a natural language. The ALGOL 68 identity declarations make it possible to introduce synonyms for identifiers and indications (indicants); the latter may also obtain synonyms by choice of representations. From this point of view it seems necessary to have additional facilities for specifying synonyms of field selectors.

As, in the authors' opinion, it is undesirable to change either the standard prelude or, the more so, the quasisyntax structure, they think it useful to change the structure of an ALGOL 68 program in the Original, that is, to replace rule 2.1.a by

program : open symbol, standard prelude, national prelude, library
    prelude option, particular program, exit, national postlude, library
    postlude, library postlude option, standard postlude, close symbol.

and to add in Ch. 2 the following rules for national prelude and postlude:

national prelude : declaration prelude sequence option.
national postlude : label sequence option, statement interlude option.

It is meant that the national prelude may contain all the transitive identity declarations for the renaming of the standard prelude objects and that the first label of the national postlude may happen to be the corresponding synonym of *exit:*.

Thus, a concrete version of a fixed modification of a chosen variant of the language in which respective national prelude and postlude are specified, can be fixed as the canonical National ALGOL 68 for a given natural language.

In particular, the canonical English ALGOL 68 coincides with the canonical ALGOL 68, and in this case the national prelude and postlude are empty. (For the sake of logical completeness it would be helpful to write the canonical Report in Latin or Esperanto.)

The version chosen for the National ALGOL 68 should naturally contain all those representations which are available in the canonical ALGOL 68 so that any correct text in the canonical ALGOL 68 should be so in the canonical National ALGOL 68 and have the same meaning.

Starting from the canonical National ALGOL 68 one can build its variants, modifications and versions according to the above rules.

In other words, we have in mind the following scheme:

	International language	National language
Canonical language	1.1	1.2
Variant	2.1	2.2
Modification	3.1	3.2
Version	4.1	4.2 → Implementations

Sector 1.1 represents the strict language as defined by the Original, and moving along the table downwards means further concretization of the language (though any such step can, in a particular case, leave the language unchanged). The complete concretization of the language is achieved only in 4.2 and it is for this "version of the modified variant of the National ALGOL 68" that concrete implementations are made. The above phrase in " " can naturally be abbreviated, where it does not cause ambiguity, to "ALGOL 68".

Besides, some alteration should be made in the canonical description of the language in order to regulate translation of the Original, reducing to a minimum the changes in the description structure.

The main difficulty arising here is to conserve the mnemonical meaning of syntactical objects denoted in the Original by English words and phrases. Even in the Original its authors were confronted with some difficulty when trying to identify different grammatical forms of the same word (Ch. 1.1.6.c, point v), although analytical languages, to which English belongs, have in fact very few flexions which are so important for synthetical languages such as Russian, German, etc.

However, it seems valuable that representations of metanotions, notions, hypernotions and paranotions should remain, after the translation, meaningful and grammatically correct phrases of the respective language without violating a one-to-one correspondence between objects and rules of the metasyntax and the quasisyntax of the Original and the Translation, thus ensuring one-to-one correspondence between a text of the formal language of the Translation and that of the Original.

For this purpose we suggest that the "principal form" of metanotions and notions (hence, paranotions) should be defined in the canonical description as the form which they have when occurring in the left-hand part of the corresponding production rule. A form obtained from the principal one according to the grammar of the respective language is regarded as a form "related" to the latter. The description should postulate that the occurrence of the form related to some (single) principal form stands everywhere for this principal form of a given metanotion or notion (paranotion). The latter rule will replace, in particular, the text of 1.1.6.c.v

According to this a special section should be incorporated into the Report which regulates the method of creating national ALGOL 68-s. This section should explicitly enumerate the parts of the Original to be replaced in the Translation. These parts are: the section where the concept of closeness is defined, the section containing the national prelude and postlude, etc.

The remaining part of the Original must be translated, maximally retaining the meaning of the Original. The translation of the formal language (FL-type fragments) requires a new national terminology corresponding to that of the Original but having its own mnemonic contents. The translation of EF-type fragments must generate a new text since it should describe the formal language of the Translation rather than of the Original. As for the EA-type fragments, it is sufficient to translate them literally using glossaries of technical terms and paranotions. In translating pragmatic remarks one has more freedom. In particular, the quotations should be translated literarily and might possibly be replaced by quotations which are more suitable from the point of view of the corresponding language.

(Omnia mutantur nihil interit)

REFERENCES

[1] Van Wijngaarden, A. (Editor), Mailloux, B.J., Peck, J.E.L. and Koster, C.H.A., Report on the Algorithmic language ALGOL 68. Mathematisch centrum, Amsterdam, MR 101, October 1969.
[2] Algorithmic Language ALGOL 68. Edited by A.P.Ershov. "Kibernetika" No.6, 1969 and No. 1, 1970. Kiev (in English and Russian).
[3] Majnagasheva, G.I., Syntactic charts for ALGOL 68. Computing Centre Report. Novosibirsk, 1970 (in Russian).
[4] Bährs, A.A. and Grushetski, V.V., Syntactic charts of ALGOL 68. In ref. [2].

DISCUSSION

Lindsey:

The word NATIONAL is clearly a metanotion which produces the protonotions English, French, and so on, and I think if this proposal is adopted, it must be clearly stated that English-prelude produces EMPTY.

Rar:

Yes. English produces empty, of course!

Lindsey:

Even more importantly, it must be stated that American-prelude is EMPTY.

Rar:
(with much amusement) Whether the English language and the American language are different is out of the realm of our discussion.

Van der Poel:
What have you done about constructions such as 'NOTION-option', which in the English is affixed. How does it work in Russian?

Rar:
We have not done it very well, I confess, but we have done something, namely, we have given some forms and declared that protonotions may be in other forms and some protonotions may be close to one another. This depends on the Russian grammar and references are made to it.

Lindsey:
Can you give an example of 'NOTION list'?

Rar:
Yes. 'NOTION list' is 'список ПОНЯТИЙ'. In the metasyntax there is not such a metanotion as 'ПОНЯТИЙ' but there is the metanotion 'ПОНЯТИЕ'. Now it is said that two sequences of large syntactic marks which are the same in different grammatical forms, according to the rules of the Russian grammar, are close and may replace one another.

Van der Poel:
That was not exactly my question. My question was: In English the word 'option' follows 'notion'. And here as I understand it, it precedes.

Rar:
This is not so in Russian.

Van Wijngaarden:
You see, we had in English the choice between one of two possible orders because we could have said "optional this or that" or "this or that option". We chose in English, for some reason or other, the last formulation. Now it turns out that in most of our Western languages you can always have the first formulation but not always the second one, and in Russian too. Now, what they did in Russian is to use the other form consistently. Your 'NOTION list proper' is translated into 'properly listed NOTION'.

Koster: (with a smile)
Are you considering having a companion volume to your publication which contains the Russian grammar?

Rar:
No, we are not.

Koster:
With your national prelude, you open the door for a company prelude. Just imagine the IBM prelude or the Burroughs prelude. (irreverent laughter)

Rar:
(with a twinkle) I propose that our approach will use the national point of view, not the point of view of the companion.

Van Wijngaarden:
May I add to this that if you have the IBM with you, then you also have the international prelude! Moreover, I had a question myself. You have been talking about indicants and you made a scheme by having a letter-a-tag-symbol, a letter-b-tag-symbol, and so forth. In some implementations those representations might look like a or ab and so on. However, the indicants that we allow are not necessarily sequences of letters.

Rar:
If in some variant we include the question mark, then the following representations will be possible: ? or a̱?ḇ.

Van Wijngaarden:
But that is not sufficient.

Rar:
If we have the question mark on our keyboard, it is all right, but if we do not have it, we do not use it.

Van Wijngaarden:
That is fine. Obviously, nobody has to have all the representations, but it is the other way around. I have not only on my keyboard a question mark but also a symbol I do not tell you now, you see, because I implement my keyboard after the Report is written.

Rar:
Of course, but it is a matter of a variant. You see, what we suggest is to have an international canonical variant, which does not include the question mark at all. But then some special variants may have the question mark and so on. When we want to implement the language, we choose a concrete variant, concrete modification and concrete version, and when we chose all of it, we may have a question mark. It is upon this base that we may construct an implementation.

Van Wijngaarden:
I still do not quite get it. This is not a question of a national prelude.

Rar:
No. When some people want to have a national variant, a canonical national language variant, then they may include that or other indicants, but I suppose that they will offer only those letters which are in their national alphabet as elements of the special alphabet ('SPALPHA').

Van Wijngaarden:
But that is not my point. Suppose there was at some moment a Dutch national variant of the language, and after this Dutch national variant has been printed I am going to use an indicant which is not in that and no document whatsoever and that is why I said that everyone who is going to intro-

duce a new symbol is writing a new Report. I give him the right to write his Report.

Rar:

You see, only those who implement have the need to write their Report in the form of some companion volume, but not every programmer that uses the language and wants to use xyz as his own indicant. Your point of view was that if one wants to use a new indicant, it is as if he writes a new volume, though in invisible ink. But in our point of view, that is not the case. If in our concrete variant, we have defined in a way which I have described, all the underlined sequences of letters as indicated, then everyone uses them without asking.

Van Wijngaarden:

I agree completely that for a lot of indicants, namely all the, let us say, underlined ones, you could define them syntactically once and for all. I think it would have been a wise way to do it. But my point of view was that, apart from those, there are many other symbols which you cannot enumerate because you do not know what they are.

Rar:

You see, in a concrete implementation you can enumerate these. There are those that can be used practically.

Van Wijngaarden:

Let us say, for instance, the Chinese alphabet, the national Chinese version ...

Rar:

The Chinese alphabet consists of some primitive hieroglyphs, from which their numerous hieroglyphs are constructed.

SOME PROBLEMS IN COMPILING ALGOL 68

GERHARD GOOS
Rechenzentrum der Technischen Hochschule, Munich, Germany

1. INTRODUCTION

Implementing a new programming language begins by analysing existing implementations of similar languages. This analysis should detect language differences which may create problems in the implementation of the new language:
1.1 The difficulty of distinguishing between declarations and statements without the knowledge of certain other declarations;
1.2 The internal representation of modes both at compile-time and at run-time, including the problem of finding out whether two modes are equivalent or not;
1.3 The verification of the context conditions [9, 4.4];
1.4 The application of the rules for coercing and the identification of operators;
1.5 The checking of scopes at compile-time and run-time;
1.6 Linkage editing of separate pre-compiled procedures;
1.7 The treatment of formats at run-time;
1.8 The storage allocation at run-time including the problem of garbage collection;
1.9 The implementation of parallel processing.

We concentrate here mainly on problems arising during the compilation phase.

The implementation of parallel processing as described in [9] is largely dependent upon the particular operating system. It requires a dynamically varying and a priori unknown number of processes when implemented in full generality.

We define a "pass" of a compiler to be a sequential scan without backtracking, generating sequential output and possibly some tables. It follows immediately that we have to cope with lexical analysis, syntactic analysis, and the problems 1.1 - 1.3 in a pass preceding the one in which coercing and operator-identification are done. This latter pass, however, has to precede that in which code is generated due to some implications of coercing which are found "too late" in the sequential reading. Finally we have to have a very simple pass which inserts addresses, etc. into the generated object program. We therefore start the discussion by assuming a 4 pass-compiler with a distribution of functions roughly as described previously. For the simplification of program logic, it is, however, advantageous to insert two passes, one between 1 and 2, and the other between 2 and 3. These additional passes scan the program from right to left. This scheme of a 6 pass-compiler is discussed in the second part of the paper. In particular, this is the scheme underlying current work on an implementation of ALGOL 68 for a Telefunken TR4 at the Technische Hochschule, Munich [2].

2. CONTEXT DEPENDENCIES IN THE FIRST PARSING

Consider the examples

$$\textit{proc } \underline{a}\, x\,;\quad\quad\quad\quad\quad\quad\quad\quad\quad\quad\quad\quad\quad\quad\quad\quad\quad\quad\quad (2.1)$$
$$p := (\underline{real}\, x\,;\, \underline{a}\, y) \ldots \quad\quad\quad\quad\quad\quad\quad\quad\quad\quad\quad\quad (2.2)$$
$$(l1 : l2) \ldots \quad\quad\quad\quad\quad\quad\quad\quad\quad\quad\quad\quad\quad\quad\quad\quad (2.3)$$

(2.1) is an identity-declaration if $\underline{a}$ is declared by a mode-declaration; it is a formula if $\underline{a}$ is declared by an appropriate operation-declaration, in which case $\textit{proc}$ is a generator.

The constructions (2.2) and (2.3) show special cases of the problems encountered in scanning parentheses. Without knowledge of the context to the right or the meaning of $\underline{a}$, it is impossible to decide whether the parentheses in (2.2) form a formal-parameters-pack or a closed-clause. The object (2.3) may be the beginning of

$$(l1 : l2)\ \underline{real}\ x$$

or it may be read as

$$(l1 : \underline{goto}\ l2). \quad\quad\quad\quad\quad\quad\quad\quad\quad\quad\quad\quad\quad\quad\quad\quad (2.4)$$

The local ambiguity indicated by (2.1) can be overcome by a somewhat sophisticated algorithm in the first pass of the compiler (for details see [2]) which picks out all these ambiguous constructions and resolves the ambiguity by the end of the first pass. Mailloux [7] proposes to solve the problem by using the first scan of the program to find the mode- and operator-declarations only. In the second pass the meaning of the newly introduced symbols is then known and it is easy to distinguish the two syntactic interpretations of constructions such as (2.1).

An opening parenthesis may occur in one of three different situations:
(i) Preceded by one of the symbols $\underline{struct}$, $\underline{union}$, $\underline{proc}$, $\underline{ref}$, $\underline{op}$, $\underline{loc}$, $\underline{heap}$ or the equals-symbol of a mode- or operation-declaration;
(ii) Preceded by a sequence of symbols which may be interpreted as a primary;
(iii) Elsewhere.

It is easy for a compiler to distinguish these three situations. Case (i) very easily allows the interpretation of the parenthesis to be found. Case (ii) causes the usual problem of distinguishing between calls and slices as in many other languages.

In the other cases, the opening parenthesis may open a closed-, conditional-, collateral- or case-clause as well as a formal-parameters-pack or a declaration of a multiple value. The general idea for solving this kind of ambiguity is to check each symbol following the opening parenthesis as to whether it is suitable to reduce the number of possible syntactic interpretations until a unique interpretation is reached. The constructions (2.2) and (2.3) show that this may sometimes require scanning beyond the corresponding closing parenthesis.

Moreover, the fact that

$l1$:

in (2.4) is a label definition, is discovered only after all other interpretations of (2.3) have been eliminated. Such late recognition of the correct interpretation of the symbols also causes problems in determining the range in which a defining occurrence of an identification or indication is valid. The construction (2.2) shows an example in which this range cannot be determined at the time the definition of x is encountered. Problems concerning the meaning of parentheses and the recognition of ranges are discussed in greater detail in [1] and [5].

3. REPRESENTATION OF MODES

Every compiler for a high-level programming language has to build up a "declaration-table" in which the modes and further attributes associated with identifiers and other newly introduced symbols are recorded.

For most languages the format of table-entries can be based on the assumption that there exist only a finite - and in fact small - number of different modes and other attributes. This assumption is invalid for ALGOL 68. Although in each program to be compiled we have only a small number of modes, nevertheless the number of possible modes is infinite. There are two ways in which this can occur.

The first is theoretical in nature and is that by use of the symbols *ref* and *long* and by forming arrays (= multiple values) of arbitrarily many dimensions, an infinite number of modes can be constructed; in practice the number of modes constructed in this way is usually limited by restricting the number of times the prefixes *ref*, *long* and *row* (standing for one-dimensional array) can be repeated*.

The second way is the infinity of modes which can be classified as procedures, structured and united modes. Examples are

mode s = *proc*(*real*, *s*) *real*	(3.1)
mode s = *struct*(*ref s pointer*, *q value*)	(3.2)
mode s = *union*(*int*, *ref s*).	(3.3)

As a consequence it is impossible to represent a mode in ALGOL 68 by

---

* E.g.. The author knows of no practical case in which the symbol *ref* has to be used more than three times in front of a mode.

able-entry of fixed length. Instead we have chosen a scheme in which the declaration-table is split up into two tables: a declarator-list finally containing internal representations of the modes as list-structures and a connection-list, in which each entry connects an identifier or an indication with a mode. The content of these lists for the mode-declarations (3.1) - (3.3) is shown schematically in figure 1 - 3.

Figure 1 shows the state immediately after all three declarations have been recognized the first time. Any mode-indications occurring in the RHS's are not further processed.

Figure 2 shows the state when the declarations of $\underline{s}$ and $\underline{q}$ have been associated with all the applied occurrences of these symbols.

Figure 3 shows the final state after all indications have been removed from the declarator-list and have been replaced by pointers to the unique entry for the appropriate mode.

From the figures it is apparent that the cases in which a field of an entry contains a pointer to some mode and in which it contains a direct representation of the mode are treated as being equal.

In the transition from figure 2 to figure 3, a set of algorithms is involved. Most of them have to check whether the context-conditions [9, 4.4] are fulfilled, i.e. they have to detect such illegal constructions as

$\underline{mode}\ v = union(real,\ \underline{ref}\ real)$
$\underline{mode}\ w = struct(\underline{w}\ a,\ real\ b).$

These algorithms are straightforward although very lengthy exercises in list-handling.

More interesting are two other algorithms which check whether two modes are equivalent or not. The first algorithm determines the equivalence of such modes as $\underline{s1}$, $\underline{s2}$, defined by

$\underline{mode}\ \underline{s1} = struct(\underline{ref}\ struct\ (\underline{ref}\ \underline{s1}\ p,\ real\ x)\ p,\ real\ x)$
$\underline{mode}\ \underline{s2} = struct(\underline{ref}\ \underline{s2}\ p,\ real\ x).$

The internal representations of these modes are shown in figure 4; one of the possible solutions to the problem is published in [6].

The other algorithm deals with the equivalence of united modes. This algorithm first replaces united modes which are members of other united modes by their member modes e.g., it determines that

$\underline{union}(\underline{real},\ \underline{union}\ (\underline{int},\ \underline{compl}))$

and

$\underline{union}(\underline{real},\ \underline{int},\ \underline{compl})$ (3.4)

are equivalent.

Secondly the equivalence of united modes e.g., (3.4) and $\underline{union}(\underline{int},\ \underline{real},\ \underline{compl})$, which differ only by a permutation of the members of the mode, has to be shown. This is done by assigning to each mode an ordinal number and by reordering each united mode in such a way that the members follow one another in ascending order. Then the equivalence can be shown by pairwise comparison of the members. Since these ordinal numbers have to be

SOME PROBLEMS IN COMPILING ALGOL 68

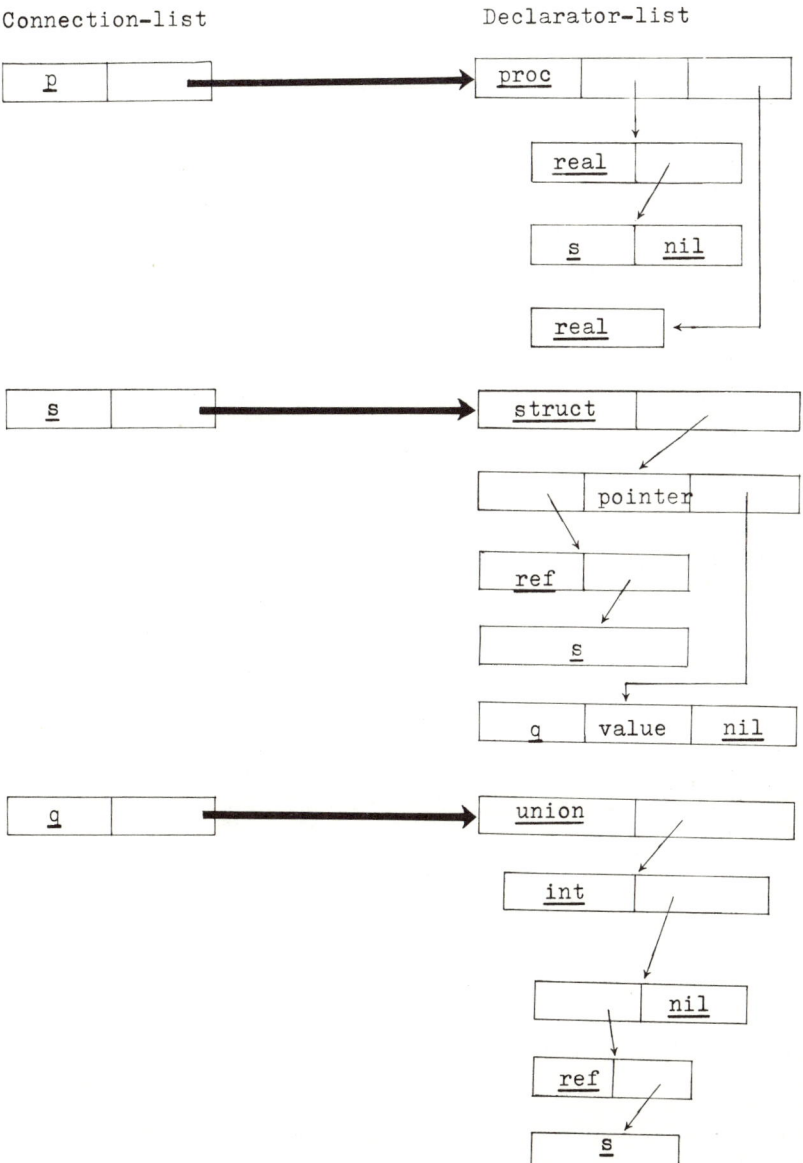

Figure 1.

mode p = **proc**(**real**, s) **real**
mode s = **struct**(**ref** s pointer, q value)
mode q = **union**(**int**, **ref** s)

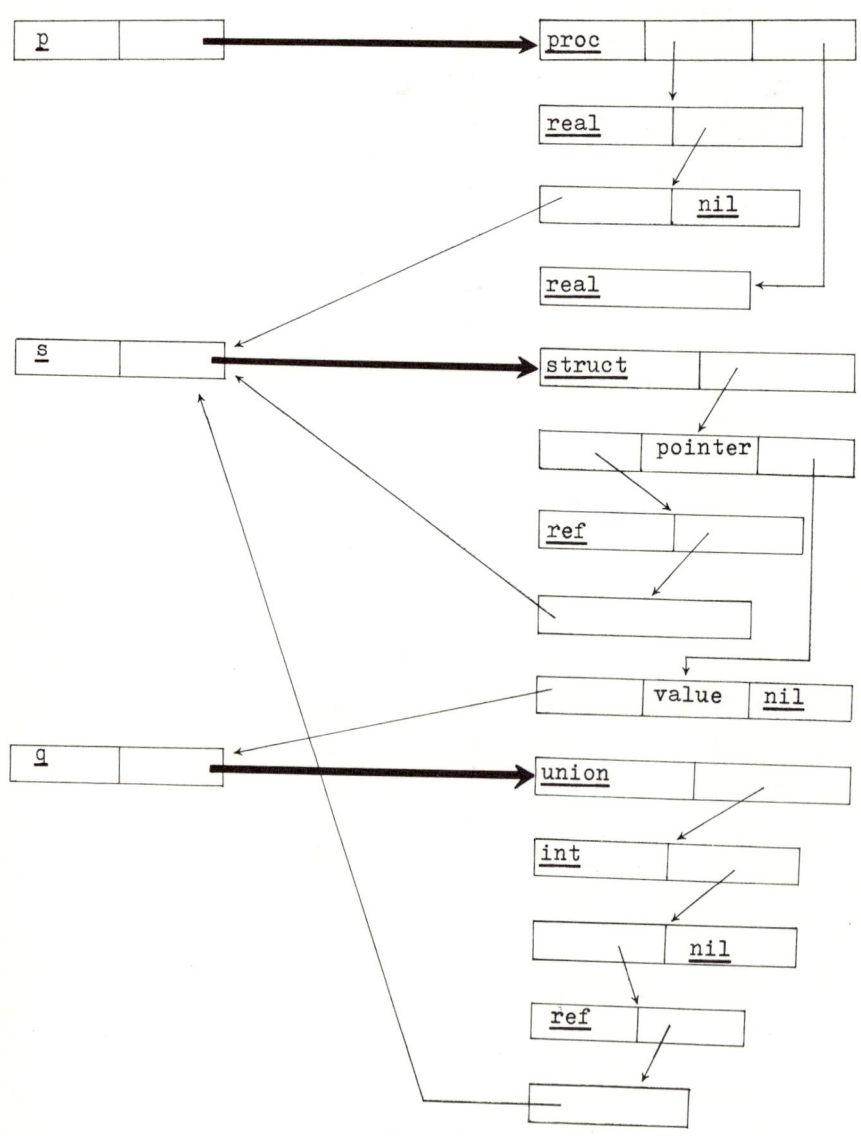

Figure 2.

SOME PROBLEMS IN COMPILING ALGOL 68

mode p = *proc(real, s) real*
mode s = *struct(ref s pointer, q value)*
mode q = *union(int, ref s)*

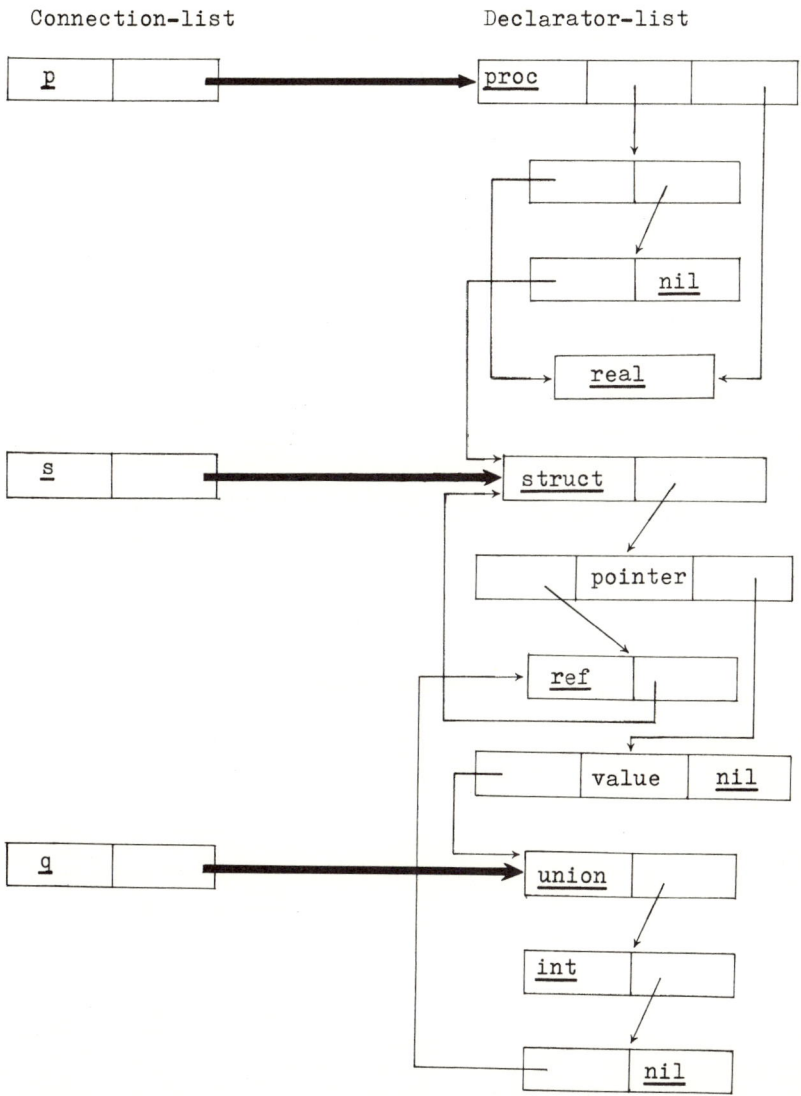

Figure 3.

$\underline{mode}\ \underline{s1} = \underline{struct}\ (\underline{ref}\ \underline{struct}\ (\underline{ref}\ \underline{s1}\ p,\ \underline{real}\ x)\ p,\ \underline{real}\ x)$
$\underline{mode}\ \underline{s2} = \underline{struct}\ (\underline{ref}\ \underline{s2}\ p,\ \underline{real}\ x)$

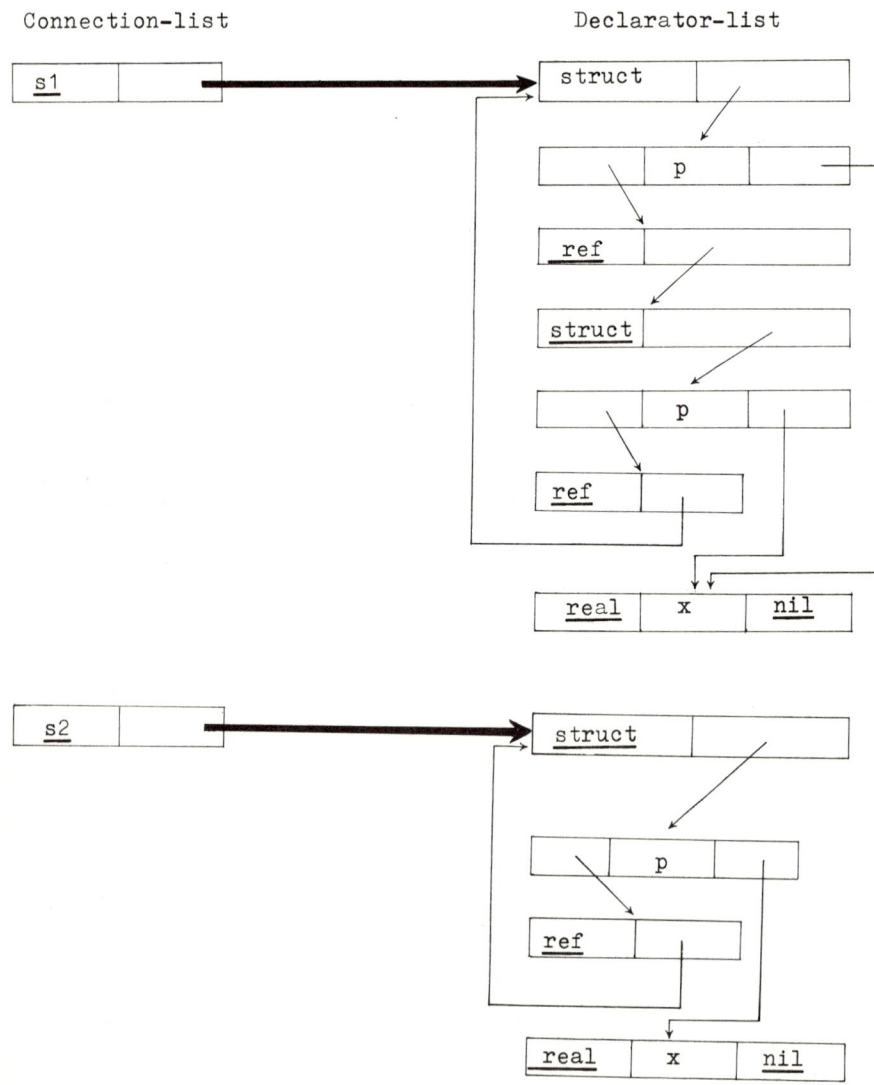

Figure 4.

represented internally in the computer they must have a fixed maximum length. For this reason and since there is an infinite number of modes, a solution which consists of a Gödelization of the modes is impossible. An ordinal number with a fixed maximum length is possible only if we choose the numbers dependent on the particular program at hand.

On the other hand, assume that we have variables a, b declared by

$\underline{union}(\underline{int}, \underline{real})\ a\ ;$
$\underline{int}\ b$

and we want to assign the value of a to b using the conformity-relation

$b\ ::=\ a\ ,$

we then have to check at run-time whether the present value of a is integral. This can be done only by storing a pair, consisting of the current value and its mode for each variable of united mode. Clearly we need a representation of modes at run-time also. Obviously, the ordinal numbers introduced above are well-suited to this purpose; in fact there are no other possibilities which differ in principle from this solution. This method, however, has a serious disadvantage: since the ordinal numbers are program-dependent we run into difficulties if we have to bind more than one program together, e.g., a main program and some precompiled procedures. Consequently, we cannot use the general linkage-editor of the system to bind ALGOL 68 programs together, and a special-purpose linkage-editor must be constructed.

4. COERCION AND OPERATOR-IDENTIFICATION

In all high-level programming languages some implicit changes of modes, usually called type-conversions, are provided. Each such "coercion" is split up into two algorithms. The first, and more difficult one, is executed at compile-time and determines which change of modes are to occur. The second one is prepared at compile-time and executed at run-time in most cases. It computes the new value corresponding to the changed mode *.

In an interpretive implementation of some languages it is possible to execute both algorithms at run-time ("dynamic type-checking"), but this is impossible for ALGOL 68 due to the problems involved in balancing and proceduring (see below).

The difference between ALGOL 68 and other languages concerning coercion is twofold. On the one hand, which coercions are to be applied is determined by the syntax and not by the semantics of the language. This allows for a much more systematic treatment of the problem than e.g. in PL/I. On the other hand deciding which coercions have to be applied is much more context-dependent than in other languages. This increases the complexity of the algorithms involved.

---

* In case of hipping the second algorithm is empty.

There are eight possible coercions: dereferencing, deproceduring, proceduring, uniting, widening, rowing, hipping and voiding. The application of these coercions depends, amongst other things, on the syntactic position of the "coercend", i.e. the syntactic entity which is being coerced. There are four such positions.

In strong positions, e.g. the RHS of an assignation or the actual-parameters of a procedure call, all coercions are allowed. The a posteriori mode of the coercend is completely determined by the context, normally by the preceding symbols; e.g., in the case of an assignation the a posteriori mode of the RHS is given by the mode of the LHS minus the first *ref*. The problem here consists therefore in determining whether a coercend is in a strong position and which sequence of coercions leads from the a priori mode of the coercend to the given a posteriori mode.

In firm positions, e.g. the operands in a formula, only the first four coercions are allowed. Two different problems are encountered with firm coercends.

The first one is that there exist some syntactic constructions in which an operand is composed of more than one component as in

$$(1, 1.2, 1.2 \quad 5) + (1, 1, 1),$$

or is chosen from a set of alternatives, as in

$$\underline{if}\ x < y\ \underline{then}\ 1\ \underline{else}\ 2.1\ \underline{fi} + 4. \tag{4.1}$$

Here one of the alternatives or components is in a firm position and determines the a priori mode of the whole operand. The others are in strong positions and, e.g. have to be widened to that a priori mode. It is, however, not at first known which one of the alternatives or components is in the firm position. The process which determines this is called balancing.

It is mainly this process of balancing which makes the run-time determination of the coercions impossible. If, e.g. in (4.1), the first alternative is chosen dynamically, then the first operand and the result of the whole formula would be found to be integral. However, it should be real, because 2.1 and not 1 is in the firm position. This mistake may have disastrous consequences.

The second problem with firm coercends is that the a posteriori mode of the operands is not immediately known in most cases since it depends on the operator applied and there may be more than one declaration, only one of which is applicable. In the example

$$\underline{real}\ x\ ;$$
$$\&x\ \ldots$$

the symbol & may be declared by

$$\underline{op}\ \& = (\underline{real}\ a)\ \underline{real}\ :\ \ldots$$

or by

$$\underline{op}\ \& = (\underline{ref\ real}\ a)\ \underline{real}\ :\ \ldots$$

or by

$\underline{op}$ & = $(\underline{proc}\ \underline{real}\ a)\ \underline{real}$: ...

The a posteriori mode is different in each of these cases. The algorithm for finding the coercions in these firm positions therefore consists of three steps:
(i) Determine the a priori mode(s) of the one (or two) coercend(s) and all possible a posteriori modes. (There are infinitely many such a posteriori modes.)
(ii) Compare the a posteriori modes with the modes of the parameters of all operator-declarations valid for the given operation-symbol until the declaration is found which is applicable to the given case. The fulfillment of the context-conditions, checked before, guarantees that there is at most one declaration applicable.
(iii) Determine the sequence of coercions which have to be applied to the operands in order to obtain the modes of the parameters of the operator-declaration chosen.

The second step of this algorithm is called operator-identification. Any implementation of this algorithm will be very time-consuming, even in such trivial cases as

$$1 + i$$
$$x/y + z\ *.$$

It is therefore desirable to have a simplification of the algorithm which works for at least the most common cases of modes of operands. Scheidig, Wössner and the author [3] outline such a simplification which works as long as none of the modes of the actual operands and of the parameters of the possible operator-declarations is a united mode. The general idea behind this simplification is that, for each a priori mode m of an operand and each mode m' of a parameter, there exist "reduced" modes m_r, m'_r such that the identity

$$m_r = m'_r \tag{4.2}$$

of modes is a necessary and in most cases also a sufficient condition for the applicability of an operator-declaration. The reduction of a mode m to m_r consists of removing any $\underline{ref}$s and $\underline{proc}$s in front of m. Therefore, (4.2) implies that m and m' are related [9, 4.4.3b].

The two other syntactic positions in which coercions may be applied are called weak and soft. It is very easy to determine whether a coercend is in a weak position; e.g., a primary which is followed by an index. This is also true for soft positions; e.g., the LHS of an assignation. However, in identity-relations such as

$$i :=: jj$$

a simple version of balancing has to take place in order to decide whether it is the LHS or the RHS which is in the soft position. Further treatment of

---
* Note that + and / could be redefined (overloaded) by the programmer for integral and real operands as well!

weak and soft coercion causes no difficulties since only dereferencing (weak) and deproceduring (soft or weak) are performed and the a posteriori mode is deduced very easily from the a priori mode.

The practical implementation of the different coercions involves no new problems; with the exception of rowing all coercions occur in other well-known languages also. Rowing involves the establishment of a new array-descriptor for an array of zero elements or for one whose single element is the same storage-cell as occupied by the value which has to be rowed.

Proceduring is an extension of the call-by-name-concept of ALGOL 60 to other syntactic positions than actual parameters. While all other coercions eventually change the computed value of the coercend, proceduring prohibits this computation and saves the coercend for later evaluation. Proceduring therefore creates problems if output of a pass is generated sequentially. The need for proceduring, e.g., of the first operand of a formula, is recognized only very late, e.g., after the whole formula is processed. But forming a procedure requires the insertion of some instructions in front of the procedure-body, which by the time the need is recognized, may already be on the backing store.

5. SCOPES OF REFERENCES, PROCEDURES AND FORMATS

Any variable has a scope, outside of which it cannot be used. At the end of the execution of a closed-clause or a procedure the storage allocated to local variables or parameters is freed, and therefore references to such variables or procedures containing global variables should end their existence when the scope of these variables is left.

Therefore the program

$$\begin{array}{ll} & \underline{begin} \quad \underline{ref}\ \underline{int}\ ii\ ; \\ & \quad \underline{int}\ i\ ; \\ \\ (*) & \quad \underline{begin}\ \underline{int}\ j := 0\ ; \\ & \qquad\quad ii := j \\ \\ & \quad \underline{end}\ ; \\ (**) & \quad i := ii + 1\ ; \\ \\ & \quad print\ (i) \\ & \underline{end} \end{array}$$

should fail because in (**) an attempt is made to access the value of the variable j which has already ceased to exist*. Since it is nearly impossible to check this mistake at compile-time, there is a rule that no local value may be assigned to a nonlocal variable. Hence (*) is wrong.

Except when the reference is the result of a procedure, an operation or

---

* The same problems are encountered with pointers in PL/I, but while ALGOL 68 states the scope-rules explicitly, PL/I says nothing about this problem.

a dereferencing, the scope-rule can be controlled at compile-time. Unfortunately, the remaining cases require that for all references space is reserved at run-time not only for the address representing the reference but also for a mark indicating the scope*.

The same considerations apply to procedures. But while it is convenient, in the case of references, to check the scope-rules at the same time as coercing is done, this is impossible for procedures, since, due to proceduring, the set of all procedures is known only at the end of that pass. Furthermore, while the scope of a reference follows immediately from the corresponding declaration or generator, the scope of a procedure has to be computed as the minimum scope of all globally declared objects occurring in it. This can also be done only after it is known where proceduring is applied. These remarks show the use for a pass between coercing and code-generation. Due to historical reasons our compiler determines scopes of procedures during the coercing-phase also; but this solution is expensive in time and program logic and is therefore not recommended.

Formats, if they contain dynamic replicators, cause the same problems as procedures. This will be seen in the next section.

6. THE HANDLING OF FORMATS

Apart from dynamic replicators, formats cause no special problems; they can be completely compiled in the first pass. Unlike FORTRAN, ALGOL 68 does not allow for reading formats at run-time, and therefore very efficient coding of formatted I/O is possible.

If a format contains dynamic replicators, then the transition format → transformat described in the syntax and semantics of the language [9, 5.5.8.1] implies the evaluation of the replicators and the saving of the results for use in one or more I/O-operations. This transition can occur more than once, the second time before use of the first transformat has finished. As a consequence, the appropriate solution is to compile a procedure from the format which on evaluation delivers a structured value consisting of the computed values of all dynamic replicators and the format string in internal form. The mode of this structured value is internally declared and the computed value has to be stored on the heap, not in the push-down-store. This method is shown by the following example:

The format

$$\$ \, 1 \quad 2zd, \, n(2 \times i+1) \, xn(3 \times j) \, (zd.4d3x)\$$$

compiles to

$\underline{mode} \; \underline{s} = \underline{struct}(\underline{int} \; dr1, \, dr2, \, \underline{string} \, f) \; ;$
$\underline{proc} \; transform = \underline{ref} \, \underline{s} \; :$

---

* Of course this remark does not apply when a program is completely debugged and is to be compiled to get fast object-code.

(*heap s s* := (2×*i*+1, 3×*j*, "*l*2*zd*, *n*(*dr*1 *of s*) *xn*(*dr*2 *of s*) (*zd*,4*d*3*x*)") ;*s*) *

7. THE MUNICH IMPLEMENTATION OF ALGOL 68

The following list** gives an overview of the subdivision, into tasks, of the implementation which presently is in construction at the Technische Hochschule, Munich.

T1 : Preprocessing of the program in order to form a string of symbols (in this, a character, e.g. the character "(", or a group of characters, e.g. "..", which may represent different symbols, is treated as one symbol), deletion of comments. Reconstruction of tags and replacement of tags by internal keys, replacement of denotations except format- and procedure-denotations by internal values.

T2 : Syntactic analysis of formats except dynamic replicators. Construction of a procedure for each format which first calculates the dynamic replicators and then delivers the corresponding transformat.

T3 : Preliminary determination of ranges. Construction of the connection- and the preliminary declarator-list. For each mode- and priority-declaration an entry is made in these lists.

T4 : For each operator- and identity-declaration, formal-parameter of a procedure, generator and label-definition, an entry is made in the connection- and declarator-list.

T5 : Mode- and priority-independent parsing.

T6 : Development (a generalization of the development of the Report) of declarers for deleting the mode-indications from the declarator-list. Check of the declaration condition and the uniqueness condition for mode-declarations. Check of the existence of all required mode-declarations, marking of all mode-declarations from which generator-procedures have to be produced.

T7 : Identification of identifiers.

T8 : Construction of procedures from all mode-declarations which were marked by T6.

T9 : Addition of declarations for all identifiers not declared or defined in the particular-program from the library. (Only the formal-declarer is needed.)

T10: Check of the uniqueness condition for tags and operators. Addition of the appropriate priority to the entries for operators in the connection-list. The entries for priority-declarations may now be deleted.

T11: Check of the mode-condition.

T12: Deletion of all entries in the declarator-list which occur more than once. This operation constructs the final declarator-list.

---

 * Of course, the string is represented internally by a pointer to the code to which the format-string has been compiled.
** This list and the diagram are reprinted from [3].

T13: Mode-recognition, identification of operators, identification of field-selectors, coercing and balancing. Addition of operator-declarations from the library if necessary. Final determination of ranges.
T14: Transformation of the program into reverse polish form.
T15: Determination of the scope of procedures, including those procedures constructed by T2.
T16: Check of the scope-condition in assignation as far as possible and insertion of the check-operations in the program if not possible.
T17: Construction of lists containing the information which is needed later for the linear address-calculation of subscripted variables in loops.
T18: Insertion of the coercing- and scope-check-operations determined in T13 and T16 at the appropriate place in the program.
T19: Optimization by linear address-calculation.
T20: Transformation of reverse polish form into one-address form and introduction of the necessary auxiliary variables.
T21: Determination of the storage allocation for run-time and construction of the parametrization for garbage-collection.
T22: Code-generation.
T23: Construction of lists for post-mortem-routines.
T24: Final addressing.
T25: Addition of the code of procedures from libraries including the code of standard-procedures. Addition of the declarator-lists belonging to these procedures to the given declarator-list. Repetition of T12. Insertion of code-numbers for modes in the program; afterwards the declarator-list may be deleted.
T26: Loading of the program.
T27: Run of the program.

Tasks T8 and the corresponding remark in T6 refer to the fact that if storage is allocated to a value of a mode which produces array-descriptors, "storage-allocators" have to be constructed if the mode is given by a mode-declaration. These storage-allocators are non-trivial procedures, especially if the RHS of the mode-declaration contains another mode-indication with the same property.

Task T19 indicates that this implementation tries to optimize loops by linearizing the address-calculation of elements of arrays. This optimization, which is particularly useful in numerical applications, is possible in ALGOL 68 with fewer restrictions than in ALGOL 60 (see [4]).

Figure 5 shows the distribution of the tasks over the passes. The numbers refer to the list of tasks. An arrow indicates that the completion of the first task is prerequisite to the second task. Only the more important inferences are indicated; some minor ones are given by dotted arrows. As a consequence of the grouping of tasks into passes, tasks have to be treated simultaneously. This implies some additional tasks which are not shown in the diagram.

Pass 2 mainly has to clear the different tables and therefore could be avoided*. The other pass which is added to the 4-pass scheme discussed in

---
* Note that [7] discusses a scheme in which pass 2 has a much more important role.

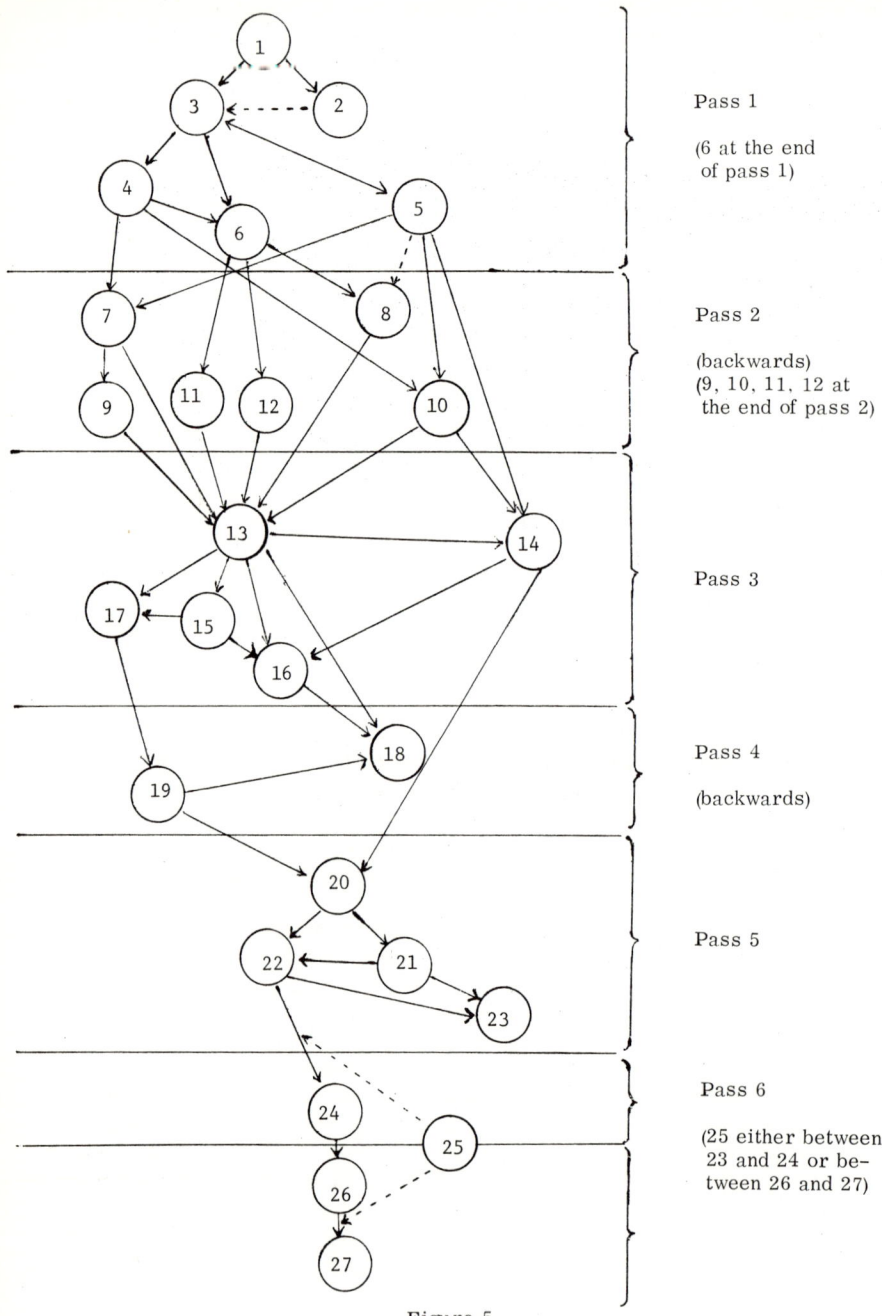

Figure 5.

the introduction is pass 4. Besides optimization its main job is to move all the internal operations determined by pass 3 (see sections 4, 5) to the correct places. The author sees no way to avoid this pass without complicating the logic of other passes to such an extent that no benefits result.

ACKNOWLEDGEMENTS

The author thanks his coworkers Miss U. Hill, Mr. H. Scheidig and Mr. H. Wössner for many useful discussions. The detailed design of the algorithms to solve the problems, especially in the area of coercion and loop-optimization, is mostly their work.

ABSTRACT

In order to compile ALGOL 68, certain problems which are not present in the compilation of FORTRAN or ALGOL 60 must be solved. Most of these problems are caused by the extensibility properties of ALGOL 68, namely the ability to introduce new modes and new operators. This paper describes some of these problems and discusses a possible decomposition of an ALGOL 68 compiler into separate tasks.

REFERENCES

[1] Branquart, P. and Lewi, J., Analysis of the parenthesis structure of ALGOL 68, Rep. R130, MBLE Brussels, April 1970.
[2] Goos, G., Eine Implementierung von ALGOL 68, Rep. Nr. 6906, Rechenzentrum Technische Hochschule München, 1969.
[3] Goos, G., Scheidig, H. and Wössner, H., Mode representation and operator identification in ALGOL 68, Proc. of an Informal Conference on ALGOL 68 Implementation, University of British Columbia, Vancouver, August 1969.
[4] Hill, U., Automatische rekursive Adressenberechnung für höhere Progammiersprachen, insbesondere für ALGOL 68, Thesis, Technische Hochschule München, Februar 1969.
[5] Koch, F., The recognition of ranges in ALGOL 68, Thesis, University of Calgary, September 1969.
[6] Koster, C. H. A., On infinite modes, Algol Bulletin AB 30.3.3.
[7] Mailloux, B. J., The implementation of ALGOL 68, Thesis, Mathematical Center, Amsterdam, 1967.
[8] Scheidig, H., Coercions in ALGOL 68, Rep. Nr. 7005, Mathematical Institute, Technische Hochschule München, July 1970.
[9] Van Wijngaarden, A. (Ed.), Mailloux, B. J., Peck, J. E. L. and Koster, C. H. A., Report on the algorithmic language ALGOL 68, Num. Math. Vol. 14 (1969) pp. 79-218.

DISCUSSION

Koster:

I would like to ask two questions about T3. In your diagram of the declarator-list some mode-indications occur, for instance this s. Should not they be accompanied by some kind of block number, in order to discriminate between the various s's that you have defined?

Goos:
   Of course, they should. I have simplified the diagram. Also it is not made in a manner whereby references and longs have a separate entry. These things are really together. We have much more information than is given in the diagram.

Kosler:
   Do you do anything to keep this declarator-list as small as possible, according to the following lines: if you are in some specific range and meet there two declarers which are the same sequence of symbols, you need to store only one of them.

Goos:
   We do not. The problem in our case is that in the first reading it may happen that, if we try to get this list short, it is still too long to hold completely in core. Therefore we just add one new entry after another and at the end of the first parsing we load the whole list into core. We have now no buffers for any other things and we process the list completely in order to shorten it.

Kosler:
   Still, I think that you could have a considerable shortening of your declarator list, for instance in programs using only *real* and *ref real*. If you are going to have 1000 copies of *real* in your list ... ?

Goos:
   The standard declarators *real* and *ref real*, etc., are identified separately.

Ershov:
   How do you implement indirect addressing as implied, e.g., by *ref real* $x = a[i]$?

Goos:
   Declarations of this form are transformed internally into *ref ref real* x' = *ref real* := $a[i]$. In the corresponding entry of the connection-list it is annotated that x' has to be dereferenced once at every applied occurrence. This dereferencing takes place also in soft positions. In the same way we handle arrays with flexible bounds:

   [1 : 2 *flex*] *real a*

is transformed into something like

   ref [ ] *real a'* := [1 : 2] *real*

with one dereferencing everytime a' is used, except in those cases in which a new array is assigned as a whole.

Ershov:
   What is the stage of development as a whole?

Goos:
   The stage of the development is that four of the six passes are coded some of which are partially running and some are in the debugging stage.

SESSION 5

(Chairman: C.H.A.Koster)

A SCHEME OF STORAGE ALLOCATION AND GARBAGE COLLECTION FOR ALGOL 68

P. BRANQUART and J. LEWI
MBLE Research Laboratory, Brussels, Belgium

INTRODUCTION

The purpose of this note is to outline a system incorporating both the schemes of storage allocation and garbage collection. In this sketch, the accent is laid rather on the basic principles and theoretical aspects than on pragmatic details and particular hardware considerations.

In developing the scheme of storage allocation and garbage collection, the following main strategy is adopted: utmost advantage has been taken of the static information on the values dealt with by the program; an important static information results from the concept of *'mode of a value'*.

This strategy is maintained for each of the four parts of the storage allocation scheme.

The first part handles the *storage structure* of the different ALGOL 68 values in memory. This part forms the kernel of the storage allocation system and it lays the basis for an efficient access scheme for values and for components of compound values.

The next two parts are concerned with an important feature which is present in most programming languages, i.e., the ability to allocate and recover storage in a dynamic way. This dynamic storage control can be done essentially in two distinct ways: by means of a stack and by means of a heap. This leads us to the respective problems of the ALGOL 68 *stack organization* (part 2) and *heap organization* (part 3).

The heap, in contrast with the stack, is a randomly organized storage zone where storage recovery is performed by an operation called *garbage collection* (explained in part 4 of this note). The construction of the garbage collector is based on the following three principles:
  (i) utmost advantage is taken of the static information (especially of the mode of the values);
 (ii) dynamic information to be stored during the garbage collection is reduced to a minimum;
(iii) program execution is not slowed down outside the garbage collection.

The first rule directly influences the speed of the garbage collection, whereas the second rule influences the amount of storage needed by the garbage collection routines at a moment this storage is scarce. The most critical point is the third rule which causes some problems related to the working stack.

Both schemes of storage allocation and garbage collection are developed for a direct access memory. In the sequel, a (memory) *cell* is considered to be the smallest addressable storage unit in the memory and by a *location* is meant a number of consecutive cells.

PART 1. THE STORAGE STRUCTURE OF VALUES

The memory representation of a value may consist of different locations (which are not necessarily contiguous in memory). The hierarchical ordering of these locations for a given value is called the *storage structure* of that value; the term *storage structure* differs from that of *memory representation* in that the former is not concerned with the exact bit patterns. As an example, by storage structure of a structured value (record) is meant the size of the location for that value as well as the sizes and the relative positions of all the sublocations for the individual fields of that value (and this in a recursive way if in turn fields are compound values). The study of the storage structure forms the basis of the storage allocation since it determines the degree of efficiency of the access scheme for different components of a given compound value.

The description of the storage structure of values is based on the recursive definitions of *static part* and *dynamic part of a value*. For any value, static part and dynamic part are such that the storage structure of the former can be deduced from the mode of the value, whereas that of the latter cannot, but depends on an elaboration in the program. As an example, the size of the descriptor of an n-dimensional real array and the place where to find its ith quintuple (with $i \leq n$) depend only on the mode of the array (on the number of dimensions), mode which is specified by the declarer "$[I_1 : J_1, \ldots, I_n : J_n]$ *real*"; the descriptor is then said to be the static part of the array. However, the number of the elements constituting the dynamic part depends on the elaboration of the bounds $I_1, J_1, \ldots, I_n, J_n$ in the program.

In the sequel, the terms *static* and *dynamic*, used for any given property, are equivalent to respectively *mode deducible* and *elaboration dependent*.

In ALGOL 68, one can distinguish five main types of value: the *ordinary values*, the *names*, the *multiple values* (arrays), the *structured values* (records) and the *values of united modes*.

(i) Ordinary values are of the modes "*int*", "*real*", "*bool*", "*char*", "*bits*", "*bytes*", "*proc* $(\mu_1, \ldots, \mu_n) \mu$", "*proc* $(\mu_1, \ldots, \mu_n)$", "*proc* μ", and "*proc*", where μ stands for any mode. They are stored into locations of static size depending on a specific hardware; one might say that their storage structure is elementary. Note that routines are stored at compile-time in the form of pieces of object code and they are manipulated by using the addresses of the locations containing these codes.

(ii) A name is characterized by the mode "*ref* μ" where μ stands for any mode as it is recursively defined in this section. Such a name refers to a value of the mode "μ" and it is represented by a *pointer* (i.e., a stored address) to the memory representation of that value. In the case an address is stored into one memory cell, the size of a pointer is one. In the sequel, a pointer will be denoted by p (possibly indexed).

(iii) A multiple value is characterized by the mode "$[,,\ldots,]\,\mu$"; its memory representation consists of a static part, the *descriptor*, and a dynamic part, the *elements* which are all of mode "μ". The static part (descriptor) of a multiple value consists of a number of *quintuples* (a quintuple for each dimension) and a *pointer* to the dynamic part (elements). Quintuples contain the coefficients of what is called in [3] the *storage mapping function* for the elements of the multiple value.

Each element of the multiple value is stored in a way depending on the mode "μ"; all their static parts are stored together into one location. Clearly, this location has a dynamic size, since the number of elements is dynamic; this size can be dynamically (at run-time) derived from the quintuples. In this sense, the descriptor of a multiple value contains dynamic storage information. In the sequel, a descriptor and a quintuple will be respectively denoted by D and q (possibly indexed). The storage structure of a multiple value M is illustrated by fig. 1, where M is of mode:

"$[,]$ *struct* (*int a, b)*"

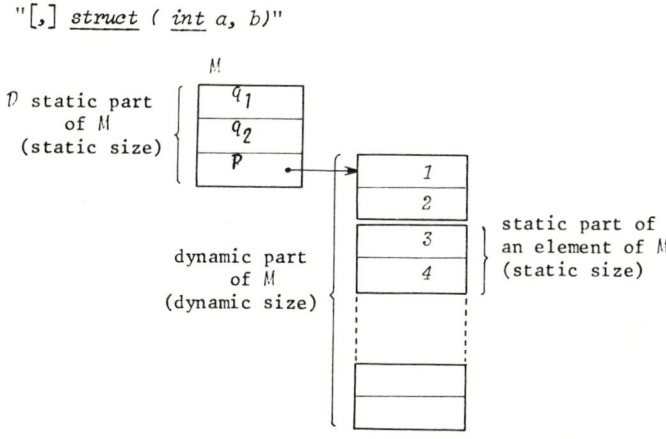

Fig. 1.

(iv) A structured value is characterized by the mode "*struct* ($\mu_1 \sigma_1, \ldots, \mu_i \sigma_i, \ldots, \mu_n \sigma_n$)", where μ_i is a mode and σ_i a field selector ($n \geq 1$); the static parts of all fields of the value constitute a location defined as the static part of the structured value. The dynamic parts, if any, of these fields constitute the dynamic part of the structured value and they are stored elsewhere in memory; their storage structures depend on the modes of their corresponding fields.

It must be emphasized that each field selector σ_i is translated into the relative address of the static part of the ith field; this results in a very efficient addressing mechanism for fields of structured values.

The storage structure of a structured value S is illustrated in fig. 2, where S is of the mode:

"*struct (int n, [ ] compl m, bool p)*"

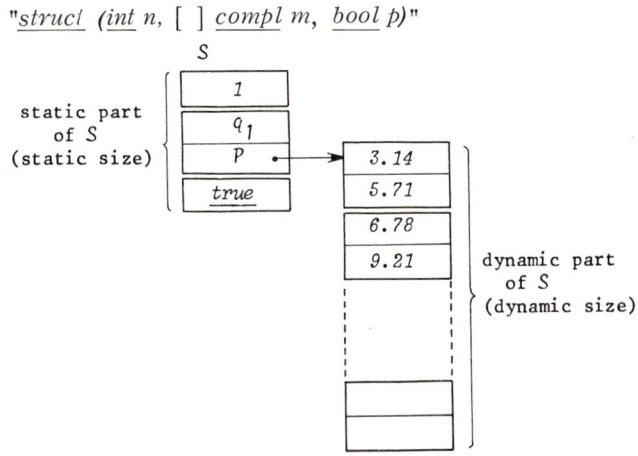

Fig. 2.

(v) A united mode is of the form "*union* $(\mu_1, \ldots, \mu_i, \ldots, \mu_n)$", $n \geq 2$, where all μ_i's are non-united modes. A value of such a mode which is a *compile-time mode* is at run-time of one of its constituent modes, say "μ_i", its *current mode*. In memory such a value consists of a static part and possibly of a dynamic part. This static part is divided into two subparts. The first one, termed the *model*, contains the current mode of the value. The second subpart contains the static part of the value stored in a way depending on the current mode "μ_i"; the size of this second subpart is the maximum static size of any value of any of the constituent modes "μ_1", ..., "μ_n". The dynamic part of the value is stored elsewhere in memory; its storage structure depends on "μ_i". Note that the storage structure of this second subpart must be deduced at run-time from the model (containing the current mode) and, in this sense, the model (as the descriptor of a multiple value) contains dynamic storage information. According to the above definition of size, the static part of a value of a united mode may have an unused storage space. This space will be termed the *residue* of that static part and it will be denoted by *res*. The model of that static part will be denoted by *m*.

The storage structure of a value of a united mode is illustrated in fig. 3, where U_1 and U_2 are values of the united mode:

"*union (int, [,] char)*"

In this example, U_1 is of the run-time mode "*int*", whereas U_2 is of the run-time mode "*[,] char*".

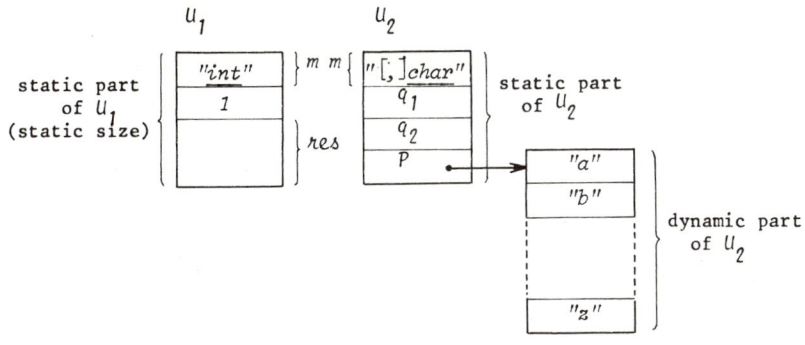

Fig. 3.

PART 2. THE STACK ORGANIZATION

One of the important features of most languages is the ability to allocate and recover storage dynamically. This dynamic storage control can be done essentially in two distinct ways: by means of a *stack* or by means of a *heap*. In ALGOL 68, stack controlled values are values of *identifiers*, partial results of *expressions* and values referred to by names of *local generators*. This classification of values (more precisely of instances of values in memory), which is based on the properties of *access*, *life-time*, and *storage control,* is such that with each class an adequate storage device, basic stack, can be associated; these three basic stacks are:

   (i) the *identifier stack (id-stack)*
   (ii) the *local generator stack (lg-stack)*
and (iii) the *expression stack or working stack (wo-stack)*.

First, we shall treat these three stacks independently from one another in order to show the basic principles (as they are defined in [1]) of storage handling of stack controlled values. Then, it will be examined how these three stacks can be merged into one, termed the *range stack,* thus leading to a practical memory organization where the only two devices of dynamic size are the range stack and the heap. Clearly, this merging must preserve the basic principles of storage handling, which are characteristic of each of the three stacks.

(i) *The identifier stack (id-stack)*

Values can be made to be possessed by *identifiers* or can be components of such values in which case they are possessed by notions called slices and field selections. E.g., the declaration "<u>compl</u> $c = (1.1, 2.2)$" causes the identifier "c" to possess the complex value "$(1.1, 2.2)$" and causes the field selection "re <u>of</u> c" to possess the real number "1.1".

Storage handling of the values of this class is based on the nested structure of ranges and it is implemented by means of a basic stack, the *id-stack*, where the values are stored in blocks $\underline{id}_i$; each block of the stack corresponds to a program range entered but not yet left. Access to the values of this class is obtained by organizing each block $\underline{id}_i$ into a static part $\underline{sid}_i$ and a dynamic part $\underline{did}_i$. This partitioning of a block $\underline{id}_i$ is identical with that of a structured value of the mode:

$$\text{"}\underline{struct}\ (\mu_1\ \sigma_1,\ \ldots,\ \mu_k \sigma_k,\ \ldots\ \mu_n \sigma_n)\text{"},$$

where n represents the number of identity and/or operator declarations of the ith range. By such a declaration an identifier or an operator σ_k ($1 \leq k \leq n$) is made to possess a value (a routine in the case of an operator) of the mode μ_k.

As long as they are created and unstacked together, in practice, static part $\underline{sid}_i$ and dynamic part $\underline{did}_i$ need not be adjacent in memory (see practical stack organization in (iv)).

It must be emphasized that the storage structure of $\underline{sid}_i$ is static, thus permitting an efficient access scheme for values in $\underline{sid}_i$. The block $\underline{sid}_i$ itself can be accessed by the classical use of a display and of a dynamic chain of block heads [3].

As an example illustrating the organization of the id-stack, consider the following declarations occurring in the range R_i of a program:

```
....  begin
            real pi = 3.14 ;
            ref real x = loc real ;
            [1 : 3] int a1 = (1, 2, 3) ;
            struct (int m, [1 : 4] char n) s =
                         (1, ("a", "b", "c", "d" )) ;
            ref real y = heap real ;
            ...
      end
....
```

The id-stack organization is then illustrated by fig. 4.

STORAGE ALLOCATION AND GARBAGE COLLECTION

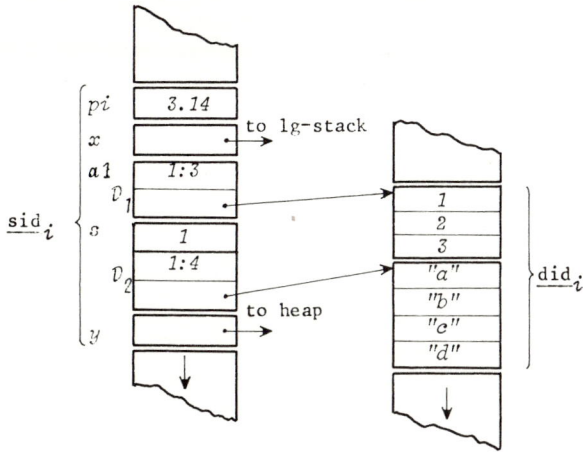

Fig. 4.

(ii) *The local generator stack (lg-stack)*

Values, more exactly names, may be created by *local generators* of the general form "loc μ" where μ specifies a given mode, e.g., "real", "*struct (int n, [1:4] char m)*", etc... When such a local generator is elaborated, storage space is reserved for a value of the mode "μ". Since local names have a life-time which is based on the nested structure of ranges, the storage reservation is done on a basic stack, the *lg-stack*. This stack is organized in blocks lg_i and the whole block lg_i is unstacked when the *i*th range is left. Since the amount of local names created in a program may depend on computations, the size of lg_i is in general dynamic.

Note that the address of the storage space reserved at the elaboration of a local generator represents the name thus created; in turn, this address appears on one of the three basic stacks or on the heap (this depends on the actual use of that local name in the program).

As an example illustrating the organization of the lg-stack (fig. 5), consider the following local generators appearing in the range R_i of a program:

> *begin*
>
> ... *loc real* := 3.14 ... ;
>
> ... *loc* [1 : 4] *int* := (1,2,3,4) .... ;
>
> ... *loc struct (int m, [1:4] char n, bool p)*
>
>   := (5,("a","b","c","d"),*true*)
>
> ....
>
> *end*

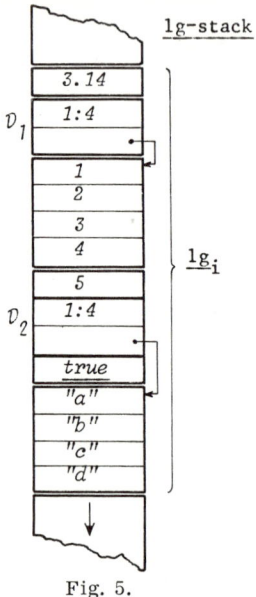

Fig. 5.

An important optimization is to be done, when local generators are used in identity-declarations of the general form "μx"; e.g., "$\underline{real}\ x$", "$[J_1:J_2]\ \underline{int}\ y$", etc. (these declarations are contractions of respectively "$\underline{ref\ real}\ x = \underline{loc\ real}$" and "$\underline{ref}[J_1:J_2]\ \underline{int}\ y = \underline{loc}[J_1:J_2]\ \underline{int}$"). The optimization consists in reserving the static part of the storage space on id-stack instead of lg-stack; the dynamic part remains on the lg-stack.

There are three cases where the values referred to by local names do not fit the last-in first-out principle of the lg-stack. These cases which are treated in part 3 of this note are entitled:

(i) the *strongly dynamic local names*
(ii) the *local names of slices*

and (iii) the *local names of rowed-coercends*

(iii) The expression (working) stack * *(wo-stack)*

Values resulting from *expressions* (and subexpressions) are handled by a basic stack, the *wo-stack*. In contrast with ALGOL 60, the wo-stack must deal with values (compound values) with dynamic parts. The access to such dynamic parts on this stack is provided by splitting it up into a *static working stack (swo-stack)*, containing all the static parts of the values, and a *dynamic working stack (dwo-stack)* containing all dynamic parts. An important point is that the maximum size of the part of the swo-

---

* In the literature, this stack is often called formula stack. In this note, we shall consider that expressions contain not only arithmetic operators and operands, but any type of operator (e.g., assignation operator, identity relator, selection and slicing, etc...) and any type of operand (e.g., names, routines, multiple and structured values, etc...).

STORAGE ALLOCATION AND GARBAGE COLLECTION

stack which corresponds to a given ith range is static and is of reasonable length; this part of the swo-stack is called $\max_i$. This property is used in (iv) where a practical stack organization is discussed.

As an example, let us consider the following expression occurring in the range R_i of a program:

$$\cdots$$
$$\underline{begin}$$
$$\quad \underline{ref}~[~]~\underline{int}~xx~;$$
$$\quad [1:3]~\underline{int}~x~;$$
$$\cdots \quad xx := x := (1,2,3+4*5)$$
$$\underline{end}$$
$$\cdots$$

Fig. 6 below must be considered a snapshot taken at the moment when the last term in the formula "$3 + 4 * 5$" constituting the collateral clause is put on the stack. (Several types of optimization in the sense of [9] and [10] could be applied to the wo-stack, but this is outside the scope of this note.)

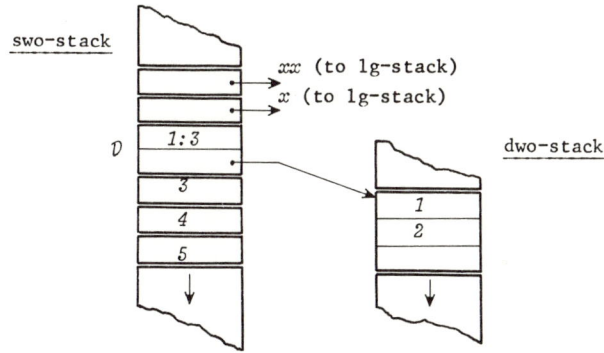

Fig. 6.

(iv) *The range stack*

Until now, attention has been focused on the efficiency of the access of values and on their storage handling for each individual basic stack: the id-stack, the lg-stack and the wo-stack. In practice, however, one should dispose of a memory organization where only two devices of dynamic size are available. This will lead to the problem of merging the three basic stacks into one, termed the *range stack*. This merging must preserve the principles of access and storage handling, which are characteristic of each basic stack.

In practice, the range stack is organized into blocks (one for each range entered but not yet left). Each block of the range stack has a static part and a dynamic part.

(a) The static part of ith block consists of both $\underline{sid}_i$ and $\underline{max}_i$; it has a static storage size. This part of the block is organized at compile-time. This permits all the values of this part of the block to be accessed by relative addresses.
(b) The dynamic part of the ith block results from the merging (which takes place at run time) of both $\underline{did}_i$ and $\underline{lg}_i$ and it has a dynamic storage size. This part of the block is organized in a dynamic way. Access to the values on this part of the block is performed by pointers which either represent accessible names or are stored in descriptors of accessible multiple values.
(c) Finally, the dwo-stack is put on the top of the range stack. This is possible if no other part varies when the dwo-stack is used. This condition is fulfilled when local generators in collateral clauses are treated in a particular way [11]. Note that when a range R_i is entered, the dwo-stack corresponding to an outer range R_j need not be empty. This residue of the dwo-stack is denoted by $\underline{dwo}_j$ (with $j < i$).

The storage organization of the range stack is schematically illustrated in fig. 7.

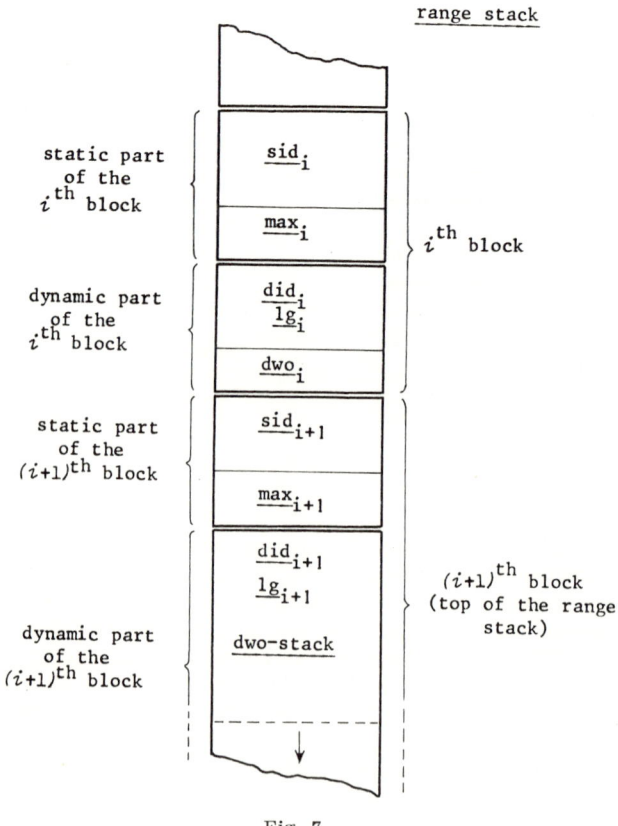

Fig. 7.

It must be emphasized that values or parts of them, wherever they may be in memory, can be accessed only through the static part of the blocks of the range stack, more precisely through $\underline{sid}_i$ and/or $\underline{max}_i$ for some i. This general principle will be used for the construction of a garbage collector (part 4) where the blocks $\underline{sid}_i$ and $\underline{max}_i$ are called *access blocks*.

PART 3. THE HEAP ORGANIZATION

ALGOL 68 deals not only with stack controlled values but also with values which do not fit the last-in first-out principle of a stack. Values of the latter type have to be stored on a random organized memory zone called the *heap*. This leads to a memory organization where the memory is dynamically partitioned into three zones: the *range stack*, the *heap* and a zone called the *free space*. When the latter is exhausted, all the heap locations containing inaccessible values are then returned to the free space by a process called *garbage collection*, explained in part 4.

According to the language definition [1], only values referred to by global names should be handled by the heap. E.g., by the elaboration of the generator "<u>heap real</u> := 3.14" in a program, a location will be reserved on the heap to store the value "3.14". Actually, there exist three distinct cases where the value referred to by a local name is not accommodated by the stack mechanism and thus must be stored on the heap. These three cases are:

       (i) the case of *strongly dynamic local names*
      (ii) the case of *local names of slices*
and (iii) the case of *local names of rowed-coercends*
    (i) *The strongly dynamic local names*

A name (local or global) is said to be strongly dynamic if its creation causes a storage space of variable size to be reserved; i.e., a space which may grow and contract during the elaboration of the program. Such names are created by generators using "<u>flex</u>" and/or "<u>union</u>", giving rise to storage spaces with a dynamic part; e.g., names created by "α[1 : 2 <u>flex</u>] <u>int</u>" and "α <u>union (bool</u>, [ ] <u>int</u>)", where α stands for "<u>loc</u>" or "<u>heap</u>", are strongly dynamic (respectively local or global) names; however, the name created by "α <u>union (bool, int)</u>" is not. The use of a strongly dynamic local name is illustrated by the following program showing that the creation of the strongly dynamic local name possessed by "x" causes a storage space to be reserved, the dynamic part of which is not accommodated by the range stack (lg-stack).

        <u>begin</u> <u>ref</u> [ ]<u>int</u> x = <u>loc</u>[1:2<u>flex</u>]<u>int</u> := (1,2) ;

          <u>begin</u> ....

                x := <u>if</u> *random* $\geqslant$ 0 <u>then</u> 1 <u>else</u> (1,2,3) <u>fi</u> ; ....

     <u>end</u>

  <u>end</u>

The storage allocation scheme for strongly dynamic local names works as follows: at the creation of such a name, the static part of the storage space is reserved on the range stack (lg-stack), whereas its dynamic part is on the heap.

(ii) *The local names of slices*

Let p represent a local name referring to a multiple value M with a descriptor D and with elements E and let p_1 be a local name referring to a subvalue M_1 of M. The descriptor D_1 of M_1 describes a number of elements E_1 of E.

This situation is schematically illustrated by fig. 8.

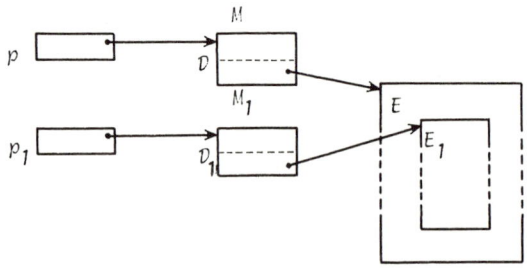

Fig. 8.

According to the language definition [1], both names p and p_1 have the same scope; let the range R_i be this scope. If the subvalue M_1 comes into existence in an inner range of R_i, then the descriptor D_1 of M_1 is not accommodated by the range stack, since D_1 must live outside that inner range; D_1 is then stored on the heap.

This case is illustrated by the following particular program where the name p is possessed by "x" and the name p_1 results from the slice "$x[2:3]$"

> *begin ref* [ ]*int xx* ;
> [1:3]*int x* := (1,2,3) ;
> ....
> *begin xx* := *x*[2:3] ;
> ....
> *end*
>
> *end*

In [8] a method has been developed, which avoids the use of the heap for values referred to by local names of slices, thus preserving the principles of 'local' (stack controlled) and 'global' (heap controlled) of the language. The main idea of this method consists in regarding the descriptor D_1 as forming part rather of the name p_1 than of the value M_1. In terms of storage structure, this means that the memory representation of a name of mode "*ref*[, ...,] μ" systematically consists of a pointer space and a descriptor space. The former space contains the pointer representing the name, the latter space is used to copy the descriptor of a multiple value as soon as this name is made to refer to that value by an assignment.

This solution gives some difficulties for multiple values referred to by a strongly dynamic name using the '*flex*' feature. The problem is caused by the fact that the contents of a descriptor of such a multiple value may change during the elaboration of a program; since different names can be made to refer to that value, there may be only one instance of that descriptor in memory. This problem is treated in [8].

(iii) *The local names of rowed-coercends*

Let again p represent a local name referring to an m-dimensional multiple value M with a descriptor D and elements E. This multiple value M can be rowed-coerced a number n of times, so that a name p_1 appears which refers to an $n+m$ dimensional multiple value with a new descriptor D_1 and the same elements E (note that D_1 is different from D). This situation is illustrated by fig. 9.

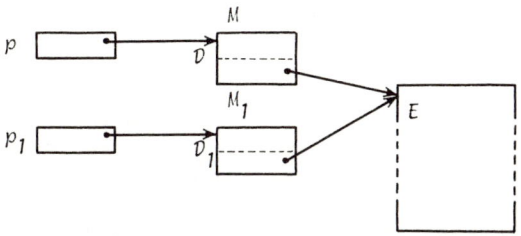

Fig. 9.

According to the language definition [1], both names p and p_1 have the same scope, say R_i. If the coerced value M_1 comes into existence in an inner range of R_i, then the descriptor D_1 of M_1 is not accommodated by the range stack and is stored on the heap. This case is quite analogous to the case (ii) where the operation 'slicing' must be replaced by the operation 'coercing'.

This case is illustrated by the following program:

$$\begin{aligned}&\underline{begin}\ \underline{ref}[,]\underline{int}\ xx\ ;\\&\quad [1:3]\underline{int}\ x\ :=\ (1,2,3)\ ;\\&\quad \dots\dots\dots\\&\quad \underline{begin}\ xx\ :=\ x\ ;\\&\quad \dots\dots\dots\\&\quad \underline{end}\\&\underline{end}\end{aligned}$$

By the declaration "$[1:3]\underline{int}\ x\ :=\ (1,2,3)$", the identifier "$x$" is made to possess a name p referring to a multiple value M consisting of a descriptor D and elements E. The value of "x" in "$xx := x$" is rowed-coerced; this means that a new name is made to refer to a subvalue M_1 of the multiple value M; M_1 consists of a new descriptor D_1 (with one dimension more than D) and the same elements E. Both p and p_1 are local to the outer range. The descriptor D_1 of M_1 is built up in the inner range and therefore is not accommodated by the range stack. There is a method to avoid the use of the heap for values referred to by names of rowed-coercends; this method is identical to that in case (ii).

Note that the problem of local names of rowed-coercends also exists when the coercend is a non-multiple value V; the value resulting from the rowed-coercion operation is then an n-dimensional multiple value M_1 with a descriptor D_1 and only one element V.

PART 4. THE GARBAGE COLLECTION

The memory is dynamically partitioned into three zones: the (range) *stack*, the *heap* and a zone called *free space* having the form either of a contiguous memory area or of a list of holes. When this free space is exhausted, all the heap locations containing inaccessible values are returned to the free space by a process called *garbage collection*. Actually, the zone in which the heap is organized consists of two merged spaces: the *active space* containing accessible values and the *garbage* containing (inaccessible) values lost by the object program. The role of the garbage collection is then twofold:
(i) to separate the active space from the garbage by *tracing* and *marking*,
(ii) to reconstitute the free space either by means of a list of holes or by *compacting* all accessible values towards one end of the zone.

1. *The tracing of list structures*

The memory can be considered to be ordered from a point of view completely different from that of stack-heap organization, namely: from a point of view of list structures. Thus, values or parts of them, whether they are stored on the stack or on the heap, can be regarded as the elements of list structures in memory.

A list structure (abbreviated into list) consists of a number of memory areas, the *nodes* n_i, linked by pointers p_i appearing within these nodes; these pointers represent the *branches* of the list; as it is explained below, nodes and branches represent well-defined values or parts of them. In ALGOL 68, list structures are of the most general type, i.e., they may have nodes of different sizes, they may share common sublists and they may even be cyclic.

The main problem is the *tracing* of list structures. Tracing is the operation through which each node of a list is recognized; this requires the knowledge of the size of each node and the exact place of the pointers contained in it. (Tracing can be compared with the operation of finding each node of an oriented graph.) In practice, tracing is done together with the operation *marking* which indicates that a branch has already been traced and must not be traced again; this is necessary to keep track of cyclic list structures.

The tracing principles are based on the fact that each value in memory is of a given *mode* and has a given memory *address*. Suppose a given value forming part of a given list has been reached by tracing that list, then the 2-uple consisting of the mode and of the address of that value characterizes the actual state of the tracing. This mode and this address are respectively called *current mode cm* and *current address ca* of the list and the 2-uple is then denoted by *(ca, cm)*. One can distinguish five basic situations each corresponding to a tracing rule. These five situations are:

(i) A node is constituted by a pointer p representing a name

Suppose the name is of the mode "*ref* μ", then p points to a value of mode "μ". The corresponding tracing step is obvious and consists in following the pointer of address ca, thus obtaining the 2-uple (ca', μ) on which in turn one of the five situations applies.

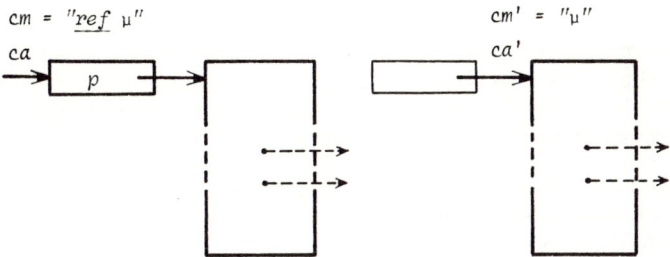

The tracing step is then characterized by the transformation rule:

$(ca, \underline{ref}\ \mu) \rightarrow (ca', \mu)$

(ii) A node is constituted by the static part of a structured value

This value is of mode "*struct* $(\mu_1 \sigma_1, \ldots, \mu_j \sigma_j, \ldots, \mu_k \sigma_k)$". According to part 1, the storage structure of this static part only depends on the mode; hence, from this mode, one can calculate the address of the ith field for any i $(1 \leq i \leq k)$, thus obtaining the 2-uple (ca', μ_i) on which in turn one of the five situations applies.

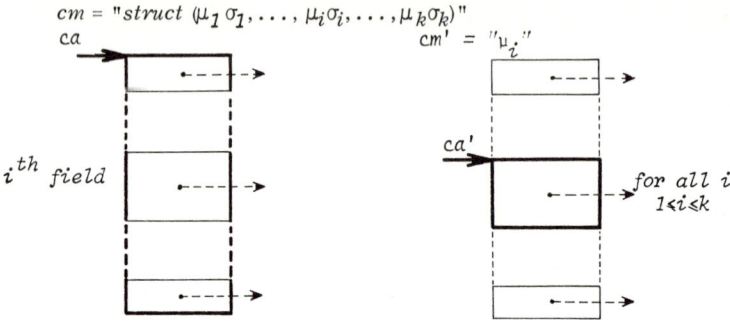

The tracing step is characterized by:

$$(ca, \underline{struct} \ (\mu_1 \sigma_1, \ldots, \mu_i \sigma_i, \ldots, \mu_k \sigma_k)) \to (ca', \mu_i)$$

for any i $(1 \leq i \leq k)$

(iii) A node is constituted by the static part (descriptor) of an n-dimensional multiple value.
This value is of the mode "$[,,\ldots,] \mu$" ($n-1$ comma's). The storage structure of the descriptor, i.e., its size and the exact place of each quintuple and of the pointer in it, can be deduced from the mode.
Since "μ" describes the storage structure of the static part of each element and since all these static parts are put together, one is able to calculate from the mode the address of the ith element for any i
$(1 \leq i \leq N)$. However, the maximum number N of elements is a dynamic information and must be calculated from the quintuples of the descriptor. This leads to the 2-uple (ca', μ) on which in turn one of the five situations applies.

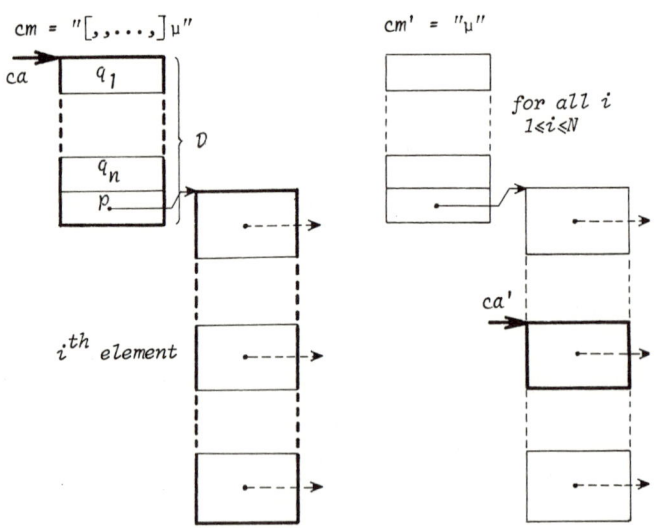

STORAGE ALLOCATION AND GARBAGE COLLECTION

The tracing step is characterized by:

$(ca, [, , \ldots,] \mu) \rightarrow (ca', \mu)$ for any i $(1 \leq i \leq N)$.

(iv) A node is constituted by the static part of a value of a united mode. This mode has the form "$\underline{union} \ (\mu_1, \ldots, \mu_k)$"; it specifies the size of the static part of the value and the exact place of the model containing the run-time mode "μ_i" of the value. This leads to the 2-uple (ca', μ_i) on which in turn another situation applies.

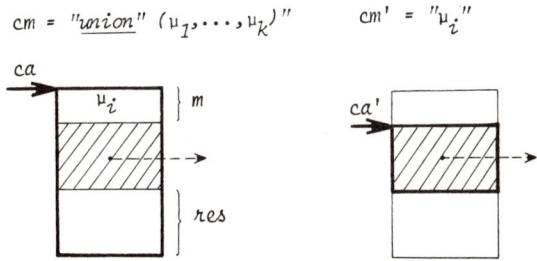

The tracing step is characterized by:

$(ca, \underline{union} \ (\mu_1, \ldots, \mu_k)) \rightarrow (ca', \mu_i)$

(v) A node is constituted by an ordinary value.
Locations containing ordinary values are the terminals of lists, where a particular branch ends; another branch, if any, can then start to be traced. Obviously, tracing requires a stack to memorize the branch points and other dynamic tracing information (see section 3).

cm = "$\underline{int}$" $\vee$ "$\underline{real}$" $\vee$ "$\underline{bool}$" $\vee$ "$\underline{char}$" $\vee$ "$\underline{bits}$" $\vee$ "$\underline{bytes}$" $\vee$
"$\underline{proc} \ (\mu_1 \ldots \mu_n)\mu$" $\vee$ "$\underline{proc} \ (\mu_1 \ldots \mu_n)$" $\vee$ "$\underline{proc} \ \mu$" $\vee$ "$\underline{proc}$".

2. The access blocks

In order to trace a list a *starting address* sa and a *starting mode* sm are required, forming the initial 2-uple (sa, sm). This sa is then the address of a particular node, called the *starting node*, which represents the static part of a value of mode sm. The memory areas containing the starting nodes of the lists to be traced are called the *access blocks* for these lists. These blocks are such that all values accessible from the object program can be reached by tracing the lists starting from these blocks.

There are two types of accessible value:

(i) Those which can be reached from the id-stack and they are called *externally accessible values*.

All these values form part of lists which have $\underline{sid}_i$'s (for all i) as access blocks.

(ii) Those which can be reached from the wo stack and they are called *internally accessible values*.

All these values constitute lists which have $\underline{max}_i$'s (for all i) as access blocks.

All other values have become inaccessible for the program. Note that values may be both externally and internally accessible.

(i) The external access blocks

From a conceptual point of view, a block $\underline{id}_i$ is organized in the same way as a structured value of the mode $\mu_{ex,i}$ obtained as follows. Suppose there is a reach R_i with n identity and/or operator declarations, by which identifiers and/or operators σ_k ($1 \leq k \leq n$) are made to possess values (routines in the case of operators) of the mode μ_k. Then, $\mu_{ex,i}$ is of the form:

$$\text{"}\underline{struct}\,(\mu_1\,\sigma_1,\,\ldots,\,\mu_k\,\sigma_k,\,\ldots,\,\mu_n\,\sigma_n)\text{"}$$

The block $\underline{sid}_i$ as a whole is now considered to be the starting node of an accessible list with starting mode $\mu_{ex,i}$.

It should be clear that there are as many such accessible lists as there are blocks $\underline{sid}_i$ on the range stack; these blocks are dynamically chained in a classical way [3]. Any externally accessible value necessarily forms part of at least one of these lists. For example, consider the program:

(mode $\underline{s}$ = $\underline{struct}$ ($\underline{int}$ i, $\underline{ref}$ $\underline{s}$ r) ;

$\underline{ref}$ $\underline{ref}$ $\underline{real}$ xx = $\underline{ref}$ $\underline{real}$:= $\underline{real}$:= 3.14 ;

...

($\underline{ref}$ $\underline{bool}$ bb = $\underline{bool}$:= $\underline{true}$;

$\underline{ref}$ $\underline{s}$ s = $\underline{loc}$ $\underline{s}$:= $(1, \underline{s} := (2, \underline{s} := (3, \underline{nil})))$

...

...

)

After the elaboration of the last declaration, there are two blocks $\underline{sid}_1$ and $\underline{sid}_2$ on the range stack, which are the starting nodes of two accessible lists with $\mu_{ex,1}$, respectively $\mu_{ex,2}$ as starting modes.

$\mu_{ex,1}$ is of the form "$\underline{struct}\,(\underline{ref}\,\underline{ref}\,\underline{real}\,xx)$" and

$\mu_{ex,2}$ is of the form "$\underline{struct}\,(\underline{ref}\,\underline{bool}\,bb,\,\underline{ref}\,\underline{s}\,s)$"

This is illustrated by fig. 10.

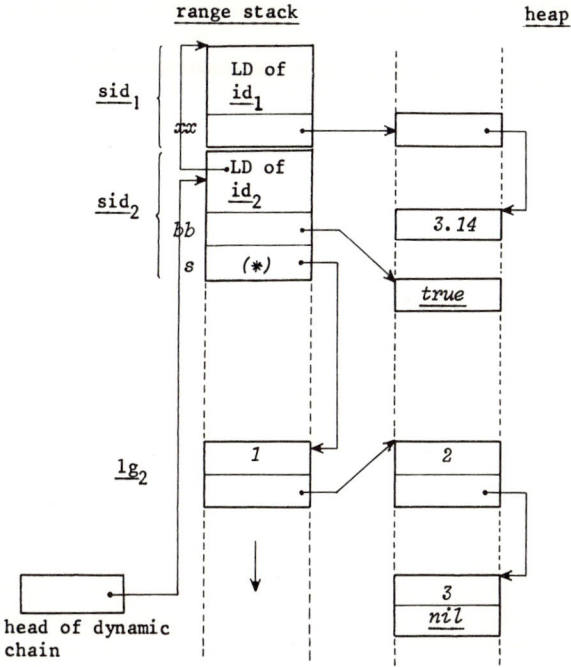

Fig. 10. $LD \equiv$ link data

(ii) The internal access blocks

As it is described above, for reasons of accessibility the two-stack is split up into a static part, the *swo-stack*, and a dynamic part, the *dwo-stack*. In the ith block of the range stack, a storage space $\underline{\max}_i$ is reserved (for each i) having the maximum size of the swo-stack for the range R_i.

In principle, in a way analogous to section 3.1, $\underline{\max}_i$ could be regarded as a starting node of a list structure with a starting mode $\mu_{in,i}$. The fundamental difference between the internal and external access blocks is that, in the former case, $\mu_{in,i}$ (for a given $\underline{\max}_i$) may vary each time a wo-stack operation is carried out, whereas, in the latter case, $\mu_{ex,i}$ (for a given $\underline{sid}_i$) remains valid as long as $\underline{sid}_i$ is on the range stack. In practice, $\mu_{in,i}$ will be implemented as a table $M_{in,i}$ of 2-uples, each 2-uple consisting of the address of an internal accessible value and of its mode; this mode and address are respectively the starting mode and the starting address of an accessible list starting from that value.

The method of using a table $M_{in,i}$ to save garbage collection information

---

* In an optimized storage allocation scheme [8], it is not this location, but the location on $\underline{\lg}_2$ which would appear on the id-stack.

for the wo-stack seems to be not very satisfactory because of a lack of run-time efficiency, which can be minimized by the following consideration. Garbage collection information has not systematically to be stored for all wo-stack values. Clearly, only those values which either are names or are structured and multiple values having names as components have to be taken into account. A more detailed optimization scheme is explained in section 6.

3. *The marking*

Marking is evidently done together with tracing. During the tracing of a list, all its active memory cells are marked by the use of an extra bit if it is provided by hardware or otherwise by the use of a bit table. This way of marking is known as *cell marking*. There exists another way of marking, *location marking*, which consists in the marking of an active location as a whole. Location marking requires each location to be provided with an overhead to store the mark and the size of that location; this method does not work here, since in ALGOL 68 in turn any sublocation may be considered a location.

Let us recall that the tracing of a list requires two things: the *starting address*, i.e., the address of the starting node of the list, and the *starting mode*, i.e., the mode of the value whose static part is that starting node. If the starting node is an external access block $\underline{sid}_i$, the starting address is the address of the block $\underline{sid}_i$ itself and it can be reached by means of the dynamic chain of blocks on the range stack- the starting mode $\mu_{ex,i}$ is composed at compile time. If the starting node appears in an internal access block $\underline{max}_j$, the starting address is contained in the corresponding table $M_{in,i}$ and again its associated starting mode is known at compile-time.

As it has been emphasized in the preceding sections, the starting mode of a list contains all the information for tracing that list from its starting address. The routine performing both the tracing and the marking of the active cells of a list can be deduced from its starting mode at the moment of garbage collection itself. This method which is known as the *interpretive method* is not very satisfactory since it slows down the garbage collection. Garbage collection can be speeded up by generating at compile-time a marking routine for each possible starting mode. This method is known as the *compiled method* (its disadvantage may be the great amount of storage space taken by the compiled routines).

(i) The interpretive method

In section 3, we have discussed the tracing principles indicating by means of five recursive rules how a starting mode sm of a list can be interpreted to trace that list from its starting address sa.

The routine *MARK* given below illustrates these principles. It consists in tracing and marking the active cells of a list with any given mode as starting mode and any given address as starting address; more precisely, *MARK* has two parameters: a current mode cm and a current address ca.

STORAGE ALLOCATION AND GARBAGE COLLECTION 219

For reasons of clarity, the routine *MARK* is described in a schematic way; so one will recognize in the routine each of the five tracing rules of section 1. A more elaborated and practical version of the interpretive marking routine can be found in [6].

Before the routine *MARK* is outlined, some frequently used subroutines are given, which are denoted by *CONT, NELEMENTS, RUNMODE, STATICSIZE, MARKCELLS* and *MARKED*.

<u>int</u> nil = <u>co</u> *integer corresponding to the pattern of* <u>nil</u> *in the memory* <u>co</u> ;

<u>proc</u> (<u>int</u>)<u>int</u> CONT =

<u>co</u> *CONT possesses a routine with an integral parameter representing the current address of a memory cell. The result of CONT is an integer representing the contents of that cell*

<u>co</u> ;

<u>proc</u> (<u>int, string</u>) <u>int</u> NELEMENTS =

<u>co</u> *NELEMENTS possesses a routine with two parameters : one is an integer representing the current address of a descriptor D, the other is a string representing the current mode (which is of the form $[,,...,]\mu$). The result of NELEMENTS is an integer representing the number of array elements and is deduced from the quintuples of D. (The number of quintuples is deduced from the current mode.)*

<u>co</u> ;

<u>proc</u> (<u>int</u>)<u>string</u> RUNMODE =

<u>co</u> *RUNMODE possesses a routine with an integral parameter representing the current address of the static part of a value of a united mode. The result of RUNMODE is the contents (which is a mode) of the model of that part.*

<u>co</u> ;

<u>proc</u> (<u>string</u>) <u>int</u> STATICSIZE =

<u>co</u> *STATICSIZE possesses a routine with a string parameter represen-*

ting a mode. The result of STATICSIZE is an integer representing the size (the number of cells) of the static part of any value of that mode.

co ;

proc (*int, int*) MARKCELLS =

co MARKCELLS possesses a routine with two integral parameters: one for a current address of a static part of a value and another for its static size. The result of MARKCELLS is the marking of all individual cells of that static part in a bit table.

co ;

proc (*int*) *bool* MARKED =

co MARKED possesses a routine with an integral parameter representing a cell address. The result of MARKED is *true* or *false* according as the cell has already been marked or not.

co ;

proc MARK = (*int* ca *co* current address in the list structure *co*,
   string cm *co* current mode associated with that current address *co*) :

rule (i)
$$\left\{\begin{array}{l} \textit{if } cm = \text{"}\underline{ref}\ \mu\text{"} \\ \quad \textit{then } \textit{if } \neg \text{MARKED (ca)} \\ \qquad \textit{then } \text{MARKCELLS (ca, STATICSIZE (cm))}; \\ \qquad\quad \textit{if } \text{CONT (ca)} \neq nil \\ \qquad\quad\quad \textit{then } \text{MARK (CONT(ca),}\mu\text{)} \\ \qquad\quad \textit{fi} \\ \quad \textit{fi} \end{array}\right.$$

STORAGE ALLOCATION AND GARBAGE COLLECTION

rule (ii)
$$\begin{cases}
\underline{elsf}\ cm = \text{"}\underline{struct}\ (\mu_1\sigma_1,\ \ldots,\ \mu_j\sigma_j,\ \ldots,\ \mu_k\sigma_k)\text{"} \\
\quad \underline{then}\ \underline{int}\ cad := ca\ ; \\
\qquad \underline{for}\ j\ \underline{to}\ k\ \underline{do} \\
\qquad \underline{if}\neg\text{MARKED}\ (cad\ +:=\ \underline{if}\ j=1 \\
\qquad\qquad\qquad\qquad\qquad\quad \underline{then}\ 0 \\
\qquad\qquad\qquad\qquad\qquad\quad \underline{else}\ \text{STATICSIZE}\ (\mu_{j-1}) \\
\qquad\qquad\qquad\qquad\quad \underline{fi}) \\
\qquad \underline{then}\ \text{MARK}\ (cad,\ \mu_j) \\
\qquad \underline{fi}
\end{cases}$$

rule (iii)
$$\begin{cases}
\underline{elsf}\ cm = \text{"}[,,\ldots,]\mu\text{"} \\
\quad \underline{then}\ \underline{if}\neg\text{MARKED}\ (ca) \\
\qquad \underline{then}\ \text{MARKCELLS}\ (ca,\ \text{STATICSIZE}\ (cm))\ ; \\
\qquad\quad \underline{int}\ n = \text{NELEMENTS}\ (ca,\ cm)\ ; \\
\qquad\quad \underline{int}\ cad := \text{CONT}\ (ca + \text{STATICSIZE}\ (cm)-1)\ ; \\
\qquad\quad \underline{int}\ s = \text{STATICSIZE}\ (\mu)\ ; \\
\qquad\quad \underline{for}\ i\ \underline{to}\ n\ \underline{do}\ \text{MARK}\ (cad\ +:=\ (i-1)*s, \mu) \\
\quad \underline{fi}
\end{cases}$$

$$\begin{cases}
\underline{elsf}\ cm = \text{"}\underline{union}\ (\ldots\ldots\ldots)\text{"} \\
\quad \underline{then}\ \underline{if}\neg\text{MARKED}\ (ca) \\
\qquad \underline{then}\ \underline{int}\ s = \text{STATICSIZE}\ (cm)-\text{STATICSIZE}\ (\text{RUNMODE}\ (ca))-1; \\
\qquad\quad \underline{co}\ s\ represents\ the\ number\ of\ cells\ of\ the\ resi- \\
\qquad\qquad due\ of\ the\ static\ part;\ the\ size\ of\ the\ model \\
\qquad\qquad is\ considered\ to\ be\ one\ cell \\
\qquad\quad \underline{co}
\end{cases}$$

rule (iv)

$\qquad$ MARKCELLS (ca + STATICSIZE (RUNMODE (ca))+1,8);

$\qquad$ MARKCELLS (ca, 1) ;

$\qquad\qquad$ <u>co</u> first, the model and the residue are marked and not the whole static part, otherwise the dynamic part, if it exists, will never be traced.

$\qquad\qquad$ <u>co</u>

$\qquad$ MARK (ca + 1, RUNMODE (ca))

$\qquad$ *fi*

rule (v)

$\qquad$ <u>elsf</u> ¬MARKED (ca)

$\qquad$ <u>then</u> MARKCELLS (ca, STATICSIZE (cm))

$\qquad\qquad$ <u>co</u> ca is necessarily the address of an atom.

$\qquad\qquad$ <u>co</u>

$\qquad$ *fi*

(ii) The compiled method

Compiled marking routines have only one parameter, i.e., a memory address. The problem is to compile a mode into a routine performing the tracing and marking of a list which has that mode as starting mode. This problem will be illustrated for three different types of mode:

$\qquad$ the structured mode <u>s</u> = <u>struct</u> <u>(int</u> i, <u>ref s</u> r),
$\qquad$ the multiple mode <u>m</u> = [,] <u>struct</u> <u>(ref m</u> a)
and $\quad$ the united mode <u>u</u> = <u>union</u> (<u>s</u>, <u>m</u>).

These modes are recursively defined ones, so that they will represent the fundamental problems of the compiled method.

The marking routines for the modes <u>s</u>, <u>m</u> and <u>u</u> are respectively denoted by $MARK_s$, $MARK_m$ and $MARK_u$. These routines frequently use five subroutines which are denoted by $\overline{MARKCELL}$, MARKED, CONT, NUMB and RUNMODE.

<u>int</u> nil = <u>co</u> integer corresponding to the pattern of <u>nil</u> in the memory <u>co</u> ;

<u>proc</u> (<u>int</u>) MARKCELL =

$\qquad$ <u>co</u> the routine MARKCELL has an integral parameter representing the address of the (memory) cell to be marked in a bit table or by the use of an extra-bit if it is provided by hardware.

$\qquad$ <u>co</u> ;

STORAGE ALLOCATION AND GARBAGE COLLECTION 223

proc *(int)* *bool* MARKED =

 co the routine MARKED has an integral parameter representing a cell address. The result of MARKED is *true* or *false* according as the cell has already been marked or not.

 co ;

proc *(int)* *int* CONT =

 co the routine CONT has an integral parameter representing the address of a cell containing a pointer. The result of CONT is the contents of that cell, which again is an integer representing a cell address.

 co ;

proc *(int, int)* *int* NUMB =

 co the routine NUMB has two integral parameters ; the former represents the address of the descriptor of a multiple value, the latter represents the number of dimensions of that value. The result is the number of elements of the multiple value and it is calculated from the quintuples of its descriptor.

 co ;

proc *(int)* *string* RUNMODE =

 co the routine RUNMODE has an integral parameter representing the address of the static part of a value of a united mode. The result is a string representing the run-time mode of the value, obtained by taking the contents of the model of that static part.

 co ;

The mode s = *struct* *(int* i, *ref* s $r)$ can be compiled into a marking routine $MARK_s$ defined as follows:

proc MARK$_s$ = (**int** add **co** *the parameter represents the address of a structured value of mode s*

co) :

(**if** ¬MARKED (add) **then** MARKCELL (add)

fi ;

if ¬MARKED (add+1)

then MARKCELL (add+1) ;

if CONT (add+1) ≠ nil

then MARK$_s$ (CONT (add+1))

fi

fi

)

The mode m = [,] **struct** (**ref** m a) can be compiled into a marking routine MARK$_m$ defined as follows:

proc MARK$_m$ = (**int** add **co** *the parameter represents the address of a multiple value of mode m*

co) :

if ¬MARKED (add)

then MARKCELL (add) **co** *the first quintuple* **co**;

MARKCELL (add+1) **co** *the second quintuple* **co** ;

MARKCELL (add+2) **co** *the pointer* **co** ;

int n = NUMB (add, 2) ;

for i **to** n **do** **if** ¬MARKED (CONT (add+2)+i-1)

then MARK (CONT (add+2)+i-1) ;

if CONT(CONT (add+2)+i-1) ≠ nil

then MARK$_m$ (CONT (CONT (add+2)+i-1))

fi

fi

fi

STORAGE ALLOCATION AND GARBAGE COLLECTION 225

The mode $u = \underline{union}$ $(\underline{s}, \underline{m})$ can be compiled into a marking routine $MARK_u$ defined as follows:

$\underline{proc}$ $MARK_u$ = ($\underline{int}$ add $\underline{co}$ the parameter represents the address of a value of

a united mode u

$\underline{co}$) :

$\underline{if}$ ¬MARKED (add) $\underline{then}$ MARKCELL (add) $\underline{co}$ the model $\underline{co}$;

$\underline{if}$ RUNMODE (add) = $\underline{co}$ the string represented by the mode $\underline{s}$ $\underline{co}$

$\underline{then}$ MARKCELL (add+3) $\underline{co}$ the residue $\underline{co}$;

$MARK_s$ (add+1)

$\underline{else}$ $MARK_m$ (add+1)

$\underline{fi}$

$\underline{fi}$

(iii) The dynamic marking information

There are two important remarks to be pointed out with respect to the marking of lists.

The first one concerns the marking of subvalues of multiple values, which is somewhat more complicated for reasons of compacting (second part of the garbage collection). In order to understand all aspects of this particular problem, it has been treated (see section 5) after the compacting has been explained.

The second remark concerns the dynamic information to be stored during the marking process. Conceptually, one can distinguish three types of dynamic information each requiring the use of a stack. First, each type of information is discussed and then some comment is given, indicating how these stacks can be actually implemented. A first type of dynamic information are the branch points in the list, which are currently traced and which must be memorized in order to be able to continue when a complete branch has been finished. This problem is quite analogous to that of tracing an oriented graph. A second type of dynamic information are the return addresses in the marking routine; these addresses must also be handled by a stack in order to cope with the recursive calls within the marking routine. Marking routines can be recursive since there exist recursively defined modes. The third and last type of dynamic information to be stored on a stack is the number of elements of a multiple value and the current number of the element traced lastly. Here, a stack is required because the elements of a given multiple value can be recursively defined in terms of the mode of that given multiple value.

There exist methods to implement these stacks such that no storage space of dynamic size must be reserved at the moment of garbage collection, a moment where storage space is rather scarce. An obvious case is the stack handling the maximum number and current number of elements of a multiple value; one can systematically add a memory cell to the descriptor of a multiple value to store the current value of a counter, indicating the current number of the element traced lastly. In [6] one can find a practical method for the implementation of the other two stacks: the stack of branch points and the stack of return addresses.

4. *The compacting*

The role of the marking is to separate on the heap the active space from the garbage such that two kinds of memory areas (locations) can be distinguished: the locations which consist of marked cells and which are called *active locations*, and the locations which consist of unmarked cells and which are termed *holes*. The free space of the heap can be reconstituted by organizing the holes into a list of holes and program elaboration can go on using these holes to store nonlocal values. There are two situations where a free space organized as a list of holes is not sufficient any more: one occurs when it is the (range) stack which causes the free space to be exhausted, the other appears as soon as a value must be stored, which does not fit any hole. In both situations the operation *compacting* has to take place. As it will be explained in detail, compacting is performed in two steps: (i) *shifting* and (ii) *updating*. In the first step, the contents of the active locations will be shifted towards one end of the memory; in the second step all pointers to active locations will be updated.

We suppose the compacting phase will immediately follow the marking phase; the technique of using holes for storing new values before compacting is not discussed in this note.

(i) The shifting of accessible values

In fig. 11, the memory organization of the heap is shown in a schematic way. For $1 \le k \le n$, the notations a_0, a_k and b_k represent machine addresses, h_k a hole and v_k an active location containing an accessible value or a part (static or dynamic) of it.

$$a_n < b_n < a_{n-1} < b_{n-1} \ldots \ldots < a_1 < b_1 \le a_0$$

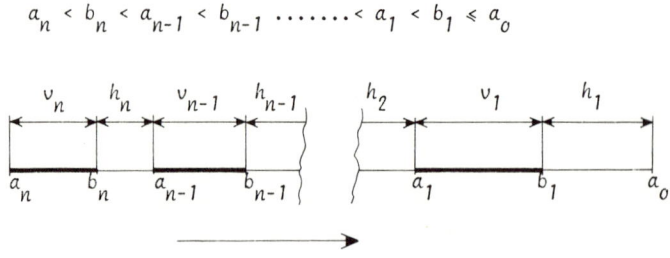

direction of the shifting of v_k's

Fig. 11.

STORAGE ALLOCATION AND GARBAGE COLLECTION 227

Shifting consists in moving the contents of all v_k's one by one towards one end of the zone constituting the heap. (In fig. 11 the direction of shifting is from left to right.)

During this shifting operation a table T_{upd} of dynamic information is set up, which will be used for the updating of pointers after the contents of the last active location, v_n, has been shifted. T_{upd} may have the form of an array of records with two fields: an *address field* selected by *add* and a *correction field* selected by *cor*. Each time the contents of a new v_i is shifted, a new record $T_{upd}[i]$ is added to T_{upd} as it is shown by the following two assignments:

$add \underline{of} \ T_{upd}[i] := a_i$

$cor \underline{of} \ T_{upd}[i] := \sum_{j=1}^{i} h_j$

Before the shifting operation starts, the table T_{upd} must be initialized as follows:

$add \underline{of} \ T_{upd}[0] := a_0$

$cor \underline{of} \ T_{upd}[0] := 0$

It should be clear that T_{upd} needs an unpredictable amount of storage space at a time when this space may be scarce. Clearly, the holes could be used for this purpose, but this possibility will not be treated in this note. A method using the holes to store T_{upd} is described in [12].

(ii) Updating of pointers

Each pointer p for which the following relation holds for some $k (1 \leq k \leq n)$

$add \underline{of} \ T_{upd}[k] \leq p < add \underline{of} \ T_{upd}[k-1]$

is updated into $p + cor \underline{of} \ T_{upd}[k]$.

Such pointers (which either are representing names or form part of descriptors of multiple values) may be located either on the range stack (id-stack, lg-stack or wo-stack) or on the heap itself. For the recognition of these pointers, list structures may be traced in the same way as it is done in the marking process by using the information $\mu_{ex,i}$ and $M_{in,j}$ respectively for each block $\underline{sid}_j$ and $\underline{max}_j$ on the range stack.

As it is the case with marking, the updating operation can be performed in an interpretive way or in a compiled way.

The compiled method is illustrated by the following example where the mode $\underline{s} = \underline{struct} \ (\underline{int} \ i, \ \underline{ref} \ \underline{s} \ r)$ is compiled into a recursive updating routine $UPDATE_s$. This routine uses the subroutines $UPDATE$, COR and the subroutines $CONT$, $MARKED$ and $MARKCELL$ as they are described in section 3.

$\underline{proc} \ COR = (\underline{int} \ add, \ cor) \ : \underline{co}$ *to the contents of the*
            cell with address add is added the value
            cor $\underline{co}$;

$\underline{proc}\ UPDATE = (\underline{int}\ add)$:

$\underline{for}\ i\ \underline{to}\ n\ \underline{do}$

$\underline{if}\ CONT\ (add) \geqslant add\ \underline{of}\ T_{upd}\ [n]$

$\underline{thef}\ add\ of\ T_{upd}\ [i] \leqslant CONT\ (add) \land$

$CONT\ (add) < add\ \underline{of}\ T_{upd}\ [i-1]$

$\underline{then}\ COR\ (add,\ cor\ \underline{of}\ T_{upd}\ [i])$

$\underline{fi}$

The compiled routine $UPDATE_s$ for the mode $\underline{s} = \underline{struct}\ (\underline{int}\ i,\ \underline{ref}\ \underline{s}\ r)$ has the following form:

$\underline{proc}\ UPDATE_s = (\underline{int}\ add\ \underline{co}\ the\ parameter\ represents\ the\ address\ of\ a$

$structured\ value\ of\ mode\ \underline{s}$

$\underline{co})$:

$\underline{if}\ \neg MARKED\ (add+1)\ \underline{then}\ MARKCELL\ (add+1)$;

$\underline{if}\ CONT\ (add+1) \neq nil\ \underline{then}\ UPDATE\ (add+1)$;

$UPDATE_s(CONT\ (add+1))$

$\underline{fi}$

$\underline{fi}$

5. The marking problem for subvalues

Given a name referring to a subvalue M_1 of a multiple value M with a descriptor D. The descriptor D_1 of M_1 describes a number of elements of M. Obviously, for reasons of access, the interjacent spaces between the static parts of the elements of M_1 must be preserved during the compacting phase of the garbage collection and, hence, these spaces are to be marked as well during the marking phase.

This situation is illustrated by fig. 12, where p_1 and p represent names respectively referring to the multiple values M_1 and M. In this example, M is of the mode "$[1:3, 1:2]\ \underline{ref}\ \mu$" and M_1 is of the mode "$[1:3]\ \underline{ref}\ \mu$", M_1 is a subvalue of M such that if M were identified by A, M_1 is the value of the slice $A[\ ,1]$.

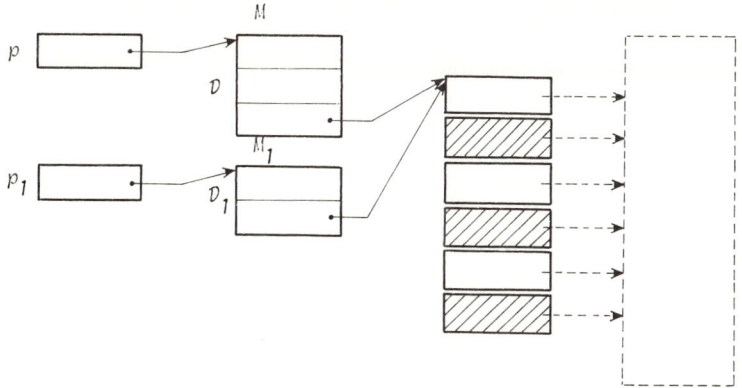

Fig. 12.

This situation gives rise to the following two complications:

(i) It should be clear that these interjacent spaces must be marked starting from D of M. Since M may be inaccessible, D must be attainable from D_1. For this reason, the memory representation of a descriptor of a multiple value, as it is given in part 1, is slightly modified as follows: storage space for a descriptor is to be reserved not only for the quintuples and the pointer to the dynamic part, but also for a second pointer. Each time, during the elaboration of a program, a subvalue of a given multiple value is made, then this second pointer in the descriptor of that subvalue will be dynamically given the address of the descriptor of that given multiple value [2].

(ii) On the one hand, the marking process of these interjacent spaces must differ from that of accessible values, since only the cells in these spaces are marked and not the list structures starting from them. On the other hand, if an element of M must be marked and if this element is an interjacent space of a given subvalue of M, then, clearly, the marking must go on through the whole list structure starting from this element. This necessitates the differentiation of the two kinds of marking. To avoid the use of two different bit tables, which is rather expensive, one can adopt the following strategy:

The memory cells constituting memory representations of accessible values on the heap are marked in a bit table. Each time a subvalue of a multiple value M is marked, the address of the descriptor of M is added to an address table T_{subv}. Only, when all accessible values on the heap are marked, the remaining interjacent spaces in multiple values, whose addresses are in T_{subv}, are marked at once in the same bit table.

6. The optimization of $M_{in,j}$

The processes of marking and updating, as they are described in sections 3 and 4, need both the same tracing information, i.e., $\mu_{ex,i}$ for each $\underline{sid}_i$ on the id-stack and $M_{in,j}$ for each $\underline{max}_j$ on the wo-stack. These two processes seem not to work very efficiently in the case of the wo-stack, since the contents of the wo-stack vary continuously with each stack operation. If j is the number of the current range (block on the top of the range stack), $M_{in,j}$ has to be dynamically adapted each time a name or a compound value having a name as component is added or deleted from the wo-stack.

An optimization consisting in minimizing the tracing information for the wo-stack will now be worked out. The main principle of this optimization is that only those values of the wo-stack have to be considered in the table $M_{in,j}$, which either have no external access block or which have an external access block but which is unstacked before these values disappear from the wo-stack. A way in which this principle may be put into practice results from the following classification of (partial) results of (sub)expressions for a given range R_i.

Class (i): contains the results of expressions E, which are values possessed either by identifiers in E, or resulting from slices, selections and coercions on such values. (Note that this class of results is recursively defined.) Such results are said to have an identifier as origin, since they are obtained by passing through a block $\underline{sid}_j$ (for some $j \leq i$); j is the number of the range where the identifier is declared.

Class (ii): contains the results of expressions E, which are values (names) created either by generators in E, or resulting from slices, selections or coercions of such values. (Again, this class of results is recursively defined.) Such results are said to have a generator as origin; in other words, the results are obtained without passing through a block $\underline{sid}_j$. It should be clear that calls and formulae cause a new range to be entered (new block to be put on the range stack). Their results fall into one of the two classes for that range.

According to the classification above, for the processes of marking and updating, only those names are to be considered in $M_{in,j}$, which have no external activation block (results of class (ii)) and which have an external activation block which is unstacked before these values are used (results of a subclass of (i)).

The last case occurs in the following example:

$$yy := (\underline{ref}\ \underline{real}\ xx := \underline{real} := 3.14;\ xx) +:= (\ldots;6.28)$$

The range where xx is declared is left before the name created by the generator "$\underline{real}$" disappears from the wo-stack. Suppose a garbage collection takes place during the elaboration of the part of the program represented by dots; this name has no external activation block.

For all the other names there is no marking process to be done, but a simple updating process. The updating process is simple because only the pointer representing a name is to be updated and there is no tracing of the list structure starting from that pointer (the modes of the names have not to be saved as tracing information). For the updating process of such names, one needs as information only the indication permitting to detect names on the wo-stack; this can be done by a bit table or an address table, if no extra bit is available.

The main problem is now to detect at compile-time the maximum number of cases for which no garbage collection information has to be stored in $M_{in,j}$. In a way analogous to [9] this compile-time detection can be done by using a simulated wo-stack dealing with information, such as the origin of the values, their modes and their block number in case their origin is an identifier.

CONCLUDING REMARKS

There exist three language design principles which are characteristic of ALGOL 68 and which have served as guide lines in the construction of a scheme of storage allocation and garbage collection:
  (i) the implementation of general *hardware considerations* in the language
  (ii) the great amount of *static information* (e.g., the mode) on the values of a program
  (iii) the *storage control* (stack or heap) by program directives ("*loc*" and "*heap*").

In the storage allocation, the principles (i) and (ii) seem to work satisfactorily. The principle (iii) gives rise to a problem: i.e., there exist three cases where intrinsically, storage space, although specified as local in the program, cannot be stack controlled.

The critical point in the garbage collection is the application of the principle (ii) when the access block is on the working stack; one should dispose of a table $M_{in,j}$ minimized by taking utmost advantage of the static information in the program.

REFERENCES

[1] Van Wijngaarden, A. (ed.), Mailloux, B.J., Peck, J.E.L., Koster, C.H.A., *Report on the algorithmic language ALGOL 68*, MR 101, Mathematisch Centrum, Amsterdam, February 1969.
[2] Mailloux, B.J., *On the implementation of ALGOL 68*, Mathematisch Centrum, Amsterdam, 1968.
[3] Randell, B. and Russell, L.J., *ALGOL 68 implementation*, Academic Press, 1964.
[4] Hoare, C.A.R., *Record handling, in programming languages* (F.Genuys, ed.) Academic Press, 1968.
[5] Schorr, G. and Waite, W., *An efficient machine-independent procedure for garbage collection in various list structures*, CACM, August 1967.
[6] Wodon, P., *Methods of garbage collection for ALGOL 68*, MBLE Research Laboratory, Brussels, April 1970.
[7] Branquart, P. and Lewi, J., *On object language and storage allocation in AL-*

GOL 68 *compilers*, "*Proceedings of an informal conference on ALGOL* 68 *implementation*", J.E.L. Peck (ed.), University of British Columbia, Vancouver 1969.
[8] Branquart, P. and Lewi, J., *On the implementation of local names in ALGOL 68*, R121, M.B.L.E. Research Laboratory, Brussels, November 1969.
[9] Samelson, K. and Bauer, F., *Sequential formula translation*, Comm. ACM, February 1960.
[10] Floyd, R.W., *An algorithm for coding efficient arithmetic operations*, Comm. ACM, January 1961.
[11] Branquart, P. and Lewi, J., *Local generators and the ALGOL* 68 *working stack*, Note N62, MBLE Research Laboratory, Brussels, April 1970.
[12] Haddon, B.K. and Waite, W.M., *A compaction procedure for variable-length storage elements*, The computer Journal, August 1967.

DISCUSSION

Lindsey:
What happens when some values have been put on the working stack during the evaluation of an expression, and a local-generator is then encountered in the expression

Branquart:
If you look at the possible constructions of the language, you can see that there are only two cases where a local-generator may be elaborated when the dynamic working stack is not empty; these cases are the collateral clauses and the assignments. In both cases, it is possible to elaborate the constituent generators beforehand, and so to eliminate the difficulty of merging the dynamic part of the working stack and the local-generator stack.

Koster:
I have a question about the relationship between the lengths of $\underline{sid}_i$ and $\underline{max}_i$. Probably you elaborate your declarations more or less from left to right and there may be some collaterality involved. That means, that if you have not had all of your declarations yet, $\underline{max}_i$ might be slightly shorter, since it has to be only the maximum up to that point.

Branquart:
No, you have to reserve the maximum size for $\underline{sid}_i$ and $\underline{max}_i$ of the range R_i as soon as it is entered; the reason is that the first declaration you elaborate in this range may give rise to a dynamic part on $\underline{did}_i$.

Trilling:
During the elaboration of a recursive procedure you have to reserve $\underline{max}_i$ each time and this could be inefficient.

Branquart:
You can also reserve space for the whole static working stack, this can be less expensive in some cases, but anyway, you get troubles with re-

cursivities for which the maximum size of the working stack cannot be foreseen. An advantage of this solution is that the values of the working stack can then be addressed by means of absolute machine addresses; this balances somewhat the inefficiencies inherent to recursivities; anyway, it is difficult to say which solution is better.

Mailloux:

The first comment I should make is that, although you attribute this idea to me, I actually got it from Paul in 1964, and I believe he got it from Samelson. This is important, because if you have a machine, as most of us do, which does not have an accumulator stack built into its hardware, then its simulation is a fantastically expensive business.

Branquart:

I should like to insist a bit more on the storage of the descriptors of slices and rowed coercends referred to by names. It is easy to understand why such descriptors can generally not be stored on the stack; an obvious solution is to store them on the heap. But this would imply heap organization and garbage collection even for programs of numerical analysis, as soon as they use slices or rowed-coercends. A solution avoiding the use of the heap, consists in associating the descriptor with the name and not with the multiple value itself. This solution is based on the following considerations:

1) Associating the descriptor of a value referred to by a name with the name implies copying this descriptor with each instance of the name in the memory. This is possible when the descriptor cannot change when an assignment is made to the name, otherwise, all instances of the descriptor should have to be changed at once, when an assignation is elaborated, and this is practically unfeasible.

2) A descriptor can only be changed when the name referring to it is strongly dynamic, in this case there should be only one instance of the descriptor. Fortunately, no slices nor rowed coercends may give rise to strongly dynamic names.

The solution is now the following:
- The memory space reserved for storing a name of mode $\underline{ref}\,[\ldots]\,\ldots$ consists of a pointer space and a descriptor space.
- When the name is not strongly dynamic, the descriptor is stored in the descriptor space of the name at each instance of this name in memory, so, if the name comes from a slice or a rowed-coercend, there is no problem for storing the corresponding descriptor.

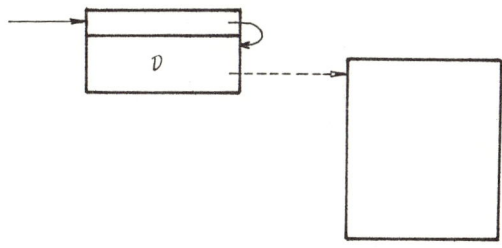

- When the name is strongly dynamic, there can only be one instance of the descriptor, and the descriptor space of the name is unused:

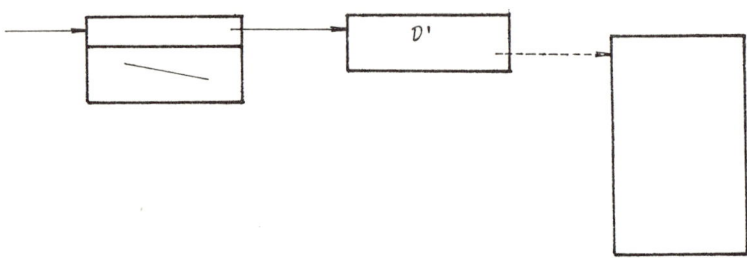

given that there are no strongly dynamic names issued from slices or rowed coercends, the problems of storing their descriptors is nonexistent.

This solution has drawbacks:
- Reserving descriptor spaces is space consuming.
- Copying the descriptor at each instance of the name is time consuming, but it is possible to avoid the copy in case the name is not issued from a slice or a rowed-coercend, by adopting the solution of strongly dynamic names in those cases.
- At each assignation of a name of mode $\underline{ref}$ [...] ... to a name of mode $\underline{ref}\,\underline{ref}$ [...] ... a dynamic check is needed in order to determine if the descriptor has to be copied or not.

The advantage of the solution is clear, it avoids the use of the heap for programs which contain neither global names nor strongly dynamic names and so facilitates the implementation of the corresponding sublanguage.

Bekič:

Can you say again precisely what you mean by a strongly dynamic name? May I repeat what I have understood? A strongly dynamic name is a subname of a flexible name, is this true?

Branquart:

No, a strongly dynamic name is a name referring to a value, the dynamic part of which is not frozen at the creation of the name. There are two cases where strongly dynamic names are created: when the corresponding generator contains the $\underline{flex}$ feature, or when it begins with $\underline{union}$ and may give rise to dynamic parts for the value referred to by the name.

Bekič:

So strongly dynamic names are just names which correspond with flexible locations, i.e., flexible arrays and unions?

Branquart:

Yes, that is right.

Koster:

The scheme you present is very complex. It is much more complex than that which we are used to in the case of ALGOL 60. Now have you, in

Branquart:

In most cases we can state that the run time efficiency of an ALGOL 68 program, equivalent to an ALGOL 60 program, will be better. The only price you have to pay for the generality of ALGOL 68 is in the block organization; the so-called link-data are a bit more complicated, but this does not influence very much the general efficiency of the programs.

Mailloux:

I am not sure if I have understood the situation exactly. Your problem, I think, is that on your identifier stack there may be some pointers into the rest of this stuff which, at a given point, may or may not be filled in. I was just wondering if there is some reason why you might not, as soon as you enter a block, fill in all pointers in this block with nil, or some special nil.

Branquart:

This is not exactly the point; of course, initializing the pointers of the static identifier stack with a special nil or putting some special bit in it solves your problem. My point is the following: suppose you have to start the garbage collection at the moment when a pointer to the heap is on the working stack. There are two possibilities:

a) The pointer has been obtained through an identifier declared in a range which has not been left at the moment of the garbage collection; this pointer has to be updated, but no tracing starting from it has to be performed, given that this tracing is already done starting from the identifier stack.

b) The range where the identifier has been declared has been left at the moment of the garbage collection, or the pointer is issued from a generator the name of which has neither yet been assigned nor made to be possessed by an identifier; in these cases, the pointer has not only to be updated but the tracing has to take this pointer as starting address; hence, such a pointer has to be provided with garbage collection information, and this is rather inefficient. But such cases are very scarce and the compiler should detect them in order to store tracing information only when strictly needed. This can be done by means of a simulated working stack at compile time.

Mailloux:

Yes, that is right! I thought you were also concerned about the identifier stack pointing further down into the stack. A second question; considering the following example:

ref [ ] *real* $a, b;\ a := [\ 1:10\ ]\ real$;

$b := a[\ 2:8@2\ ];\ a := b;\ b := a[\ 3:?@3\ ]$

where we have a *ref* to vector, like a or b, which must be stored in two parts, a pointer and a descriptor. Now all I am suggesting is that the pointer part is going to be of no use to you since in general you are going to have the descriptor part there anyway. If you look what happens dynamically in a program like this, then you can never be sure whether indeed the pointer or whether the descriptor is to be there and therefore you may as well have the descriptor there. That is not quite what I wanted to say. What I want to say is the following: in the assignation $a := b$, you may not let a point to the descriptor which you created at b, because in the next assignation you are going to change it.

Branquart:

Let us elaborate your example and see what happens in the memory.

After having elaborated *ref* [ ] *real* a, b; we have reserved space for pointers and descriptors

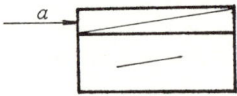

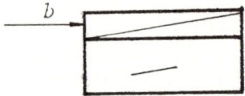

after $a := [\,1:10\,]$ *real*; $b := a[\,2:8\,\underline{at}\,2\,]$; space has been reserved for 10 elements

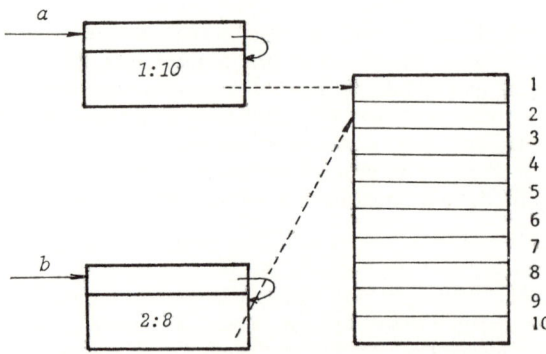

and after $a := b$; $b := a[\,3:7\,\underline{at}\,3\,]$ we have the following situation:

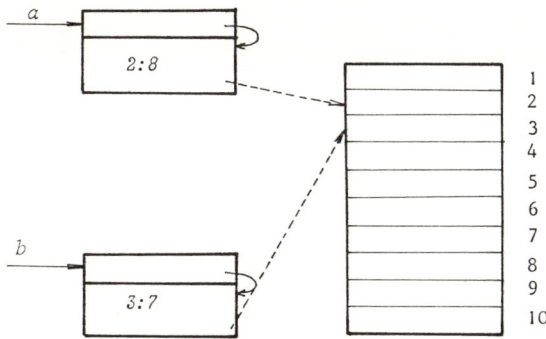

Bekič:

Let us first distinguish between fixed and flexible array names, if it is clear what that means. So flexible array names are flexible in at least one bound, etc. and you may say that with a fixed array name the descriptor is part of it. This clearly reflects your picture, because it is really part of the name, not of the multiple value. On the other hand, the descriptor cannot be part of the flexible name, at least not the current descriptor. This must really be part of the value being referred to. I think that your implementation, as far as I can see from those diagrams, corresponds with this.

van der Poel:

If I understood you correctly this is not meant for dealing with parallel-clauses, because in the case of parallel-clauses you can have a tree-like stack. You have not dealt with that problem?

Branquart:

No, we have not considered that problem.

van der Poel:

We have some experience ourselves with arranging a stack in a linked-like fashion, that is where elements are not placed in consecutive locations, but are linked. Indications are that in a machine which has no built-in stack operations this is almost as efficient. Have you thought about that scheme? Then you can treat everything, stack and heap in the same fashion and you can deal with it by the garbage collector which is called in more frequently than in the case with a real stack, but it works very well. We have an implementation of another language where we have actually done it.

Branquart:

If you have the experience and if you tell me that it is as efficient, I can trust you.

van der Poel:

You can then deal with the parallel-clauses as well. You have no restriction whatsoever and you can place everything into the same kind of storage.

Branquart:

We did not elaborate such a solution because we thought it was less efficient than the classical one.

van der Poel:

A little bit.

AN ALGOL 68 GARBAGE COLLECTOR [†]

S. MARSHALL
Kiewit Computation Center, Hanover, New Hampshire

AN ALGOL 68 GARBAGE COLLECTOR

A garbage collector generally has three parts: a marking part where all words that can be referenced by the program are marked, a compacting part where all marked words are moved to a contiguous block, and a pointer adjustment part where all pointers are modified to refer to the new locations of the marked words. For this ALGOL 68 garbage collector, free memory consists of a linear array of words which contains data structures. A data structure is a concatenation of data elements. Data elements are either primitive elements and are not pointers or are data descriptors and contain a pointer word followed immediately by zero or more index quadruples. Pointer words contain in their address field a pointer to the first word of a data structure and in their tag field a pointer to a pattern describing the data structure. The index quadruple contains four words called L_i, the lower bound; U_i, the upper bound; D_i, the stride; and P_i, the place. (The place word is used only by the garbage collector and is assumed to be initially zero.) A data descriptor refers to a collection of identical data structures each described by the pattern referred to by the pointer word. If n is the number of index quadruples in the data descriptor, then the location of a particular data structure can be found as follows: let $(X_1, X_2, \ldots, X_n)$ be a vector satisfying $0 \leq X_i \leq U_i - L_i$ where i runs from 1 to n, then let $K = \Sigma_i X_i D_i$. The addresses of all the data structures referred to by the descriptor can be found by adding all possible values of K to the data structure pointer word. If the number of index quadruples is zero then only one data structure is referenced. If any lower bound is greater than the corresponding upper bound then no data structures are referenced.

A pattern is a list of data specification words followed by a pattern terminator word. Primitive data elements are specified by a zero and descriptors are specified by a $n+1$ where n is the number of index quintuples followed by $4n$ zeros. A pattern terminator word contains minus the number of data specification words in the pattern. It is therefore also equal to minus the number of words in the data structure specified by the pattern. A mark bit is assumed to be associated with every word to be garbage collected.

[†] This research was supported by the Advanced Research Projects Agency of the Department of Defense and was monitored by the Air Force Office of Scientific Research under Contract No. F44620-68-C-0015.

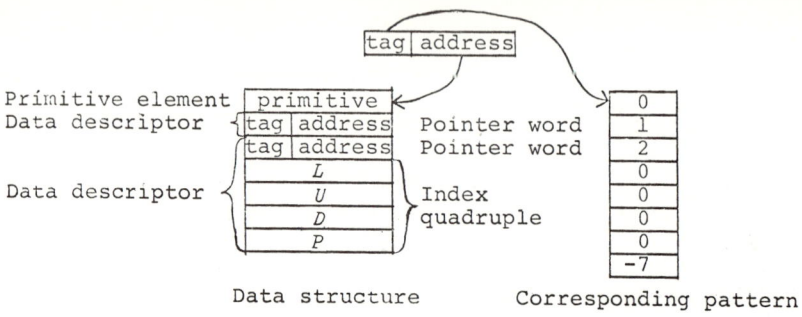

Data structure   Corresponding pattern

MARKING ALGORITHM

1. Set all mark bits to zero, set A to 0 and set B to point to the data structure to be marked. The address field of B points to the first word of the data structure and the tag field of B points to the corresponding pattern. B is a pointer word that points to the word under immediate consideration and A is a pointer word that points to a chain of reversed pointers that are constructed during the course of the marking algorithm.

2. If the address field of B points to a word that is already marked then go to step 8.

3. Mark the word pointed to by the address field of B.

4. Examine the contents of the pattern word pointed to by the tag field of B. If it is 0 then go to step 8. Otherwise B refers to a data descriptor and all the elements it refers to must be marked.

5. The address field of B refers to an array descriptor containing a pointer and $n-1$ index quadruples where n is the contents of the pattern word referred to by the tag field of B. If the lower bound in all of the index quadruples is less than or equal to the corresponding upper bound then continue. Otherwise, go to step 8.

6. Let C stand for the pointer word pointed to by the address field of B. Simultaneously put the contents of B in A, C in B, and A in C. This stores a reversed pointer in C. It will be restored in step 12.

7. Go to step 2 to mark the first data structure.

8. Increment both the address field and tag field of B by 1. This causes the address field to point to the next word in the data structure and the tag field to point to the corresponding pattern word.

9. If the contents of the pattern word pointed to by the tag field of B is not negative (is not the pattern terminator word) then go to step 2.

10. If A is zero then the marking algorithm is finished and all reversed pointers have been restored.

11. Increment both the address field and the tag field of B by the contents of the pattern terminator word pointed to by the tag field of B. This will restore both the address field and the tag field of B back to the beginning of the data structure and the pattern respectively.

12. Let C stand for the pointer word pointed to by the address field of A. Simultaneously put the contents of A in B, B in C, and C in A. This will restore the contents of the reversed pointer in C to its original value. (Compare with step 6.)

13. The address field of B refers to an array descriptor containing a pointer and $n-1$ index quadruples where n is the contents of the pattern word referred to by the tag field of B. If there is a quadruple then increment its P word by one. Also increment the address field of the pointer word by D. If P is now greater than $U-L$ then set P to zero, decrement the address field of the pointer word by $D(U-L+1)$, and repeat this step with the next index quadruple if it exists.

14. If there were no index quadruples or P in all index quadruples was set to zero, then go to step 8. Otherwise, go to step 6.

THE HADDON AND WAITE COMPACTING ALGORITHM [1]

Assume that a word can contain two addresses. The compacting algorithm proceeds from the bottom of memory to the top in the following manner:

Starting from the bottom find the next free word. Into this word store the address of the next following marked word and the address of the first unmarked word. Interchange the block of free memory and the next following block of marked memory. Continue in this way until there is no more marked memory. All of the marked words will now be compacted at the bottom of memory followed by a block of unmarked words containing old and new addresses of all blocks. After sorting these words in order, the new address of any marked word can be quickly found from the old address by table look-up. These words will be out of order only if the interchanging of marked and unmarked blocks changes the order of the unmarked block. This may happen if the interchange is made efficient.

In ALGOL 68 it is possible to construct an array descriptor that does not reference a solidly packed array of data structures. It would be a mistake to compress the elements of such an array because then index calculations would not come out right. This problem can be solved by solidly marking the interior of all arrays *after* the marking program is finished. This can be accomplished by altering step 14 of the marking algorithm to link up all array descriptors having at least one index quadruple in a chain and solidly marking these descriptors after the marking program terminates.

5	C		C		C		C		5,3
4	free		free		free		5,3		2,1
3	B		B		2,1		2,1		C
2	A		A		B		B		B
1	free		2,1		A		A		A

Picture of memory during compacting (A, B, C are marked)

PROOF OF THE MARKING ALGORITHM

It is the function of the program starting at step 2 to mark a piece of a data structure referred to by word B. This piece starts at the address referred to in B and continues to the end of the data structure. The tag field of B is assumed to point to the pattern specification word corresponding to the address field of B. Notice that if there are no pointers left in the pattern, the program marks all of the words left in the data structure in program steps 2, 3, 4, 8, and 9. When the data structure is done, step 10 checks to see if A indicates that the program is finished. The program therefore works if there are no descriptors. To mark all reachable data words when data descriptors are present it is necessary only to mark all data structures referred to by the descriptor. This marking may encounter further descriptors requiring this process to be interpreted recursively. If step 12 followed step 6 immediately, the effect is no operation. Notice that the effect of step 6 is to place in B a pointer to a data structure which is the next data structure to be marked. It also alters the contents of cell C but the mark bit of cell C was set to one in step 3, and the program never looks at a cell that is already marked. Notice that the action of step 6 never leaves the contents of A zero so step 10 will not indicate that the job is done. Step 11 restores the B pointer to its original value it had when this particular list element was first considered. Therefore, step 12 will correctly undo the effects of step 6 and we will be at the same state except for the setting of some mark bits. Since this is the case, the tag field indicates the type of descriptor referred to in B (i.e., the number of index quadruples) and the P's in the descriptor can be incremented to the next value with the proper modification of the pointer word. Since the pointer word was marked in step 3, this alteration does not affect anything. If step 13 resets to the beginning of the array, then the entire descriptor has been reset to its original state. When this happens, all of the elements of the array have been marked and step 8 correctly continues marking the data structure containing the descriptor.

There are some subtle points in the program. For example, it would be a mistake to mark an entire data structure and then follow the pointers contained in the data structure. The difficulty is that if the marker encountered the same data structure the second time through, it would be unable to distinguish the reversed pointer left behind the first time through and would attempt to follow it. Whenever a word has the mark bit on, either all words reachable from this word have been marked, or the program is in the process of marking these words. In either case, the marker can ignore marked words. It is also essential to mark words before marking the words reached from them. If this is not done, an unmarked reversed pointer may be encountered causing total calamity. The only restriction the garbage collector imposes on the list structure is that all pointers contain tags which refer to consistent patterns. This means that if an area of memory is referred to in one descriptor as a descriptor with index quadruples, then this area must always be referred to in this way. Also, primitive words must always be referenced as primitive words and never as descriptors. No other restrictions are imposed and a word may be referred to consistently as part of several different data structures of various lengths. If memory is to be compacted, then elements of an array cannot change their relative separation distance (arrays may not be solidly packed) and this can be accomplished by solidly marking the interior of all arrays; therefore, they are treated as a single block by the compacting routine.

POINTER ADJUSTMENT

After memory has been compacted, it is necessary to adjust all pointers so that they refer to the new location of all data structure. This is accomplished by modifying step 5 of the marking algorithm and executing it again. Step 5 is modified to read:

5. If all lower bounds in the data descriptor are less than or equal to the corresponding upper bounds, then the address field of B is adjusted so that it refers to the new location of the data structure rather than to the old. Then continue to step 6. Otherwise, go to step 8.

Since all pointer are encountered exactly once in step 5, this will correctly adjust all pointers in memory. A side effect of the pointer adjustment process is that an accurate mark table is constructed so that the memory allocator can use fragments of memory between the elements of arrays that are not closely packed.

REFERENCE

[1] Haddon, B. K. and Waite, W. M., A compaction procedure for variable-length storage elements, Computer J. 10, 2 (August 1967), pp. 162-165.

METHODS OF GARBAGE COLLECTION FOR ALGOL 68

P. L. WODON
MBLE, Res.Lab., Brussels

INTRODUCTION

The purpose of this working note is to sketch and compare different methods of garbage collection for ALGOL 68.

It is clear (see e.g. [2], [3]) that the form of a garbage collector depends on the properties of modes. Three of them are particularly important:
(i) a mode may be declared in a program, (ii) each value has a mode and (iii) a mode declaration may be recursive.

Property (i) means that the garbage collector cannot be completely constructed beforehand: it must be tailored to the needs of each program.

Property (ii) means that the compiler is indeed able to do so, at least partially, at compile time. This may be done either in the form of a table (table of "templates" in [3]) to be interpreted by a general routine or in the form of a set of compiled routines as in [2].

Property (iii) means that the garbage collector will be of a recursive nature and therefore that dynamically generated information will have to be stored during its execution.

A garbage collector must fulfil two obvious requirements: it must collect all or almost all the garbage and be as quick as possible. Apart from that, the ideal garbage collector should not decrease the efficiency of the programs which do not call it and should not use a too large and/or unpredictable storage area for its own purpose. As usual, there are conflicts between these four requirements and a compromise must be found.

Unfortunately, hardware characteristics have a great influence on the relative efficiency, and sometimes even the practical feasibility, of the various compromises. Furthermore, a good solution may also depend on so far unavailable statistical data about the use of ALGOL 68.

We are going to deal with a heap of the most general form in direct access memory. It does not seem that the ALGOL 68 heap can be efficiently accommodated in a secondary store, although some general indications can be given. Similarly, it does not seem that general purpose heap organization and garbage collection can be made satisfactory for special purpose problems which manipulate a great amount of data of a limited number of types, especially if a secondary store is used. It is very likely that, within ALGOL 68, one must look to pragmats and transputs for solving that kind of problems.

1. FORM OF THE HEAP

The heap contains three parts: the available space, i.e. that part of it known to be free for storing values, the active space, consisting of all accessible locations, and the garbage. The two latter parts are necessarily intermixed but the available space may be a contiguous memory area, a structure of holes or even a list of free pages.

Before discussing how the garbage collector can trace and mark all accessible locations and reconstruct the available space, we briefly describe the kind of things that are in the heap. It will be a somewhat simplified but still realistic picture based on [2].

We call "cell" the smallest directly addressable memory unit. By "location", we mean a block of contiguous cells in which is stored a non-multiple value or a descriptor. Multiple values are supposed to be stored, element by element, in contiguous locations.

In this fashion, to each mode, there corresponds exactly one "type" of location of a specific and fixed size and form, depending on the mode only. By "description" of a location, we mean the static (i.e. known at compile time) information on its type, relevant for the garbage collector.

If we forget for a moment that there are structured modes, we have four different classes of descriptions, respectively corresponding to 'reference to MODE', 'ROWS NONROW', 'UNITED' and any other mode, except 'structured with FIELDS'.

We assume that all pointers occupy the same amount of memory, i.e. one cell, so that the description of a location corresponding with 'ref to MODE' must contain the flag "pointer" and an indication permitting to retrieve the description of 'MODE'.

To 'ROWS NONROW', there corresponds a type of location big enough to contain a descriptor of the multiple value, and not the multiple value itself. Its description consists of the flag "descriptor", an indication of the description for 'NONROW' and the size of the location, which probably depends on the number of dimensions.

To process the complete array, the garbage collector must also know the number of elements and the address of the first one. In general, these are dynamic informations depending on elaboration. We shall assume that, in a location for a descriptor, the first cell contains a pointer to the elements and the second cell the number of elements. Since these informations must be present anyhow, it is not forbidden to suppose that they are in this form.

It is clear that slices must be handled in a special fashion. To start with, we will simply admit that the descriptor of a slice also contains the address of the first element and the number of elements of the complete array and that the latter is completely traced and marked.

To a mode 'UNITED', where no constituent mode is itself 'UNITED' (we can certainly assume that), there corresponds a type of location with a size large enough to contain any value of the constituent modes. Its description contains the flag "united" and the size. To process the location, the garbage collector must know the actual type corresponding to the actual value of the location. This last information is dynamic and we suppose that it is contained in the first cell of the location.

For any other mode, except 'structured with FIELDS', the corresponding type contains the flag "plain" and the location size. The garbage collector is not interested in the contents, called here "plain values", of such locations.

It remains to describe types corresponding to 'structured with FIELDS'. A location for a structured value simply is the contiguous juxtaposition of locations for its fields so that its description may simply be an enumeration of simpler descriptions. Then, the description corresponding to e.g. the mode '*struct* ($a\,a$, *struct* ($b\,b$, $c\,c$)d)' is practically the same as that for '*struct* ($a\,a, b\,b, c\,c$)'. We shall take advantage of this and ignore (or develop) structures inside structures. This permits to avoid useless recursivities within the garbage collector and it will be seen that the case where a pointer points to a subvalue of a structured value is taken care of, provided that the inside modes have their own descriptions. A possible inconvenient is that type descriptions are no more isomorphic to modes.

2. TRACING THE ACTIVE SPACE

2.1. *General remarks*.

The active space is traced in order to be marked. Obviously, both things must be done together but, for facility, they are discussed separately.

Tracing starts from known locations (in the stack) with known types. The problems this raises are discussed in [2]. In order to proceed, the tracing routine must know, as "forwards informations", the address of a location and its description. The address is contained in the location just left. The description (i.e. any number permitting to retrieve it) could be attached to the address or contained at some fixed place in the location but this has obvious inconvenience and is unnecessary since it can be obtained from the description of the location just left.

In general, when a location is left for another one, through e.g. a pointer, it is not completely marked and must be traced back. This means that "backwards information" has to be memorized: an address, a description and what is left to be marked. This dynamically generated information must be dynamically stored and the easiest way of doing it is on a stack (see [2]).

Of course, it is not very advisable to use an unpredictable amount of storage when the garbage collector is activated. An alternative method (see [3]) is to store the backwards information in the locations themselves. Room must be reserved for that purpose and this amounts to reserving in advance room (too much in general) for a "split up stack".

We shall give examples of both techniques, using two forms of type descriptions: a table and a set of compiled tracing routines.

2.2. *A table-driven tracing routine which uses a stack*.

The following example is meant to isolate the main features that any tracing routine must have. In particular, we want to find out what are the minimum forwards and backwards informations that are needed at each step.

To simplify, any value is considered as a structure with one or more fields and we suppose that a plain value uses one cell. Any cell in the heap contains either a plain value or a pointer ('a') or the number of elements of a multiple value ('*nmax*') or the current type ('*ct*') of the value in a location of "united" type.

The location descriptions are in a table built up by the compiler from the modes. For an n-cell type of location, there are n+1 entries in the table.

This is summarized by the following piece of ALGOL 68 text. (Some liberty with the language has been taken: conformity relations are not used where they should be.)

mode cell = *union (pointer, descrip, united, bits)*;

mode pointer = *struct (int a)*;

mode descrip = *struct (int nmax)*;

mode united = *struct (int ct)*; *comment*

although not strictly necessary, the use of unions and structures clarifies somewhat the reading because a mnemonic name is used for the fields

co

[1:1 *flex*] *cell* M := *comment*.

the store, stack and heap, as it is when garbage collection is activated

co;

mode type = *struct (string tag, int index)*;

[1:1 *flex*] *type* D := *comment*

the table of descriptions as built up by the compiler for the particular program. The way this table 'D' is formed may be understood with an example. If we suppose that the modes used in a program are '*int*', '*person*' = '(*int* age, *ref person* father)', '*ref int*', '[,]*int*' and '*union(person, int)*', the table is as follows:

	'tag'	'index'	
1	"plain"	skip	*int*
2	"last"	1	
3	"plain"	skip	
4	"pointer"	3	*person*
5	"last"	2	
6	"pointer"	1	*ref int*
7	"last"	1	

8	"descriptor"	1	
9	"plain"	skip	[,] _int_
10	"plain"	skip	
11	"last"	3	
12	"united"	skip	
13	"plain"	skip	_union_, (_int_, _person_)
14	"plain"	skip	
15	"last"	3	

When the tag is "plain" or "united", the index is irrelevant. When the tag is "pointer", the index is the address, in the table, of the description of the location pointed to. When the tag is "descriptor", the index is the address, in the table, of the description for an array element. When the tag is "last", the index is the size of the location and the table-entry does not correspond to a cell of the location. The descriptor is supposed to need 3 cells.

co; proc stack = (int i) : comment

this routine puts an integer on a stack

co; proc unstack = int : comment

this routine delivers the top element of the stack

co; proc mark = (int a) : comment

this routine marks the cell with address 'a'

co; proc marked = (int a) bool : comment

this routine checks if the cell with address 'a' is already marked

co;

int ad, type; comment

current address and type of the location being marked

co int A, T, N; comment

working registers for an address, a type and a number of array elements

co

next trace : comment

the routine starts from a pointer or a descriptor in a known area (this is discussed in [2]). This pointer or descriptor has a known description with address θ in D and points to a location in the heap with address α and type description θ' = index of D[θ]

<u>co</u>

ad := α; type := θ';

<u>if</u> tag <u>of</u> θ = "descriptor" <u>then</u> stack (0) <u>fi</u>;

stack (0); stack (θ);

start : <u>if</u> tag <u>of</u> D[type] = "last" <u>then</u>

T := unstack; A := unstack;

<u>if</u> tag <u>of</u> D[T] = "pointer" <u>then</u> backwards

<u>elsf</u> tag <u>of</u> D[T] = "descriptor" <u>then</u> next elem

<u>elsf</u> tag <u>of</u> D[T] = "united" <u>then</u> complete <u>fi</u>

<u>fi</u>;

<u>if</u> marked (ad) <u>then</u> next <u>else</u> mark (ad) <u>fi</u>;

<u>if</u> tag <u>of</u> D[type] = "plain" <u>then</u> next

<u>elsf</u> tag <u>of</u> D[type] = "pointer" <u>then</u> pointer

<u>elsf</u> tag <u>of</u> D[type] = "descriptor" <u>then</u> array

<u>elsf</u> tag <u>of</u> D[type] = "united" <u>then</u> union <u>fi</u>;

next : ad +:= 1; type +:= 1; start; <u>comment</u>

the location and its description are scanned in parallel

<u>co</u>

pointer : <u>if</u> a <u>of</u> M[ad] = <u>nil</u> <u>then</u> next <u>fi</u>;

forwards : stack (ad); stack (type);

ad := a <u>of</u> M[ad];

type := index <u>of</u> D[type];

start;

backwards : <u>if</u> A = 0 <u>then</u> next trace <u>else</u> ad := A; type := T;

next <u>fi</u>;

array   : <u>if</u> *nmax* <u>of</u> M[*ad+1*] = 0 <u>then</u> *next* <u>else</u>

              stack (0); forwards <u>fi</u>;

next elem : N := *unstack* + 1;

            <u>if</u> N < *nmax* <u>of</u> M[A+1] <u>then</u>

              stack (N); stack (A); stack (T);

              type := *index* <u>of</u> D[T];

              start

            <u>else</u> *backwards* <u>fi</u>;

union   : *stack (ad); stack (type);*

            type := *ct* <u>of</u> M[*ad*]; *ad* +:= 1;

            start;

complete : *type* := T + 1 + *index* <u>of</u> D [*type*];

            start;

This rather crude method permits to see (as pointed out and discussed in [2]) that tracing need not, in principle, require that extra information be put in the locations. All information used by the tracing routine either is already present in any location or can be gathered at compile time from the modes and put in the location descriptions.

The method also shows the kind of backwards information that needs to be memorized when a pointer, a descriptor or a union is met: namely an address-type pair plus a number of already processed elements in the case of a descriptor. It is worth noting that the information concerning what is left to be marked is included in the address-type pair, thanks to the description entries tagged "last".

There are obvious practical improvements to the method. For example, a pointer to a location containing only plain values should have a special tag and the index should indicate the size of the location. This would save one step of recursivity and shorten the table. Similar remarks apply to descriptors and unions.

2.3. *A table-driven tracing routine without stack.*

If, instead of using a stack, we wish to store the backwards information in the location themselves, we must find room for it. It is certainly sound to store the number of already traced array elements in the descriptor. It is possible to store the backwards address where the forwards pointer was stored. This is the technique, proposed in [5], of reversing pointers. But we need extra room for storing a type.

The example of tracing routine which we now give assumes that a pointer is contained in a cell and that, in the same cell, there are enough extra bits to store a type indication. This is an assumption whose workability depends on the size of an address, the size of a cell and the size of the description table. The latter has the same form as before but it is clear that it may be shortened in a practical implementation.

One could also use two cells for a pointer but it is certainly inadvisable.

The principle of the tracing routine is again outlined in an ALGOL 68 piece of text whose general structure is exactly the same as the one above.

mode cell = *union (pointer, descrip, united, bits);*

mode pointer = *struct (int t, int a) comment*

the field 't' represents the spare room, in a cell, suitable for storing a type

co; mode descrip = *struct (int n, int nmax) comment*

the field 'n' represents the place, in a descriptor, where the number of already traced elements may be stored

co; mode united = *struct (int ct) comment*

we suppose that the current type is stored in a cell and therefore that we are able to store a type and a pointer in the same cell.

The declarations for 'M', 'D', 'mark' and 'marked' are as before. We need the following registers

co;

int ad, type, A, T; pointer status comment

'status' will contain the backwards information of the location just left (i.e. figure the top of a stack). It is in the latter location that is stored the backwards information for the still preceding location, etc.

co;

next trace : ad := α; type := θ';

if tag of θ = "descriptor" then comment

put '0' at the right place in the descriptor from which the routine starts tracing

co fi;

status := (θ, 0);

```
start : if tag of D[type] = "last" then
            if tag of D[t of status] = "pointer" then backwards
            elsf tag of D[t of status] = "descriptor" then next elem
            elsf tag of D[t of status] = "united" then complete
            fi fi;
        if marked (ad) then next else mark (ad) fi;

        if tag of D[type] = "plain" then next
        elsf tag of D[type] = "pointer" then pointer
        elsf tag of D[type] = "descriptor" then array
        elsf tag of D[type] = "united" then union fi;

next : ad +:= 1; type +:= 1; start;

pointer  : if a of M[ad] = nil then next fi;
forwards : A := a of M[ad]; M[ad] := status;
           status := (type, ad);
           type := index of D[type]; ad := A;
           start;
backwards : if a of status = 0 then next trace fi;
            A := ad; T := type;
            ad := a of status; type := t of status;
            status := M[ad];
            M[ad] := (skip, A - index of D[T]) comment
```
here the forwards pointer is reestablished, using the location size
```
            co; next;

array     : if nmax of M[ad + 1] = 0 then next else
            n of M[ad + 1] := 0; forwards fi;
next elem : n of M[a of status + 1] +:= 1;
```

$$\underline{if}\ n\ \underline{of}\ M[a\ \underline{of}\ status\ +\ 1]\ <\ nmax\ \underline{of}\ M[a\ \underline{of}\ status\ +\ 1]$$

$$\underline{then}\ type\ :=\ index\ \underline{of}\ D[t\ \underline{of}\ status];\ start\ \underline{fi};$$

$$\underline{if}\ a\ \underline{of}\ status\ =\ 0\ \underline{then}\ next\ trace\ \underline{fi};$$

$$A\ :=\ ad;\ T\ :=\ type;$$

$$ad\ :=\ a\ \underline{of}\ status;\ type\ :=\ t\ \underline{of}\ status;$$

$$status\ :=\ M[ad];$$

$$M[ad]\ :=\ (\underline{skip},\ A\ -\ nmax\ \underline{of}\ M[ad\ +\ 1]\ \times\ index\ \underline{of}\ D[T]);$$

$$next;$$

union : $T\ :=\ ct\ \underline{of}\ M[ad];\ M[ad]\ :=\ status;$

$$status\ :=\ (type,\ ad);$$

$$type\ :=\ T;\ ad\ +:=\ 1;$$

$$start;$$

complete : $A\ :=\ a\ \underline{of}\ status;\ T\ :=\ type;$

$$type\ :=\ t\ \underline{of}\ status\ +\ 1\ +\ index\ \underline{of}\ D[T];$$

$$status\ :=\ M[A];$$

$$M[A]\ :=\ (\underline{skip},\ T\ -\ index\ \underline{of}\ D[T]);$$

$$start;$$

Again, this is a rather crude sketch which admits obvious improvements. In any case, it is clear that this method will be slower than the preceding one. One can also imagine an intermediate way: backwards address stored into locations and backwards types on a stack.

2.4. *Compiled tracing routines without stack.*

Instead of putting the descriptions of the locations into a table, the compiler, when processing the modes, may insert them directly into the tracing routines. This is the method in [2]. We give here an example which does not use a stack. It is in fact still the same example, except that types are now materialized by labels, i.e. return addresses. In practice, these addresses may be put in a table and a table index stored in the locations in order to minimize the number of bits occupied by a description.

We will show, using texts in ALGOL 68, how a tracing routine may be compiled. No table 'D' is used and the memory 'M' is as before, except for

$$mode\ pointer\ =\ struct\ (string\ r,\ int\ a);$$

GARBAGE COLLECTION FOR ALGOL 68

The field 'r' again represents the place where the backwards type is stored. It is only for description facility that we suppose it a string. We also suppose an operator '<u>lab</u>' which transforms a string into a program label. The working registers that are needed by the complete set of tracing routines are the following:

int ad, A, size;

string type, T;

pointer status := ("next trace", 0);

Then, to each type of location, there will correspond a compiled tracing routine, constituted as outlined below for a location of type "t1" and size 'n1':
At the beginning, insert, to represent the address of the routine:

<u>lab</u> "t1" :

If the ith field contains a plain value, supposed to use one cell, insert:

mark (ad) ; ad +:= 1;

If the ith field contains a pointer to a location of type "t2", insert:

<u>if</u> marked (ad) <u>then</u> <u>lab</u> "t1$_i$" <u>fi</u>;

mark (ad);

<u>if</u> a <u>of</u> M[ad] = <u>nil</u> <u>then</u> <u>lab</u> "t1$_i$" <u>fi</u>;

A := a <u>of</u> M[ad] ; M[ad] := status;

status := ("backt1$_i$", ad);

ad := A;

<u>lab</u> "t2";

<u>lab</u> "backt1$_i$" : <u>if</u> a <u>of</u> status = 0 <u>then</u> next trace <u>fi</u>;

                    A := ad; ad := a <u>of</u> status;

                    status := M[ad];

                    M[ad] := (<u>skip</u>, A - size);

<u>lab</u> "t1$_i$" :   ad +:= 1;

If the ith field is a descriptor (supposed to use d_i cells) to an array of elements of mode "t2", insert:

$\underline{if}$ marked (ad) $\underline{then}$ $\underline{lab}$ "t1$_i$" $\underline{fi}$;

$\underline{for}$ j $\underline{from}$ ad $\underline{to}$ ad + d_i-1 $\underline{do}$ mark(j);

$\underline{if}$ nmax $\underline{of}$ M[ad + 1] = 0 $\underline{then}$ $\underline{lab}$ "t1$_i$" $\underline{fi}$;

n $\underline{of}$ M[ad + 1] := 0;

A := a $\underline{of}$ M[ad]; M[ad] := status;

status := ("backt1$_i$", ad);

ad := A;

$\underline{lab}$ "t2";

$\underline{lab}$ "backt1$_i$" : n $\underline{of}$ M[a $\underline{of}$ status + 1] +:= 1;

$\quad\quad\quad$ $\underline{if}$ n $\underline{of}$ M[a $\underline{of}$ status + 1] < nmax $\underline{of}$ M[a $\underline{of}$ status + 1] $\underline{then}$

$\quad\quad\quad\quad\quad$ $\underline{lab}$ "t2" $\underline{fi}$;

$\quad\quad\quad$ $\underline{if}$ a $\underline{of}$ status = 0 $\underline{then}$ next trace $\underline{fi}$;

$\quad\quad\quad$ A := ad; ad := a $\underline{of}$ status;

$\quad\quad\quad$ status := M[ad];

$\quad\quad\quad$ M[ad] := ($\underline{skip}$, A - size × nmax $\underline{of}$ M[ad + 1]);

$\underline{lab}$ "t1$_i$" : ad +:= d_i;

If the ith field contains a "united" value (supposed to use u_i cells), insert:

$\quad\quad\quad$ $\underline{if}$ marked (ad) $\underline{then}$ $\underline{lab}$ "t1$_i$" $\underline{fi}$;

$\quad\quad\quad$ mark (ad);

$\quad\quad\quad$ T := ct $\underline{of}$ M[ad]; M[ad] := status;

$\quad\quad\quad$ status := ("backt1$_i$", ad);

$\quad\quad\quad$ ad +:= 1;

$\quad\quad\quad$ $\underline{lab}$ T;

$\underline{lab}$ "backt1$_i$" : A := a $\underline{of}$ status; status := M[A];

$\quad\quad\quad$ M[A] := ($\underline{skip}$, type);

$\quad\quad\quad$ $\underline{for}$ j $\underline{from}$ ad $\underline{to}$ A + u_i-1 $\underline{do}$ mark(j);

$\quad\quad\quad$ ad := A;

$\underline{lab}$ "t1$_i$" : ad +:= u_i;

At the end, insert:

size := *n1; type* := *"t1"*;

lab r *of status;*

Of course, developed like that, the tracing routine corresponding to a structure with 10 fields would look rather formidable. In fact, many parts of it may be replaced by non-recursive procedure calls.

2.5. *Discussion.*

If we try to imagine how these tracing routines may be actually implemented in machine code on a computer, then there are questions that come up, the answers to which usually depend on the hardware itself. For example: is there room enough in a cell to store a pointer and a type indication? If yes, can the latter be easily, i.e. quickly, obtained and transformed either into a jump or into a description address? It is certain that the overall efficiency of a garbage collection will very much depend on the answers, but we cannot say more.

Even if we think of a particular machine, it is difficult to evaluate in advance the comparative efficiency of different methods. We should need statistical data on the form of the heap and anyway too much depends on adequate bit-twisting. Ideally, one should experiment with all sound-looking methods.

There is still a point to make on the inherent recursivity of the methods: it is not quite true to say that recursivity is only allowed when strictly needed since, in fact, a location which contains only one pointer or descriptor need not be traced back. This remark is easy to implement when the recursivity uses a stack and when therefore nothing is changed in the locations themselves.

If, however, we erase forwards pointers to store backwards information, we must reestablish and therefore know the forwards pointers when tracing back. The above outlined methods can do that simply because, when going backwards, they come from the locations to be pointed at. In other words, they demand that a location containing e.g. only one pointer is included in the recursivity because its address will be needed and not because something has still to be marked in it or from it. Therefore, if we want a method which uses recursivity only when strictly needed without implementing it on a stack, backwards information stored in locations must not erase anything and special room must be provided for it. One may accept to append extra cells to locations containing at least two pointers and/or descriptors but it is perhaps more advisable to reserve dynamically this room elsewhere.

Still another kind of problem is raised by subarrays (slices). We have supposed that, when meeting a subarray, we mark completely the complete array. Of course, this is not necessary (see [2]) and only the first layer, so to speak, must be completely marked. This is discussed in [2], where a solution is given. There are other ones. For example, when meeting a subarray, we could trace and mark completely only the relevant elements and afterwards mark the first layer of the rest, indicating in the descriptor of the complete array that this has been done. Subsequent tracing in the same array may then unmark the first layer, do what it has to do and mark the first layer again.

3. MARKING THE ACTIVE SPACE

To mark the active space, one may mark either each cell of it or only each location. This is discussed in [4]. Let us simply recall that marking only each location imposes that the mark is put in an overhead to the location which must also contain the size of the location. This seems to forbid location marking for ALGOL 68 since any sublocation may also be a location.

With the current type of hardware, cell marking imposes the use of a bit table. Practically, this means that the routines 'mark(ad)' and 'marked(ad)' are rather inefficient. The idea of marking locations in an overhead should not be discarded too quickly, especially because the same overhead can be used to speed up the compacting routine quite a bit.

Of course, if we allow overheads to creep everywhere, about 50% of the heap will be occupied by them, which is certainly not acceptable. But we could, for example, give an overhead to any location which is not a field of a structure. Any pointer to a field would then be accompanied by a (small) index permitting to find the overhead of the structure. The execution would ignore that index but the garbage collector would use it.

Even if this method looks odd, it should be considered because it is possible and much more efficient in the case where mainly large structures are in the heap. For mainly small structures, the overall efficiency decreases rapidly because garbage collection is called more often. One could imagine compilers with both methods of marking (and compacting), with a possibility of choice. Of course, if locations have overheads, the tracing routine could use them with profit.

If marking is done in a bit table, the routine 'marked(ad)' can still be made efficient. For a cell containing a plain value, it need not be used. On the contrary, it must be used for a cell containing a pointer and it is advisable to use it for a descriptor or a union. In these cases, it is very likely that there is room enough in the cell itself to put another mark there, besides the one in the bit table. The routine 'marked(ad)' can thus make its test without looking in the bit table. This other mark, for example the sign bit, can be advantageously used and in any case erased during the compacting phase.

4. RECONSTRUCTION OF THE AVAILABLE SPACE

The various ways of reconstituting the available space are also discussed in [4]. We only recall the main points.

Reconstituting a list of holes is easily and quickly done, but this kind of available space slows down the execution of the program and, because of the generality of modes, it may eventually lead to a situation where the free store is a scattering of unusable small holes. It also imposes a fixed limit between the stack and the heap.

Paging the heap is a possibility which should be considered, although, at a first glance, the generality and the recursivity of modes do not make it simple to organize.

Compacting the accessible locations cannot be made in the simple fashion used for e.g. LISP 1.5 since locations are of any size. They must be all moved down (or up) and all pointers updated. Even so, compacting is the easiest solution.

Let s_i be the size of the ith hole. All accessible locations between hole i and hole $i + 1$ have to be moved down n_i cells, with

$$n_i = \sum_{j=1}^{i} s_j.$$

Any pointer p to data in this area must be replaced by $p - n_i$. The way this can be done is explained in [4] and [2]. Let us repeat that the numbers n_i can be easily computed from the bit table but that they must be stored somewhere. Since there are as many of them as there are holes, the latter may be used.

Finally, updating all pointers means that all pointers must be retrieved. For locations without overhead, this means that the tracing routines are called again. If there is an overhead, a much faster linear scan of the heap may be used.

5. CONCLUDING REMARKS

We have here written down a series of ideas about possible schemes of garbage collection. It certainly remains to discuss them and to confront them with reality.

As an example, some tracing and compacting methods are going rather a long way to avoid using a stack. Isn't it simpler, after all, to make room for that stack by sending something in secondary memory when garbage collection starts?

As another and important example, is the situation in which we have supposed the heap to be implemented, realistic enough?

ABSTRACT

This working paper collects a series of ideas about garbage collecting methods for ALGOL 68. Various methods of tracing the active space are sketched in order to illustrate the features that any tracing routine must have. The form and the reconstitution of the available space are briefly discussed. Some hypotheses have been made which are based on [2], where a complete description of one method of storage allocation and garbage collection can be found.

REFERENCES

[1] Branquart, P., Lewi, J.: *On object language and storage allocation*, Proc. of an Informal Conf. on ALGOL 68 Implementation, Univ. of British Columbia, 1969.
[2] Branquart, P., Lewi, J.: *A scheme of storage allocation and garbage collection for ALGOL 68*, these Proceedings.
[3] Fites, P.: *Storage organization and garbage collection in ALGOL 68*, Proc. of an Informal Conf. on ALGOL 68 Implementation, Univ. of British Columbia, 1969.
[4] Wodon, P. L.: *Data structure and storage allocation*, BIT 9-3, 1969.
[5] Schorr, H., Waite, W. M.: *An efficient machine-independent procedure for garbage collection in various list structures*, Comm. ACM 10, Aug. 1967.

DISCUSSION

Mailloux:
Can you tell the maximum size for a stack? If so, might it not be too pessimistic?

Wodon:
When you put a location on the heap, if you provide it with extra room for garbage collection at that time, for example one extra cell, you may as well add 1 to a counter which will then contain at any time an upper bound of the stack size. That's all. It will take exactly the same amount of space but you must count and that may take time.

Bowlden:
You asked a question about the implementation of a heap on a machine with virtual memory or in a secondary store? Most of the machines that have some sort of virtual memory have some kind of paging scheme where the store is kept in chunks in some way. The main problem, it seems to me here, is figuring out a means of ensuring that related things in the heap are in the same page, so that whenever you are tracing or linking through lists, or whatever kinds of things you do, you will tend to stay in the same page, for some reasonable length of time. That cuts down the amount of paging effort that has to be done. One possibility is to use the garbage collector to help in this process. If you use the process of mapping active space into the other half, which has been proposed in the case where you have an unlimited amount of space, then indeed the tracing scheme itself would probably do more or less this, so that after the mapping was done, related items would tend to be on the same page. I don't know how good that one is. Perhaps even more important is enabling the user somehow or other, the programmer, to give some kind of information about this, perhaps by a pragmat.

Wodon:

Well, that's why I raised this question of pragmats or transputs, which may give a means for organizing the secondary memory. The main problem is what kind of informations are closely related. One obvious way is to put in one page only those locations corresponding to one mode. This makes tracing and compacting very easy. But now we have the problem, I think it is specific to ALGOL 68, that a structure may contain a substructure, and that you may have a situation where you have a pointer here, but no pointer there. Then you are in trouble of course. In which page are you going to put that? Will it be in the pages of that mode, when it should be in the pages of that other one? Well, there is a solution of course. You may point here in any case and give some kind of indication saying that this is this thing you have in mind or the other way around. I don't see any neat solution.

Currie:

I have just a few points on the tracing, the backward and forward tracing. On our machine we do not have enough room to keep the full type information for tracing. In fact we find that it isn't necessary. You can always reconstruct the backward information from just a few bits in the word. In fact we only use four spare bits in a word, to see what kind of thing we've got in our hand and what type it is. We can reconstruct the full type from this and the pointer pointing to the map area, we call it. It appears to work remarkably well. So you don't actually have to carry the full type information if you don't have enough room.

Wodon:

I didn't mean that you have to do it exactly as I said. You may have tables or some kind of machine code, or what not, to reduce the exact amount of bits which are necessary to code a particular piece of information.

Currie:

In references, for instance, we carry around references as single 24 bit words, 20 of which are address, so that we have only four bits left to use for marking and to make sure that we don't go round the list twice and don't update it twice and all the rest of it. And all in all we only use I think six of these 8 different possible marks.

Wodon:

And how many modes can you accommodate like that?

Currie:

It depends what you mean by how many modes. I think there is a bit too much said about seeing them as specific modes. In fact, what you are dealing with inside the machine are pointers. Some of them may not be actual physical modes mentioned inside your programs, because the particular implementation might work in terms of pointers which aren't actually the same as the formal specifications of the modes.

Wodon:

How many types of locations?

Currie:

All in all about 1024, or something like that. All that we have to remember about a volatile entry is the depth of pointers associated with it, and what is at the end of the chain, i.e. whether it is a structure, a union, or an array. If it is an array we also have to remember it is dimensionality. Nobody ever has used more than three depths of reference. Plenty of people do use *ref ref ref*. but never any more.

Lindsey:

I think there has been some talking at cross purposes going on here. As far as I know Currie's garbage-collector is the only one which has a separate map area. The other ones we have been talking about haven't had a separate map area.

Currie:

Which map area do you mean?

Lindsey:

With your heap you ought to have a separate map, which contains the pointers to your heap proper.

Currie:

No, that wasn't the map I was meaning. I was meaning the map which tells you which part of a structure is a reference.

Lindsey:

Nevertheless, you have this map which takes some storage space which, I suppose, is roughly the equivalent of these two little words in here.

Currie:

Nevertheless, I think that's independent of the tracing and updating problem.

Lindsey:

What is it for then?

Currie:

Well, I couldn't be bothered setting up a bit map, quite honestly, so I decided to do it in a slightly different way.

Lindsey:

By a word map instead!

SESSION 6

(Chairman: G.Goos)

PANEL DISCUSSION

ALGOL 68 SUBLANGUAGES

Chairman: G. Goos

Panelists: H. J. Bowlden, P. Branquart, B. J. Mailloux,
J. E. L. Peck, P. M. Woodward.

Goos:

Ladies and Gentlemen, may I open this panel discussion on implementation of ALGOL 68 sublanguages. I would like first to set the frame. I have provided the panelists with some questions which I shall comment upon first; I hope then that we shall have some comment from the panel which would lead to a public discussion later. I would like to start first by defining what is meant by a sublanguage for the purpose of this panel discussion. The definition is given by example. I consider ALGOL 68-R to be a sublanguage, although it is not truly a sublanguage according to the Report. This means that we should concentrate not only on problems which can be solved by leaving out certain rules, by weakening certain rules of the Report or by shortening them, but also on problems solved by making slight changes of the kind that were made by the Royal Radar Establishment, for example in proceduring.

The questions which I pose are as follows:
1) What are the reasons for having sublanguages from the implementers' point of view?
2) Is there any possibility for simplifying the recognition of the meaning of parentheses in such a way that the context required to the right has a fixed maximum length?
3) What can be done to ease the distinction between mode- and operator-indications in the first parse?
4) Is the generality of coercing appropriate? What simplifications might be considered for proceduring or uniting?
5) What kind of restriction can be made to simplify storage allocation at run-time (garbage collection, generators for rows of structures containing a row as a field etc., with arbitrary combinations of flexible and fixed bounds)?
6) What are the problems in connection with separately compiled procedures, especially in case of parameter modes which enter a union mode either in the main program or in the procedure?
7) Is the I/O-package appropriate?

8) What are the considerations on parallel processing?
9) Is there a consistent way to describe restrictions? Can these restrictions be checked by the compiler?
   Can a description for a sublanguage be derived from the ALGOL 68 Report?
   What other relations are there between the description of a sublanguage and the Report?
10) What is the relation between making sublanguages for ease of implementation and defining sublanguages for specific application areas?

May I now invite the panelists to start.

Peck:

I look at the first question and, taking out the last phrase, address myself to that. What are the reasons for having a sublanguage? One very good reason is the fact that we shall have to teach students this new language. Now, when you have to teach a large number of students a programming language, it is very essential to have a small, fast compiler and perhaps an in-core compiler, so that you get fast turn-around. This is achieved very well, as most people know, with the WATFOR compiler in the case of FORTRAN. For the language PL/I, there are now appearing such compilers for sublanguages. One of those languages is SPL, which comes from Stanford, and is now used for the instruction of students. It is not quite a sublanguage of PL/I, but it is close enough to be called a sublanguage in the sense that was outlined. I think that if ALGOL 68 is to be successful, it is very essential to have a sublanguage of this type for which there can be a small, fast compiler and which can be used to put through perhaps a thousand student jobs a day. What the restrictions should be for such a language I do not yet know. I certainly think that unions should be absent, but I leave others to suggest perhaps, what further restrictions would be necessary.

Woodward:

The question is worded rather strangely, "from the implementer's point of view", because in a sense the implementer does not really have a point of view, except to get the job done sufficiently quickly to meet users' needs and to get a rapid feedback from them. The users are the people who matter. It could be that this is a good justification for a sublanguage which enables you to get your compiler into practical use quickly.

Bowlden:

There is a problem with that, though, in the sense that one of the major things we want to be trying to sell with ALGOL 68 as compared with ALGOL 60 is the increased power. If you give them a subset that looks just like ALGOL 60, they will say, "Why bother?"

Woodward:

Well, perhaps what I would then say would come into the scope of another question, I am not quite sure. Clearly there are subsets which are at such a trivial level that we should not take them very seriously.

Goos:

May I ask you this question more precisely? What properties of the language would you identify to be necessary for not having a trivial subset?

Woodward:

Well, let me tell you straight why we had to make the decision to implement this language. Users, who were hitherto all on ALGOL 60, required structures, and it is the data structures which enabled us to sell the language ALGOL 68-R to them.

Goos:

What kind of fields? Any kind?

Woodward:

Even very simple structures are of considerable value. It is not always that you want to find the place numerically, and we have to bear in mind the psychological value of being able to use field-selectors which look like identifiers. Our users are already exploiting structures of arrays.

Goos:

Does anyone else wish to comment?

Branquart:

In my opinion, one can distinguish two kinds of reason for having language restrictions from the implementer's point of view:

The first reason is the optimization of the run-time efficiency of the compilers; though ALGOL 68 has been designed with the Bauer-principle in mind, it may happen that some sophisticated features of the language influence the efficiency of the compiliation of more current ones. The introduction of restrictions eliminating such features is, I think, quite justified.

The second reason is the minimalization of the time of compilation, and at the same time the minimalization of the time of designing and programming a compiler. There is a very striking point which all compiler builders are aware of: they devote the greatest part of their lives to taking into account very special features of languages and intricate combinations of such features, which will probably never be used by any programmer. It would be very useful to have a reasonable subset of ALGOL 68 which would be designed for current use.

Goos:

Such restrictions would be difficult to formalize.

van Wijngaarden:

May I interrupt here. I am wondering about his remark. Could you give some examples? We tried to design a language in such a way that all its concepts are orthogonal, and I think that if you implement each concept correctly, then automatically you get correct all those which you call improbable combinations.

Branquart:

That is right, but in some cases, if you can suppress improbable combinations it simplifies the job of the compiler. For example, you admit generators which are dereferenced immediately, and which have not even been initialized.

van Wijngaarden:
Of course, these are nonsense programs.

Branquart:
But if you want to have a very general compiler, you have to take such cases into account.

van Wijngaarden:
But what is there to trouble you? The local-generator is an address. If you do not initialize it, then you do not put anything in that address. So what?

Branquart:
Consider the case of recognition of parentheses; if you eliminate the possibility of having uninitialized generators which are immediately dereferenced, you forbid the possibility of having *int*: *i* as bound pair, and the job of the compiler is made easier.

Woodward:
But one cannot design a language which, from its very nature, would remove the nonsense programs. You can write a nonsense program in any language.

Branquart:
Yes, but it would be advantageous to suppress what is possible to suppress.

Goos:
Are there languages restricted in such a way that you cannot program at all in them?

van Wijngaarden:
That is the other extreme.

Goos:
I think that the basic problem underlying your question is that of efficiency at run-time or at compile-time. You quickly find out certain cases in which the compiler writers have to solve not only the recursive case, which comes from the orthogonal design, but they have to split up this general case and see whether they can optimize the usual case which requires only one or two levels of recursion. It turns out that some of the orthogonalities in the language are very hard to handle if you try that. But this has to be tried for optimization.

Bowlden:
There are three cost features that are involved really. One is the cost of developing the compiler in the first place, one is the feature of compilation speed, and one is the problem of run-time speed, execution speed. They all have to be considered. Really what it amounts to is that you have

to decide on the point of diminishing returns as far as increasing the cost. It seems to me that a good criterion is that if the inclusion of any particular feature would add heavily, whatever that means, to the cost of programs that do not use it, then it should be omitted, or at least be relegated to a larger version of the compiler for the use of those people who really have to have it.

Goos:
This criterion is very difficult to handle because I do not know any language in which the generality does not contribute to complexity of certain programs even if they do not use the full generality.

van Wijngaarden:
Here we did our best according to the Bauer-principle not to let the generality weigh on those people wo do not use it. But we have always decided that a very tiny little bit of tax should be paid by everyone for recursion.

Bowlden:
Well, in some cases it is not just a tiny bit. Certainly there are certain things that on certain machines would be expensive to implement for everybody who uses the system, unless you provide him with a pragmat or something to enable him to tell the compiler "I do not intend to use this feature, so do not build it into my program."

Woodward:
I think there is one overriding principle which we have tended to bear in mind in decisions which we have had to make, and that is never to stop people from being able to do the things that they want to do. We do not mind if, for ease of implementation, the way in which they have to express themselves is a little bit more cumbersome than it would be in ALGOL 68. But we do not like to withdraw real facilities.

Goos:
I believe that we have now established certain criteria, according to this first question, about the reasons for having sublanguages. These criteria seem to be, first, we want to be efficient at run-time as far as possible and this in a general way, which of course has to be split up into the two points, efficient in time and efficient in space. The second point is that we want to minimize the design time and programming time for the compiler itself. The third point are the advanced properties of the language, according to the question, whether these properties contribute to the complexity of the generated program or of the generation process in such a way that people who do not use these features have to pay for it. The last point is the one which was expressed by Woodward, in asking which features could be weakened or removed from the language in order to fulfill these criteria. We should not reduce the expressive power of the language but only make it somewhat more cumbersome to express things. I think these are the criteria we can generally establish.

Scheidig:
Does there exist a group which would implement the whole language without restriction?

Ershov:
Yes.

Scheidig:
But it seems to me that most groups make restrictions and so there is the danger that we have many sublanguages. Perhaps we should come to a general sublanguage.

Goos:
So this question is: What can we do to get a unified look at the different problems the compiler builder is concerned with, and what can we do to solve them in a uniform manner in different implementations?

Bowlden:
Really, what we are probably thinking here is that we do not want to go the way ALGOL 60 has gone, with sublanguages that are not nested. This makes it so that in effect you have different languages because different features are implemented. If we can define a nested set of sublanguages to start with, then this reduces the chance of that sort of thing happening.

Mailloux:
I should just like to remark again that there are perhaps two different kinds of subset and that one might have two different reasons for having them. One is essentially for teaching because you want to compile and probably reject thousands of programs every day; we intend to implement some such subset, probably a very large subset, while at the same time constructing a second implementation, of the entire language. The other reason that one might want to have a subset is that one has a small machine and feels incapable or unwilling to go to the trouble, which might be considerable, of implementing the full language on it, and still getting it efficient.

Wodon:
What Branquart has said gives me the impression that there are two kinds of restriction: one just suppresses a concept and orthogonally all its consequences; and another suppresses 'side effects'. But if we have to suppress this kind of thing, it is very difficult to express this formally. We would easily come out with a list of unformalized restrictions, let us say some kind of PL/I stuff. The question is: are we ready to accept that, or are we not? Practically, it would be nice, of course.

Goos:
This is one of the possible answers which we should give to that first meta-question which I posed [9]. What kind of description can be visualized for sublanguages? As you just said, we may see a PL/I-like description consisting of many special cases, or we may drop certain features of the language completely, with the consequence that all things that follow by the principle or orthogonality from that must also be dropped.

Branquart:
I think that it is always possible to use the two level syntax of the Report

for describing the suppression of a side effect, but this could give rise to huge swellings in the syntax; generally speaking, it is easier to cut out a whole feature than only its side effects.

van der Meulen:
With regard to the teaching aspects of the language, only structures were mentioned. I should like to remark that in particular, operation definitions and the whole slicing mechanism are as important and appeal immediately to students as soon as they have some experience with them.

Woodward:
I would say that physicists using the language will find the slicing extremely important.

Mailloux:
I would like to ask Peck just why unions in particular are so difficult. I do not see it.

Peck:
Well, the inclusion of unions means the inclusion of the conformity-relation with run-time mode checking and I would think that exclusion of this would simplify the compiler.

Mailloux:
I agree that it would simplify it, but it cannot really see that it would be all that much, since you still have to check at compile-time for equivalence of modes which might have been defined in different ways. It seems to me that is the really tough part and kicking unions out is not going to simplify that very much.

Goos:
I think we come now to the more specific questions. I would like to give the panelists first an opportunity to express their views on those facts which are difficult to implement and to see what they believe can be done to remove difficulties.

van Wijngaarden:
Who came first on this question between Mailloux and Peck? I thought I heard that if you took unions out then also the conformity relations should go. Is that true? But this is without any reason, because in the syntax of the conformity relation, unions do not occur.

Goos:
Can you tell me what expressive power remains in the conformity relation if unions have gone?

van Wijngaarden:
May I say something about the possibility of simplifying the recognition of the meaning of parentheses in such a way that the context to the right is of fixed magnitude in length. Well, I think there is only one solution and it is to give all the different parentheses a specific representation. Why? After an opening parenthesis, an identifier can always follow. This identifier

is of any length. It will supersede any given fixed maximum length. Therefore, all we need to do is to have a specific opening parenthesis. You can manage with the same closing parenthesis because it is just a matter of matching, you see. The opening parenthesis must be different.

Branquart:
   I agree with you, but not for the same reason.

van Wijngaarden:
   That makes the point even stronger! That means I have more arguments in favour.

Branquart:
   I do not think the example of 'identifier' is a good one: an identifier is recognizable by a finite state automaton and in practice, I do not consider the context 'identifier' as unbounded.

van Wijngaarden:
   I am sorry, I do not understand at all. I have an opening parenthesis, then <u>int</u>, and then *a*, then I shall not know whether I have to do with a structure or the opening of a closed-clause.

Branquart:
   I agree with you; I was only against the example of identifier. Here is a display of all possible kinds of parentheses, which may happen in a program; this display shows clearly that the context allowing one to recognize the left parentheses are generally not bounded.

1) Let us first enumerate the trivial cases where the contexts are bounded;

   <u>struct</u> (...

   <u>union</u> (...

   <u>struct</u> ⟨indication⟩ = (...

   <u>union</u> ⟨indication⟩ = (...

   <u>op</u> (...

   <u>proc</u> (   ) ...   ⎫ parentheses of virtual bounds
   <u>proc</u> (, ...   ⎪
   <u>proc</u> (: ...   ⎬
   <u>proc</u> (...   ⎪ parentheses of virtual plan (other contexts)
   <u>par</u> (...

   ⟨tail of primary⟩ (...   slice or call

2) The detection of extensions needs a special state to be stored on a stack, and even with the help of such a state the necessary context is unbounded:

<u>struct</u> (...) s , (...,)   <u>real</u> r
                  bounds

<u>struct</u> (...) s , (...,)   sl
                  fields

There is one single solution for solving these cases without using specific brackets: suppression of the extensions.

3) The remaining cases are not bounded either, I have tried to characterize them rather roughly; note that the order in which they are written is important:

  ((...   )   declarer : ...   )
      formal-parameters

      routine-denotation

  (...)   declarer
  bounds

  (... ; ...)   closed-clause

  (... , ...)   collateral-clause

  (... | ...)   conditional-clauses
  (... | ... | ...)
  (... |: ...)

  (... | ... , ...)   case-clauses
  (... | ... , ... | ...)
  (... , ... | ... , ...)
  (... , ... | ... , ... | ...)

Goos:
I think you have stated the problem of parentheses now and also the cases in which a parenthesis is not preceded by a primary. Is this true?

Branquart:
  Yes it is.

Goos:
  Yes, and the question that we should be concerned with now is: what can we do in this situation, not by inventing tricky compiling routines but by changing the situation?

Bowlden:

Can we change the situation without extensive alterations? We certainly cannot do it by making a sublanguage out of it. I am inclined to think that the question hinges on how much you are trying to do in the first pass.

Goos:

That is the question I have. You should not discuss the question of having a tricky compiling routine, because this is not the question put to this panel.

Peck:

I think there is one obvious thing and everybody knows it. It is that the representation of the sub-symbol should be different from the representation of the open-symbol. This is an obvious simplification.

van Wijngaarden:

The representation of the sub-symbol *is* a different one from that of the open-symbol. But it is an extension that allows another representation under certain circumstances.

Lindsey:

I think that Branquart's second example, under 3), could also be a routine-denotation because a formal-parameters-pack can contain commas, and a comma can be a go-on-symbol. So in fact you have to go even further before you know the context.

van der Meulen:

Many of these troubles arise from two sources. One of them is the 48 character set, and the other is the different possible ways of representing certain extensions. I think we could come a long way by saying that the implementation requires a 64 character set including in particular, square brackets, and secondly, prescribing certain extensions and excluding others so that a lot of troubles of this kind disappear.

Goos:

This is a proposal for attacking the problem by restricting the possibilities of expressing certain things in different ways.

van der Meulen:

It is only a choice in the representations.

Goos:

Is it only a choice of the representation, or do you suggest the use of certain extensions everywhere while forbidding other extensions in some places?

van der Meulen:

Yes, for example, for the declarations of a new mode by means of a *struct* you can say *mode m* = *struct* ... . You can also say *struct m* = ... , and you can use it without an intermediate mode-declaration. In my opinion the implementer could help himself very much by requiring that you have always to declare a new mode by one of the three possibilities of extension.

The same applies to the square bracket and the round bracket. By simply requiring that an implementation presupposes square brackets and only uses square brackets where the sub-symbol and the bus-symbol are meant and for all other cases round brackets, you have done away with some other problems of this kind. Then I think you can make a certain choice of possible extensions, prescribe some of them and say here you cannot use the strict language but you have to use a certain extension. By making an intelligent choice of this kind (not restrictions, but just suppositions of the compiler) you can come a long way. Many of these problems arise from the many choices you have. Others arise from the restrictions of the 48 character set.

Mailloux:

First, I should like to say that yes, indeed, I would very much like to choose different representations, but I cannot. I am sorry, but I just cannot, because the boss of my computing center has bought a large number of keypunches with the character set that they have got on them. The same thing is true in most of the world, and although, of course, we would like to do everything we can to change it, I am afraid we are not quite in power yet. Soon we shall take over from FORTRAN, but it has just not happened yet. Secondly then, perhaps in a constructive vein, and I hope you will not tear me apart for this, in something that we might call an array-declaration, we might reinstate the ALGOL 60 *array*. It is slightly unfortunate but I suppose I could be put up with. We could probably also put up with something or other in front of a routine-denotation, whether it is *expr* or *rout*, or whatever. I think that the other cases essentially either take care of themselves or are not serious in the sense that, you do not really need to know, when generating code for whatever follows any other left parenthesis, what the exact nature of the parenthesis is. Just compile along to the end of the serial-clause; if you there encounter a vertical bar, then the mode of the unitary-clause last compiled distinguishes between conditional-clause versus case-clause; if you encounter a comma instead, then you have a collateral-clause; or if you encounter a right parenthesis, then it was a closed-clause. I think the problem can probably be handled with those two additions, distortions, or whatever you want to call them, to the language.

Goos:

Did your first proposal mean that you want the sub-symbol to be represented by something like *row* (in some places only?

Mailloux:

I am saying you can do this. This is a possibility. I do not like it but it might make life livable.

Goos:

The question here is: can this be considered to be a property of a sublanguage, or not?

Mailloux:

Well, I must insist that if Currie can get away with the things he is getting away with, and this can still be considered a sublanguage by our chairman, then this must also be a sublanguage in his sense.

Goos:

Then I do not doubt the question!

Bowlden:

This is not just a matter of a 48 character set either. The set in question is a 128 character set, which is becoming a de facto standard, which has no square brackets.

Koster:

There is some point in looking at the restrictions or changes that Currie has used in his implementation. One of them is an old friend of mine, the reintroduction of the void-symbol as the virtual-void-declarer with maybe a corresponding extension to be deleted at nearly all places again. There is another thing in his proposal which I found much less to my taste and which I think people should now have a fight over, and that is his leaving out of the formal-declarers. It is quite clear that if you follow this example, then you are rid of both a number of local ambiguities in parsing and some problems in your compiler, but is it worth it. To begin with, you might envisage some system where you restrict what may occur as bounds in such a way that you can never have a closed-clause there because the closed-clause as bound is really the dangerous thing.

Currie:

I suppose I should rise up in defense at this point. I do not think it is going to make any difference at all, on the analysis side of it. It does not make it any easier having virtual bounds there instead of formal bounds. It makes no difference at all on the analysis side. That is the first thing. The second thing is that my reason for omitting it, besides the standard laziness, was that most users will never put anything in formal bounds — just sheer laziness. You know, they will assume they will always have the bound right and when it goes wrong, it goes wrong — and that is it. In a sense it is putting redundancy on top of redundancy. As far as any of the really tight library procedures are concerned, these are generally written in code anyway and they test bounds in the text. It did make some difference to the code production. It is slightly easier to produce code, but it does not make any difference in the analysis at all.

Goos:

May I comment on the last point. I think you need not reflect on the question of procedures written in code but should say that it is possible for the routine, by using the correct operators, to ask what the values of the bounds are so that you can check them.

Lindsey:

I think it was quite a reasonable thing myself to omit the bounds from the formal-declarers but I think it was a terrible crime to omit the *either* or the *flex*, particularly the *flex*, because that is the point at which you cease to be a strict sublanguage. I think you should at least have accepted a formal bound with a flexible-symbol. You could ignore this and pretend it was not there and do nothing about it. I am not saying that you must do the check when you actually put in the actual-parameters. At least you should have accepted it. We now have a state where a program which will run on your implementation, which does not happen to contain a flexible-symbol in a particular place, will not run on anybody else's implementation.

Currie:

I would suggest that most of the programs that are written for a particular installation will not work anyway when you go across to another completely different installation.

Woodward:

We are talking about sublanguages and you only need two different sublanguages to encounter exactly the same problem.

Goos:

I think that this whole discussion is at a point where we violate the principles underlying a higher-level language. One of those principles - is the portability of programs from one installation going to another one. Also, if we have doubts that this is effective in any case, we should not restrict languages in such ways that it is impossible.

Currie:

That does not make it impossible. Our machine is a 24 bit machine. That is the length of the integers. Do you think that everybody is going to be writing their programs in such a way so that they do an environment inquiry to find out how big their integers are going to be, and using it in some way to modify the program later on so that it can run on a machine that has got 18 bit integers perhaps, or maybe 36 bit integers?

Goos:

That is a rather strange idea. I think that experience with ALGOL 60 and FORTRAN has proven that in very many cases these kinds of restrictions are not so important.

Currie:

No, but there is always something which has to be changed in the program.

Goos:

I think we should close now on the point of parentheses and go on to another problem.

Bowlden:

I think that on this third point perhaps, with reference to the distinction between mode- and operator-indications in the first pass, maybe we ought to postpone that until after coffee and let Lindsey give us a little presentation on that subject, since he seems to have given more thought to it than anyone else, I am aware of, on that sort of thing.

Goos:

Do you want to comment on another point?

Bowlden:

This question as to the passing of united parameters to a separately compiled procedure seems to be a very difficult one to handle, and it may be that extensive extra tables will have to be kept if we are going to do this. Now maybe this is one of the reasons why Peck feels that unions are to be avoided, I am not sure. The other thing of course is simply to say that in a sublanguage you do not allow separately compiled procedures. This would be one direction to go. It is not even a sublanguage in that sense of the term. You could indeed argue that if you want to simplify the problem, do not allow separately compiled procedures. But if you are going to allow it and you are going to allow united modes, then you are going to have to keep a mode table with representations, I think, just as you are going to keep an identifier table for separately compiled procedures.

Goos:

May I first comment on the possibility of leaving out the precompiled procedures. You should note that the problem of passing the mode numbers in case of unions applies also to the case of procedures written in code, and I can see that it is possible to make an implementation which allows procedures written in code introduced implicitly, but not by explicit call. explicit call.

Currie:

Well, I think I must have misunderstood this problem when you were describing it because as far as I can see, you could put it right by not allowing the commutation of the modes inside the union.

Bowlden:

No. The problem is having a unique number assigned to each mode, which obviously depends on the order in which the declarations of these modes are processed by the compiler. If in the two separate compilations they are to be given the same number so that the test can be made to work, you have to have a complete list.

Koster:

I do not quite see this union problem. If you are to have a precompiled procedure, it is clear that you have to accompany it with part of a table, a declarer table. Your main program has its own declarer table. At a specific moment you are trying to insert the library routine into your main program. That means also a merging of the tables. Only after that can you find your unique integers, etc., for the modes in this case. But I see no problems there. It is some work, but no problem.

Goos:

But difficult work. I think that Peck was right when he said: "I leave out unions for such reasons because it slows down the speed, just that".

Mailloux:

If you have got independent compilation, it does. Otherwise it does not. I mean, it follows the proper Bauer-principle that you should not pay for something unless you use it, and in this case you do not. Furthermore, the process which you have to go through to knit these independent pieces of program together is a process which you essentially included in the first or second pass when the compiler went through and found out, i.e., that this mode is equivalent to that mode, so you do not really even have to write a new piece of program. You have to modify it slightly to get at these things, but I do not see it as a real problem, any more than independent compilation of things at all is a problem in any language. Now in fact it might be considered to be a very bad thing in general. On our machine you cannot get a FORTRAN compilation in less than 18 seconds, and the main reason for this is that they have a thing called the linkage editor, which has all sorts of disk files and goes and compares things and spends most of its time doing transput and a very little time calculating and fixing things up. This would not be any worse, I think, in ALGOL 68, at least not significantly.

Goos:
    I think we have no new ideas on this problem so one of my questions was the following: is there any possibility of designing specific garbage collectors which run, not with the full language but perhaps with a subset, so that we are able to recognize, at compile-time, whether some programs belong to that subset which may be handled by that garbage collector or not? I think for instance of the following. Suppose somebody has written, by suitable mode-declarations and operator-declarations, a LISP system in ALGOL 68. Then at the first look, all that is needed is a LISP-like garbage collector, and nothing of all those generalities for structured values and so on. Of course, the second look shows that there are certain problems, for instance, the fact that formats generate something on the heap, that unions containing arrays generate something on the heap, that arrays with flexible bounds generate something on the heap. So the question I would like to pose is: what can we do to avoid all these special cases which prevent the construction of special garbage collectors? One of the possibilities would be to say in advance that all things which are on the heap are declared by such and such mode-declarations which come in the first part of the program. And later on the compiler can check that it has no global-generator and no other kind of storage allocator which puts things on the heap and which does not fit into these modes we have declared in advance. This is my proposal.

Currie:
    I am not at all clear as to why this would help. We have still got the problem of the intermediate working results. Why would ...

Goos:
    This you can put on the stack.

Currie:
    No, but we still have to remember that these intermediate results, or intermediate references as it might be, have got to be stored somewhere, and they are still in the stack and you still have to remember them. I think that is the point in the whole garbage collection setup that you have got to attempt to optimize. I feel that if garbage collection takes more than 10%

of your program, then there is something wrong anyway. You are running on too small an installation. I agree that there are times when 99% of the time is spent in garbage collection, but nevertheless it is not a good way to use store. Making your garbage collector two or three times as fast is not really going to gain you so much as reducing the amount of code that you use to keep all these pointers updated correctly so that the garbage collector can be aware of them. I think this is a far more important point.

van der Poel:

Our experience with garbage collectors of a rather complicated kind, namely for LISP with variable length element structures, is that the only thing which a garbage collector has to do is to see whether it deals with a pointer, which it has to displace or whether it deals with a plain value, which it is not allowed to touch. I have the strong impression, from my own experience, that it would not matter that the garbage collector would not become any more difficult for the general case as for a specialized case. And even in a general case, such a garbage collector is within 700 instructions or so.

Goos:

It is not the length of the garbage collector. It is just the execution time.

van der Poel:

Oh, not even the time because you can describe garbage collection as the number of times you have to visit each particular cell. It is practically a linear process which can be expressed as a coefficient times the total number of cells. So it goes up linearly with the number of storage cells you have and nothing else.

Branquart:

I should like to ask you how many extra bits you have at your disposal in your system.

van der Poel:

Three.

Lindsey:

I think there may be some programs in which you could use a garbage collector which does not need to compact. If all your garbage is in units of the same size, as in the LISP system it probably would be, then you can go back to conventional chaining of your free store together, allocating pieces out of the chain as you wanted it. This would save the whole of the compaction.

Bowlden:

Certainly it would not be hard to keep what amounts to a statistical table of sizes of spaces that have been allocated on the heap and if they are all of one size you could do exactly that. But the trouble with this, it seems to me, is that you are adding to overhead in the case where, as may often happen, you never have to do a garbage collection, and, in particular, I think this applies too to the handling of the working stack. I agree with what

Currie was saying about the business of trying to keep track of what is on the working stack. If you put in a code to do that, you are penalizing people who will never use garbage collection, to keep track of something that the garbage collector could do if it ever gets called.

Goos:
Do you see any way to avoid that?

Currie:
In fact our implementation does not include any of that code if the garbage collector is not present in core, i.e., if there had not been any generators or two-dimensional collaterals, or similar things used in the program, then the garbage collector will not be loaded into use, neither will 99% of the code required for manipulating the pointers. The other point was this point about getting areas of the same size together. This only makes sense when you have got a segmented store, when you can afford really to have disjoint areas in core. If you have got just a linear chunk of core, as I have got, which the stack and the heap have got to go into, then it just is not worth it. It does not pay. You might as well compact every time because most of the time the garbage collection is invoked by the stack expanding and hitting the heap. So you might as well compact every time. There is no point in messing about in that case. However, if you did have a machine architecture which did allow you to separate out your core into reasonably disjoint areas, then I agree that would be the way to do it.

Wodon:
The subject of this panel discussion was sublanguages, and I did not hear anything about a sublanguage which could ease the burden of garbage collection. I must say I do not see one either. The only thing I can see was expressed by Lindsey. In a case when we have only a small number of different structured modes without structures in them, then I can imagine very fast garbage collection of course, using pages and things like that. But as far as sublanguages are concerned, I do not see anything.

Goos:
But the question is exactly that one. How can you recognize how many different structures you have?

Wodon:
I just have the compiler count them.

Branquart:
One more comment. In my opinion, the efficiency of the garbage collection itself is not so important. What I am afraid of is the influence of the necessity of the garbage collector on the execution of the normal programs.

SOME ALGOL 68 SUBLANGUAGES

C. H. LINDSEY
University of Manchester, UK

This note introduces three proposed sublanguages known as CHL1, CHL2 and CHL3, whose purpose is to satisfy those implementations which prefer their defining occurrences to precede their applied ones.

It is also hoped that these examples will establish a satisfactory precedent for rigour in the definition of sublanguages. Note that I have been careful to apply my restrictions only to particular-programs since it is not necessarily the case that the standard and library preludes should be expressible in the sublanguages.

SPECIFICATION OF THE ALGOL 68 SUBLANGUAGE CHL1

{This sublanguage is intended to place the minimum restriction on the language, whilst yet enabling new indicants to be recognised as either mode-indications or ADIC-indications as soon as they are encountered during a single forward pass through the source text. It is essentially a formalisation of an informal proposal made by Goos during the Banff meeting of WG2.1.}

An "excluded object" is a terminal production of a notion, contained within a sequence of symbols which is to be replaced by a second sequence of symbols in the course of an extension {9.a}, which is not contained within that second sequence. {Thus, in *ref real* x = *loc real*, when it is to be extended to *real* x, *ref real* is an excluded object}.

If a given {applied} occurrence of a terminal production of 'MODE mode indication' where "MODE" stands for any terminal production of the metanotion 'MODE' indentifies a defining occurrence of the same terminal production and is the textually first occurrence of that terminal production, excluding any such occurrence contained within an excluded object, within the smallest range containing that defining occurrence, then the given occurrence is an "establishing" occurrence of that terminal production.

No proper particular-program in the sublanguage contains a heap-generator whose constituent heap-symbol-option is empty (a local-generator which is to undergo the extension given in 9.2.a) and whose constituent declarer is an establishing occurrence of a mode-indication.

{Thus, in a particular-program commencing with

<u>begin</u> <u>proc</u> p = : (<u>goos</u> a; . . . . . .

<u>goos</u> must be the representation of a monadic-operator, for otherwise

goos a would be an extension of *ref goos a* = *loc goos*, in which the second occurrence of *goos* would be an establishing occurrence, and the particular program would be improper in the sublanguage. On the other hand, in a particular-program commencing with

begin proc p = : *(mode a* = *ref c; c a;* .... ,

c must clearly be the representation of a mode-indication, as it must also be in both of its occurrences in

begin mode c = *real; proc p* = : *(c a;* .... ,

since no symbol can be a terminal production of both 'MODE mode indication' and of 'monadic indication' (1.1.5.b).}

SPECIFICATION OF THE ALGOL 68 SUBLANGUAGE CHL2

{This sublanguage is intended to place the minimum restriction on the language, whilst yet enabling the identification of mode-identifiers, indications and operators to be performed during a single forward pass through the source text. The main restriction is that all defining occurrences must precede their applied occurrences, and a consequence is some difficulty with regard to mutually recursive pairs of procedures or operators (for the solution to this see CHL3). This sublanguage is a sublanguage of CHL1.}

An "excluded object" is a terminal production of a notion, contained within a sequence of symbols which is to be replaced by a second sequence of symbols in the course of an extension {9.a}, which is not contained within that second sequence. {Thus, in *ref real x* = *loc real*, when it is to be extended to *real x*, *ref real* is an excluded object.}

If a given {applied} occurrence of a terminal production of 'MABEL identifier' ('MODE mode indication', 'PRIORITY indication', 'PRAM ADIC operator') where "MABEL" ("MODE", "PRIORITY", "PRAM", "ADIC") stands for any terminal production of the metanotion 'MABEL' ('MODE', 'PRIORITY', 'PRAM', 'ADIC') identifies a defining occurrence of that same terminal production and is the textually first occurrence of that terminal production, excluding any such occurrence contained within an excluded object, within the smallest range containing that defining occurrence, then the given occurrence is an "establishing" occurrence of that terminal production.

No proper particular-program in the sublanguage contains an establishing occurrence of a mode-identifier (dyadic-indication, operator).

{Thus *(proc a* = : *b; proc b* = : *a; skip)* is improper because the first occurrence of *b* is an establishing one. Likewise, *(op a* = *(real p,q)* : *p b q, b* = *(real p, q)* : *p a q; priority a* = 7, *b* = 7; *skip)* is improper for two reasons.}

If an idication-applied occurrence of a mode-indication identifies an indication-defining occurrence of that mode-indication, then it must also "ultimately" identify one or more indication-defining occurrences of mode-indications found by the following steps:

Step 1: Each mode-indication is said not to have been encountered; the given indication-applied occurrence is considered;

Step 2: The considered {indication-applied} occurrence and all mode-indications consisting of the same sequence of symbols are said to have been encountered; the indication-defining occurrence identified by the considered occurrence is said to be ultimately identified by the given occurrence, and is itself considered;

Step 3: If the constituent declarer of the mode-declaration, of which the considered {indication-defining} occurrence is a constituent contains one or more indication-applied occurrences of not yet encountered mode-indications (other than occurrences contained within a boundscript contained within that declarer), then each such {indication-applied} occurrence of each such mode-indication is considered in turn, and for each one Step 2 is taken.

{Thus in

(*union a* = (*real*, *ref b*);

a p;

mode b = *bool*; *skip*)

the second occurrence of *a* identifies the defining occurrence of *a*, and ultimately identifies the defining occurrences of both *a* and *b*.}

No proper particular-program in the sublanguage contains a generator (a formal-parameter) whose constituent declarer contains a mode-indication (other than a mode-indication contained within a boundscript contained within that declarer) which ultimately identifies an indication-defining occurrence of a mode-indication which occurs later in the textual order than that given declarer.

{Thus (*struct a* = (*real p*, *ref b q*), *b* = (*real p*, *ref a q*); *a x*, *b y*; *skip*) is perfectly proper, whereas

(*op q* = (*union* (*real*, *ref bool*) *a*) : *skip*;

union a = (*real*, *ref b*);

a p;

q p;

mode b = *bool*; *skip*)

is not (and must not be, for the identification of the applied occurrence of *q* cannot be made until the mode of *b* is known).}

No proper particular-program in the sublanguage contains a jump whose constituent label-identifier is an establishing occurrence of that label-identifier and whose constituent go-to-symbol-option is empty. {For otherwise, in *proc p* = *skip*; (*p*; *p* : *skip*)), the second occurrence of *p* could not be recognised as a jump during a single forward pass.}

SPECIFICATION OF THE ALGOL 68 SUBLANGUAGE CHL3

{The purpose of this sublanguage is the same as that of CHL2, except that a provision is made for the creation of mutually recursive pairs of procedures and operators by means of pragmats. CHL3 is a sublanguage of CHL1. CHL2 is a sublanguage of CHL3.}

Let the definitions of "excluded object", "establishing occurrence", and "ultimate identification", given in the specification of CHL2 be deemed to have been made.

Let the restrictions on the occurrences of dyadic-indications, jumps and mode-indications {but not of mode-identifiers or operators} given in the specification of CHL2 be deemed to have been made.

It is necessary in this sublanguage to make use of pragmats {2. 3. c} and that the following production rules be included in the language with the restriction that they may only be used inside pragmats:
   a) pragmat unitary declaration : identity warning declaration;
      operation warning declaration.
   b) identity warning declaration : formal PROCEDURE parameter,
      equals symbol, skip symbol.
   c) operation warning declaration : PRAM caption, equals symbol,
      skip symbol.
   d) * warning declaration : identity warning declaration;
      operation warning declaration.

{It follows from this syntax that occurrences of mode-identifiers (operators) in warning-declarations are applied occurrences, and may be establishing occurrences.}

The elaboration of a warning-declaration involves no action.

If a given operator-applied occurrence of a terminal production of 'PRAM ADIC operator' where "PRAM" ("ADIC") stands for any terminal production of the metanotion 'PRAM' ('ADIC') is the constituent operator of an operation-warning-declaration then it may identify an operator-defining occurrence of the same terminal production found by using the steps of 4.1.2.b, with Step 3 replaced as in 4.3.2.b. {The identification of mode-identifiers in identity-warning-declarations is already covered by 4.1.2.b.}

{4.4.1.a,b now ensures that the mode specified by a warning-declaration is the same as that specified by the unitary-declaration with which it is associated by the identification process.}

No proper particular-program in the sublanguage contains an establishing occurrence of a mode-identifier (operator) unless that establishing occurrence is contained within a warning-declaration.

{Thus the following particular-program, which was improper in CHL2, is proper in CHL3:

   (pr proc b = skip; pr proc a = : b; proc b = : a; skip).}

DISCUSSION

van Wijngaarden:
What is the purpose of the goto restriction in your sublanguage CHL2?

Lindsey:
The main purpose of the restriction is to ensure that an applied occurrence of *p* is properly identified as a jump, rather than a procedure call. At least we then know we can compile a jump into the program (and maybe let the loader fill in the address later). There is then no risk of compiling in a procedure call, which might be longer. However, I don't think you need to have the restriction which Currie has put in, where he has insisted that a goto should occur in every jump.

Currie:
I think the reason why I insisted on the goto appearing is that it is too complicated to explain where one could leave it out.

Lindsey:
Oh, it may very well be that in teaching your students, particularly when you are teaching them to write readable programs, which I hope you will teach them, that you may not tell them that they can leave this out until they are very skilled programmers and they have already discovered it in the primer anyway. I am trying to put on the minimum restriction which is necessary. There may be other restrictions in the language desirable for good programming.

Lindsey (in answer to a question about mode-indications):
The restriction I have placed on mode-indications is a little different because there are some more problems. Consider the following:

(union a = (real, ref b ¢ an establishing occurrence ¢);

    op q = (union (real, ref bool) a) : skip;

    a p ;

    q p ;

    mode b = bool;

    skip)

I don't want to say that the establishing occurrence of *b* is illegal because then I would have some difficulty in treating recursive pairs of modes, and I want to be able to do this. In any case, most compilers are not particularly interested at this point in knowing exactly what *b* was. The compiler can tell it is a mode-indication because otherwise it would not have followed a ref. The *a p* declares one of these objects of mode *a*, quite properly identifying the defining occurrence of *a*, which precedes the applied occurrence. Is there any reason to complain at this point? To show that there is, we must consider the applied occurrence of the operator *q*. It turns out that you cannot perform the identification of this q until you know this mode $\underline{b}$, because the mode $\underline{a}$ turns out to be exactly the same mode as the formal parameter of q. But as I have written this program, we don't know this until we get to the mode-declaration for $\underline{b}$. I now define a new term. We already know that $\underline{a}\ p$ contains an applied occurrence of $\underline{a}$ which identifies the defining occurrence; but this in turn contains an applied occurrence of some other mode-indication $\underline{b}$ which identifies its own defining occurrence $\underline{mode}\ \underline{b} = \ldots$. And so I'm going to say that $\underline{a}\ p$ identifies the defining occurrence of $\underline{a}$ and, also, it "ultimately identifies" this defining occurrence of $\underline{b}$. I now make the following restriction in my sublanguage. No proper particular-program in the sublanguage contains a generator (such as $\underline{a}$ in $\underline{a}\ p$) which contains a mode-indication which ultimately identifies an indication-defining occurrence of a mode-indication which occurs later in the textual order than that generator (and therefore this program is improper in my sublanguage).

Currie:
I did not see why you had to go all the way around the houses like that to show that it was improper. You see, all you have to do is to put an assignation by that p. Then how are you going to manage that in a one-pass compiler?

Lindsey:
All that I am saying is that once you get down to this point here ($\underline{a}\ p$) you must already have met $\underline{mode}\ \underline{b}$.

Currie:
Yes.

Lindsey:
There are several reasons why this should be so. I have shown a particularly nasty reason by showing that I could not identify q. There are probably lots of other cases. For example, you cannot really assign storage for an $\underline{a}$ until you know exactly what sort of beast it is. So this line ($\underline{mode}\ \underline{b} \ldots$) must be moved up to earlier than $\underline{a}\ p$ and then there is no problem. This is merely a particularly nasty consequence of what happens if you don't do it.

van Wijngaarden:
Why can you not assign the storage?

Lindsey:
It depends. If $\underline{b}$ is going to turn out to be a row-of mode, it may well be, if you adopt Branquart's system, that a reference to a row-of mode takes several words of space. A reference to a $\underline{bool}$ is presumably just one word. So you may well want to know that. Incidentally, in this sublanguage, of course, you cannot do recursive pairs of procedures. The sublanguage CHL3 shows how you might get around that one.

PANEL DISCUSSION

ALGOL 68 SUBLANGUAGES

(Second part)

Goos:
  I think that what Lindsey has shown us is a proposal for how we can build a one-pass compiler as far as things like mode-indications, operator-indications, and operator identification are concerned. He said that recursive procedures are not in at the moment, so I think we should not discuss that point. How can we teach that kind of language to users? I think it was not sufficiently clear how you could state all these rules (or some sharper rules) so that a user may have quick information on what is permitted and what is forbidden.

Bowlden:
  It seems that the last restriction is the only one that poses any problem. As Currie suggested, a solution is to teach the beginning student that you always put <u>go to</u>'s in jumps. As far as identifiers are concerned the simple rule is that the declaration must precede any use. That takes care of that one without any ambiguity and it is easy to say it. This last one is the problem. For the guy who is not writing recursive mode-declarations, that is no problem either, and this is not a beginning student.

Mailloux:
  I would like to know at what point you can detect infringements against the rules. In your example, when the compiler gets to <u>ref b</u> in the first line, it either discovers that there is no global defining occurrence of <u>b</u> and issues an error message, or it finds that there is such an occurrence of <u>b</u>, uses it, and carries on. The problem arises when it reaches the fifth line, with the local declaration of <u>b</u>; somehow, the compiler must remember about its earlier assumption, and signal the contradiction. It is not immediately clear how this remembering can be done without fairly heavy overhead.

Lindsey:
  I think, in one-pass compilers of this sort, you must keep your mode tables up to date as you go along. So when you meet the declaration of <u>a</u>, the first check is whether all the entries in the mode table for <u>a</u> are complete. Now, in that case they would not be complete. There would be a pointer to the undeclared mode <u>b</u>. Now let us consider this problem:

  <u>begin</u> <u>proc</u> a = : b ; <u>proc</u> b = : a ; <u>skip</u> <u>end</u>

with nice simple things like identifiers, which have not got nasty overtones associated with them. Suppose that the identifier *b* had been declared in an outer range. The compiler comes along and thinks it is compiling a proper program in the sublanguage. It has *b* correctly entered in its tables. It comes across that first occurrence of *b*, and thinks "Ah! yes we know this man. *proc a* is equal to some procedured version of this man." At that point it should make a note in the tables for *b*, that *b* has been encountered in this range. It must do this; otherwise, when it gets to the second occurrence of *b* it cannot detect that it has made a mess of itself. If it makes this note in the table, it knows it has made a mess of itself and it can immediately proceed to produce rude messages, and that is the end as far as correct compilation goes.

Currie:
I think this is throwing away a lot of the advantages of one-pass compilation though. You are going to have to keep very extensive tables of usages of identifiers, and of modes in particular.

Lindsey:
If in that program I had an outer block in which I declared *b*, how would your compiler discover that it was improper?

Currie:
I would not.

Lindsey:
It would just make a mess?

Currie:
It would not discover that it was improper because I do not keep usages of identifiers.

Lindsey:
It would have yielded a program which would have failed to run?

Currie:
Yes.

Bowlden:
I think that the table organisation that I described in my paper on Monday, or something of that type, would answer this problem. For every identifier, the first time it is encountered in a range, you make an entry for that range because at this point you do not know what it is going to be. If at the end you decide indeed that it referred to the exterior range, the link is there and you can proceed in the identification process that way. But you have got an entry in the range and now when you try to declare it you say: "Oh, but there is already an entry in this range." There is no extra labor involved here, I believe.

Scheidig:
Without defending these rules as such, I would say that they are no more complicated than some which are in the Report.

van Wijngaarden:

Do you mean just that the rule is more complicated or that it is more difficult to find out whether the rule is satisfied?

Woodward:

I have the impression it would be difficult to teach.

Trilling:

Perhaps my questions fall outside of the subject, but I would like to ask Currie and Lindsey whether they have considered the conversational situation where the user is writing his program on the console and is conversing with the compiler. In such cases, the compiler can ask him: "Well, I never met this thing. Give me the declaration for the mode of this procedure" (in the case of recursive procedures, for example).

Lindsey:

I think if you are in this conversational situation, and it came across b and said: "Please, tell me what b is." I think you must now look to the sublanguage CHL3, which I did not describe, in which there is a facility to tell it in advance what b really is, and then you can go ahead compiling on that basis.

Currie:

I am not quite sure whether I understand the question. Are you meaning to imply that for every known local that you come across in the block you have to ask whether or not this is really a known local or whether I am really going to declare it later on the next line? Surely, that is out.

Lindsey:

I think what Trilling meant was that, if you came across this b, and b was completely unknown to you as an identifier at that point, then the compiler is immediately aware that something is wrong and can type out a message to you, inviting you to put it right. If on the other hand, b had already been declared in an outer range, I think any reasonable compiler would have presumed that its mode fitted and so on, and that was the b you meant.

Trilling:

Do you have the possibility to say this beforehand?

Lindsey:

Of course, if the programmer remembers to say beforehand that this is a new b (assuming he has this facility in CHL3) that is fair enough. But I would imagine, if we have the given program that the conversational compiler would complain at the first occurrence of b. If on the other hand b had already been declared in an outer range, then the compiler would not complain until it came to the *proc* b. Then it would complain. By that time it would be more difficult for the user to mend.

van Wijngaarden:

If I declare a b and then seven ranges inwards I use that b again, I must not only make a note that I found this b but also for all those ranges inside

I must keep notes. In each of those ranges the *b* may still be declared, may still become proper. It is not sufficient to make one note; you must make a recursive note.

Lindsey:
I think you only need to make a note if you follow what Bowlden was describing earlier, if you actually encounter an instance of *b* in one of these ranges.

Bowlden:
No, it has to be copied back into each range.

van Wijngaarden:
When you come out of the range, you can throw away that range, but you still have the problem for the range to which you have reverted, so you have to make a note for all the nestings. It multiplies your identification table.

Goos:
I think that this is a problem which occurs in finding out the scope which procedures have, for there one must do the same things. You have to note that a certain identifier or indication appears some *n* ranges inside and you have to bring it out.

van Wijngaarden:
But you first scan the whole program so you know the scope of the identifiers.

Goos:
Perhaps you do not know if you want to make a one-pass compiler.

van Wijngaarden:
No, not in the one-pass compiler, of course, but that was not the usual way in which you scan an ALGOL program. If you read it in one-pass, then you get into this difficulty. We do not need one identification table, we would need one on each level.

Goos:
If you do this and make a one-pass compiler, you are involved in the same problem, another solution to which is also that of the scope problem. Identification is not the only problem.

van Gils:
The problem can be solved by requiring rigorously that each applied occurrence has to be preceded by a defining occurrence, and this is usually not possible with recursivity. You must make a new kind of syntactic object like <u>mode</u> *a* and then you can declare <u>mode</u> *b* in terms of *a* and *a* in terms of *b*; but it is an extension to the language and not a sublanguage; however, this is a good solution for implementation.

Bowlden:
I think that the question of whether this business of copying the table information back from range to range is bad in terms of space can be taken

care of because we are talking about doing this in a one-pass compiler and, in a one-pass compiler, as soon as you are through with that inner range, you throw away that part of the table. So this is not a table explosion problem really.

van Wijngaarden:
What? This *is* a table explosion!

Bowlden:
You throw away the inner-most range. Now you copy the thing into the next range. You have not added to the size of the table.

van Wijngaarden:
Oh! You have then seven times. If you are in the seventh block you have to take the outermost x ...

Bowlden:
No, not until you exit from the inner range and when you exit from a range you throw away that range table.

van Wijngaarden:
Yes, but still there are the other seven ranges outside, and in each of the ranges you have to make a note that you have seen the x.

Bowlden:
No, you do not make that note until you exit from the range.

Currie:
Oh, but you must have made it somehow.

Bowlden:
No. It is very simple. If you have a defining occurrence of that x in the innermost range, then you do not need to copy it out. Now, in the case where the order does not matter, indeed you do not know yet until you have hit the end of the range whether you want to copy it out. So why insist on copying it out?

van Wijngaarden:
No, no. It is a check that you must perform. We do not trust that the program is proper in the new sense.

Bowlden:
Yes. But there is no need to copy it into the next outer range until you get back to compiling the next outer range. You do not have to do it until you are through with this range because you do not get to the next outer range until you are through with this range.

Goos:
I think we are now discussing a problem which can be solved in some way or another but has nothing directly to do with the proposal Lindsey has made.

van Wijngaarden:
Oh, I think it has very much to do with it.

Goos:
   I think it is a solvable problem.

van Wijngaarden:
   I assert, for the moment, that it will result, not in an exploding identifier table but in a much bigger identifier table, actually in a multiple identification table.

Mailloux:
   I feel I have to come to van Wijngaarden's support here. It said in my thesis that the trouble you might have to go to in enforcing such a condition in a one-pass compiler, might amount to almost the same trouble you would have to go to in building a two- or three-pass compiler anyway. It is probably a wee bit exaggerated, but I feel there is quite a high price to be paid if you are actually going to check that rigorously.

Lindsey:
   Well, Bowlden thinks there is not a table explosion. I think I agree with him, but this is a technical matter which is probably better discussed in a smaller circle. I think I understand what he is getting at, and I do not see the problem.

Goos:
   May I close this part of the discussion. Is there anybody who wants to make other proposals for solving the same kind of problem?

van Wijngaarden:
   May I add to this that if you want to have some announcement of mode-indication, then you can do it by staying exactly in the language. You do not need an extension for it, just use a pragmat. That is what they are for.

Bowlden:
   I believe this is in the CHL3 as a means of getting around recursive procedures.

Goos:
   This seems to be the same kind of solution that ALGOL 68-R contains, because if you say *mode a*, then this is a kind of pragmat, although it is not written in that form.

van Wijngaarden:
   Why not?

Goos:
   That is a question Currie should answer.

Currie:
   Three symbols instead of one! I think it is fairly irrelevant which particular symbol you use.

Mailloux:
   No, it is not irrelevant. It is a question of morality. We have a Bible, and you are sinning! Furthermore a way has been given for walking down

the straight and narrow path while still getting all the good things in life, so why the devil do you not stick to the rules?

Goos:
Do you allow only one type of theology?

Mailloux:
Yes!

Griffith:
It may well be that it is the test of a good language that everybody follows the Bible.

Lindsey:
If you look at my note on pragmats you will find that my standard example, which I use in various places, is this mode thing contained within pragmat-symbols.

Woodward:
Let me just say that your various criticisms will be accepted in the spirit in which they are offered!

Goos:
I close this point by stating that it seems that we have several proposals, one by Lindsey, one by van Gils and one by Mailloux which can be extended to be proper in the sense of sublanguages. I would like to invite discussion on other points, and would first like to ask Woodward the following. You have taken out proceduring from the language and replaced it by something else. What other solutions had you discussed before for coming to this solution? Are there other solutions possible to overcome the problem posed by proceduring? The problem is that you have to return some information to the front of the coercend but you find this out mostly only at the end of that coercend or in a later scan.

Woodward:
The only thing it would be proper for me to say, since our compiler writer is with us, would be that without automatic proceduring we are not really withdrawing a facility; you can still have a dynamic parameter by simply expressing yourself slightly differently.

Mailloux:
(pontificating:) You are expressing yourself outside the language. It is a sin!

Goos:
The point is correct that the expressive power of the language is not reduced but the syntax is changed and we are outside of the language as Mailloux points out. Are other solutions possible which perhaps remain inside the language?

Woodward:
Could we clear this point? I did not know what was meant when somebody said: "Outside the language". It seems to me that if you write a

routine-denotation when you want a dynamic parameter, you are within the language.

Currie:

Could I perhaps expand on that point? The point is that we have a new representation of the cast-of-symbol, namely *val*.

Mailloux:

It is a new representation, but it has a different meaning, I believe.

van Wijngaarden:

Could you have obtained the results that you wanted to obtain by putting a colon instead of the *val*?

Currie:

No. What I intended to say was that if you replace any *val* in your program by a colon, it should come out to ALGOL 68.

van Wijngaarden:

All right then, why did you not use the colon?

Currie:

Because I wanted to distinguish strongly between casts and routine-denotations.

Woodward:

This is a similar point to a suggestion made in quite a different connection, that reintroducing the word *array* would be a useful thing to do. It is similar to this, is it not, and therefore it is a variation in the strict sense?

Lindsey:

May I, for a change, come to Currie's defense. I am quite satisfied that in this respect, what he has created is a proper sublanguage, in the strict sense. Any program which is acceptable to ALGOL 68-R as far as procedures are concerned is acceptable to the full language, provided that when offering such a program to the full language you say that *val* is another representation, of the cast-of-symbol. You are perfectly entitled to say that.

Mailloux:

No, we do not! Technically, the definition of a sublanguage says that anything in the sublanguage should have the same meaning as in the full language. Now, what about the fellow who actually does write a colon Then he has written something which apparently does not get the same meaning as in the full language.

Lindsey:

Well, as a macro effect, it does in ALGOL 68-R, I checked up on this this morning. If you write a cast containing a real, genuine colon in ALGOL 68-R, then it says: "Ah here is a procedure" and it proceeds to consider the procedure. And then it says: "Ah, we can deprocedure this procedure", which gets it back to exactly where the cast would have been, taking up 60 more instructions than it should have done to do this. In fact, it has the required property.

Goos:

I think that generally speaking, we are now discussing the following problem. Given a certain symbol in the language, and somebody comes and splits the possible uses of this symbol into two classes; he prescribes one representation if the symbol is used as a member of the first class and another representation if the symbol is used as a member of the second class. Do we consider such a rule as being a rule of a sublanguage or as an extension?

van Wijngaarden:

No, a sublanguage.

Goos:

I think that is exactly the point that was made.

van Wijngaarden:

Because you can define a set of restrictions whereby, ... and so on and so forth, and that is what you are doing.

Goos:

Any further comment on that? We seem now to have proved that ALGOL 68-R, in this respect, is a sublanguage.

Koster:

I suppose then that you might give the following representations of the cast-of-symbol: (*void* and :). You would hardly use this, except in the case of void-casts. Am I correct?

Woodward:

Yes and no.

Goos:

Is there anybody who has thought about the problems which are posed for the language and for the compiler by the handling of transput? There is one special question on that, viz. the efficient treatment of united modes occurring as parameter modes of the transput procedures.

Mailloux:

We have considered it. In fact we have a transput package almost ready to go. It takes about 6000 bytes of memory essentially to do the whole of section 10.5, assuming that we do have an operating system to move the tapes around and some of those odds and ends. Unions are a nuisance. In fact, it is interesting that you could not output a union until someone thought up the wonderful idea of making unions commutative, distributive and all those wonderful things; then it suddenly popped out. (I think it was discovered later to be a fortunate accident.) Essentially, it is a nuisance, but it is not terribly difficult. What it means is that, not within the input or output routines but in the program calling them, you have to construct a conformity case clause, find out which case it is we are worrying about now and call the appropriate part of the transput routine.

Goos:

Your opinion is that it can be implemented easily without doing anything restrictive.

Mailloux:

That is right, and furthermore, only those who use it have to pay.

Bowlden:

You mean the people who do not do any transput at all do not have to pay for it?

Mailloux:

No. Only those who transput unions have the extra overhead.

Woodward:

May I ask what the question means when it says: "Is the I/O package appropriate for use in sub-sets?"

Goos:

It means: "How can one implement it?" and "Is it useful to implement it as it stands?"

Woodward:

I had better not comment on this because we have submitted a short paper to the Working Group, by our expert Dr. Jenkins, giving constructive comments on transput facilities in ALGOL 68. Since this paper is more concerned with criticizing the definitions, it does not really come within the terms of reference of this discussion on implementation.

Currie:

Our transput depends essentially on expanding each of the calls of the appropriate routines, depending on the modes which you are trying to input or output. It only pulls in the routines that it requires.

Lindsey:

There is great scope here for individual implementations, putting more procedures into their library preludes to do different things in I/O, to give different facilities and so on. This is not strictly on the subject of this discussion, but I think it is something which will come and of which some degree of standardization may have to be kept.

van der Meulen:

Is an implementation of ALGOL 68, without formatted transput, a sub-language?

van Wijngaarden:

Yes. You can formulate a set of restrictions to reduce the set of programs to those not containing formatted transput.

Woodward:

It might be appropriate here to say what facilities we are providing to gain flexibility in unformatted output. We provide a global structure, a library structure if you like, the fields of which describe parameters controlling the number of digits before and after the point and that kind of thing. If you are not aware of the existence of this structure, you will get the ordinary default read and print. If you are aware of it, you can reassign to the fields of that structure so as to get a certain flexibility and still have something that is very easily explained to beginners.

Mailloux:
  Sin!

Goos:
  I think that this means that you allow the programmer to act as the intermediate step, which usually is the result of compiling a format.

Koster:
  I think there is nothing sinful in this. But there is a practical difficulty..

A voice:
  It is heretical!

Koster:
  Well, no, it is just a new catechism. There is one problem on the input side. I mean, it is clear that on output you may have wanted to make some changes to the standard format of your reals. But on input you have, in unformatted transput, a flexibility which you can never get by one format. I wonder how you have solved that.

Woodward:
  I regret to admit that the programs I have written in ALGOL 68-R, have made no use of this facility so I cannot answer the question. The implementer of this part is not with us. Perhaps his paper will explain it.

Branquart:
  There was another question concerning parallel processing. I should like to draw attention to the point that a compiler built for a machine with one single central unit can very well take the semaphores into account; it has just to control a queue of jobs.

Goos:
  But to me, the main effect of your idea was to express the well-known fact that if you have only one CPU and if your operating system does not allow you to do multi-programming, then nevertheless you are able to construct a run-time system for your ALGOL 68 programs which allows implementation of parallel processing and implementation of semaphores. Thus you hold, in the run-time system, a pointer which tells you which of those parallel processes must get the CPU. This pointer is switched if and only if you come either to the end of that process or to an operation on a semaphore.

Currie:
  What do you do with the intermediate results in the meantime in your strict language? I do not understand this. This seems to me a contradiction in terms. If we are speaking about ALGOL 68 and crossing out any parallel processing, then the *up*s and *down*s are meaningless.

Lindsey:

It would be possible for an implementation in its library-prelude to declare some *sema*. The use of the parallel-symbol is nevertheless forbidden in this implementation...

van Wijngaarden:
What do you do?

Lindsey:

I have an implementation. I forbid the use of the parallel-symbol in any form. In the library-prelude there is declared a certain *sema*, and the intended use of this is, for example, you do some computation, you then obey a *down*, or an *up*, whichever it is, according to this *sema*, and the effect is that your program is then thrown off the machine until such time, for example, as the transput you have initiated previously has been completed. So this gives you a way of latching yourself on to some real time through your operating system. This is perfectly possible. I think this is the sort of thing that Branquart had in mind.

Goos:

I think we have seen, this afternoon, some proposals for a one-pass scheme for the solution of the problem of mode-indications, operator-indications, and mode-identifiers. We have also seen that there seem to be possibilities for reducing the complexity of the recognition of parentheses and to reduce the problems encountered in proceduring, by stating that certain symbols in different contexts may have different representations. We shall not be able to go into the details of the transput and parallelism and I think that we should close the discussion by saying that we have to consider it as input to WG2.1.

SESSION 7

(Chairman: A.P.Ershov)

A GARBAGE COLLECTOR TO BE IMPLEMENTED ON A CDC 3100 [*]

PIERRE GOYER
Université de Montréal

INTRODUCTION

This paper describes a garbage collector for a subset [9] of ALGOL 68, to be implemented on a CDC 3100. This subset treats non-local structured values and names but does not include unions, multiple values and routines. However, the garbage collector is believed to be easily extensible to the general case of ALGOL 68.

The CDC 3100 computer is word-addressable (24 bits), and our installation has a 16K central memory and a mass storage provision consisting of two disc packs (# 854).

THE GARBAGE COLLECTOR

Two phases can be distinguished in a Garbage Collector routine for ALGOL 68 [5]:
- tracing and marking
- compacting.

Tracing can be done with two different kinds of algorithms, those which need only a predetermined amount of storage (static) ([8], appendix) and those for which we need a stack (dynamic) [4]. Dynamic algorithms have been found to be faster [8]. However they present a major problem: being dynamic, we cannot know for sure the space they will require for the stack, so the G.C. must be called soon enough to allow sufficient space for the stack. If the reserved storage space proves to be insufficient then in principle, the algorithm cannot be resumed.

Static algorithms, when applied to ALGOL 68, need the adjunction of "fences" [7] to structured values comprising one or more fields which are "fingers" [7]. All users thus pay for the extra space needed to represent a structured value contained in the "heap" [2]. The main advantage of these algorithms resides in the fact that only the heap is necessary to insure completion of the tracing phase.

[*] Ce document a été rendu possible grâce aux nombreux conseils de monsieur Laurent Trilling, professeur au Département et de son assistance dans la description ALGOL 68 de la simulation.

The Haddon and Waite method [7] for compacting is mostly interesting when considering ALGOL 68, because it preserves the order of the values contained in the heap and does not need any supplementary storage space (provided that the size of the smallest value one is able to "free", is greater or equal to the size of one entry for the "break table").

Our computer's word size (24 bits) does not permit building the break table inside the heap. To build it outside of it means that we need an extra storage space which is dynamic in nature. (We cannot predict exactly what will be the table's size.) Moreover, we have to trace the pointers inside the heap in order to modify them. This tracing could be done by going down into the heap with a dynamic tracing routine or can be overcome, while executing the tracing and marking routine, by filling a "pointers' table" (where one bit represents one computer word in the heap). Then one dynamic storage space is to be taken care of while compacting and marking.

Our approach is then to provide the system with a "Service Space", which is furnished to the user whenever he needs garbaging. This way the user pays only when he calls G.C. routine. Our final approach to the G.C. problem is described below.

Tracing and marking

The starting point for a list contained in the heap is found in an "access block" [3]. Our algorithm uses a stack [4] (the Service Space being necessary anyway for the compacting phase, nothing now prohibits us from using a dynamic routine), the values in the heap being traced "interpretatively" [5], by the use of "templates" [6]. One will find in the appendix a static routine deduced from the one adopted. Marking is done with the help of a bit table and furthermore the pointers' positions are kept in a bit table called "pointers' table".

Compacting

Haddon's and Waite's compaction procedure has been retained with the notable exception that the break table is now directly built in the Service Space and consequently it is not rolled in the heap during the compaction process.

The Service Space

As we mentioned before the Service Space is provided to the user only when he needs it, i.e. when he calls the garbage collector routine.

The Service Space fulfills two goals:
During the first phase, it must provide sufficient storage space for
- the bit table
- the pointers' table
- the stack
and during the second phase:
- the bit table
- the pointers' table
- the break table.

Conclusion
This garbage collecting should prove to be fast enough since
1. tracing is done with a stack
2. it is done only once
3. the break table is not "rolled" into the heap.
Moreover, one pays for garbage collecting only when needed.

THE SIMULATION

We have written an ALGOL 68 simulation of our Garbage Collector. The purpose of this chapter is to introduce the main features of the program presented below.

In our simulation, the heap (*tas*) is a row of integer values and the integer variable *taille tas* is the upper bound. Two rows of boolean represent the bit table and the pointers' table (*table marquage* and *table pointeurs*). Also, six integer values (*type, niveau, lieu, compteur, type P, lieu P*) are titled *registers* because of the role they play during the tracing and marking phase. Two rows of structured values have a flexible upper bound due to their dynamic nature. These are the break table (*table modification*) and the stack (*pile*).

Models and their display
A model (value of mode *modèle* in our simulation, see p. 310) is used to describe a value that is being traced and of which the type is not a reference to mode.
With the considered subset [9], only three kinds of model are required.
- Plain values and structured values containing no name.
  In this case, the size (field selected by *taille*) is the only information needed.
- Structured values in which one field is or contains only one name.
  We need the size of this value and three more informations (field selected by *pointeur*) about the name contained in this value. These are the type (field selected by *type*), the number of references (field selected by *niveau*) and the offset (field selected by *adresse*, used to locate the name in the value).
- Structured values in which more than one fields are or contain names.
  We need the size of the value and for each name in it, the information mentioned above.
In each model, its kind (field selected by *genre*) has been added.
The type of a value that is a name corresponds to the dereferenced mode of that value.
The models' display (*display modèle*) is a row of reference to *modèle*.

Example:
Assuming the following declarations in a user's program:
  struct tata = *(int a, toto b, ref tata c)* ;
  struct toto = *(int a, ref int b)* ;

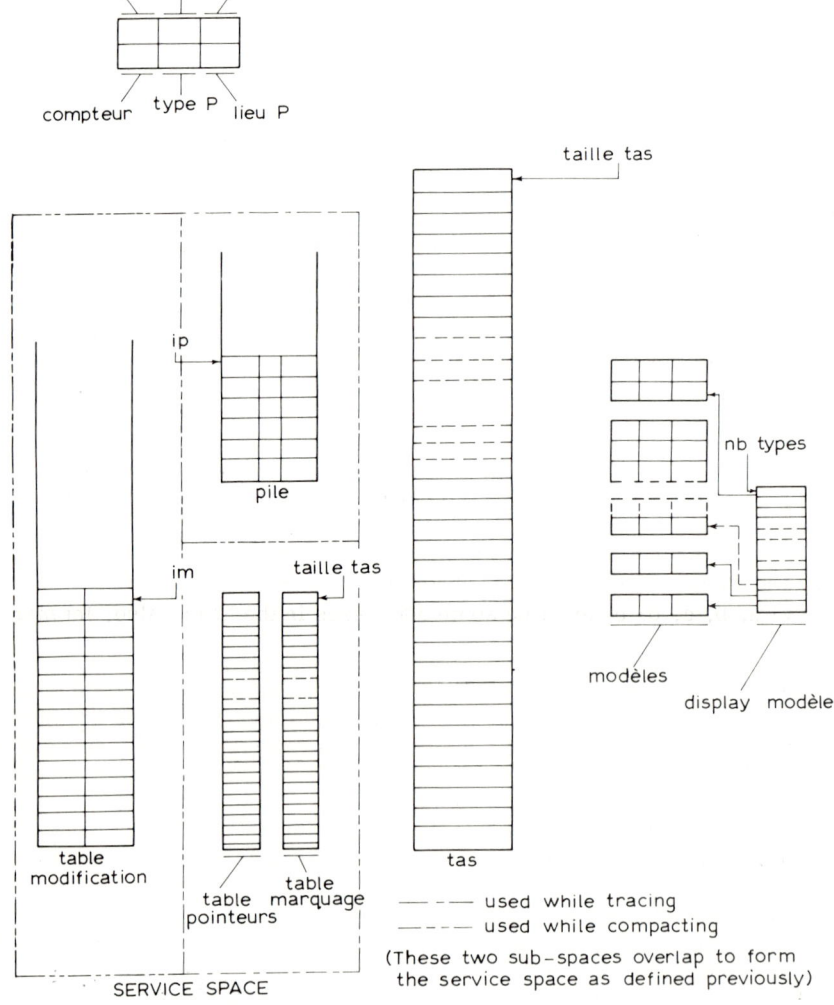

Fig. 1.

Then with the declarations for our simulation program, the following would be found:

    modèle int   := *(1, 1, skip) ;*
    modèle toto   := *(2, 2, (type int, 1, 1)) ;*
    modèle tata   := *(4, 3, ((type int, 1, 2), (type tata, 1, 3))) ;*
    int type int   = 1 *;*
    int type toto   = 2 *;*
    int type tata   = 3 *;*
    display modèle   := *(int, toto, tata) ;*

Tracing and marking

Tracing starts from an access which provides informations necessary to initiate the scanning of a list. These informations are:
- the type (*type*) corresponding to a model,
- the number of references (*niveau*), and
- the address in the heap (*lieu*) corresponding to the first value in the list.

The integer variable *début* is the location of this access.

Furthermore, three integer values, *compteur*, *type P* and *lieu P* represent the top of the stack. The counter (*compteur*) is used to remember which branches have been traced.

During the forward scan, values are marked and when the model of a value belongs to the third kind, information on this value is stacked and tracing continues with the first pointer (figs. 2 and 3).

During the backward scan, the branching point designated by the top of the stack is considered and if all branches have been traced, unstacking is accomplished.

Example (illustrating the use of registers)

Let a, b, c, d, e, and f be some addresses in the heap. Also, let *tata*

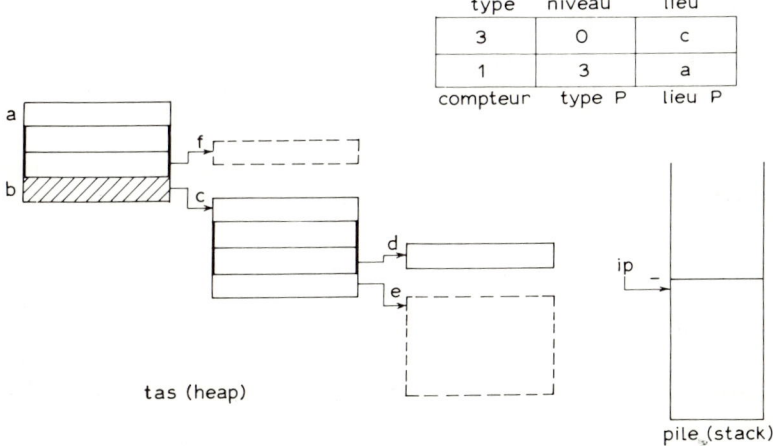

Fig. 2. Prior to the scan of the value located at c.

308   P. GOYER

be declared as in the previous example for models. The values located at b, d and f are declared to be *int* and those at a, c and e to be *tata*.

The graphs picture the situation prior to and after a forward scan where the value located at c is to be considered.

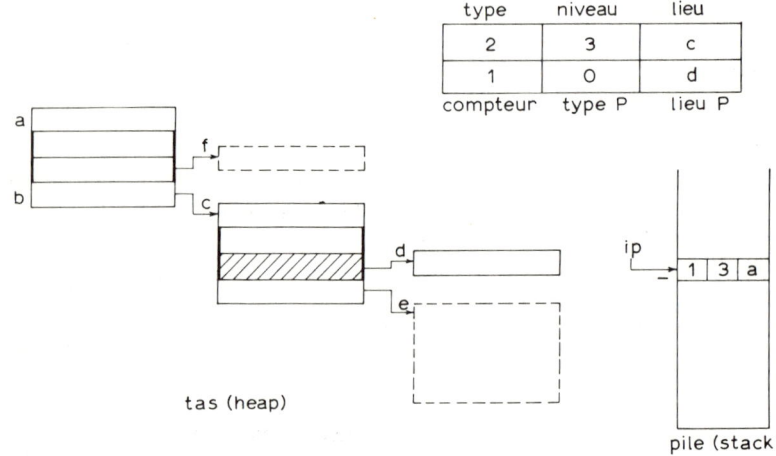

Fig. 3. Immediately after the scan.

Compacting

Compacting is executed in two steps:
- shifting of accessible values,
- modification of pointers.

The bit table (*table marquage*) is used to shift the values. Each time a marked word is encountered, it is shifted up to the location indicated by *marque* and if this word immediately follows a non-marked word then one entry is added to the break table (*table modification*). This entry is a structured value with two fields selected by *adresse* and *décalage* which respectively represent the address of an accessible block (contiguous locations) of values and the number of holes encountered up to this address (fig. 4).

Modification of pointers is done with the help of the pointers' table (*table pointeurs*) which has been constructed during the tracing phase and shifted accordingly to the heap. Pointers are scanned linearly and modified with the help of *table modification*.

The main program

Each time garbage collection is called upon, an *INITIALISATION* occurs and *TROUVER ACCES* searches for accesses. When an access is found, *RECUPERER* is called. After all accesses have been scanned, *DEPLACER* takes care of the compaction and accesses are then modified by *MODIFIER ACCES*.

IMPLEMENTATION OF A GARBAGE COLLECTOR

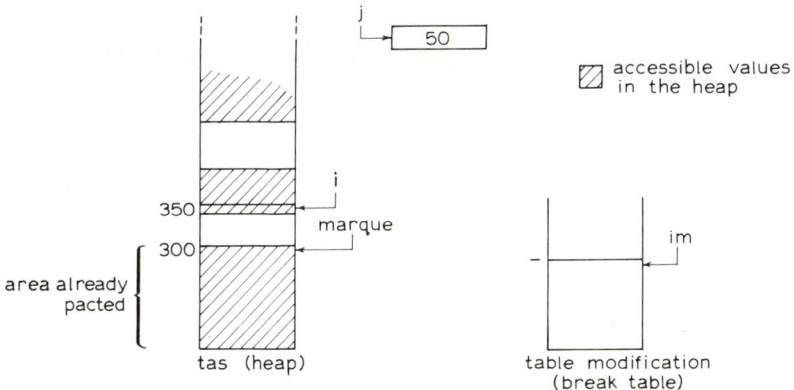

Reaching an accessible value and ....

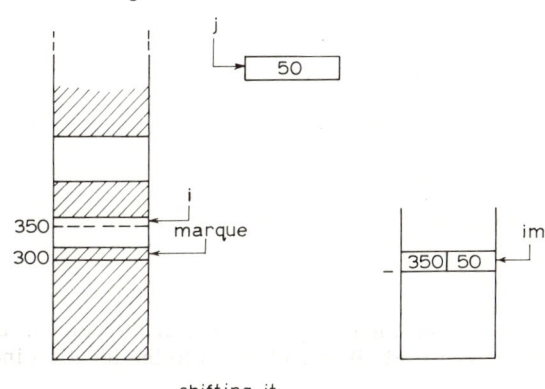

shifting it

Fig. 4.

THE GARBAGE COLLECTOR PROGRAM

co Global variables co ;

    int nb types, taille tas, début, ip, im, nil := -1 ;

    co nb types : number of models co

    co début : an address in the access block co

    co im : table modification index co

    co ip : stack index co

    taille tas := c ? c ? c ; nb types := c ;

    ip := 0 ; im := 1 ;

<u>co</u> *Models* <u>co</u>

 struct <u>modèle</u> = (<u>int</u> *taille, genre,* [1:0 <u>flex</u>]<u>constituant</u> *pointeur*) ;

 struct <u>constituant</u> = (<u>int</u> *type, niveau, adresse*) ;

 [1 : *nb types*] <u>ref</u> <u>modèle</u> *display modèle* ;

 <u>co</u> *a model contains information to trace and mark a value in the*

  heap. There are three kinds of model, describing respectively

  values without names, values comprising one name and

  values that are branching points <u>co</u>

<u>co</u> *Tables, the stack and the heap* <u>co</u>

 [1 : *taille tas*] <u>bool</u> *table marquage, table pointeurs* ;

 [1 : 0 <u>flex</u>] <u>struct</u> (<u>int</u> *adresse, décalage) table modification* ;

 [1 : 0 <u>flex</u>] <u>struct</u> (<u>int</u> *c, t, l*) *pile* ;

 [1 : *taille tas*] <u>int</u> *tas* ;

 <u>co</u> *"table marquage" is the bit table,*

  "table pointeurs" is the pointers table,

  "table modification" is the break table,

  "pile" is the stack and "tas" is the heap <u>co</u>

<u>co</u> *Registers* <u>co</u>

 <u>int</u> *type, niveau, lieu* ;

 <u>co</u> *these registers describe the value being traced* <u>co</u>

 <u>int</u> *compteur, type P, lieu P* ;

 <u>co</u> *these registers represent the top of the stack* <u>co</u>

<u>co</u> *Procédures* <u>co</u>

<u>co</u> <u>proc</u> *INITIALISATION = initialization of "table marquage" and "table*

   pointeurs".

IMPLEMENTATION OF A GARBAGE COLLECTOR

proc TROUVER ACCES = *this procedure finds an access in the access block and does the initialization of : "début" and the six registers.*
When all accesses have been taken care of, this procedure is a jump to "second phase".

proc RECUPERER = *this procedure does the marking.*
proc EMPILER = *this procedure does the stacking.*
proc DESEMPILER = *this procedure is used to unstack.*
proc DEPLACER = *this procedure does the compacting.*
proc MODIFIER ACCES = *accesses are modified consequently to the compacting phase.*

NOTE: *"INITIALISATION", "TROUVER ACCES" and MODIFIER ACCES" are not described in ALGOL 68* **co**

    proc RECUPERER = :
    begin
        proc EMPILER = :
          (pile [ip +:= 1] := (compteur, type P, lieu P) ;
          compteur := **upb** pointeur **of** modèle ;
          type P := type ; lieu P := lieu
) ;

        proc DESEMPILER = :
          (compteur := c **of** pile [ip] ;
          type P := t **of** pile [ip] ;
          lieu P := l **of** pile [ip] ;

        ip -:= 1

) ;

modèle modèle ;

descente:

   (modèle := display modèle [type] ;

     int taille = (niveau > 0 | 1 | taille *of* modèle) ;

     if (lieu = nil | *true* |

              (*bool* marque = *true* ; *for* i *from* lieu *to* lieu +

              taille - 1 *do*

                (¬ table marquage [i] marque := *false* ; e) ; e :

              marque))

     then remontée *else*

if niveau > 0 *then*

   table marquage [lieu] := table pointeurs [lieu] := *true* ;

   lieu := tas [lieu] ;

   niveau -:= 1 ;

   descente

   else

   for i *from* lieu *to* lieu + taille -1 *do* table marquage [i] := *true* ;

   case genre *of* modèle *in*

           remontée,

           suite,

           (EMPILER, suite)

   esac ;

suite: (*constituant* c = (pointeur *of* modèle [1] ;

         int dec = lieu + adresse *of* c ;

         table pointeurs [dec] := *true* ;

```
                        type := type of c ;
                        niveau := niveau of c - 1 ;
                        lieu := tas [dec] ;
                        descente
                                )
   fi fi
) ;
        remontée :
            if lieu P = début then terminé else
            if compteur > 1 then
                constituant c = (pointeur of display modèle [type P])
                                                        [compteur] ;
                int dec = lieu P + adresse of c ;
                table pointeurs [dec] := true ;
                type := type of c ;
                niveau := niveau of c - 1 ;
                lieu := tas [dec] ;
                compteur -:= 1 ;
                descente
                else
                                DESEMPILER ;
                                remontée
            fi fi ;
        terminé : skip
    end

proc DEPLACER = :
    begin
        int marque := 0 ;
```

```
        ( int i := 0 , j := 0 ;
            while (i +:= 1) ≤ taille tas do
          ( if table marquage [i] then
                table modification [im +:= 1] := [i,j] ;
              e :tas [marque +:= 1] := tas [i] ;
              table pointeurs [marque] := table pointeurs [i] ;
              if ((i +:= 1) ≤ taille tas | table marquage [i] |
                                              sortie) then e
                fi
          fi ;
          j +:= 1
          ) ;
  sortie: skip
  ) ;
  adresse of table modification [im + 1] := taille tas + 1 ;
  for i to marque do
      if table pointeurs [i] then
          ref int lieu = tas [i] ;
              for k to im do
                  if lieu ≥ adresse of table modification [k] ∧
                     lieu < adresse of table modification [k+1] then
                     lieu := lieu - décalage of table modification [k]

                  fi
          fi
  end ;
```

<pre>
        co   Main program co ;

                            INITIALISATION ;

                first phase :   TROUVER ACCES ;

                            RECUPERER ;

                            first phase ;

                second phase : DEPLACER ;

                            MODIFIER ACCES
)

)
</pre>

ABSTRACT

This paper deals with a problem related to the implementation of ALGOL 68. The problem is the one of "garbage collection" occurring with storage allocation for non-local values. A general description and a simulation (described in ALGOL 68) are given for the proposed solution. The whole is considered in the context of an implementation on a small computer with many terminals.

REFERENCES

[1] Van Wijngaarden, A. (Editor), Mailloux, B. J., Peck, J. E. L. and Koster, C. H. A.: Report on the algorithmic language ALGOL 68, MR 101, Mathematisch Centrum, Amsterdam, February 1969.
[2] Mailloux, B. J.: On the implementation of ALGOL 68, Mathematisch Centrum, Amsterdam, 1968.
[3] Branquart, P. and Lewi, J.: General principles of an ALGOL 68 garbage collector, Technical Note N60, M.B.L.E., January 1970.
[4] McCarthy, J. et al.: LISP 1.5 Programmer's Mannual, The MIT Press, Cambridge, Mass., 1962.
[5] Wodon, P. L.: Data structure and storage allocation. Bit 9 (1969) p. 270.
[6] Fites. P.: Storage organisation and garbage collection in ALGOL 68, Proceeding of an Informal Conference on ALGOL 68 Implementation, Department of Computer Science, University of British Columbia, Vancouver, 1969.
[7] Haddon, B. K. and Waite, W. M.: A compaction procedure for variable length storage elements, Computer Journal, Vol. 10, 1967-68, p. 161.
[8] Schorr, H. and Waite, W. M.: An efficient machine-independent procedure for garbage collection in various list structures, Communications of the A.C.M., Vol. 10, Number 8, August 1967, p. 501.
[9] Trilling, L.: Un sous-ensemble d'ALGOL 68, Université de Montréal, to be published.

APPENDIX

A static tracing algorithm

By "Static" it is meant that no storage reservation is done at the moment the Garbage Collector is called upon. That is, no extra space is needed for a stack.

Branching points

A branching point is defined to be any value containing more than one pointer. In the subset of ALGOL 68 considered, only structured values having more than one field consisting of a "name" [1] or another structured value containing "names" are branching points.

The method's principle

If each time we generate a non-local value which is a branching point we add to the representation of the value being generated in the heap sufficient space (called "stackelem") to enter in it one stack entry (that is, one entry one would normally put in the stack with a dynamic algorithm), then, one always has sufficient space to build a stack into a list. This is demonstrated by the fact that, when using a dynamic procedure, stacking is done only when one encounters a branching point during the forward scan of a list.

Practical consideration

This method can easily be compared to that of Schorr and Waite as adapted for ALGOL 68 by Fites [6].

Indeed, with the exception that a structured value containing only one "finger" is not a branching point, one sees that stackelems correspond to "fences" used in a different way.

Accepting the fact that stackelem can be one computer word, we have a static algorithm functioning under the same principle as for a dynamic algorithm and which requires less storage reservation than the procedure described by Fites.

This method, which utilises a stack built into a list, should prove to be faster [8] than the method of Schorr and Waite adapted for ALGOL 68, since no reversing of pointers is needed.

Modifying the dynamic algorithm into a static one

Only two procedures in the program described above are to be changed.

From these modifications, one can see that, in a non-local value representing a branching point, stackelem is simulated by three integers values representing respectively: the counter, the type and the heap address of the last branching point encountered previously to the one located at *lieu*.

IMPLEMENTATION OF A GARBAGE COLLECTOR

<u>proc</u> EMPILER = :

    (tas [lieu] := compteur ;

                     tas [lieu+1] := type P ; tas [lieu+2] := lieu P ;

                     compteur := <u>upb</u> pointeur <u>of</u> modèle ;

                     type P := type ; lieu P := lieu

) ;

<u>proc</u> DESEMPILER = :

    (compteur := tas [lieu] ;

                     type P := tas [lieu+1] ;

                     lieu P := tas [lieu+2]

) ;

Example

         <u>mode</u> <u>lisp</u> = <u>struct</u> (<u>ref</u> <u>lisp</u> car, cdr) ;

A value generated by <u>heap</u> <u>lisp</u> is represented as follows:

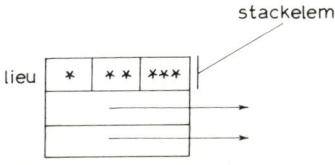

Fig. 5. (During the tracing phase, * *tas* [*lieu*] will contain the counter, ** *tas* [*lieu*+1] the type, *** *tas* [*lieu*+2] the address, of the last branching point encountered prior to this one located at *lieu*.)

SESSION 8

(Chairman: F.L.Bauer)

PANEL DISCUSSION

IMPLEMENTATION

Panel-Moderator: F. L. Bauer.
Panelists: H. J. Bowlden, P. Branquart, I. F. Currie,
A. P. Ershov, C. H. A. Koster,
B. J. Mailloux, M. Paul.

The discussion was based on a list of questions compiled by M. Paul:
- How far have you come?
- How many man years are needed?
- Space needed?
- Run time characteristics – batch or interactive?
- Are you in accordance with your time schedule as planned?
- What do we hope to win?
   Learn the handling of the implementation problem for a highly complex language such as ALGOL 68?
   Make programming in ALGOL 68 possible
      in order to allow the actual use of the language by users?
      in order to have a powerful language for teaching computer science in general?

Bauer:

We have a panel discussion today on a number of questions which arose, I think, during the work most of you are engaged with. These questions have been put into shape by Paul. Some of them may seem to be trivial. If so, then we can hopefully discard them or simply answer them and thus solve the problem. Others may turn out to be very difficult to answer. Those are probably the ones we are most interested in. If we get answers after a while, fine; if we do not get an answer, that is also an answer to the the question. This is also an open discussion, which means that the floor should take part in the discussion. We have seven panelists here, carefully selected so that we are sure that at least certain experiences made by certain implementing groups will be brought to the attention of the public. And you may comment on them of course.

Is there any objection to putting the direct question "How far have you come?" to the seven panelists?

Paul:

This group, here in Munich, consisting of about three seniors and two 'mathematical-technical assistants', started just about a year ago. They have designed the compiler to consist mainly of five passes, three of which are coded and are now being tested. The last two passes are beyond the designing phase and we are about to start coding them. I should mention in addition that the run-time operating system needed for our compiler has to be coded by us because the present one does not provide us with file handling and things like library routines and so on.

Koster:

I must begin by saying that I am here under false pretenses, but the false pretenses are not mine. That is, I am sitting here as an implementer, but the Mathematical Center has not started implementation yet. What we have done is some preparatory study in the syntactic field, which is my main interest. I have looked at the possibilities and impossibilities of using syntax-directed techniques for implementation of ALGOL 68 on the semantical side. De Bakker has given the compiler considerable thought. On the syntactic side, I spent my free time on a compiler, which is strong enough to allow implementation of ALGOL 68, but which was such a job in itself that hardly any time has been spent on the syntax of ALGOL 68. We have three unchecked syntaxes for the three first passes of our compiler, which would consist of four passes and maybe something after that.

Bowlden:

We have a recognizer coded and working, which operates on a state transition matrix method. We have not yet put the full ALGOL 68 syntax into it. As a matter of fact, we have not done much on that at all. It is currently working with the partial syntax that we have in it. There is a good deal more that needs to be done about this. It does a parenthesis recognition and produces trees. It is coded in an ALGOL dialect.

Branquart:

We have designed a six-pass compiler, four of which have been programmed and partly debugged — partly, because you can never be sure. There remain the last two phases to be programmed and we are thinking of reprogramming our coercion routines in a more efficient way and of introducing new static checks in order to increase run-time efficiency.

Ershov:

First of all I would like to mention that in the Soviet Union there exist three groups which have some implementation aims. Let me say a few words about the other two groups.

The group which first began to implement ALGOL 68 is headed by Levenson of the Institute of Mathematical Economics of the Academy of Science in Moscow. He has a group of students of Moscow University, and they have planned to implement the ALGOL 68 strict language. They are now in the stage of flow-charting and particular programming. It will be a several pass scheme. They will implement first of all some core of the language and then, through bootstrapping, have the full strict language. Their plans to make some experimental operations are for the end of the next academic year. They are implementing their version for the BESM-6 computer.

IMPLEMENTATION

Another group is headed by Professor Tseytin of Leningrad State University. They have a plan to implement ALGOL 68, in full, for a new line of computers. Their approach is to construct a very fast compiler. Another important approach is to save a full and strict correspondence between language patterns in the source program and corresponding organization of the object program. They consider their compiler mainly as a tool for debugging and for some one-run programs. They are at the stage of development of the technical specification of the language and the search for a syntactic algorithm. They hope to begin actual coding of the compiler in the next year and to finish the work within the nex two years, say in 1972.

As for us, I have mentioned, in my talks, that we now are at the research stage and are mainly involved in the search for a specification of the internal language, which we hope to have at the end of the year. Then we are involved in researching the appropriate method for the syntactic analysis of the text. We hope to make our decision by the end of this year. As I told you, it will be mainly a separation of the syntactic analysis into two parts; one of them is the context-free parsing, and another the inductive determination of all modes and other characteristics for internal quantities introduced during the decomposition of the program.

Bauer:

Thank you. On behalf of the organizing committee for the working conference, I may say that we tried to have Tseytin and Levenson here, the leading people from the groups which you mentioned, but it was unfortunately not possible for them to come to this country. I am especially thankful to Ershov that he has mentioned the work done by these other two groups.

Mailloux:

We have a garbage collector coded. Unfortunately we cannot test it since, for the time being, we have nothing to generate garbage with. We have the transput package almost coded. Beyond that, we have a document almost completed describing the internal storage organization and a translation of external objects into internal ones. One of our compilers will have five passes and will include linkage editing and loop optimization. Our other compiler will be a one-pass compiler, the intention being to use it for teaching students. Therefore, we want to compile as quickly as possible and we are not too concerned as to how fast the object program runs. It should be super-diagnostic. We hope to have both of these done in about a year. They will make considerable use of sections from each other, in particular the garbage collector and the transput package.

Currie:

We have been running an ALGOL 68-R system on our machine since April, with a somewhat restricted transput operation. The complete transput is now available, although still under test. That is basically how far we have come.

Bauer:

Thank you. These answers are a kind of basis for some additional questions, which may make sense only when you know, more or less, in what frame the work is being done. For example in our next question, "How many man years are needed?", the answer depends on what you are doing, whether you do a compiler for the full language or for a restricted set, whether you do it for a pilot model or whether you do it for a production type of compiler.

van Wijngaarden:
There is a question to Ershov. You said that in the Moscow implementation they restrict themselves to the strict language. I mean hardly anyone would ever write a program in the strict language.

Ershov:
Well, he considered his project as an experimental one so he really begins with the strict language but after that he will expand the compiler.

Scheidig:
I would be interested to hear about the size of the groups, say how many persons.

Bauer:
May we go on with the next question, "How many man years are needed?". I would like the panelists, if they give figures about estimated man years or established man years, please add for what kind of a compiler, full or restricted, more of the experimental or pilot type or more of the production type.

Branquart:
We intend to implement a compiler for the full language. Up to now we have consumed a total of eight man years, only taking into account people who are directly involved in the project, namely Lewi, Cardinael, Delescaille and van Begin. These man years ask for some comments:
- Two man years have been consumed for learning of the language, but I must add that we had undertaken the study when the language was not yet settled, and on the other hand, that we took profit from the advice of Sintzoff, who undertook the study of the language from the very beginning.
- Three man years have been consumed for the design of the compiler. Here it is important to note that I have personally the experience of an ALGOL 60 compiler and, together with Lewi, of various syntactic analysers. Moreover, we take profit from the advice of Wodon, who has the experience of LISP and SNOBOL compilers.
- Two man years for programming and debugging proper. Only one of our programmers was experienced.
- And one man year for documentation and reports. We estimate that we still need at least six man years for obtaining a compiler with a very simplified input/output. This compiler is not designed for being incorporated into the system, nor for being provided with a specialized library.

Bauer:

Thank you. It would be useful if now we could have other figures on a similar basis, that is for the unrestricted or practically unrestricted language.

Bowlden:

The amount of time that has been spent to date on the processor that we have is about six man months. If I run over two man years, I am in trouble. That is my estimate. This is for a full compiler.

Bauer:

For the whole thing?

Bowlden:

For the whole thing.

Bauer:

Design and coding?

Bowlden:

Yes.

Bauer:

Now this is a little bit less than Branquart indicated. But Branquart had, I think, included that phase where he studied the language.

Bowlden:

I did not include my evening and morning time and things like this.

Bauer:

So Branquart's figure would have been lower if he had stated them on the same basis you have. But still it is larger than yours.

Peck:

Is it possible that some people are not including coders whereas others are?

Bowlden:

That is not so in my case, we have no coders.

Bauer:

Branquart did?

Branquart:

I did.

Bauer:

Anyhow, so far the design phase seems to be in the order of magnitude of a few man years. The production phase seems to be of a similar order of magnitude, is this right?

Bowlden:

Yes.

Ershov:

We have to make some estimate because, as I told you, we do our work on a contract basis. We have the following schedule of consumption of man power during the period of development. In 1970 we write the specification of the internal languages and do all the necessary research using 10 persons for one year. In 1971 we shall write technical projects concerning the beginning of the language specification and the constructing of tables and other information projects for the compiler. This period will require about 20 people. The next year, 1972, is a period for flow-charting and coding the compiler and all the necessary language tables. The next year, 1973, is a period for debugging the compiler, i.e., its pilot model. These two years will require about 30 people to take an active part in the work. And now 1974 is a period for field tests, experimental running, and finalization of documentation. This period will require about 20 people. Thus it is about 100 man years to do the job. I would like to stress that these figures are based on our previous experience in constructing productive compilers. The ALPHA compiler, which is a reasonable extension of ALGOL 60, including some multi-dimensional complex arithmetic and so on, required for us 30 man years, but the documentation was not adequate. So this estimate includes also the documentation, and what is more important, the field testing on actual programs.

Bauer:

Thank you. It has been said clearly that it aims at a productive kind of a compiler.

Ershov:

Also I have to say that it is a joint implementation of three languages.

Bauer:

It also includes many things one would certainly not include in an experimental or pilot work. We have Bowlden, who is on the extreme side, if I may say so, of being short in resources and being forced to do the best he can with the very limited amount of man years he has available; and we have Ershov, who is estimating 100 man years and I am sure he went on the safe side. I think this is a good spectrum now, and I would like to see how the others fit in.

Paul:

We aim at the full compiler, really compiling almost the whole language, minor restrictions can be discussed later, but it is really a full compiler. We had one very experienced programmer and one very experienced translator, if I may say so, compiler-builder, in the group. Altogether I would say they take (if you do not count the time they spend for teaching, i.e., if you only consider the time that they spend for the compiler during a year) about $2\frac{1}{2}$ to 3 full workers. They have been working now for almost a year, so it is about 2 to $2\frac{1}{2}$ man years that they have spent on the first three passes. I am expecting them to finish their work, if the group stays together, perhaps at the end of next year. So add another 4 to 5 man years to my estimate, i.e., at least 6 to 7 man years, which is at least two more than we estimated in the beginning.

Bauer:

Language learning was not particularly counted. Is documentation included?

Paul:

It includes documentation and includes field testing and debugging. So we should have a running and productive compiler by the end of next year, I think.

Bauer:

Productive, that means embedded in an operating system, including library routines to be provided.

Paul:

Yes.

Currie:

When we started on the restricted ALGOL 68-R project in January 1969, I estimated three man years for the basic compiler, i.e., just the compiler itself, that 24K of code I was speaking about. In fact, it is spread out to about 5 man years. Fortunately the machine was late. That was for the basic compiler itself. The transput routines have probably taken about 3 man months to write, in sort of interactive mode between the compiler writers and the one who is doing the transput routines. The other library operations seem to be taking roughly the same time as that, perhaps a bit more. The documentation is not complete. It is impossible to separate it from the documentation of the operating system itself. So all and all I suppose, up to now, we have had six man years perhaps to get a running, practical compiler.

Bauer:

Thank you. There was a general remark that Koster wanted to make and then I shall invite the audience to ask questions or give further information.

Koster:

We have seen a big spread in the spectrum of man years, which comes, more or less, from the different way of operating in the various implementation groups. Bowlden probably works alone and other people speak about working with 20 or 30 people. I think the ideal group is a 3 to 5 person group, which will then spend 2 to 3 years on it, but from our experience of designing the language, we know that it is good to have a shadow group double-check everything you are doing. Therefore the group could, on those lines, be larger.

Ershov:

I have a remark to Koster's remark and also want to give some characteristics of our group. I am not fully in agreement that 3 to 5 people is the optimal group to do the job. It depends on the style and what you have to do. If you can convert the art of programming into a technology of programming, you can use many more people to do the job in a proper manner and with high productivity. I refer again to our experience in constructing modifications of new versions of compilers for the same language when you have already developed a scheme of translation. Then you simply need to program, debug, check, and deliver a compiler. At such a stage of work (for example we are now making a compiler from ALGOL to the URAL computer), it is fairly technical work. We can assemble a group of 15 people, who cooperate well, who can finish their work in one year with full documentation and all the other necessary technical requirements. Of course, when you are on the preliminary study and when you are developing a pilot model, I agree with Koster, that his group is optimal from the point of view of the exchange of information. I would like to make some specific points about our group. The manner in which people join the group is as follows: The initial group consists of five people, three of them with experience of various compilers, two of them are experienced people who have changed their interests from other fields to become compiler writers. We have about seven graduate students coming with ordinary training and no special knowledge in programming. But now we can capture the ten best 4th year students from one course, and they are now working on a version of the ALPHA compiler for the BESM-6 computer. They will finish their work before graduation. That will be the core of the main group. They will have two years of experience in writing compilers. We consider that we can involve them in the work very quickly over several weeks or maybe two months to get the necessary initial experience. So I consider it is quite possible to have a large project with students, but only if you have a possibility to influence their approach and to teach them properly during the last two years of their education.

Bauer:

Thank you. Here I would like to make one direct remark concerning the estimate of man years, which perhaps is wrong. I do not think you have to take the number of people times the number of years, although this is what is usually the financial concern. This is no proper measure for the work that you do. I think you have to take the logarithm of the number of people multiplied by the time that they work, and you get roughly an indication of the work to be done. For example, if 8 people can do it in one year, then one man would not need 8 years, he would need 3 years. I think that would be more reasonable. Unfortunately, it is not true that the cost of wages goes up with the logarithm of the number of people, it is directly proportional.

Bowlden:

My estimate does not include documentation, but it does lean heavily on the fact that I have a good operating system. There is an awful lot that I do not have to worry about. The run time package is practically nothing.

Bauer:

Thank you. That again explains the discrepancy a little and where it is coming from.

Branquart:

I think that the figures are influenced by the language people have at their disposal for writing compilers. I should like to know in what language other people write their compilers.

Bauer:

We can ask this question. What language are you using, Branquart?

Branquart:

Assembly, with macro facilities.

Bauer:

What language are you using or plan to use, Ershov?

Ershov:

For system programming we use a specially designed language, a machine oriented language, with some properties of high order languages, designed especially for symbol manipulation. We call it the EPSILON language. It is a kind of macro assembler which also incorporates string manipulations, list manipulations, table manipulations and such things. We use this language first of all as a way of expression of our algorithms. After that we have a double way. One of them is to compile from EPSILON to machine code; and for a not very responsible part of the compiler we use this compiler. Sometimes if we have to write a difficult part, we use assembler language doing the translation from EPSILON to this assembler language by hand.

Bauer:

May I ask Bowlden?

Bowlden:

It is in Burrough's extended ALGOL.

Bauer:

May I ask Paul?

Paul:

It is assembler code directly into machine code.

Bauer:

Last, not least, what are you using, Mailloux?

Mailloux:

We expect to spend six man years to produce both compilers. This is because the work will overlap very considerably. In fact I expect the one-pass compiler will require an additional man year over the full compiler. The language will be the full language with the exception of parallel processing and the semaphores. The language we are writing it in, I am ashamed to admit, is PL... oh, you know that one. The reason for this is that we have no suitable ALGOL 60 translator on our machine, and even if we did, we would find ALGOL 60 less suitable because we want to translate our compiler as quickly as possible into ALGOL 68 and perhaps produce it as a model compiler. Since PL/I does have some features which look a little bit like some of the things in ALGOL 68, this seems a more appropriate choice. We expect to have an extremely inefficient compiler in the beginning, and of course this will improve, possibly by translating it into ALGOL 68 and having it compile itself. We shall also have it translated into assembly. The time for translating into ALGOL 68 and assembly is not included in the estimates.

Bauer:
Does anyone else want to make Geständnisse?

Peck:
I shall also admit that the efforts that we are making are written in PL/I. I am not as ashamed as Mailloux to admit it.

van Wijngaarden:
A direct question to Ershov. You said that you were making an ALGOL compiler for the URAL computer? Is that right?

Ershov:
That is right.

van Wijngaarden:
Which ALGOL?

Ershov:
Well,...

van Wijngaarden:
number?

Ershov:
This is a kind of socialist ALGOL, namely ALGAMS, so called, because it was officially adopted in a group of socialist countries, a subset of ALGOL which includes the IFIP-subset.

van Wijngaarden:
Well, fine, I thought it might perhaps have been ALGOL 68. Thank you.

Bauer:
There is not yet a socialist form of ALGOL 68. Other questions? Then we shall come back to documentation. We spoke about it here and whether it is included in the count and what time is needed. I think it is a very important topic, documentation, and I think it fits in here. Does anybody care to say something about documentation, about its problems and in particular about the time it needs. I think documentation, at least in our circles, has very often been a time problem, and I have seen it insufficiently done. An excuse was usually: "We did not have the time."

Ershov:
I have a question for the panelists, please. It seems to me that some kind of machine independent documentation for a compiler is necessary, and I need to know what kind of such machine independent documentation are you planning to prepare.

Bauer:

I was really trying to ask the same question. Thank you very much and we can start at the other end with Paul.

Paul:

We are certainly hoping that we shall have a good machine independent documentation, as we had it in the past for the ALCOR compilers. You all know that it was published about four or five years after the compilers were built. It took the longest time to get this documentation finally published.

Bauer:

It was a very ambitious publication.

Paul:

All right, but it was machine independent, and its purpose was to say exactly what the basic ideas in this compilation were and how it was fitted together in a modular way. If we can make this gap between completion of the compiler and completion of documentation shorter, then we would consider it a big success.

Bauer:

In what language will the documentation be?

Paul:

We have not yet made up this documentation language.

Scheidig:

For each pass which we have in the test phase, we have two kinds of documentation. One is internal and is necessarily machine dependent. On the other hand we have our machine independent documentation, first a description in words, and as an appendix the description of the compiler in ALGOL 68 itself.

Bauer:

Well, so there is even a description in ALGOL 68 which is a kind of machine independent documentation.

Bauer:

Sorry for interfering about the ambitiousness of the documentation, but I am quite sure that documentation can be looked at from several levels. You may only want to give the documentation, for later reference to what you have done or for your going into maintenance, I think this is the minimum level. The maximum level is if you want from the project, as in the ALGOR project, to derive and publicize the utmost in knowledge that you gain from the project. In the case which Paul has mentioned, when it took quite a long time, I know that most of the time came from the polishing, which is a very complicated and time-consuming thing, so we should not suggest that documentation will always need five years after the completion of the compiler. I think Paul certainly did not want to do this.

Paul:

I mean to warn people that if you have completed your compiler and you have debugged it, then you are so happy that it works, you are usually not so concerned with completing this burdensome task of documenting the whole thing. Of course you tried to document it while you were programming, and this of course is good advice to every group of programmers, but beware that as soon as the thing works and you can give it to people to program in that language you are so happy, you go away and you leave the documentation in the state it is at that time. That is the danger.

Koster:

There is a connection between part of the documentation problem and the language used for the detailed description of your compiler. What you should aim for is that other people can use, fully or in part, what you have done, especially in the present situation, the beginning of implementation of ALGOL 68. Therefore, we are thinking of using syntax-directed techniques for the parser, that is, having a grammar describe all of parsing and translating. This grammar, together with the compiler described in itself, is a complete informal documentation. One may use as intermediate, let us say for testing the object code, ALGOL 60. No good ALGOL 68 compiler is available but ALGOL 60 is quite sufficient for describing your compiler and even testing it on a machine. Only lastly you get into machine code. That is, you need a set of well-defined macros, as small as possible, as well thought out as possible, which you have trouble in documenting.

Branquart:

As far as we are concerned, we spent one man year for documentation, but rather high-level documentation where principles are settled. As an emphasis of the statement of Koster, I think that for a compiler which is written in a high-level language, the program itself can already be considered as good documentation. We use an assembly code with macro facilities, and we try to define, as Koster said, a set of primitive macros in such a way that the machine dependency appears only in the macro definitions.

Ershov:

As to our approach to documentation, I should say that we are happy with the flow charts but they require some means of automation for producing them. But now some means exist. It is only one level of documentation and of course there has to be some detailed method of documentation. As for us, maybe we shall use the same EPSILON language, but of course, we shall have some experiments in expressing our compiler in ALGOL 68. We do not know whether it will come into the technical documentation. Perhaps it will be the way to have a scientific publication about the main parts of the compiler.

Mailloux:

I am perhaps in a good position, since most of my workers are students who need to write theses in order to graduate, and so they will write documentation or else! One of the things that we are doing is trying to invent a universal ALGOL-oriented language (UNALGOL). This is somewhat like what Ershov has been mentioning, I think, but we are not trying to be quite as ambitious. We shall be sufficiently happy if we can invent a small language of about 50 instructions which is sufficient to describe what ALGOL 68 does and yet can still be translated into the order code of present-day machines. Our final pass will produce code in this intermediate language. This is essentially the output of the compiler and after that, you have to write a machine dependent thing to translate this output into your own machine language. Quite likely, people will tend to rewrite the whole last pass, but we hope at least to have given them some guidance as to how they should do this. I hope that a complete description of this will be available in a few weeks.

Bauer:
 This is in fact the problem of portability which you are mentioning here. As on many other occasions, we have here also the problem: can you arrange your documentation in a language that, if you go to a different and unforeseen machine configuration or machine structure, you have to change as little as necessary? In your case, and this I think is the classical way, it is done by introducing language layers.

Bowlden:
 I would say it is intended that our compiler be self-documenting and about 25% of the current ALGOL program is comment. Of course my own choice for the most important immediate documentation for a project like this, is a user programming manual. If you do not have this, you will not get people using it.

Bauer:
 Now you mention manuals, and this is perhaps a key word to which we may return later. It is generally something that cannot be taken away completely from the compiler building, and that is from the job we are discussing here during this week. But it is not our main point.
 Our next question is: "How much space is needed?" Who will volunteer to give such information?

Bowlden:
 Our experience with our processors so far is that we can run two copies easily, three copies with difficulty, together in our 32K core. This is a page on demand multi-programming system. This is the only way we can make an estimate: the core usage of the program is rather soft.

Bauer:
 Has somebody other information?

Ershov:
 I cannot estimate the actual necessity for core memory for our compiler, so I make only some extrapolation based on our experience. If you have no very diverse method for using multi-dimensional arrays or structures, then you can reduce the actual requirements of core memory. But if you write large programs which make full use of the ALGOL 68 language, then no less than 16K of memory has to be in the possession of

the running problem to make things comfortable.

Boulden:
Pardon me. Are we talking about space for the compiler or for the run-time system?

Bauer:
Our question left it open. Our question allowed you to include both. But perhaps Branquart will say something.

Branquart:
We count an average of 5K instructions per pass. That is 30K instructions for the whole compiler.

Paul:
Well, that really comes exactly to the same amount that we estimate right now 30K for the compiler.

Bauer:
So on this we got quite obviously a certain agreement. At least the order of magnitude seems to be not too different.

Ershov:
I have one more remark about space. In our case we shall have program processor and language tables. Our estimate is that the program processor will occupy about 50K words, but language tables will occupy much more space and we consider that languages such as ALGOL 68 and PL/I, each require no less than 50K to 60K words. Thus, as a whole, this joint implementation will occupy about 200K words in the secondary memory.

Currie:
The size of our compiler is 32K. That includes table space. The amount of actual program is about 24K. This is for the one-pass compiler.

Bauer:
Here I think I would like to say that your compiler, as far as the language goes, will be restricted. It is a compiler for a restricted language. This is right. This should be said clearly because some of the other gentlemen are not speaking about a compiler for a restricted language.

Currie:
I think everybody is aware that it is a restricted language.

Bauer:
Do we really have to say much about run-time characteristics, against interactive?

Paul:
Are there any installations that plan interactive systems in the near future? Because I should like to know some of the basic ideas that have been considered already.

Currie:

We have plans for running an ALGOL 68-R interpreter interactively, in such a mode that it can run with previously compiled segments, using our compiler. This is, I would say, about half done. It is estimated at one man year. Previously we had another version of much the same project running, last year some time, of a very slow interpretive system for ALGOL 68, our subset, and this has been running but it was not much use, it was too slow. It will still be just as slow at the outermost level but at least you will be able to use the previously compiled segments so that you can test them perhaps with different inputs on line.

Paul:

I would like to ask Currie directly again if I may, would you provide for initializing names that have not got any values at a certain point, if you want to test the program interactively while you are writing it? Is there any plan that the system provides reasonable values for identifiers, or is this up to the programmer that the system will ask him to initialize, for instance?

Currie:

In general what will happen is that he will come to a run-time error, if he has forgotten to initialize or something like that. Perhaps it has got some good numbers which are illegal in certain circumstances.

Ershov:

We do not yet have immediate plans to make conversational compilers for ALGOL 68, but we hope to organize some cooperation with the Grenoble group. We begin our own implementation not earlier than in two years. Our first version will be specifically for batch processing and for remote batch processing.

Lindsey:

In our implementation we shall try to make it such that all diagnostic error messages come out during the first pass, which means we have to restrict the language, of course. The intention then is that the same implementation could be used. You could type in your program and if you made an error, the diagnostic message would come out immediately and you would have the chance to correct it on the spot.

Bauer:

Now inevitably I think the discussion leads us into another question. That is, do you have to restrict the language and what are suitable restrictions if you want to do interactive compiling? Has anybody any ideas about it?

Lindsey:

You have to restrict it at least to the level of CHL2, which I defined yesterday.

Currie:

What do you do with the labels in that case? Are you going to keep your complete source string?

Lindsey:

I think you have to restrict it at least that far.

van der Meulen:

Are the restrictions of ALGOL 68-R established now, or is there some chance that after the discussions of this conference, and perhaps some deliberations of the WG2.1, you could consider a modification of your restrictions in such a way that you are more in the line of an official sublanguage of ALGOL 68?

Currie:

I doubt it. I cannot say much more than that. It depends critically on the sort of installation parameters that you are dealing with. We have got real programs running and all the rest.

Bauer:

I think the question is much more the kind of question to be discussed next week in WG2.1 meetings and I hope we shall discuss it at that conference.

Paul:

Especially I think the term sublanguage has not really been established yet. I mean, apart from what is in the Report, which says something about sublanguages.

van der Meulen:

But ALGOL 68-R being, as far as I know, the first ALGOL 68-like compiler which is operative, I think this is a crucial question.

Bauer:

Now, if you agree, our next question is: "Are you in accordance with your time schedule as planned originally? If not, what are the unforeseen difficulties?" Does the panel have ideas about this?

Bowlden:

It depends on whether you are asking about elapsed time or processor time figures. On elapsed time we are behind; processor time I think we are on schedule. And the reason is that there is a fair amount of unforeseen or more than expected time in preparing for and attending meetings and preparing for a new computer and a few other incidentals.

Branquart:

We never had a very precise time schedule but I estimate that we are four man years late. We had external reasons for that. Let us say quickly that our single experienced programmer had an accident and we had approximately one year delay in the delivery of our drum, so we had to work with only 32K. There are also internal reasons.

Bauer:

And these are the ones we are more interested in, may I say this?

Branquart:

The more we enter into details of the compilation, the more we see the possibility of introducing new compile-time features to ameliorate the run-time efficiency, and it is very time consuming.

Bauer:

May I say that you have changed your concept a little, during your work. That of course may sometimes cause you delay. Of course you gain something by it, but you usually do not keep to your schedule.

Paul:

Well, we are behind schedule, about a year I should say.

Bauer:

A year or a man year?

Paul:

A year just in time, one year behind schedule. We wanted to have the five passes far enough to give, for instance, the participants of the working conference a chance to run some example programs. That was at one time our idea for this conference. And of course since we have only three passes, it is impossible to do it. So I should say we are one to one and a half years behind. Now, what are the reasons, or what could be the reasons? One certainly is that you cannot so easily communicate and convey the experiences that you have made in earlier ventures of the same sort. We have many experts in the Munich group, who have been writing compilers for ALGOL 60 in all kinds of system, and some of them have experience with two or three of these interpreters, generators. One of these people that have been working on ALGOL 60 compilers is still active in this group. And still it was not so easy to convey all the experience gained during those past ventures. I think this is one main reason. They have to learn it again and even if you tell them that is the trick that they should use, and these are nice easy ways to go, it is not so easy without once jumping into the water yourself and trying to swim.

Scheidig:

I would say that 50% of our difficulties arise because of our installation. The details are not interesting, but it is so. And the other 50% arise because we have too few persons for coding. That is a dirty job.

Paul:

Yes, you are quite right. The coding itself is, as everyone knows, a burdensome task. You do not have the coders and it is too hard to explain the flow charts and such things. What you then do is, you just code it yourself and, of course, it is frustrating and all the rest of it. Still, I think one reason remains: this difficulty of conveying to other people the experience which would allow one to repeat compiler writing in the same institution.

Bauer:

I would like to go to our next point: "What do we hope to win?" Essentially two things are mentioned here: handling the implementation problem on the one side, and making possible programming in ALGOL 68 on the other side. So the one aspect is a pure research aspect: we want to make progress without looking at the product. The other is a purely economic aspect: we want to have a product. Now, I am sure that some people do their implementation more under the one aspect and that some do it more under the other aspect. I hope that in most implementations at least both aspects are somehow present, but I can imagine that at present some implementations are really, to a large extent, pilot implementations only.

Branquart:

We work in a research laboratory. Our main goal is not to produce an effective operational compiler. We essentially try to learn the methodology of compilers, and ALGOL 68 appears to be very well fitted for it.

Bowlden:

We have a dual role in our research laboratory. One is to do research and the other is to serve the research scientists in the laboratory. So we really have a split personality on this matter: we are doing both. We have developed a special purpose extension package in the current ALGOL which has meant extensions. It looks as if ALGOL 68 is much more suited for this purpose and we are planning so to use it. We plan to make a production compiler, but in the sense of an experimental compiler too.

Ershov:

Please, let me cover both points. What do we hope to win, what are the real goals for this work Now, one of them is, of course, obvious — that is to construct a productive compiler for actual usage. From the point of view of programming technology we are trying to make language description directed compilers economically feasible. It seems to me that this approach to writing compilers, up to now, if you consider the spectrum of existing compilers in real usage, has not produced so many compilers. So we are trying to study this subject and gain some real knowledge. From the scientific point of view, our main interest is in searching for universal optimization algorithms. Next, what are the reasons for having a compiler for ALGOL 68. I believe that for several years the main language for teaching will be ALGOL 60. It is difficult to see that many teachers can switch from ALGOL 60 to ALGOL 68 very soon. They would begin to do it only after the first successful implementation and very wide publication about this implementation. The problem of dissemination of the information on how the work on ALGOL 68 is done is very important because up to now we are a rather closed group.

Currie:

I would like to say that our motivation in implementing ALGOL 68-R was simply to provide a reasonable language for users actually to solve problems with it, and not for any particular academic exercise in writing the compiler.

Mailloux:

One of the things I feel is an aspect of this is that the language and its definition have brought some clarity (at least to me) about what it is we are doing when we are computing. Now the world seems, at least on my side of the ocean, to be cluttered with people who have what I call "FORTRAN minds". It seems to me that we have a 'mission', if you will, to clean up these minds, but we shall need compilers to help us do it, and some good reading material.

Bauer:

Mailloux has introduced a point to be discussed which is 'educating the community'. I think it is an important point that we should have listed here. Is there someone who wants to speak in particular to the point "in order to have a powerful language for teaching computer science in general"? Is it true that it is a powerful language for teaching computer science? It is implied by Mailloux's remark that it is. But is this the question?

van der Meulen:

Since ALGOL 68 is an ideal vehicle for teaching computer science, it is important to have some compiler available, because swimming in the dry is not so amusing. Therefore I think it is wise for every compilation to have this point foremost in mind, because after some people have been taught in ALGOL 68, they will want to use the language for programming problems. This is in my opinion the natural order. ALGOL 68 is a much better language for teaching computer science than ALGOL 60 is. For example, the mode concept, the reference concept, the possibility of declaring structures, the possibility of declaring new operators, appeal immediately to students. Therefore, it is important to have a compiler for teaching purposes in the first place and the rest will come as a consequence.

Bauer:

I may say, as others in Munich could have said, that in fact we look very much at ALGOL 68, at the moment, from the point of view of using it in teaching. I have used it in teaching my students since 1967, i.e., even before it existed. I used the form that existed at that moment. I used it to the extent that I understood or misunderstood it; sometimes I misunderstood it on purpose (laughter); that was the first year, the next year I was already more orthodox and it was not that easy to misunderstand it on purpose. The next year, that is the academic year that is just now over, Samelson gave that course here. He also used ALGOL 68 as a basic language, the language in which you learn to think, the language in which you explain concepts. By the way, we are not orthodox, as you know we still deviate sometimes unintentionally, and we have not exhausted it. I do not think that in using ALGOL 68 in teaching you have to teach people every corner of it. By no means, we only give the basic philosophy. I have not the slightest doubt that it is much better than any other thing I could do – chosing among the other existing languages, whatever names they have, or trying to concoct, as one usually did, one's own language, which usually ends up in a mess.

van der Meulen:

Until now we do not have a regular computer science curriculum in Utrecht. I gave in total four courses in ALGOL 68, there and elsewhere, and many from the audience told me afterwards, it really was a course in computer science. You cannot teach ALGOL 68 without teaching essential things about computer science. The language forces you to be exact about a lot of points you can never be exact about if you are teaching ALGOL 60 or something.

Bauer:

We still have a question left: we have minus 8 minutes left. Is somebody willing to speak on the question? "What could be the reason that manufacturers are so hesitant to implement ALGOL 68?" I take it for granted that we agree that this is a fact.

van der Meulen:

Manufacturers are not hesitant. I think it is entirely a matter of the customers. If the customers require ALGOL 68 with all their force, the manufacturers will do it.

Bauer:

Well, that is quite clear, but the question is, why do customers not require it and so the manufacturers can do nothing but be hesitant.

Paul:

I do not believe van der Meulen's statement. Because you teach your customers to wish something, to want something. Everybody knows that advertising is just to create wishes and this is done in the computer community by "Big Brother" as well as by others. Therefore, I am still of the opinion that there is mainly a certain resistance among some of the manufacturers to implement ALGOL 68, as they did in the past with ALGOL 60. Most efficiently working compilers for ALGOL 60 were built by university people and people involved mainly in research, and not so much by manufacturers' software houses.

van der Meulen:

Of course, manufacturers are hesitant. We now know how much effort you have to invest in implementing ALGOL 68. But, if in a small computer center like the University of Utrecht, I speak with manufacturers and I say I personally want to have an ALGOL 68 compiler, I do not even then get a flat refusal. If I were backboned, for example, by the ARA Center, which will have the largest computer in Western Europe as we were told before, and if the people there require from their manufacturer an ALGOL 68 compiler, well, it will not be so difficult. This is a big chance to press them.

Bauer:

What is the big chance: to get a bad compiler instead of no compiler?

van der Meulen:

Oh yes, you will always start with a bad compiler. I think, perhaps, if the manufacturer realizes that the customer requires such a thing and he can really sell the biggest computer in Western Europe...

Paul:

You see, I am really concerned about something which is different from what you think is the main point. My concern is that there seem to be indications that on asking for the profit that you will make by implementing this language, the answer for any manufacturer is: "The profit is not there, I cannot make profit with it, so I shall not put money into it" — is not that so? I mean, every good businessman will, of course, try to get the best compiler there is, if he can make business with it. I think we should try to find out why this is not a possible break-through for software construction. PL/I probably has failed, as far as I can see, and so ALGOL 68 will be a candidate, that is my opinion.

Bowlden:

I think it may be that a few manufacturers have gotten stung in a way. The decision of Burroughs when they started back in 1960 on the design of the B 5000, to implement ALGOL and not FORTRAN, really hurt them, not because they were providing ALGOL, but because they did not provide FORTRAN. The computer community in the United States is basically very conservative. They know it, and now Burroughs is being much more careful, and not looking seriously at ALGOL 68, as far as I can find out, not until they get some real pressure from users. I think it is this kind of experience in the past which is responsible.

Griffiths:

Can we also make the point that the manufacturer always takes a lot longer to make up his mind to do something Two years is not a long time for them to make a similar decision, which implies for them an awful lot more money than for us. Their hesitance merely means they are being as cautious as usual.

Branquart:

I think manufacturers hesitate to adopt ALGOL 68, not for isolated reasons, but for a combination of reasons, at least two of the main reasons are: the language seems to be difficult to learn and we have no compiler.

Bauer:

He said, "seems to be".

Branquart:

Yes, on purpose. Now, another remark: different universities and laboratories have taken the burden of showing the way; manufacturers prefer to wait and see, it is more sure and less expensive.

Bauer:

Exactly, and less expensive in particular. In fact, if universities again will provide ALGOL 68 compilers and if the compilers will be good enough to convince the manufacturers that they could take them over, why should this not happen? It happened with ALGOL 60 in Europe. I think the question is a really complicated one under the surface of the wording we have here. Hesitant may have two meanings. Someone is 'hesitating', but if you would do it for him or if you would convince him, then you could bring him on your side – as it has happened with ALGOL 60 with some manufacturers. And the other 'hesitant' can turn out to be hostility. The more you show that it is possible, the more hostile the manufacturer becomes, because he now sees that some difficulties are coming to his market. This could of course happen again with ALGOL 68, that some manufacturer would think there is a deadly danger for his market position. Of course it would not be our duty to keep manufacturers from making silly decisions, but on the other hand it does not help us a bit, if the manufacturer makes a wrong decision. We are also hurt by it, as the community has been in the United States at least, with respect to ALGOL 60, and the way it was suppressed there.

Paul:
I would like to find out what failures we have made with ALGOL 60 and not so much the wrong thing the other side has done. I have discussed this question about ALGOL 60 so often with people involved and I know that there were some things which a theorist would call minor flaws. Since manufacturers, of course, have to do with people who want to input and output a language, if it is good, it has to have good input-output facilities with it. I am sure that is one of the main reasons for ALGOL 60 to be a failure in the United States.

Bauer:
Of course, one would expect that people in Europe would also want input-output.

Paul:
Since the manufacturers in Europe have not built a decent compiler by themselves, they took it over and maintained it after it was given to them. That is right in one sense.

Bauer:
In fact, I cannot see why the input-output argument explains anything for the Unites States. If it would hold, it would also hold for Europe, or...

Paul:
I mean, of course, one can close one's eyes, but I think it is quite clear that I/O shortcoming was one of the main reasons for ALGOL 60's state in the United States.

Bauer:
Yes, but what I am saying is that the lack of input-output in ALGOL 60 did not do the same harm in Europe, as it did in the United States, and that makes me think about it.

Bowlden:
It did not stop Burroughs either.

Bauer:
It might very well be that for a number of people this lack of input-output was only a very easy excuse. It certainly was used for an excuse. It was very handy.

Paul:
I am not so sure whether this is true.

van der Meulen:
It is also a matter of the right approach to the manufacturers. If you say to a manufacturer: "I want to have your computer, if you have an implementation of ALGOL 68", perhaps you are asking too much. Another question could be: "If we make, together with you as a customer, an ALGOL 68 compiler, will you support it?", then I think for ALGOL 68 this could be the best approach. So I think we really should speak about how to get the right support from the manufacturer for implementations made by customers and not give them the whole burden of the responsibility.

Bauer:
Let me bring to this discussion a kind of conciliatory note now: I do not want it to end in any aggressive mood. What we should hope for is good cooperation with the manufacturer, be it "Big Brother" or smaller brothers, in establishing the best for the community. Thank you.

SESSION 9

(Chairman: W.L.van der Poel)

MAKING THE HARDWARE SUIT THE LANGUAGE

C. H. LINDSEY
University of Manchester

1. INTRODUCTION

There is at present under construction, in the Department of Computer Science at Manchester, a machine known as MU5, whose design has been a joint venture by all the members of that department. The principle features of this machine have already been described [1, 2]. The motivation behind this project was to produce a piece of hardware especially suited to the implementation of high level languages, and it therefore contains special features to facilitate the run time performance of such languages, and it omits those features which had been common in earlier machines (notably large numbers of addressable registers) of which high level languages (as distinct from machine code programmers) cannot make effective use.

The purpose of the present paper is to describe the new machine, showing how its features are especially suited to ALGOL-like languages, and to ALGOL 68 in particular.

2. THE VIRTUAL STORE

The programmer has at his disposal a large virtual store, a 32 bit address being needed to specify any byte in it. The actual word length is 64 bits, but the user can readily handle, 64, 32, 16, 8, 4 or 1 bit quantities. The 32 bit address is subdivided as follows:

14 bit segment address	18 bit byte address

It is therefore possible to address 16K segments, each of 64K 32 bit words. Of these, the top 8K segments are common to all processes (and contain a library of pure procedures, including the compilers themselves and the run time routines which their object programs will require). A user may use as few or as many segments as he wishes, but the operating system will expect him, within each segment, to restrict his usage to some continuous region at the beginning of that segment. A given segment may be shared between several processes (who may know it by different segment numbers), each of whom may have permission to "read", "write", or "execute" it.

This virtual store is implemented by a fairly conventional paging scheme, using a 32 word associative store to perform the page look-up. The page size is variable in powers of 2 from 16 to 1024 32 bit words (the user is invited to suggest a page size for each segment he creates). Infrequently used pages will find themselves paged out to a mass core store, and thence to a fixed-head disc.

Alternatively, a segmented store of this nature can be implemented by means of multiple base and limit registers, this solution being more appropriate to a smaller machine which has to be compatible with the larger one.

Apart from the virtual store, there are comparatively few central registers known to the user. There is an accumulator known as A, in which 64 bit *real* and 32 bit *int* arithmetic may be performed, and a 32 bit *int* register known as B with a more limited arithmetic repertoire. There are also registers D, XD, NB, XNB and SF, whose use will be described presently. It is also possible that 128 bit *real*, 64 bit *int* and decimal arithmetic could be performable in A, but at present these are being implemented by software.

3. THE NAMING SEGMENT

In the context of this project, the word "name" has a special meaning, different from its usage in ALGOL 68. A name will exist, roughly speaking, for every identifier declared in a program, and for each such name a space will be reserved in the "naming segment". When I have occasion to speak of 'names' in the ALGOL 68 sense, I shall therefore use the word "reference" instead.

Each process must possess a naming segment (normally its segment zero), whose contents will always be laid out according to the following plan:

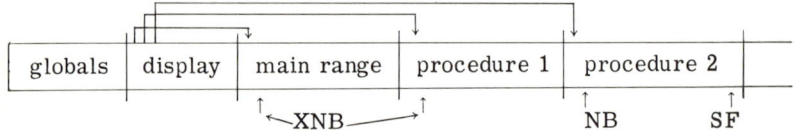

The naming segment is to be used for the storage of fixed length data (i.e. primitives, *struct*s, *ref*s and descriptors, but not the elements of multiple values). The register NB (name base) points to the start of the name space of the current procedure and, since all the names within this space are of fixed length, the displacement from NB of any such name is known at compile time. Hopefully, the majority of store accesses within a typical program are to names local to the current procedure, and the normal and most efficient means of access is therefore by means of a small displacement relative to NB.

Consider the following program:

MAKING THE HARDWARE SUIT THE LANGUAGE

```
begin
real x, y, int i, j ;
proc p = :
    begin
    int k, l, m, n, struct (real a, b, c, int d) s ;
    real e = 2.718281828 ;
    proc q = :
        begin
        real q, r, t ;
        ...
            begin
            real a, b, c, d ;
            ...

            a of s := r ;
            ...
            end ;
        ...

    end ;
    ...

    q
    ...

    end ;
...

p
...
end
```

During the assignation of r (which is local to q) to a of s (which is local to p), which occurs during the call of q which occurs within the call of p which occurs within the main program (which can also be regarded as a procedure for the present purpose), the state of the naming segment will be as follows:

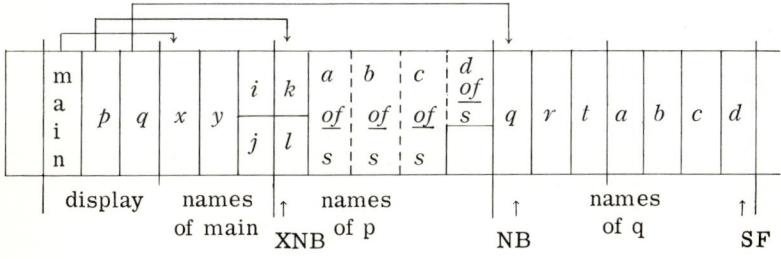

The code compiled for this would be something like:

```
XNB  - µ              ¢ set XNB from display ¢
A    = 1 (rel NB)
A    ⇒ 2 (rel XNB)
```

Thus any reference to a name not local to the current procedure requires a setting of the register XNB (extra name base). Note, however, that no new level on the display needed to be created for the inner range within q in which a, b, c and d were declared and that NB only needs to be moved during procedure entry and exit (there are of course various links and pointers not shown which also require attention at these times). Note also that no space on the name stack was reserved for the identifier e, since this possesses a literal, and literals of up to 64 bits can be stored within the operand field of an instruction.

It has been estimated that 80% of store accesses during typical programs will be to the naming segment and even, in the short term, to a comparatively small number of words within that. Perhaps these words should be stored in fast central registers; but which words, and what happens if we have 32 registers and 33 words we would like to keep there? In fact, there is a fast store of 32 words but it is addressed associatively. I.e. each time a word is brought from the naming segment in the main store, it is entered into this associative store, together with its address (another word, not recently referred to, may have to be taken out to make room for it). Each time a word is needed from the naming segment, it is first sought in the associative store (by associating on its process number and address) and only if it is not found there is a main store cycle necessary. A word can be brought from this store every 45 ns, whereas the main store cycle time is 250 ns. Simulations have shown that, for many programs, the required word will already be in the associative store 99% of the time so that, for sequences of simple instructions, the rate of execution will be one every 45 ns, or say one every 70 ns averaged over all instructions. If a particular program happens to be using more than 32 names, in the short term, then nothing disastrous happens, but the performance is degraded correspondingly. However, the compiler need have no knowledge of what is going on, and can compile on the assumption that there is one large, fast store.

4. THE ORDER STRUCTURE

Most instructions will be 16 bits long. These contain an operand field of 6 bits, enabling 64 names to be addressed relative to NB. However, escape bits are provided to extend the operand field to 16, 32 or 64 bits, thus enabling access to any displacement ahead of NB, or to displacements relative to XNB or to the start of the naming segment, or to provide literal operands and various other special cases.

Thus, up to 8 instructions can be extracted in one (128 bit wide) main store access. An instruction buffer is provided to smooth out the flow, and to contain small loops of instructions in their entirety.

MAKING THE HARDWARE SUIT THE LANGUAGE 351

The functions provided are of an essentially straightforward character. For example, for the *int* accumulator there are:

A =	operand	(load)
A *=	"	(stack and load - see later)
A ⇒	"	(store)
A +	"	
A -	"	
A *	"	(times)
A /	"	
A ≠	"	(exclusive or)
A ∨	"	(or)
A &	"	(and)
A ↑	"	(shift)
A θ	"	(reverse subtract)
A φ	"	(reverse divide)
A COMP	"	(compare - see later)
A CONV	"	(convert to *real*)

Note in particular the reverse divide and subtract operations, which enable the most efficient order of elaboration of the operands to be chosen with the operators '-' and '/'.

5. THE STACK

A working stack is kept at the head of the naming segment, the last word in it being pointed to by the register SF (stack front). The instruction "A *= operand" mentioned above first advances SF and stacks the current value of A, and then loads A from the operand. Conversely, it is possible to specify STACK as an operand, as in "A + STACK", in which case the word indicated by SF is taken as the operand, after which SF is retarded. There is also a special instruction "STACK operand".

The normal way to enter a procedure is first to stack the link and the current NB (a special instruction is provided to do this). Then the values of the actual parameters are obtained and stacked and then the procedure is entered. The first thing it must do is to set NB pointing to the link, and to advance SF so as to leave space for the names local to the new procedure. Also, if the procedure is likely to call other procedures, it must now update the display. Upon exit, SF is reset from NB and NB is reset from the link.

6. THE BOOLEAN AND TEST REGISTERS

The COMP instruction mentioned above does not alter the value of A. It compares the values of A and of the operand, and puts the result in a test register T, which is capable of storing (in two bits of information) the following states:

= ≠ > ≥ < ≤

Instructions are then provided to jump upon any of these six states. However, a jump upon the result of a comparison is not always what is required. Frequently, it is to be stored in a _bool_ variable, or operated upon by a _bool_ operator. For these purposes, there is a boolean accumulator BN, which can be combined with T or with an operand in various ways. Consider (in the range of the well known declarations) the following:

$$\underline{if}\ i < j\ \&\ k - 3 * m \geq n \vee p\ \underline{then\ go\ to}\ grenoble\ \underline{fi}$$

which would compile into:

```
A     =     i
A     COMP  j
BN    =     T<
A     =     3
A     *     m
A     θ     k
A     COMP  n
BN    &     T≥
BN    V     p
IF    BN    grenoble
```

7. THE VECTOR SEGMENT

The vector segment of a process is another segment which, by convention, contains a stack which grows and contracts with the name stack, but whose contents consist of items whose length is not known at compile time - notably the elements of multiple values. Thus the access to such objects is always indirect, via pointers (i.e. descriptors) on the name stack (or elsewhere). Clearly, the address of the front of the vector stack (we shall call it VSF) must be kept in some global location, and it must be stacked and reset every time a range is entered or left, if the outermost reach of that range contains phrases which could alter it. The following example illustrates these points:

$$\underline{begin}\ \cent\ of\ the\ range\ in\ which\ x1\ is\ declared\ \cent$$
$$\underline{int}\ m,\ n\ ;$$
$$read\ (\ (m,\ n)\ )\ ;$$
$$[m\ :n]\ \underline{real}\ x1\ ;$$
$$\underline{proc}\ p = (\underline{real}\ a)\ :$$
$$\quad \underline{begin}\ \cent\ of\ a\ reach\ which\ does\ not\ alter\ VSF\ \cent$$
$$\quad \underline{real}\ b,\ c,\ d\ ;$$
$$\quad ...$$

MAKING THE HARDWARE SUIT THE LANGUAGE

```
        begin ¢ of the range in which x2 is declared ¢
        real e ;
        [1 : m-n] real x2 ;
        ...
        e := x2[6] ;
        ...

            end ;
   ...
        end ;

   p (x1[m]) ;
   ...

   end
```

At the time the declaration of $x2$ is encountered (during a call of p), the stacks will appear as follows (note that the link stacked by the procedure call is also shown here):

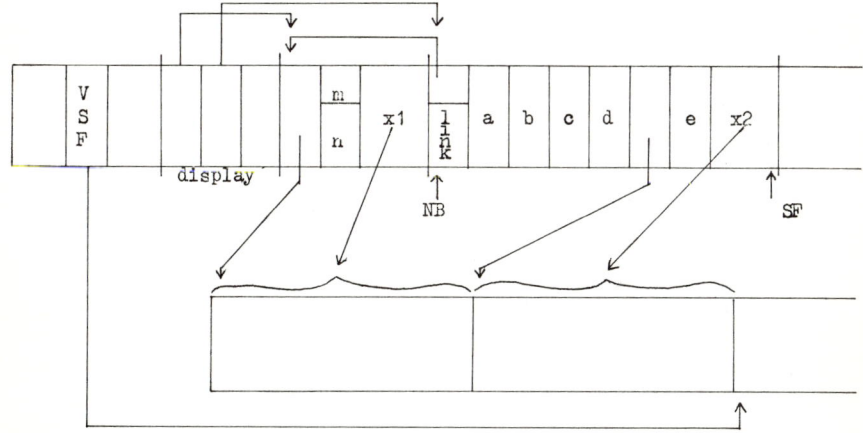

The vector stack will also be used for objects created by *loc* generators (other than those which are the constituent actual parameters of identity declarations), since the number of these that may be created within the life of a range is not known at compile time. They are simply stacked at VSF as they are created, and they disappear automatically when VSF is reset at the end of the relevant range.

8. PROCESSES

A process is an instance of the execution of a program, and takes place in a "virtual processor". A virtual processor buys real time from a real processor (of which there could be more than one) whenever the supervisor permits. Each process has its own virtual store, but some of the segments in this may be shared with other processes, thus permitting a program to be in execution simultaneously by several processes (pure procedures), and enabling processes to cooperate with each other. A process can spawn other processes subordinate to itself, at the same time arranging for some (perhaps usually most) of its own segments to be available to the new process.

This will happen, in ALGOL 68, upon entry to a parallel clause. From within a constituent clause of a parallel clause, it must be possible to access two kinds of objects - those declared outside the parallel clause (there is some risk here if *up*s and *down*s are not used correctly) and those declared within the constituent clause itself, which are quite distinct from any (possibly similar) objects declared within the other clause(s).

Therefore, upon entry to a parallel clause (with two constituent clauses, say), the old naming segment must remain accessible to both the new clauses, and two new naming segments must be created for the two processes that will now take over:

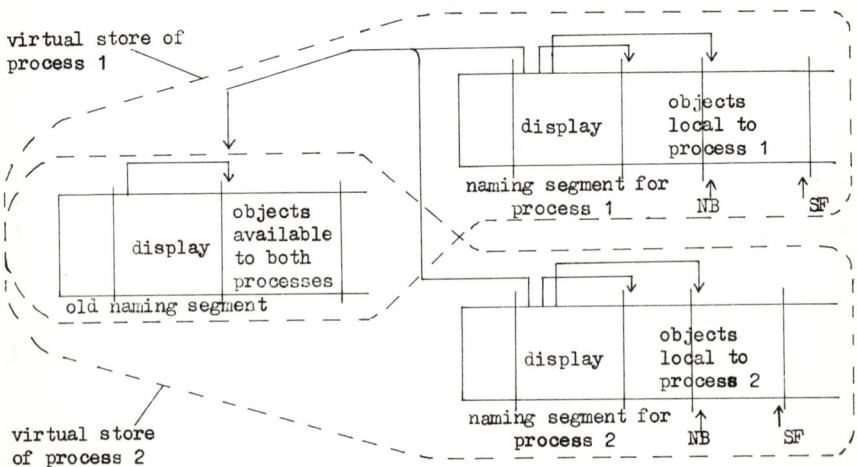

The displays for the two new processes are initialized by taking copies of the display of the parent process, thus enabling the XNB of either virtual processor to be set to points in the old naming segment as well as in the new. The vector segment must also be split in the same way as the naming segment. Apart from these, all other segments in existence at the time of the split will continue to be shared by the new processes.

A special hardware facility, guaranteed inseparable, is provided which will read a word of store, at the same time clearing it to zero. It is then quite easy to implement *sema*s, *up*s and *down*s using it.

9. OPERANDS

In general, the various functions provided and the various methods of operand access may be combined orthogonally. Some of the operand types have already been introduced - a more complete list is as follows:

> name at operand, relative to NB (always in naming segment)
> name at operand, relative to XNB (might be in any segment)
> name at operand, relative to start of naming segment
> literal (of 6, 16, 32 or 64 bits)
> some central registers (e.g., B, D, NB, XNB, etc.)
> STACK
> S[B]
> S[0]
> D[B]
> D[0]

The last four provide the normal means of access to segments other than the naming segment. Before they can be described, however, it is necessary to introduce another central register.

10. THE D REGISTER AND DESCRIPTORS

2	3	1 1 1	24	32
TYPE	SIZE	U B / S C	BOUND	ORIGIN

The D register is a 64 bit register which holds objects known as "descriptors" (not to be confused with the word 'descriptor' in the ALGOL 68 sense, although there is some similarity). Of the four types of descriptor (2 type bits), only type zero need concern us just now. Briefly, a type 0 descriptor specifies a vector anywhere within the virtual store. The 32 bits of its origin field are enough to specify any byte in any segment and are used to specify the start of the vector. The bound field gives the number of elements in the vector, the element size (1, 4, 8, 16, 32 or 64 bits) being specified by the size field.

If you now refer back to section 7 above, you will see that these descriptors are just those objects which need to be kept on the name stack (or elsewhere) in order to point to regions of the vector stack. The statement:

$e := x2[6]$

in the example might be then translated as:

> B = 5   ¢ i.e. 6 - $\underline{lwb}$ $x2$ ¢
> A = $x2[B]$
> A $\Rightarrow e$

The operand $x2[B]$ is an example of the type $S[B]$, and its effect is as follows:

The descriptor at $x2$ is loaded into D. If the value of B is <0 or $\geq$ the bound field of D, then (unless BC = 1), the process is interrupted because the subscript is out of range. Otherwise, the element whose store address is the origin field of D plus the value of B (scaled according to the size field, unless US = 1) is yielded as the value of the operand. Thus the element is obtained and the bounds are checked, all in one operation.

Unfortunately, there is only room in a descriptor for one bound, so that the lower bound must be subtracted from B before the element can be obtained. However, in deference to those languages in which the use of a lower bound of 1 is encouraged (i.e. FORTRAN and ALGOL 68), a special instruction is provided:

B =' operand

the effect of which is to load B with the value of the operand minus 1. Frequently, in ALGOL 68, the value of the lower bound will be known at compile time to be 1 (from the formal parameter at the time of its declaration), so this facility will be of benefit.

The S[0] type of operand operates similarly, except that B is not added to the origin field in order to locate the element. The types D[B] and D[0] use the descriptor already in D, instead of obtaining a new one from the operand.

11. FLEXIBLES

The vector segment is an excellent place to keep objects whose size is known at declaration time, but objects such as:

[1 : 0 *flex*] *real* x2

must be kept elsewhere. The heap is not really a good place for these either, because these objects disappear at well defined times (upon range exit) and the full generality of a garbage collector is wasted upon them. In a machine with a large virtual store, another region can be made available (call it the "pile"). In the pile, a brand new segment will be provided for each multiple value with a flexible bound. This segment can grow and contract as the number of elements in this multiple is changed, and it can be abolished entirely upon exit from the range. A descriptor pointing into this segment will, of course, be kept on the name stack in the usual manner, and therefore access to a flexible multiple is achieved by exactly the same instructions (and in the same amount of time) as access to a fixed one.

There will be some system overhead whenever such a segment is created or abolished or has its size changed but, in a machine with paging, the supervisor should never have to move blocks of data around within the real store, so that the compaction problems which would arise if the object code were to attempt its own store management are avoided. Even in a machine which achieves its segmentation by means of base registers, the supervisor should be able to make a better job of the compaction than the object code could have done, since it can avoid doing any movement until it becomes absolutely essential.

12. DOPE VECTORS

The use of the D register is a simple and quick way of accessing a multiple value of one dimension. For two or more dimensions, or where each element of the multiple is itself a sizeable object, something more elaborate is needed:

$[a:b, c:d, e:f]$ <u>struct</u> ($\underline{c}$ some object occupying g words $\underline{c}$) $t3$;

For $t3$, the following storage structure will be set up:

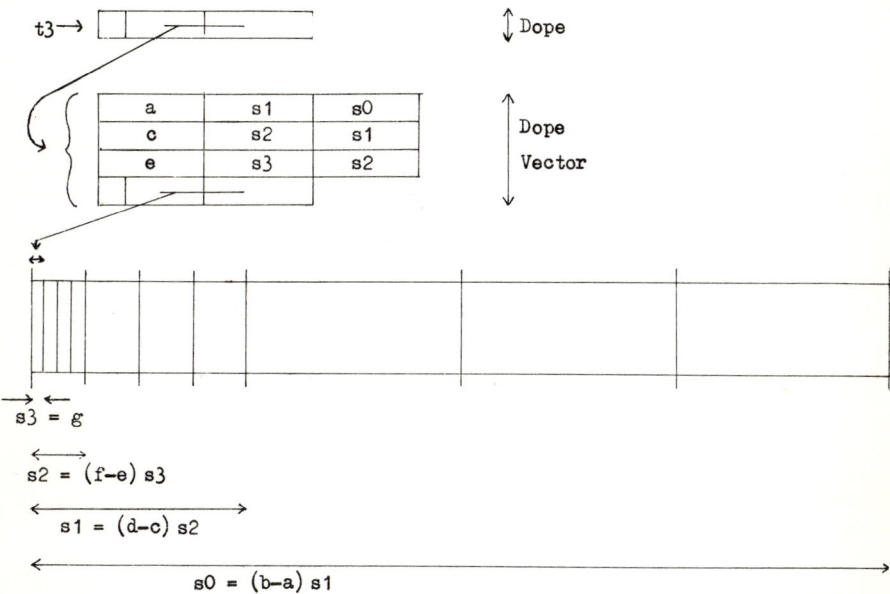

Now, in order to access the slice:

$t3[i, j, k]$

the code compiled would be:

```
B = i
SUB1 t3
B = j
SUB2
B = k
```

SUB2
RMOD XD[0]*
A - D[0] ¢ to get the first word of the *struct* ¢

This introduces several new instructions. The effect of "SUB1 t3" is defined by the following equivalent sequence:

```
XD = t3      ¢ XD is another register similar to D. It is loaded with
               the descriptor pointing to the dope vector ¢
D = 0        ¢ D is cleared ¢
B - XD[0]    ¢ subtract the lower bound ¢
B * XD[1]    ¢ multiply by the stride ¢
B check XD[2]   ¢ to check that this subscript is within its range ¢
XD + 3       ¢ increment the origin field of XD, ready for the next di-
               mension ¢
MOD    B     ¢ add B to the origin field of D ¢
```

The effect of SUB2 is identical, with the omission of the first two instructions. After SUB1 and some number of SUB2s, the origin field of D will contain the displacement (in bytes) of the required *struct* from the beginning of the element space of t3. The instruction RMOD XD[0] now takes the descriptor at the end of the dope vector (to which XD now conveniently points), adds to it the origin field of D, and puts it into D. There, it may be used to access the inside of the selected *struct* in any manner.

13. REFERENCES

It will now be seen how references (or 'names' in ALGOL 68 terminology) are to be implemented in this machine. A reference to a multiple value will consist of a dope pointing to a dope vector, the two being kept together as one unit. Thus, rows of such references and structures containing them can easily be manipulated. Such a reference can be made to point to a subvalue of a multiple value. On the other hand, if a reference to the whole of a flexible multiple value is assigned, it is important that a new copy of the dope vector is not made since, if this multiple value should subsequently acquire new bounds, these must become effective for the assigned copy also. Therefore, in the assignation of a reference to the whole of a flexible multiple, only the dope is copied across, and it is left pointing at the original dope vector (which will be the one and only master copy made when that multiple was generated in the first place). When a reference to the whole of a fixed multiple is assigned, it does not matter whether the dope vector is copied or not. Essentially the same technique has been described by Branquart [3].

It will be seen that the dope vector is equivalent to the 'descriptor' in the ALGOL 68 sense. The descriptor at the end of it corresponds to the

---

* This instruction no longer exists in the hardware being built. An alternative sequence of instructions is possible.

offset, and the triples correspond to the quintuples. There is no need to keep a record of the states, except with the master copy of the dope vector, since any reference to a multiple with one or more flexible states must inevitably lead back to such a master copy. If it does not, then the states were fixed.

Clearly, references to NONROW objects will be straightforward descriptors.

14. VECTORS

Clearly a multiple value of mode row-of-PRIMITIVE can be referred to by a single descriptor (with an associated record of its lower bound), or by a dope vector containing just one triple. The former leads to a rapid and convenient access, but in general the latter is necessary because the reference to such a multiple might be a formal parameter of a routine, and the actual parameter might be a reference to a column of a two dimensional object. Single descriptors cannot point to columns.

In order to get the best of both worlds, a straightforward vector (such as will be found 99% of the time) will be stored as follows:

[$m : n$] *real* $x1$;

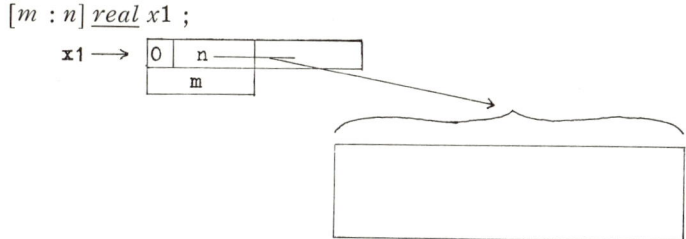

and accessed by the following code:

```
B = i
B - x1+2      ¢ i.e. the lower bound m ¢
A = x1[B]
```

However, the occasional vector of an odd shape would be stored as follows:

ref[ ]*real* $x2$ = (c *some slice* c) ; (see scheme on next page)

This would be accessed by exactly the same code as before (the compiler does not know any better), but the instruction "A = x2[B]" then finds that the descriptor at x2 is a type 3 descriptor (so far we have only met type 0 ones). The type 3 descriptor points to a vector, the first word of which contains the address of a procedure. This procedure is now automatically entered, with a link pointing to the instruction which caused the trouble. The procedure called in this case would look like:

```
NB = SF         ¢ procedures always start by setting NB ¢
MOD 1           ¢ add 1 to D, so that it points to the dope vector
                  proper ¢
```

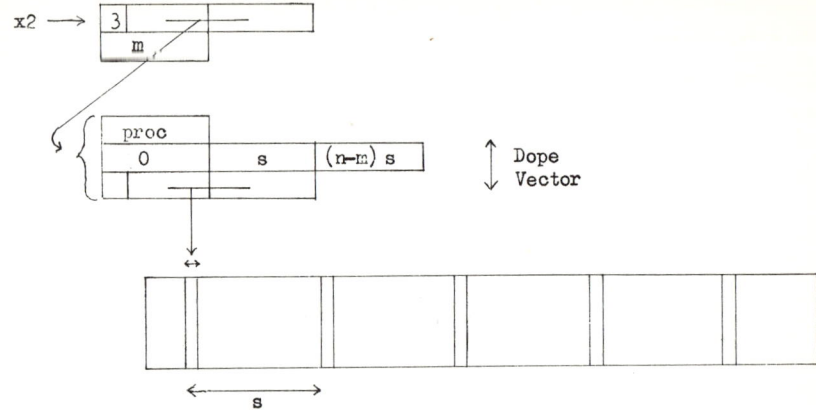

```
SUB1 D      ¢ the usual dope vector operations, using the con-
            tents of D as the dope ¢
RMOD XD[0]  ¢ D now points to the required word ¢
B = 0
DSET
RETURN
```

The instruction DSET sets a special flip-flop such that, when the procedure returns and tries to obey the "A = x2[B]" again, it will take the descriptor already in D, rather than trying to get the one in x2 again.

Thus, the compiled code can always happily assume that its vectors have the simplest kind of descriptor. Therefore, a type 3 descriptor will also be needed where the descriptor on hand should really be pointing to a master copy because the bounds are flexible. In this case, the procedure entered will quietly substitute the master copy for the one the code thinks it is using.

15. STRINGS

Objects of mode [ ]*char* can (and must) be handled in the same way as other multiple values (a *ref string* is entitled to point to a column of a [1: , 1:]*char*). However, to keep a separate segment on the pile for every *string* might be uneconomic, since the language encourages the use of lots of short *string*s which appear and disappear with great rapidity. Moreover, there must be an easy way of concatenating *string*s (for the operators +, *plus* and *prus*). Therefore, it might be better to keep objects declared as *string* in the form of chained lists, in which case a descriptor pointing to such a *string* would be of type 3 and would call a procedure which would work along the chain until it found the required element.

16. THE HEAP

Heap management in a machine with a large virtual store is rather different from that with a conventional store. The storage space does not suddenly run out, with a consequent necessity to take sudden and drastic action (with no store left to take it in). Rather, if too much store is used, the system overheads start gradually to climb, due to the amount of page turning which begins to take place. The decision when to collect garbage must therefore be taken by observing this degradation in performance in some way, and it may be necessary also to have regard to the actual current needs of other users on the machine.

Once the decision has been taken, the actual collection can be done by copying the useful parts of the heap into a fresh area, and then abandoning the old heap entirely, as has been described by Fenichel and Yochelson [4]. However, as with all compacting schemes, this does mean that a large number of pointers throughout the system has to be amended.

An alternative scheme is possible, which might turn out to be better. Suppose that, for all the multiple values which are generated on the heap, only their references are kept on the heap, their elements being put on the pile (i.e. a separate segment for each multiple value, whether its bounds are flexible or not in this instance). Then the actual object to be put on the heap for any given generator is of a fixed size, determined entirely by its mode. Suppose now that a separate segment were to be provided for each length of object generateable by the program; or, better still (since typical programs actually contain very few heap generators, although each of them may be encountered many times), let there be a separate segment for each generator occurring in the program (its private heap). Within each of these heaps, because the objects are of a fixed size, a conventional free chain technique can be used. Therefore there is no compaction and no need to alter any pointers. The marking process can be quite conventional and, in addition to showing which objects on the heaps can be thrown away, it will also show those segments on the pile which are no longer referred to (or into).

ACKNOWLEDGMENTS

As stated at the beginning, all members of the Department at Manchester, under the direction of Professor T. Kilburn, have had a hand in the design of this machine, and my thanks are therefore due to them for making this paper possible.

REFERENCES

[1] Kilburn, T., Morris, D., Rohl, J.S. and Sumner, F., A system design proposal, Information Processing 68 (proc IFIP Cong 68), North-Holland, Amsterdam.

[2] Aspinall, D., Kinniment, D. J. and Edwards, D. B. G., Associative memories in large computer systems, Information Processing 68 (proc IFIP Cong 68), North-Holland, Amsterdam.
[3] Branquart, P. and Lewi, J., A scheme of storage allocation and garbage collection for ALGOL 68, this volume, p. 37.
[4] Fenichel, R. R. and Yochelson, J. C., A LISP garbage-collector for virtual memory systems. Comm. ACM 12, 11 November 1969, p. 611.

DISCUSSION

Van der Meulen:
What happens if you violate bound checks?

Lindsey:
An interrupt.

Van der Meulen:
What kind of an interrupt?

Lindsey:
Well as far as ALGOL 68 is concerned, the further elaboration is undefined; in the case of this particular machine the operating system would clearly give the user the opportunity to be told that this interrupt had happened and take some action. But, of course, in ALGOL 68 there is nothing that can be done further. Presumably the operating system would have some default action, such as throwing you off the machine with a suitably rude message.

Prentice:
You say that the top of the stack is always to be associated with the scratch pad store. What is the idea of having the A register as a separate register? Would there be any objection to a totally stack organized operation with "Add the two top things on the stack" as an example of an instruction?

Lindsey:
This was thought of. It is essentially the zero address machine, instead of the one address we have. I think we concluded there was some inconvenience. Obviously this A register and the hardware associated with it have got to exist. I think we decided that, to specify a given piece of program, you could specify it in less bits if you did it this way than if you had done it the other way. This is essentially what it came to. It was considered.

Ershov:
Let us suppose that you have for an operating system several compilers for various languages. What is your opinion on how to divide memory allocation or linkage facilities between the operating system and the administrative system attached to a particular compiler? For example, is it possible to have a garbage collector common to various problems?

Lindsey:

It is quite possible that several of the compilers that we write will use, for example, the same dictionary routines. So that if two processes are simultaneously compiling ALGOL 68 and PL/I, they may nevertheless be using this one copy of this dictionary routine. Similarly, the run-time systems will share most of their library routines, certainly the obvious things, like sines and cosines, where you cannot really come to much harm. I imagine transput routines for any language are going to be rather specific. So every opportunity is taken to share code between different systems where this can de done.

Branquart:

You do not use the block structure of programs for addressing values possessed by identifiers, do you? When you want to address the value possessed by an identifier, you use only one register, so I think, you do not use the block structure of programs?

Lindsey:

If I show you now this picture here again (see page 349). We have here for example a block containing another block, and a new major range (we might say a new procedure, a new superblock) must start here (*proc* q). This is a procedure and this could be called from anywhere. So we have a range on the stack which has got to start here (see NB, bottom of page 349). Now we do not need to start a new range on the stack at this point (*real* a, b, c, d), because all these objects are of fixed length and therefore we can specify this a (bottom of page 353) as an address relative to this point (NB) and we know this at compile time. So the chances are that the number of different levels that we have to keep in our display is much less and therefore the number of times we have to load the XNB register, and so on and move pointers around, is reduced.

Branquart:

In the figure on page 353, I do not see clearly how you manage to update the pointer of the top of the vector stack when the block is left.

Lindsey:

Essentially you recognize two kinds of range. You recognize ranges such as this one (*real* a, b, c, d on page 349), which are not going to create anything on the vector stack, and those which are, such as the one which presumably started at that point (just after d on page 353). Now I said that no code is compiled at the point (*real* a, b, c, d on page 349) and in this particular example that is true. However, had there been a row of something declared at that point, then on entry to this block you would have had to compile code to dump the present value of VSF in there (just after the link) (page 353) and here (after the matching *end*) I would compile code to restore it. But I am still referring to the objects inside here, in this case this e (on the stack on page 353) relative to the same base as I referred to these things (a, b, c, d) declared out here. (Note: Lindsey was using the program on page 349 with the diagram on page 353, which does not quite match it. Ed.)

Branquart:

Do you recuperate the space for the descriptor?

Lindsey:

If, for example, there had been a second block (after the block <u>real</u> *a, b, c, d* on page 349) in which I declared various things, then essentially these things - let us call them *l, m* and *n* - then these would be mapped over the same storage as *a, b, c, d.*

Van der Poel:

You said that for a fixed length object on the heap, you take a segment of the store for its own purpose. That limits that number of segments to 2^{14}. I could imagine that, for example, in administrative applications this would be far too low for ranging over a large number of objects.

Lindsey:

I think we are at cross purposes somewhere. You certainly would not run out of segments unless there were 2^{14} generators in your program.

Van der Poel:

Yes, that can very well happen in an administrative application.

Lindsey:

But it would take you years to write a program with 2^{14} generators in it.

Van der Poel:

Recursively?

Lindsey:

Oh no! We are talking about occurrences. What I essentially propose in the case of generators is that each time a heap-generator occurs in the program, I will say, right, "Here is probably a new kind of generator with a mode we have not met yet - we will have a new segment for it." (and in fact, if there were several generators for the same mode, we could possibly save a little here, if it is worth it). And this essentially means that every time I come to this generator when evaluating the program, I create another object in this particular segment.

Van der Poel:

Oh, I see. OK.

Lindsey:

Particularly, I think it is the case that programs which do a lot of heap work (list processing sorts of applications) actually have comparatively few occurrences of generators in them. But they come round and use them an awful lot.

Currie:

If you are going round a loop a hundred times, you are going to fill up that particular segment very quickly. And you have got no compaction of this.

Lindsey:

A segment can hold 2^{16} 32 bit words, which is quite a lot, and it is possible, in fact, for it to continue into the next segment.

Currie:

But you might have grabbed the next segment for the next generator.

Lindsey:

This is all chained and we can arrange to point into another segment somewhere else - we have got plenty of virtual space - or we can try to collect some garbage and see if we can recover some of it. You see, the other point about garbage collection is that you do not suddenly find that your stacks run into each other in a virtual store system; you just find that the overheads start to go up rather sharply. So you can postpone garbage collection, to some extent, to when it suits you.

CONFERENCE PARTICIPANTS

Bauer, F. L., Mathematisches Institut, Technische Hochschule München, Arcisstr. 21, 8000 Munich 2, Germany.
Bekić, H., IBM-Laboratory Vienna, Parkring 10, A-1010 Vienna, Austria.
Björk, Harry, Mickelsbergsv 136, S-126 63 Haegersten, Sweden.
Bond, Susan G., Ministry of Technology, Royal Radar Establishment, St. Andrews Road, Great Malvern, Worcs., England.
Bowlden, H. J., Westinghouse Research Center, Beulah Road, Pittsburgh, Pennsylvania, USA.
Branquart, P., M.B.L.E. Research Laboratory, 2 Ave. van Becelaere, Brussels 17, Belgium.
Caracciolo di Forino, A., IEI-CNR, Via S. Maria 46, I-5600 Pisa, Italy.
Currie, I. C., Ministry of Technology, Royal Radar Establishment, St. Andrews Road, Great Malvern, Worcs., England.
de Bakker, J. W., Stichting Mathematisch Centrum, 2 E Boerhaavestraat 49, Amsterdam, The Netherlands.
Duby, J. J., IBM European Systems Research, Institute 40, Rue du Rhoene, 1211 Geneva 11, Switzerland.
Ershov, A. P., Morskoyprospekt 34, KV. 14, Novosibirsk 90, USSR.
Goos, G., Rechenzentrum, Technische Hochschule München, Arcisstr. 21, 8000 Munich 2, Germany.
Grau, A., Department of Engineering Science, Technical Northwestern University, Evanston, Illinois 60201, USA.
Griffiths, M., Mathématiques Appliquées, Université de Grenoble, Cedex 53, Grenoble-Gare 38, France.
Harkema, L. B. D., Bosboom Toussaintplein 188, Delft, The Netherlands.
Hill, U., Mathematisches Institut, Technische Hochschule München, Arcisstr. 21, 8000 Munich 2, Germany.
Jorrand, Ph., Cedex 247, Grenoble-Gare 38, France.
Koster, C. H. A., Mathematisch Centrum, 2E Boerhaavestraat 49, Amsterdam-O., The Netherlands.
Král, Jaroslav, Ustav Výpočtové Techniky ČVÚT (Computing Center of ČVÚT), Horská 3, Prag 2, CSSR.
Kudielka, V., IBM-Laboratory Vienna, Parkring 10, A-1010 Vienna, Austria.
Lindsey, C. H., Department of Computer Science, University of Manchester, Manchester 13, England.
Lyall, C., Department of Computing Science, University of Alberta, Edmonton 7, Alberta, Canada.
Mailloux, B. J., University of Alberta, Department of Computer Science, Edmonton 7, Alberta, Canada.
Molnar, G., Consiglio Intern. delle Ricerche, Centro Studi Calcolatrici Elettron., Presso Universita di Pisa, Via. S. Maria, 44, I-56100 Pisa, Italy.
Morison, J. D., Ministry of Technology, Royal Radar Establishment, St. Andrews Road, Great Malvern, Worcs., England.
Paul, M., Mathematisches Institut, Technische Hochschule München, Arcisstr. 21, 8000 Munich 2, Germany.
Peck, J. E. L., Department of Computer Science, University of British Columbia, Vancouver 8, British Columbia, Canada.
Prentice, J. A., The University of Nottingham, Crips Computing Centre, University Park, Nottingham, Ng 72 Rd., England.

Rar, A. F., Computing Centre, Novosibirsk 90, USSR.
Rekdal, K., Computing Centre at the Technical University of Norway, Department of SINTEF, 7034 Trondheim - NTH, Norway.
Scheidig, H., Mathematisches Institut, Technische Hochschule München, Arcisstr. 21, 8000 Munich 2, Germany.
Sintzoff, M., M.B.L.E. Research Laboratory, 2 Ave. van Becelaere, Brussels 17, Belgium.
Trilling, L., Département d'Informatique, Université de Montréal, Montréal, Québec, Canada.
van Gils, T., Philips Electrologica NV, Postbus 245, Apeldoorn, The Netherlands.
van der Meulen, S., Univers. Mathemat. Inst. (E.R.C.), Boedapestlaan, Utrecht Uithof, The Netherlands.
van der Poel, W. L., Technological University of Delft, Julianalaan 132, Delft, The Netherlands.
van Wijngaarden, A., Mathematical Centre, 2E Boerhaavestraat 49, Amsterdam-O., The Netherlands.
Wodon, P. L., M.B.L.E. Research Laboratory, 2 Ave. van Becelaere, Brussels 17, Belgium.
Wössner, H., Mathematisches Institut, Technische Hochschule München, Arcisstr. 21, 8000 Munich 2, Germany.
Woodward, P. M., Ministry of Technology, Royal Radar Establishment, St. Andrews Road, Great Malvern, Worcs., England.
Zemanek, H., IBM - Laboratory Vienna, Parkring 10, A-1010 Vienna, Austria.

BIBLIOGRAPHY OF ALGOL 68

Andrews, M. P.,
  Practical considerations in the storage of modes, Proc. Informal Conf. on ALGOL 68 Implementation, Univ. of British Columbia, Aug. 1969, pp. 78-84.

Andrews, M. P., Peck, J. E. L.,
  Cross reference of the ALGOL 68 transput routines, Univ. of British Columbia, March 1970.

Arnal, P., Buffet, J., Quere, A. et al.,
  Projet de traduction du rapport ALGOL 68, Faculté des Sciences de Lille, Laboratoire de Calcul, 1969.

Assabgui, M., Trilling, L.,
  Entrées-Sorties ALGOL 68, Université de Montréal, Départment d'Informatique, Publ. No. 13, Nov. 1969.

Baecker, H. D.,
  The use of ALGOL 68 for trees, Computer Journal, Vol. 13, No. 1, Feb. 1970, pp. 25-27.

Baecker, H. D.,
  Implementing the ALGOL 68 heap, BIT (Nordisk Tiskrift for Informationsbehandlung) Vol. 10, 1970.

Baecker, H. D.,
  Garbage collection for virtual memory systems, Univ. of Calgary, Nov. 1970.

Bährs, A. A., Ershov, A. P., Rar, A. F.,
  On the description of syntax of ALGOL 68 and its national variants, these Proceedings.

Baker, J. L.,
  The syntax of ALGOL 68, property grammars, and context-sensitive languages, Univ. of Calgary, Sept. 1970.

Baker, J. L.,
  Acceptors from van Wijngaarden grammars, Univ. of Washington, Comp. Sci. Group, Tech. Rep. 70-02-10, Feb. 1970.

Baker, J. L.,
  Some formal properties of the syntax of ALGOL 68, Computer Science Group, Univ. of Washington, May 1970.

Berry, D. M.,
  The importance of implementation models in ALGOL 68, or how to discover the concept of necessary environment, SIGPLAN Notices, Vol. 5, No. 9, 1970, pp. 14-24, Sept. 1970.

Boussard, J.C., Pair, C.,
  Introduction à ALGOL 68. Revue française d'Informatique et de Recherche Opérationnelle. 1969-No. B3, pp. 17-52, Dec. 1969.

Boussard, J. C., Duby, J. J. (Editors),
  Rapport d'évaluation d'ALGOL 68, IMAG, Grenoble and Centre Sci. IBM France, July 1970.

Bowlden, H. J.,
  A comparative introduction to ALGOL 68, Westinghouse Research Labs. No. 69-1C4-COMPS-P2 (obsolete).

Bowlden, H. J.,
  Environmental factors in computer language design and implementation, Proc. Informal Conf. on ALGOL 68 Implementation, Univ. of British Columbia, Aug. 1969, pp. 97-109.

Bowlden, H. J.,
  ALGOL 68 structural flowchart, Westinghouse Research Labs., Report 69-1C4-COMPS-R2, Oct. 1969.

Bowlden, H. J.,
  A symbol table for the B-6500, Westinghouse Research Labs. No. 70-1K4-COMPS-R1, Pittsburgh, April 1970 (obsolete).

Bowlden, H. J.,
  A symbol table with scope recognition for the B-6500, these Proceedings.

Bowlden, H. J.,
  ALGOL 68 - Comments and recommendations, Algol Bulletin 31.3.3, March 1970, pp. 28-32.

Branquart, P., Lewi, J., Cardinael, J. P.,
  A context-free syntax of ALGOL 68, Technical Note N66, MBLE Research Lab. Brussels, Aug. 1970.

Branquart, P., Lewi, J.,
  On object language and storage allocation in ALGOL 68 compilers, Proc. Informal Conf. on ALGOL 68 Implementation, Univ. of British Columbia, Aug. 1969, pp. 25-34.

Branquart, P., Lewi, J.,
  General principles of an ALGOL 68 garbage collector, Technical Note N60, MBLE Research Lab. Brussels, Jan. 1970.

Branquart, P., Lewi, L.,
  On the implementation of coercions in ALGOL 68, Report R123, MBLE Research Lab., Brussels, Jan. 1970, and Proc. International Computing Symposium, Bonn, 1970.

Branquart, P., Lewi, J., Cardinael, J. P.,
  Local generators and the ALGOL 68 working stack, Technical Note N62, MBLE Research Lab., Brussels, Sept. 1970.

Branquart, P., Lewi, J., Sintzoff, M., Wodon, P. L.,
  Structural composition of semantics in ALGOL 68, Report R125, MBLE Research Lab., Brussels, April 1970.

Branquart, P., Lewi, J.,
  Analysis of the parenthesis structure of ALGOL 68, Report R130, MBLE Research Lab., Brussels, April 1970, and these Proceedings.

Branquart, P., Lewi, J.,
  Structure d'un compilateur d'ALGOL 68, Report R131, MBLE Research Lab., Brussels, April 1970, and Congrès d'Informatique AFCET, Paris, 1970.

Branquart, P., Lewi, J.,
  A scheme of storage allocation and garbage collection for ALGOL 68, Report R133, MBLE Research Lab., Brussels, July 1970, and these Proceedings.

Branquart, P., Lewi, J.,
  Quelques aspects de l'implémentation d'ALGOL 68, Séminaire de Programmation IMAG 1968-69, Grenoble, 1970.

Brown, W. E.,
  The cross-referencing of ALGOL 68 syntax, Univ. of Calgary, June 1969.

Chastellier, G. de, Colmerauer, A.,
  W-grammar, Proc. 24th National Conf. ACM, 1969, pp. 511-518.

Currie, I. F., Bond, Susan G., Morison, J. D.,
  ALGOL 68-R, these Proceedings.

Currie, I. F.,
  Working description of ALGOL 68-R, RRE Memorandum No. 2660, Royal Radar Establishment, Malvern, Worcs., U.K. (to be published).

Dijkstra, E. W., Duncan, F., Garwick, J., Hoare, C. A. R., Randell, B., Seegmüller, G., Turski, W., Woodger, M.,
  Minority Report, Algol Bulletin, AB 31.1.1.1, March 1970, p. 7.

Ershov, A. P.,
  A multilanguage programming system oriented to languages description and universal optimization algorithms, these Proceedings.

Finch, P. M.,
  Defining and applied occurrences of identifiers, Proc. Informal Conf. on ALGOL 68 Implementation, Univ. of British Columbia, Aug. 1969, pp. 110-117.

Fites, P. E.,
  Storage organization and garbage collection in ALGOL 68, Proc. Informal Conf. on ALGOL 68 Implementation, Univ. of British Columbia, Aug. 1969, pp. 85-96.

Fites, P. E.,
  On error classes in ALGOL 68, Univ. of Alberta, April 1970.

Garwick, J. V., Merner, J. M., Ingerman, P. Z., Paul, M.,
  Report on the ALGOL X 1/0 Subcommittee W. G. 2.1 Working paper, July 1967.

Goos, G., Scheidig, H., Seegmüller, G., Walther, H.,
  Another proposal for ALGOL 67, Bavarian Academy of Science, Munich, May 1967.

Goos, G.,
  Eine Implementierung von ALGOL 68, Report, Computing Centre, T. H. München Nr. 6906, 1969.

Goos, G., Scheidig, H., Wössner, H.,
  Mode representation and operator identification in ALGOL 68, Proc. Informal Conf. on ALGOL 68 Implementation, Univ. of British Columbia, Aug. 1969, pp. 36-41.

Goos, G.,
  Einige Eigenschaften von ALGOL 68, Elektronische Datenverarbeitung, Vol. 11, Sept. 1969.

Goos, G., Scheidig, H.,
  Une implémentation d'ALGOL 68, Séminaire de programmation IMAG 1968-69, Grenoble, 1970.

Goos, G.,
  Some problems in compiling ALGOL 68, these Proceedings.

Goyer, P.,
  A garbage collector to be implemented on a CDC 3100, Département d'Informatique, Université de Montréal, No. 34, April 1970, and these Proceedings.

Hill, U.,
  Automatische rekursive Adressenberechnung für höhere Programmiersprachen, insbesondere für ALGOL 68, T. H. München, Feb. 1969.

Hoare, C. A. R.,
   Critique of ALGOL 68, Algol Bulletin, AB 29.3.5, 1968.

Hodgson, G. S.,
   ALGOL 68 extended syntax, Univ. of Manchester, Dept. of Computer Science, March 1970.

Jorrand, P.,
   Intersection de deux langages "context-free". Application à la grammaire du langage ALGOL X, Université de Grenoble, Mathématiques Appliquées, Oct. 1967.

Jorrand, P.,
   Tutorial on ALGOL 68, Proc. third annual Princeton conference on information sciences and systems, March 1969, pp. 403-407.

Koch, F.,
   The recognition of ranges in ALGOL 68, Univ. of Calgary, Sept. 1969.

Koster, C. H. A.,
   On infinite modes, Algol Bulletin AB 30.3.3, Feb. 1969, pp. 61-69.

Koster, C. H. A.,
   Syntax directed parsing of ALGOL 68 programs, Proc. Informal Conf. on ALGOL 68 Implementation, Univ. of British Columbia, Aug. 1969, pp. 61-69.

Koster, C. H. A.,
   Two level grammars, Amsterdam, Mathematisch Centrum, May 1970.

Koster, C. H. A.,
   Affix grammars, these Proceedings.

Kral, J., Moudry, J.,
   An implementation of identifier tables in multipass ALGOL 68 based on hash code techniques, these Proceedings.

Landell, A., Pleyber, J.,
   A definition of the translation of ALGOL 60 to ALGOL 68, Proc. Informal Conf. on ALGOL 68 Implementation, Univ. of British Columbia, Aug. 1969, pp. 49-60.

Landelle, A., Pleyber, J.,
   Traduction d'ALGOL 60 en ALGOL 68, Séminaire de Programmation, 1968-69, IMAG Grenoble, 1970.

Lewi, J., Branquart, P.,
   Implementation of local names in ALGOL 68, Report R121 MBLE Research Lab., Brussels, Nov. 1969, and International Computing Symposium, Bonn, 1970.

Lindsey, C. H.,
   ALGOL 68 with fewer tears, Algol Bulletin AB 28 (obsolete).

Lindsey, C. H.,
   An iso-code representation for ALGOL 68, Proc. Informal Conf. on ALGOL 68 Implementation, Univ. of British Columbia, Aug. 1969, pp. 1-24, and Algol Bulletin AB 31.3.6, March 1970.

Lindsey, C. H.,
   Making the hardware suit the language, these Proceedings.

Lindsey, C. H.,
   Some ALGOL 68 sublanguages, these Proceedings.

Mailloux, B. J.,
   On the implementation of ALGOL 68, Mathematisch Centrum, Amsterdam, 1967.

Mailloux, B.J., Fites, P.E.,
  Storage organization and garbage collection for ALGOL 68 implementation, Univ. of Alberta, Feb. 1970.

Mailloux, B.J., Peck, J.E.L.,
  ALGOL 68 as a self extending language, Proc. Extensible Language Symposium, SIGPLAN Notices, Vol. 4, No. 8, Aug. 1969, pp. 9-13.

Marshall, S.,
  Preliminary report on ALGOL 68 implementation, Proc. Informal Conf. on ALGOL 68 Implementation, Univ. of British Columbia, Aug. 1969, pp. 42-48.

Marshall, S.,
  An ALGOL 68 garbage collector, Technical Report TM 0111, Dartmouth College, Dec. 1969, and these Proceedings.

Mazurkiewicz, A.W.,
  A note on enumerable grammars, Information and Control, 1969, Vol. 14, pp. 555-558.

Meek, B.L.,
  ALGOL X, some comments, Computer Bulletin, Aug. 1969, p. 298.

Meertens, L.,
  On the generation of ALGOL 68 programs involving infinite modes, Algol Bulletin, AB 30.3.4, pp. 90-92.

Nadrchal, J.,
  Guide to the language ALGOL 68, Math. Inst. Czechoslovakia Acad. of Sciences, Praha.

Pair, C.,
  Concerning the syntax of ALGOL 68, Algol Bulletin, AB 31.3.2, March 1970, pp. 16-27.

Peck, J.E.L.,
  The syntax of ALGOL 68, Department of Mathematics, Univ. of Calgary, March 1968 (obsolete).

Peck, J.E.L.,
  On storage of modes and some context conditions, Proc. Informal Conf. on ALGOL 68 Implementation, Univ. of British Columbia, Aug. 1969, pp. 70-77.

Peter, R.,
  Zur zweistufigen Satzstruktur-Grammatik, Studia Sci. Math. Hung., Vol. 2 pp. 455-456, Vol. 3 pp. 181-194.

Scheidig, H.,
  Anpassungsoperationen in ALGOL 68, T.H. München, Feb. 1970.

Scheidig, H.,
  Syntax and mode check in an ALGOL 68 compiler, these Proceedings.

Schneider, V.B.,
  A translation grammar for ALGOL 68, AFIPS Spring Joint Computer Conf. 1970 and International Computing Symposium, Bonn, 1970.

Schneider, V.B.,
  A one-pass algorithm for compiling ALGOL 68 declarations, Purdue Univ., 1970.

Simonet, M.,
  Une grammaire context-free d'ALGOL 68, Congrès d'Informatique AFCET Paris, 1970, p. 5.3. 119-135.

Sintzoff, M.,
  Calculating the properties of programs by valuation on specific models, MBLE Res. Lab., Brussels, N64, May 1970.

Sintzoff, M.,
  Existence of a van Wijngaarden syntax for every recursively enumerable set, Annales Soc. Scientifique de Bruxelles, Vol. 81, No. 2, 1967, pp. 115-118.

Sintzoff, M.,
  Grammaires superposées et autres systèmes formels, Journées d'Etude sur l'Analyse Syntaxique, Centre d'Automatique Fontainebleau, 1969.

Sintzoff, M.,
  Introduction à la description d'ALGOL 68, Revue Française d'Informatique et de Recherche Opérationnelle Vol. B-3, 1969, pp. 3-16.

Sintzoff, M. (Ed.), Branquart, P., Lewi, J., Wodon, P. L.,
  Remarks on the Draft Reports on ALGOL 68, Report R96, MBLE Res. Lab., Brussels, Jan. 1969.

Trilling, L., Verjus, J. P.,
  An attempted definition of an extensible system, these Proceedings.

Lindsey, C. H., van der Meulen, S. G.,
  Informal Introduction to ALGOL 68, North-Holland Publishing Company, Amsterdam, 1971.

van Wijngaarden, A.,
  Orthogonal design and description of a formal language, MR 76, Mathematisch Centrum, Amsterdam, Oct. 1965.

van Wijngaarden, A.,
  On the boundary between natural and artificial languages, Linguaggi nella societa e nella tecnica, Edizioni di Comunita - Milano 1970, pp. 165-175.

van Wijngaarden, A.,
  Generalized ALGOL, Annual review in Automatic Programming, Vol. III, 1963, pp. 17-26.

van Wijngaarden, A. (Ed.), Mailloux, B. J., Peck, J. E. L., Koster, C. H. A.,
  Report on the algorithmic language ALGOL 68, Mathematisch Centrum, MR 101, Amsterdam, Oct. 1960, and Numerische Mathematic, 14, 1969, pp. 79-218.

van Wijngaarden, A., Mailloux, B. J., Peck, J. E. L., Koster, C. H. A.,
  Report on the algorithmic language ALGOL 68 (Russian and English), Kibernetika, Vol. 6, 1969, and Vol. 1, 1970.

Wegner, P.,
  Some remarks on VWF notation, Report No. 69-12, Center for Computing and Information Sciences, Brown Univ., Dec. 1969.

Westland, J.,
  An ALGOL 68 syntax and parser, Univ. of Calgary, Sept. 1969.

Wodon, P. L.,
  Methods of garbage collection for ALGOL 68, MBLE Research Lab., Brussels, April 1970, and these Proceedings.

Woodward, P. M.,
  A narrative preview of ALGOL 68, R. R. E. Memorandum No. 2499, Royal Radar Establishment, Malvern, Worcs., U. K., Oct. 1968.

Woodward, P. M.,
  A primer of ALGOL 68-R (2nd Edition), R. R. E. Memorandum No. 2601, Royal Radar Establishment, Malvern, Worcs., U. K., Feb. 1970.

Wössner, H.,
  On identification of operators in ALGOL 68, these Proceedings.
Yoneda, N.,
  New algorithmic language ALGOL 68, Surikagaku 1969, Vols. 5-?

sg
12-15-71